A Practitioner's Guide to the City Code on Takeovers and Mergers 2019/2020

CW00822488

A Practitioner's Guide to the City Code on Takeovers and Mergers 2019/2020

Introduction by

Simon Lindsay
Director General
The Panel on Takeovers and Mergers

SWEET & MAXWELL

THOMSON REUTERS

1st Edition   1989
31st Edition   2019

Published in 2019 by Thomson Reuters trading as Sweet & Maxwell. Thomson Reuters is registered in England & Wales, Company No.1679046. Registered office and address for service: 5 Canada Square, Canary Wharf, London, E14 5AQ.

For further information on our products and services, visit *http://www.sweetandmaxwell.co.uk*.

Typeset by Letterpart Limited, Caterham on the Hill, Surrey, CR3 5XL.

Printed and bound by CPI Group (UK) Ltd, Croydon, CR0 4YY.

No natural forests were destroyed to make this product: only farmed timber was used and replanted.

A CIP catalogue record of this book is available for the British Library.

ISBN: 978-0-414-07171-1

Thomson Reuters, the Thomson Reuters Logo and Sweet & Maxwell ® are trademarks of Thomson Reuters.

Crown copyright material is reproduced with the permission of the Controller of HMSO and the Queen's Printer for Scotland.

Biographies

Simon Lindsay is Director General of the Panel on Takeovers and Mergers, a position he took up on 2 July 2018. Simon is on secondment from Citigroup where he was a Managing Director within UK Investment Banking and the Head of UK M&A. Simon has been an M&A-focused investment banker for almost 30 years and has focused principally on the UK since joining Schroders (subsequently forming part of Citigroup) in 1997.

Piers Prichard Jones is a partner at Freshfields and co-heads the firm's M&A practice in London. He focuses on domestic and cross-border M&A and corporate work and has advised on a number of significant UK public transactions in recent years. For example, in the last 12 months, he has advised Berry Global Group on its acquisition of RPC, Barrick Gold on its merger with Randgold Resources and ZPG on its acquisition by Silver Lake.

Rob Innes is a partner at Slaughter and May with broad corporate and corporate finance experience, with a focus on public takeovers, international private M&A and equity capital markets.

Public M&A highlights include advising Merlin on its proposed takeover by a consortium led by Blackstone and KIRKBI, esure on its takeover by funds managed by Bain Capital, Virgin Group in connection with Clydesdale's offer for Virgin Money, GKN on its defence against Melrose Industries Plc, Royal Dutch Shell Plc in relation to its cash and share offer for BG Group, RSA on the proposed bid for it by Zurich Insurance, Mediclinic on its combination with Al Noor Hospitals Group and its potential offer for Spire Healthcare, Novae on its takeover by Axis Capital and Centrica on its un-recommended takeover of Venture Production.

Rob was commended at the 2016 FT Innovative Lawyers Awards for his work on the Mediclinic/Al Noor combination, which won the award for innovation in M&A, and lectures to the Masters in Law and Finance course at Oxford on public takeovers.

Chris McGaffin is a partner at Slaughter and May, with a focus on domestic and cross-border M&A, currently based in Hong Kong working primarily on Asia-PAC deals.

Public M&A highlights include advising ARM Holdings on the offer by SoftBank, Cadbury on the hostile offer by Kraft, WS Atkins on the offer by SNC-Lavalin, Wood Group on its offer for AMEC Foster Wheeler, Platform Speciality Products on its offer for Alent and PTT Exploration and Production on its contested offer for Cove Energy.

Chris is listed in The Lawyer's Hot 100 2017 and was voted second in the Financial News Partner of the Year Award 2017, and has been recognised in IFLR Asia-PAC as a rising star for M&A since moving to the Hong Kong office in 2017.

Nick Adams is a Partner at Norton Rose Fulbright LLP, specialising in corporate finance. Nick has extensive experience of public company takeovers. Deals Nick has worked on include Barrick Gold/Randgold Resources; Mannesmann/Orange; Mannesmann/Vodafone; Texas Utilities/The Energy Group; Trinity/Mirror Group; Siemens Financial Services/Broadcastle; Mechel/Oriel Resources; BA/Iberia; Jelf Group/Marsh; Aermont/Pinewood Group; and Blackstone/Japan Residential Investment Company Limited. During 2000, Nick spent a year working as an investment banker at Citigroup.

Paul Whitelock is a Partner at Norton Rose Fulbright LLP with a particular focus on public M&A and capital markets transactions. Paul spent two years on secondment as Secretary at the UK Takeover Panel where he was responsible for regulating various high profile public M&A transactions, as well as developing the Panel's policies on a number of issues. Deals Paul has worked on include Melrose/GKN, Volcan/

Vedanta Resources, SNC Lavalin/WS Atkins, Blackstone/ Taliesin, Sacturino/Polyus Gold, Terra Firma/Infinis Energy, Marsh & MacLennan/Jelf Group plc, BMO Financial Group/ F&C Asset Management plc, Conforama/Darty and Muller Group/Robert Wiseman Dairies.

Seth Jones is a corporate partner at Allen & Overy LLP. Seth regularly advises clients on takeover situations. His recent work includes advising 21st Century Fox on its contested offer for Sky Plc, Worldpay on its merger with Vantiv, Virgin Money on its merger with CYBG Plc and HarbourVest on its hostile offer for SVG Capital and subsequent asset purchase. Between 2013 and 2015, Seth was seconded to the Takeover Panel as Secretary. During his secondment, Seth oversaw many of the high profile takeover bids of that period, including Shell's offer for BG Group, Anheuser-Busch Inbev's offer for SABMiller and Pfizer's possible offer for AstraZeneca. Seth was also heavily involved in policy and Code revision matters, including the introduction of the regime on post-offer undertakings, and he wrote many of the recent Practice Statements published by the Panel.

Carlton Evans has been a Corporate Partner at Linklaters since 1997 and was a Senior Executive at the Takeover Panel for the two years ending June 1998. He is Directory-rated and an M&A and private equity expert, including having advised on deals such as: Carlyle's P2P of The Innovation Group; the £7.6bn merger of Siebe and BTR to form Invensys; the £17bn break-up takeover of Cable & Wireless Communications by Cable & Wireless and ntl; Bright Foods' and Barings PE's US$ 1.7bn sale of Weetabix; Hony Capital's acquisition of Pizza Express; the P2P offer by TPG for GlobeOp; P2Ps of LA Fitness by MidOcean, of Caffè Nero by its founder Gerry Ford and Paladin, and of Willis Corroon by KKR; sales by Apax/Nordic Capital/Capio of Capio UK and Capio Spain and Apax's acquisitions of Invent Farma and Neuraxpharm; the $1.8bn investment in BTG Pactual by a consortium including GIC and Ontario Teachers; and the EUR 2.5bn takeover to redomicile New World Resources in the UK.

Lee Coney is a Partner in the Corporate Finance practice at Clifford Chance LLP. Lee advises UK and international companies, private equity houses and investment banks on a range of corporate finance transactions and has extensive experience in public company takeovers. Significant transactions include advising the Co-operative Bank on its formal sales process, Provident Financial on its successful defence against the hostile offer by Non-Standard Finance, Inmarsat on its takeover by a consortium of private equity houses, Patron Capital on its takeover of Punch Taverns and associated disposal to Heineken UK, Booker Group on its merger with Tesco, Mastercard's competitive offer for Earthport, Imagination Technologies on its takeover by Canyon Bridge, EADS on its proposed combination with BAE Systems, Babcock International on its acquisition of VT Group, Just Retirement Group on its merger with Partnership Assurance Group, George Wimpey on its merger with Taylor Woodrow and Kraft Foods on its acquisition of Cadbury. Lee has also spent 12 months in one of the UK M&A teams at Citigroup.

Rui Huo is a Senior Associate in the Corporate Finance practice at Clifford Chance LLP. Rui specialises in UK public takeovers and UK and cross-border M&A transactions, as well as general corporate advice to UK listed companies. Significant transactions include advising Sainsbury's on its competitive takeover of Home Retail Group, Mastercard's competitive offer for Earthport, Inmarsat on its takeover by a consortium of private equity houses, Provident Financial on its successful defence against the hostile offer by Non-Standard Finance, Booker Group on its merger with Tesco, French Connection on its formal sale process, Just Retirement Group on its merger with Partnership Assurance Group, Patron Capital on its takeover of Punch Taverns and associated disposal to Heineken UK, and Apollo and CVC on their takeover of Brit Insurance. Rui has also spent six months as a secondee to Morgan Stanley's UK Investment Banking Team, during which she advised on a number of takeovers including Vantiv's merger with Worldpay, Michelin's takeover of Fenner and AMEX GBT's takeover of Hogg Robinson.

Ursula Newton is a Partner in the PwC Capital Markets Group and has specialised in capital markets for over 20 years. In addition to executing transactions, Ursula advises companies on the applications of the rules applicable for listing on London's main market and on AIM, the Standards for Investment Reporting (SIRs) and the Takeover Code. She has an active interest in the development of regulation in the market, having been a member of the Auditing Practices Board SIRs sub-committee and Chair of the working party which produced SIR 1000. Ursula leads PwC's response to the Takeover Panel on changes to the City Code and is a member of the FCA Listing Authority Advisory Panel and of the Primary Markets Group of the London Stock Exchange.

Ursula has extensive experience of working with companies operating in the London capital markets having worked on a significant number of major listings and transactions including the takeover of RPC by Berry Global; the takeover of Hogg Robinson by American Express; the proposed takeover of intu by the Peel Group; the Hammerson Plc offer to acquire intu properties plc; the possible offer by Redrow Plc for Bovis Homes Group Plc; the BT acquisition of EE; the TUI AG/TUI Travel Plc merger; the demerger and IPO of the Pharmaceuticals business of Reckitt Benckiser; the Barclays rights issue and the main market IPOs of Funding Circle and Autotrader.

Mark Bardell is a partner at Herbert Smith Freehills, based in the London office, specialising in mergers and acquisitions. He is recommended in Legal 500 for M&A premium deals and noted for his public takeover expertise. He is a contributor to leading practitioner's texts on topics including market abuse, schemes of arrangement and takeovers and is a General Editor of Butterworths Takeovers: Law and Practice, the leading UK takeover reference work. He regularly lectures at Cambridge University to postgraduate MCL students as part of the Deals Course. In September 2011, he completed a two-year secondment as Secretary to the UK's Takeover Panel and acts as Secretary to the Takeover Appeal Board. Mark has been a partner at the firm for over 10 years and has helped clients to close more than US$225 billion worth of transactions, including

Sky on the competing takeover situation involving 21st Century Fox, Disney and Comcast Corporation.

Antonia Kirkby practiced as a transaction lawyer specialising in corporate finance and M&A before becoming a professional support lawyer at Herbert Smith Freehills. Her focus is providing the firm's lawyers with technical advice on company and corporate finance law issues and analysing law and regulation. Antonia was secretary to the City of London Law Society's Company Law Sub-Committee and to the Sub-Committee's Joint Working Party on Takeovers for a number of years, which involved considering and lobbying on a wide range of corporate law issues including changes to the Takeover Code. She has written a number of articles and contributes to a number of books, particularly on public M&A, market abuse and the listing regime.

Contents

1 The Panel on Takeovers and Mergers

Simon Lindsay
Director General
The Panel on Takeovers and Mergers

2 The Approach, Announcements and Independent Advice

Piers Prichard Jones
Partner
Freshfields Bruckhaus Deringer LLP

3 Share Dealings and Holdings: Restrictions and Disclosure Requirements

Robert Innes
Partner
Slaughter and May

Chris McGaffin
Partner
Slaughter and May

7   Conduct During the Offer; Timing and Revision; and Restrictions Following Offers

Lee Coney
Partner
Clifford Chance LLP

Rui Huo
Senior Associate
Clifford Chance LLP

8   Profit Forecasts, Quantified Financial Benefits Statements and Asset Valuations

Ursula Newton
Partner
PricewaterhouseCoopers LLP

Chapter 1

The Panel on Takeovers and Mergers

Simon Lindsay
Director General
The Panel on Takeovers and Mergers

1.1   Introduction

The Panel on Takeovers and Mergers (the Panel) is an independent body whose main functions are to issue and administer the Takeover Code (the Code) and to supervise and regulate takeovers and other matters to which the Code applies.

The Panel was established in 1968, since when its composition and powers have evolved as circumstances have changed. On 20 May 2006, the Panel was designated by the Secretary of State for Trade and Industry as the supervisory authority to carry out certain regulatory functions in relation to takeovers pursuant to the European Directive on Takeover Bids (the Directive). Its statutory functions are set out in Pt 28 of the Companies Act 2006 (the Act), which, among other things, implemented the Directive. The Rules set out in the Code also have statutory effect in the Isle of Man, Jersey and Guernsey by virtue of legislation applying in those jurisdictions.

The Code is designed principally to ensure that shareholders in an offeree company are treated fairly and are not denied the opportunity to decide on the merits of a takeover, and that shareholders in the offeree company of the same class are afforded equivalent treatment by an offeror. The Code also provides an orderly framework within which takeovers are conducted. In addition, it is designed to promote, in conjunction with other regulatory regimes, the integrity of the financial markets.

The Code is not concerned with the financial or commercial advantages or disadvantages of takeovers. These are matters for the companies concerned and their shareholders. In addition, it is not the purpose of the Code either to facilitate or to impede takeovers. Nor is the Code concerned with matters of public interest, such as competition policy, which are the responsibility of Government and other bodies such as the Competition and Markets Authority, the Office of Fair Trading and the European Commission.

The Code has been developed since 1968 to reflect the collective opinion of those professionally involved in the field of takeovers as to appropriate business standards and as to how fairness to offeree company shareholders and an orderly framework for takeovers can be achieved.

The Code applies to all offers for companies which have their registered offices in the UK, the Channel Islands and the Isle of Man, if any of their securities are admitted to trading on a regulated market or multilateral trading facility (each as defined) in the UK or on any stock exchange in the Channel Islands or the Isle of Man. The Code also applies to offers for other public companies and certain private companies which have their registered offices in the UK, the Channel Islands or the Isle of Man and which are considered by the Panel to have their place of central management and control in one of those jurisdictions (the residency test). In addition, under the Directive, the Panel has "shared jurisdiction" with regulators in other Member States of the European Economic Area in certain circumstances, although, as a consequence of Brexit, the shared jurisdiction system will cease to apply in the UK on "exit day" (within the meaning of s.20 of the European Union (Withdrawal) Act 2018).

The Code comprises six General Principles, 38 Rules, the accompanying Notes on these Rules and nine Appendices, as well as the Introduction and Definitions section. The six General Principles (which are taken directly from the Directive) apply to takeovers and other matters to which the Code applies. The General Principles are expressed in broad terms and the Code does not define the precise extent of, or limitations on, their application. They are applied in accordance with their spirit in order to achieve their underlying purpose. The General Principles are as follows:

1. all holders of the securities of an offeree company of the same class must be afforded equivalent treatment; moreover, if a person acquires control of a company, the other holders of securities must be protected;
2. the holders of the securities of an offeree company must have sufficient time and information to enable them to reach a properly informed decision on the bid; where it advises the holders of securities, the board of the offeree company must give its views on the effects of implementation of the bid on employment, conditions of employment and the locations of the company's places of business;
3. the board of an offeree company must act in the interests of the company as a whole and must not deny the holders of securities the opportunity to decide on the merits of the bid;
4. false markets must not be created in the securities of the offeree company, of the offeror company or of any other company concerned by the bid in such a way that the rise or fall of the prices of the securities becomes artificial and the normal functioning of the markets is distorted;
5. an offeror must announce a bid only after ensuring that it can fulfil in full any cash consideration, if such consideration is offered, and after taking all reasonable measures to secure the implementation of any other type of consideration; and
6. an offeree company must not be hindered in the conduct of its affairs for longer than is reasonable by a bid for its securities.

These General Principles, which are essentially statements of standards of commercial behaviour, encapsulate the spirit of the Code and form the foundation upon which the Rules and the accompanying Notes are based. With effect from "exit day", minor amendments will be made to the General Principles in order to bring them into line with equivalent general principles that will be set out in the Act (as amended by the Takeovers (Amendment) (EU Exit) Regulations 2019) and which will replace those set out in the Directive.

1.2 Key characteristics of the Panel: Application of the Code according to the underlying purpose

The essential characteristics of the Panel are flexibility, certainty and speed, enabling the parties to an offer to know where they stand under the Code in a timely fashion. These characteristics are important in order to avoid over-rigidity of the Rules and the risk of takeovers becoming delayed by litigation of a tactical nature, which may frustrate the ability of shareholders to decide the outcome of an offer. Central to this approach is the concept that it is the spirit of the Code which must be observed as well as the letter.

Situations frequently arise in takeovers which could not reasonably have been envisaged and the Panel Executive (the Executive) which carries out the day-to-day work of takeover supervision and regulation is able to respond to such situations by applying the General Principles and the Rules in accordance with their spirit in order to achieve their underlying purpose in the particular circumstances. The Panel is able to derogate or grant a waiver to a person from the application of a Rule, provided that, in the case of a transaction and Rule subject to the requirements of the Directive, the General Principles are respected.

When a person or its advisers are in any doubt whatsoever as to whether a proposed course of conduct is in accordance with the General Principles or the Rules, or whenever a waiver or derogation from the application of the provisions of the Code is sought, that person or its advisers must consult the Executive in advance. To take legal or other professional advice on the interpretation, application or effect of the Code is not an appropriate alternative to obtaining a ruling from the Executive.

1.3   Some key Rules

Most of the individual Rules of the Code are accompanied by Notes which provide guidance on the application of the Rules in certain given circumstances. In addition, as more particularly referred to below, the Executive from time to time issues Practice Statements which provide guidance as to how the Executive normally interprets and applies relevant Rules in particular circumstances.

In this Chapter, some particular Rules of the Code which reflect the General Principles are highlighted; later chapters deal with some of the specific Rules in more detail.

As will be noted, a number of these Rules refer to the concept of "acting in concert". Under the Code, persons acting in concert comprise persons who, pursuant to an agreement or understanding (whether formal or informal), co-operate to obtain or consolidate control (see 1.3.1 below) of a company or to frustrate the successful outcome of an offer for a company. Without prejudice to the general application of this definition, persons who fall within certain prescribed categories are presumed under the Code to be acting in concert with each other unless the contrary is established. These categories include, broadly, companies within the same corporate group, companies with their directors and pension funds, fund managers with any funds that they manage on a discretionary basis, a person with their close relatives and related trusts, the close relatives of a founder of a company with their close relatives and related trusts, financial advisers and corporate brokers with any parties to an offer that they are advising in relation to the offer, and shareholders in a private company who sell their shares in exchange for shares in a company to which the Code applies. In practice, given the importance of this definition to the application of a number of Rules, the Executive is frequently consulted on the composition of so-called "concert parties".

1.3.1 General Principle 1: Equivalent treatment and protection of non-controlling shareholders

Perhaps the best-known Rule of the Code is Rule 9, which prescribes the circumstances in which a mandatory offer must be made, the terms on which it must be made and the person who is primarily responsible for making it. The mandatory offer Rule reflects the requirement for equivalent treatment of all shareholders and seeks to ensure that de facto control of a company cannot be bought by a person paying a premium price to one or more shareholders, whilst at the same time leaving the remaining shareholders behind with a new controller and no opportunity to exit at the same premium price. For the purposes of the Code, shares carrying 30% or more of the voting rights of a company are regarded as conferring control.

The requirement under Rule 9 for a person to make a mandatory offer arises in circumstances where:

1. that person acquires (whether by a series of transactions over a period of time or not) an interest in shares which, taken together with shares in which persons acting in concert with him are interested, carry 30% or more of the voting rights of a company; or
2. that person, together with persons acting in concert with him, is interested in shares which in aggregate carry not less than 30% of the voting rights of a company, but does not hold shares carrying more than 50% of such voting rights, and that person, or any person acting in concert with him, acquires an interest in any other shares which increases the percentage of shares carrying voting rights in which he is interested.

A mandatory offer under Rule 9 must be made in cash, or include a full cash alternative, at a price not less than the highest price paid by the person who is subject to the mandatory offer requirement (or anyone acting in concert with him) for any interest in shares in the offeree company during the 12 months prior to the announcement of the offer. In addition, the offer can be conditional only upon the receipt of sufficient acceptances so as to result in the offeror and persons acting in concert with him holding shares carrying more than 50% of the voting rights in the offeree company.

Rule 11 is also based on the requirement that shareholders should be afforded equivalent treatment, specifically in relation to the type of consideration that they receive from an offeror. Broadly speaking, Rule 11 requires an offer to be in cash or accompanied by a full cash alternative whenever an offeror or any person acting in concert with him acquires, for cash, any interest in shares in the offeree company during the offer period. Further, it provides that where an offeror or any person acting in concert with him acquires, for cash, interests in shares in the offeree company carrying 10% or more of the total voting rights in the offeree company during the offer period and within 12 months prior to its commencement, the offer must be in cash or accompanied by a cash alternative at not less than the highest price paid by the offeror (or any person acting in concert with him) during that period.

Rule 6 relates to the value of the consideration that shareholders receive from an offeror, and provides that where an offeror or any person acting in concert with him acquires an interest in shares in the offeree company either during the offer period or in the three-month period prior to its commencement, the offer to shareholders must be on no less favourable terms.

In addition, favourable deals between an offeror and particular shareholders and other persons interested in shares in the offeree company, which are not made available to all shareholders, are generally prohibited under Rule 16.

1.3.2 General Principle 2: Sufficiency of time, information and advice

Rule 31.1 requires an offer to be open for at least 21 days following the date on which the offer document is published. Once an offer has become or has been declared unconditional as to acceptances (other than an offer which is unconditional from the outset), the offer must, under Rule 31.4, then remain open for at least 14 days after the date on which it would otherwise have expired. Rule 32.1 requires that, if an offer is revised, the offer must be kept open for at least 14 days following the date on which the revised offer document is published. In addition, Appendix 7 sets out similar timetable requirements in relation to an offer being effected by means of a scheme of arrangement, including the requirement that the shareholder meetings required in order to implement the scheme must be held on at least 21 days' notice, and that any revision of the terms of the scheme should normally be made by no later than 14 days prior to the date of those meetings.

Rule 23 requires shareholders to be given sufficient information and advice to enable them to arrive, in good time, at a properly informed decision regarding the offer. The obligation under Rule 23 is reinforced by the requirements of Rule 3 and also Rules 24 and 25.

Under Rule 3, the board of the offeree company must obtain competent independent advice as to whether the financial terms of the offer are fair and reasonable. The substance of that advice must be made known to all shareholders. As a result, shareholders in the offeree company have the benefit of that adviser's views, as well as the opinion of the directors.

Rule 24 requires an offeror to send an offer document to shareholders in the offeree company and to persons with information rights as well as making it readily available to the pension scheme trustees and employee representatives (or the employees themselves, if they have no representatives). Rule 25 requires the board of the offeree company to send a circular to shareholders in the offeree company and persons with information rights as well as making it readily available to pension scheme trustees and employees/employee representatives. The circular must set out the board's opinion on the offer and its reasons for forming its opinion. Rules 24 and 25 also set out detailed requirements as to the contents of these documents, which may be combined into a single document in a recommended offer. These include, amongst other requirements, a requirement that the offeror explains the long-term commercial justification for the offer and states its intentions with regard to the future business of the offeree company (including its strategic plans and their likely repercussions on employment, the balance of skills and functions of the employees and management, the offeree company's research and development functions and the locations of the offeree company's places of business), and a corresponding requirement that the board of the offeree company sets out its views on these matters. In addition, both the offeror and the offeree company must disclose certain financial information in relation to themselves, including, in relation to the offeror, details of the way in which it is financing the offer. It is also a requirement that the offeror and offeree company disclose details of the fees and expenses expected to be incurred by them in relation to the offer.

Rule 20.1 requires information about companies involved in an offer to be made equally available to all offeree company shareholders as nearly as possible at the same time and in the same manner.

Rule 19.1 requires that each document, announcement or other information published, or statement made, during the course of an offer must be prepared with the highest standards of care and accuracy. The language used must clearly and concisely reflect the position being described and the information given must be adequately and fairly presented.

Other Rules also set out the consequences of making certain specific statements during an offer period, for example Rule 2.8 ("no intention to bid" statements), Rule 31.5 ("no extension" statements) and Rule 32.2 ("no increase" statements).

1.3.3 General Principle 3: Shareholders to be given an opportunity to decide on the merits of a bid

Rule 21.1 provides that during the course of an offer, or even before the date of the offer if the board of the offeree company has reason to believe that a bona fide offer might be imminent (an expression on which guidance is given in Practice Statement No.32), the board must not, without the approval of shareholders in general meeting, take any action which may result in any offer or bona fide possible offer being frustrated or in shareholders being denied the opportunity to decide on its merits. However, shareholder approval may not be required where:

1. the proposed action is conditional on the offer being withdrawn or lapsing;
2. the offeror has consented to the proposed action;
3. holders of offeree company shares carrying more than 50% of the voting rights provide approval in writing to the proposed action;
4. the proposed action is in pursuance of a pre-existing contract or other pre-existing obligation; or
5. a decision to take the proposed course of action had been taken before the date of the offer or, if earlier, the date on which the offeree company had reason to believe that a bona fide offer might be imminent, and the proposed course of action had either been partly or fully implemented before such date or is otherwise in the ordinary course of the offeree company's business.

Under Rule 21.2, except with the consent of the Panel, neither the offeree company nor any person acting in concert with it is permitted to enter into any offer-related arrangement (as defined) with either the offeror or any person acting in concert with it during an offer period or when an offer is reasonably in contemplation. This is because offer-related arrangements between one offeror and the offeree company (for example inducement fee agreements, implementation agreements or other "deal protection" measures) might have the object or effect of deterring another offeror or offerors, thereby denying offeree company shareholders the possibility of deciding on the merits of a competing bid or bids.

Practice Statement No.29 provides guidance on the interpretation and application of Rule 21.2 in relation to:

1. certain exclusions from the prohibition on entry into offer-related arrangements, which are set out in Rule 21.2(b);
2. agreements which are entered into between an offeror and an offeree company relating to the conduct, implementation and/or terms of an offer ("Bid Conduct Agreements"); and
3. the limited circumstances in which an offeree company may agree to pay an inducement fee to an offeror.

1.3.4   *General Principle 4: Avoidance of false markets*

Transparency and disclosure are fundamental to the way in which the Panel seeks to avoid false markets in the securities of companies subject to bids. The importance of secrecy prior to the announcement of an offer or possible offer is paramount and Rule 2.2 of the Code provides that prior to any such announcement only a very restricted number of people (typically comprising not more than six outside parties) should have knowledge of a possible offer.

If a potential offeror is actively considering an offer or has entered into talks with the offeree company, and the offeree company is the subject of rumour or speculation or there is an untoward movement in the offeree company's share price, an announcement will typically be required in order to avoid a false market developing in the offeree company's shares. The obligation to make such an announcement will rest with the potential offeror if it has yet to approach the offeree company regarding its possible offer but will pass to the offeree company after the making of such an approach—provided the approach is not unequivocally rejected.

The announcement of a possible offer in relation to an offeree company will commence what is called an "offer period" (not to be confused with the formal offer timetable, as mentioned in 1.3.2 above and 1.3.6 below), during which time a number of Rules in the Code will come into effect. One of these is Rule 8, which requires prompt disclosure of positions and dealings (which includes, in the case of the latter, the entering into of options and derivatives) in relevant securities by the parties to an offer and any person who is interested (directly or indirectly) in 1% or more of any class of relevant securities of either the offeree company or any offeror that is offering its own shares as consideration under the offer.

1.3.5 General Principle 5: Certainty of bid funding

Rule 2.7 provides that an offeror should announce a firm intention to make an offer only when that offeror has every reason to believe that it can and will continue to be able to implement the offer.

Rule 2.7 also requires that when the offer is for cash or includes an element of cash, the announcement must include confirmation by an appropriate third party (usually the offeror's financial adviser) that resources are available to the offeror sufficient to satisfy full acceptance of the offer. Rule 24.8 contains a similar "cash confirmation" requirement in respect of the offer document itself.

1.3.6 General Principle 6: Offeree company not to be hindered in its affairs for longer than is reasonable

The Code contains detailed Rules relating to the timetable within which a potential offeror that has been publicly identified must confirm its intentions, and also within which an offer must be implemented. These Rules seek to prevent the offeree company from being the subject of an extended period of unwelcome "siege" as a result of an offer period continuing for longer than is reasonable, as well as to provide an orderly framework within which takeovers may be conducted.

Rules 2.4 and 2.6 set out the so-called "put up or shut up" regime which is designed principally to protect offeree companies against a protracted "virtual bid" period (i.e. a situation where a potential offeror announces that it is considering making an offer, often setting out indicative terms, but without formally committing itself to doing so).

Rule 2.4 requires that an announcement by the offeree company which commences an offer period must identify any potential offeror with which the offeree company is in talks or from which an approach has been received (and not unequivocally rejected). Further, any subsequent announcement by the offeree company which refers to the existence of a new potential offeror must identify that potential offeror, except where the announcement is made after an offeror has announced a firm intention to make an offer for the offeree company under Rule 2.7.

Rule 2.6 requires that an identified potential offeror must (subject to certain exceptions), by not later than 17.00 on the 28th day following the date of the announcement in which it is first identified, either:

1. announce a firm intention to make an offer (i.e. "put up"); or
2. announce that it does not intend to make an offer (i.e. "shut up"), in which case the potential offeror will normally be restricted from making an offer for the offeree company for a period of six months,

unless the Panel has consented to an extension of the deadline.

The Panel will normally consent to an extension of a "put up or shut up" deadline at the request of the board of the offeree company and after taking into account all relevant factors. The requirement for an identified potential offeror to make one of the announcements referred to above by the "put up or shut up" deadline will cease to apply if another offeror has already announced, or subsequently announces (prior to the relevant deadline), a firm intention to make an offer for the offeree company under Rule 2.7.

1.4   Code amendment

The Panel, through the Code Committee, is responsible for keeping the Code under review and for proposing, consulting on, making and issuing amendments to the Code. Matters leading to possible amendments to the Code might arise from a number of sources, including specific cases which the Panel has considered, market developments, and representations from third parties (such as shareholders). The Committee welcomes both suggestions from interested parties for possible amendments to the Code and the valuable responses to consultations which it receives.

In the ordinary course of events, once it has been agreed that a particular matter is to be pursued, the Committee will, with the assistance of the Executive, prepare and publish a Public Consultation Paper (PCP) seeking the views of interested parties on the proposals and setting out the background to, reasons for and (where applicable) full text of the proposed amendments. Consultation periods in relation to PCPs vary depending on the complexity of the subject but will usually be between one and two months. It is the Committee's policy to publish written responses it receives to a PCP, unless the respondent requests otherwise. Following the end of the consultation period, and once it has considered the responses received, the Committee will, with the assistance of the Executive, publish its conclusions on the proposed amendments, together with the final text of the Code amendments (if any), in a Response Statement (RS).

In certain exceptional cases, the Committee might consider it necessary to amend the Code on an expedited basis, for example because a particular market development appears to the Committee to require that the proposed amendment be made more quickly than the usual public consultation process would permit. In such cases, the Committee will publish the amendment with immediate effect, together with a public statement explaining the rationale for the amendment and its effect but without prior formal consultation. Publication of a Code amendment on such an expedited basis will be followed in due course by a PCP seeking views on the amendment, which might be modified as a result, or removed altogether, depending on the Committee's conclusions following the consultation process.

Where, in the opinion of the Committee, any proposed amendment to the Code either does not materially alter the effect of the provision in question or is a consequence of changes to relevant legislation or regulatory requirements, the Committee may publish the text of the amendment without any formal consultation process. The amendment will, however, be made public before the date on which it comes into effect, wherever practicable.

1.4.1   Recent Code Committee publications

1.4.1.1   Asset valuations

On 6 March 2019, the Committee published RS 2018/1, having considered the responses to the consultation set out in PCP 2018/1 of 17 October 2018 which proposed amendments to the Code with regard to asset valuations. Whilst PCP 2018/1 proposed a wholesale redraft of Rule 29, the revisions did not seek to alter materially the way in which Rule 29 was being applied by the Executive in practice but instead sought to codify that practice more explicitly and logically within the wording of the Rule. The proposed amendments included, among others, the following:

1.   codifying the asset valuations to which Rule 29 applies, both in relation to the time period within which such a valuation is published and the types of asset to which it relates;

2. requiring a valuation to be in the form of, accompanied by, confirmed by or updated by (as applicable) a valuation report;
3. clarifying both the content of such a valuation report and the requirements applicable to the valuer that will provide it; and
4. requiring a no material difference statement in certain circumstances.

The Committee adopted the amendments to the Code proposed in PCP 2018/1 with only minor modifications.

The rule changes came into effect on 1 April 2019.

1.4.1.2   The UK's withdrawal from the EU

On 6 March 2019, the Code Committee also published RS 2018/2. RS 2018/2 set out the results of the Committee's deliberations on the responses to the consultation set out in PCP 2018/2 of 5 November 2018, which proposed amendments to the Code to, amongst other things, cater for the consequential changes to UK law resulting from the UK's withdrawal from the EU and, in particular, the replacement of relevant provisions of the Directive with equivalent UK legislation. The proposed amendments set out in PCP 2018/2 included, among others, the following:

1. the deletion of the "shared jurisdiction" provisions, such that the Code would:
    (a) cease to apply (instead of applying partially) to a company which has its registered office in a remaining EEA Member State (i.e. not in the UK) and whose securities are admitted to trading on a UK regulated market (but not on a regulated market in that EEA Member State);
    (b) cease to apply (instead of applying partially) to a company which has its registered office in the UK and whose securities are admitted to trading on a regulated market in a remaining EEA Member State (and not on a UK regulated market) and which does not

satisfy the "residency test" set out in s.3(a)(ii) of the Introduction to the Code; and

(c) apply in full (instead of only partially) to an offer for a company which has its registered office in the UK and whose securities are admitted to trading on a regulated market in a remaining EEA Member State (but not on a UK regulated market) if the company satisfies the residency test set out in s.3(a)(ii) of the Introduction to the Code; and

2. minor amendments to the General Principles in order to align them with the equivalent general principles that will be set out in the Act.

The Committee adopted the amendments to the Code proposed in PCP 2018/2 with one minor clarificatory amendment.

The rule changes are currently not in effect as they are dependent upon the timing of the UK's withdrawal from the EU. In that regard, further to Instrument 2019/3 published by the Panel and the Code Committee on 4 April 2019, the rule changes will come into effect on "exit day" (within the meaning of s.20 of the European Union (Withdrawal) Act 2018). RS 2018/2 sets out how the new rules will apply to any offer for a "shared jurisdiction" company that is on-going at that point.

1.5   Practice Statements

The Executive, from time to time, publishes Practice Statements in order to provide informal guidance to companies involved in takeovers and practitioners as to how the Executive normally interprets and applies relevant provisions of the Code in particular circumstances. Practice Statements do not form part of the Code and, accordingly, are not binding on the Executive or the Panel and are not a substitute for consulting the Executive to establish how the Code applies in a particular case. Practice Statements are periodically reviewed by the Executive and are amended or withdrawn, as necessary. All current Practice Statements can be found on the Panel's website (*http://www.thetakeoverpanel.org.uk* [Accessed 26 June 2019]).

1.6 The Panel and its Committees

A brief description of the membership, functions, responsibilities and general activities of the Panel and certain of its Committees is set out below.

1.6.1 The Panel

The Panel assumes overall responsibility for the policy, financing and administration of the Panel's functions and for the functioning and operation of the Code. The Panel operates through a number of Committees and is directly responsible for those matters which are not dealt with through one of its Committees.

The Panel comprises up to 36 members:

1. the Chairman, who is appointed by the Panel;
2. up to 3 Deputy Chairmen, who are appointed by the Panel;
3. up to 20 other members, who are appointed by the Panel; and
4. individuals appointed by each of the following bodies:
   (a) the Association for Financial Markets in Europe (with separate representation also for its Corporate Finance Committee and Securities Trading Committee);
   (b) the Association of British Insurers;
   (c) the Association of Investment Companies;
   (d) the Confederation of British Industry;
   (e) the Institute of Chartered Accountants in England and Wales;
   (f) the Investment Association;
   (g) the Pensions and Lifetime Savings Association;
   (h) the Personal Investment Management and Financial Advice Association;

(i)   the Quoted Companies Alliance; and

(j)   UK Finance.

The Chairman and at least one Deputy Chairman are designated as members of the Hearings Committee. Up to 12 Panel members appointed by the Panel as referred to in para.(3) above are designated as members of the Code Committee and up to eight Panel members appointed by the Panel as referred to in para.(3) above are designated as members of the Hearings Committee.

The members appointed by the bodies referred to in para.(4) above become members of the Hearings Committee without further designation by the Panel. In performing their functions, these members act independently of the body which has appointed them (and not as that body's agent or delegate) and exercise their own judgment as to how to perform their functions and how to vote.

No member of the Code Committee may simultaneously or subsequently be a member of the Hearings Committee.

1.6.2   The Code Committee

The Code Committee is drawn from a spread of shareholder, corporate, practitioner and other interests within the Panel's regulated community. Up to 12 members of the Panel are designated as members of the Code Committee.

As noted above, the Code Committee carries out the rule-making functions of the Panel and is solely responsible for keeping the Code (other than certain matters set out in the Introduction, which are the responsibility of the Panel itself) under review and for proposing, consulting on, making and issuing amendments to the Code.

The Terms of Reference of the Code Committee and the procedures it has adopted for amending the Code can be found on the Panel's website.

1.6.3   The Hearings Committee

The Hearings Committee comprises the Chairman, at least one Deputy Chairman, up to eight other members designated by the Panel and the individuals appointed by the bodies listed at 1.6.1(4) above.

The principal function of the Hearings Committee is to review, on application, rulings of the Executive. The Hearings Committee also hears disciplinary proceedings instituted by the Executive when the Executive considers that there has been a breach of the Code or of a ruling of the Executive or the Panel. The Hearings Committee may also be convened for hearings in certain other circumstances.

The Rules of Procedure of the Hearings Committee are set out in Appendix 9 of the Code and its Terms of Reference can be found on the Panel's website.

Rulings of the Committee are binding on the parties to the proceedings and on those invited to participate in those proceedings unless and until overturned by the Takeover Appeal Board (see 1.8 below).

1.7   The Executive

The day-to-day work of takeover supervision and regulation is carried out by the Executive. This includes, either on its own initiative or at the instigation of third parties, the conduct of investigations, the monitoring of relevant dealings in connection with the Code and the giving of guidance and rulings on the interpretation, application or effect of the Code. The Executive is available both for consultation and also the giving of rulings on the interpretation, application or effect of the Code before, during and, where appropriate, after takeovers or other relevant transactions. In carrying out these functions, the Executive operates independently of the Panel.

The Executive is staffed by a mixture of employees and secondees from law firms, accountancy firms, investment banks and other organisations. It is headed by the Director General, usually an investment banker on secondment, who is an officer of the Panel. The Director General is assisted by Deputy and Assistant Directors General (who are permanent staff), Secretaries (both permanent staff and including one or more solicitors on secondment from prominent law firms) and other members of the Executive's permanent and seconded staff (including a number of secondee Assistant Secretaries). In performing their functions, the secondees act independently of the firms which have seconded them.

The Assistant Secretaries are primarily responsible for dealing with casework and the daily volume of general enquiries. They have the main responsibility for communicating with practitioners and parties to bids. They receive the initial enquiries and they disseminate the Executive's responses and rulings.

The nature of the Executive's rulings will depend on whether or not the Executive is able to hear the views of the other parties involved. If the Executive is not able to hear the views of other parties involved, it may give a conditional ruling (on an ex parte basis) which may be varied or set aside when any views of the other parties have been heard; if the Executive is able to hear the views of other parties involved, it may give an unconditional ruling. An unconditional ruling is binding on those who are made aware of it unless and until overturned by the Hearings Committee or the Takeover Appeal Board. In addition, such persons must comply with any conditional ruling given by the Executive for the purpose of preserving the status quo pending the unconditional ruling.

The Executive keeps under review and carries out research into issues which might require a Code amendment and, if appropriate, recommends Code changes to the Code Committee. Most changes to the Code are subject to public consultation (as described in 1.4 above) and the Executive manages the consultation process, including the preparation of PCPs and RSs.

The Executive also monitors market dealings in shares of companies which are either in an offer period or which the Executive has been informed might go into an offer period. The Executive focuses on enforcing compliance with the disclosure requirements of the Code (in particular, Rule 8), monitoring for abuses of the "exempt" status of the principal trading and fund management divisions of financial institutions, and of recognised intermediary status, and checking for breaches of the Code through dealings by parties to a takeover on the various trading platforms. Securities firms and market operators regularly receive enquiries from the Executive as to the identities of their clients, why transactions have not been disclosed and, occasionally, requests for a more detailed account of the reasons for a particular transaction. The Executive also seeks to identify transactions which might require an announcement under Rule 2 of the Code where there is evidence of speculation or informed dealing in the market but where no announcement has been made of an offer or possible offer.

1.8   Takeover Appeal Board

The Takeover Appeal Board (the Board) is an independent body which hears appeals against rulings of the Hearings Committee. The Chairman and Deputy Chairman of the Board will usually have held high judicial office and are appointed by the Master of the Rolls. Other members, who will usually have relevant knowledge and experience of takeovers and the Code, are appointed by the Chairman (or, failing that, the Deputy Chairman) of the Board. The names of the members of the Board are available on the Board's website (*http://www. thetakeoverappealboard.org.uk* [Accessed 26 June 2019]).

Any party to a hearing before the Hearings Committee (or any person denied permission to be a party to a hearing before the Hearings Committee) may appeal to the Board against any ruling of the Hearings Committee or the Chairman of the hearing (including in respect of procedural directions).

Proceedings before the Board are generally conducted in a similar way to those before the Hearings Committee, using the procedure set out in the Board's Rules which are available on its website. The Board may confirm, vary, set aside, annul or replace the contested ruling of the Hearings Committee.

1.9 Relationship between the Panel and the courts

The proceedings of the Panel are, in the same way as other bodies performing public functions, open to judicial review by the courts. There have been very few instances in which leave to apply for judicial review has been sought. One example was the *Datafin* case, which related to rival bids for McCorquodale in December 1986 (*R. v Panel on Takeovers and Mergers Ex p. Datafin Plc* [1987] Q.B. 815; [1987] 2 W.L.R. 699 CA (Civ Div)). The Master of the Rolls, Lord Donaldson, held that:

> "… in the light of the special nature of the Panel, its functions, the market in which it is operating, the time scales which are inherent in that market and the need to safeguard the position of third parties, who may be numbered in thousands, all of whom are entitled to continue to trade upon an assumption of the validity of the Panel's Rules and decisions, unless and until they are quashed by the court, I should expect the relationship between the Panel and the court to be historic rather than contemporaneous. I should expect the court to allow contemporary decisions to take their course, considering the complaint and intervening, if at all, later and in retrospect by declaratory orders which would enable the Panel not to repeat any error and would relieve individuals of the disciplinary consequences of any erroneous finding of breach of the Rules."

The Guinness/Distillers case was the subject of a Court of Appeal judgment in July 1988 (*R. v Panel on Takeovers and Mergers Ex p. Guinness Plc* [1990] 1 Q.B. 146; [1989] 2 W.L.R. 863 CA (Civ Div)). In this case the Court also indicated its reluctance to interfere in the Panel's decisions. Lord Diplock held that there was a public interest in the Panel acting to enforce the Code and, since no injustice had been done by the Panel's refusal to adjourn its case against Guinness, there was no case for judicial review.

The Court of Appeal's approach was confirmed in late 1988, when Grand Metropolitan sought judicial review of the Panel's decision not to require any remedy for breaches of the Code that the Panel held had been committed by Irish Distillers and Pernod Ricard, when the latter was gathering irrevocable undertakings to support its successful offer. The High Court refused to grant Grand Metropolitan an expedited order for the judicial review hearing on the grounds that the Court of Appeal had made it plain that such proceedings were not intended to reverse Panel decisions taken in the course of takeovers. As a result, the proceedings were discontinued. Judgments such as these demonstrate the courts' support for the Panel and thereby lend authority to its decisions.

The Court of Appeal's decision in the *Datafin* case underlies the approach taken at the time of the implementation of the Directive. For example, following implementation, rulings of the Panel have a binding effect; parties to a takeover are not able to sue each other for breach of a Rule-based requirement, and a transaction, once completed, may not be unpicked (see ss.945 and 956 of the Act).

The support of the court for the Panel, and the Rules contained in the Code, in establishing a framework for the conduct of public offers, was reinforced in the *Expro* case in June 2008 (*Re Expro International Group Plc* [2008] EWHC 1543 (Ch); [2010] 2 B.C.L.C. 514). In that case, certain shareholders submitted to the court that the decision of the directors of Expro to reject a proposal from a competing offeror was wrong and, therefore, the court should not sanction the proposed scheme of arrangement being used to implement the initial offer in order to permit the competing offeror to make its proposal to Expro's shareholders. As part of his judgment rejecting the shareholders' arguments, Richards J concluded that there should, if possible, be a common approach to bids whether they are structured as an offer or a scheme of arrangement and that it would not be desirable if the court procedures involved in a scheme of arrangement should introduce a level of uncertainty which the provisions of the Code had successfully eliminated or reduced in the course of contractual offers. More recently, the Panel has interacted with the courts in the context of enforcement pursuant to the exercise of its powers under s.955 of the Act (as to which see 1.10.3 below).

1.10   Enforcement of the Code

The Panel focuses on the consequences of breaches of the Code, rather than simply on disciplinary action, with the aim of providing appropriate redress. In certain circumstances the Panel may issue rulings to restrain a person from acting in breach of Rules or from following a particular course of action pending a Panel ruling on whether that action would be in breach of the Code. Furthermore, in respect of certain breaches of the Code, disciplinary action may be appropriate (see 1.11 below). Following implementation of the Directive, the Panel has certain statutory enforcement powers, further details of which are set out below.

1.10.1   Compliance rulings

If the Panel is satisfied that:

1. there is a reasonable likelihood that a person will contravene a requirement imposed by or under Rules; or
2. a person has contravened a requirement imposed by or under Rules,

the Panel may give any direction that appears to it to be necessary in order:

(a) to restrain a person from acting (or continuing to act) in breach of Rules;

(b) to restrain a person from doing (or continuing to do) a particular thing, pending determination of whether that or any other conduct of his is or would be a breach of Rules; or

(c) otherwise to secure compliance with Rules.

1.10.2 Compensation rulings

Where a person has breached certain Rules of the Code which relate to the equal treatment of shareholders as regards the terms of an offer (for example, Rules 6, 9 and 11), the Panel may make a ruling requiring the person concerned to pay, within such period as it specifies, to the holders, or former holders, of securities of the offeree company, such amount as it thinks just and reasonable so as to ensure that such holders receive what they would have been entitled to receive if the relevant Rule had been complied with.

1.10.3 Enforcement by the courts

Under s.955 of the Act, the Panel has the power in certain circumstances to seek enforcement by the courts. If the court is satisfied that:

1. there is a reasonable likelihood that a person will contravene a requirement imposed by or under Rules; or
2. a person has contravened a requirement imposed by or under Rules or a requirement imposed under s.947 of the Act,

the court may make any order it thinks fit to secure compliance with the requirement. Any failure to comply with a resulting court order may be a contempt of court.

The Panel has only exercised its powers under s.955 of the Act once in the case of *Panel on Takeovers and Mergers v David Cunningham King* [2017] CSOH 156; 2018 S.L.T. 79; and [2018] CSIH 30; 2018 S.C. 459. The *King* case was heard before the Outer and Inner Houses of the Scottish Court of Session and related to the enforcement of a requirement imposed by the

Executive, Hearings Committee and, ultimately, the Takeover Appeal Board, for Mr King to announce and thereafter make a mandatory offer for Rangers International Football Club Plc in compliance with the Code.

Both the Outer and Inner Houses of the Court of Session agreed to the request by the Panel to grant an order to enforce the ruling of the Takeover Appeal Board. In so doing, the Court also clarified that the reference to "may make any order it thinks fit" in s.955 gave a wide discretion to the court as to whether or not to grant an order, rather than empowering the court to act as no more than a rubber stamp. Nevertheless, the Lords Carloway (the Lord President of the Court of Session), Drummond Young and Glennie of the Inner House went on to confirm that the court should normally enforce an order made by the Panel in the absence of exceptional circumstances and that:

> "… we would expect that cases where the Court decides not to enforce a ruling by the Panel would be rare, especially where the Panel's ruling has been upheld by the Hearings Committee and the Takeover Appeal Board. The most obvious case where enforcement might be refused is where material changes in circumstances have occurred subsequently to the last decision by those bodies. For example, subsequently to the relevant decisions, the offeror might have become insolvent, or an offer by a third party for the relevant shares might have been made. It is only in such relatively exceptional cases that the discretion to refuse a remedy is likely to be relevant. Otherwise, the Court's function is to enforce the rulings of the Panel."

1.10.4 *Power to require information and documents*

The Panel expects any person dealing with it to do so in an open and co-operative way. It also expects prompt co-operation and assistance from persons dealing with it and those to whom enquiries and other requests are directed. Under s.947 of the Act the Panel has the power to require documents and information where they are reasonably required in connection with the exercise of its functions. A document describing how the Executive will exercise this power on behalf of the Panel is available on the Panel's website.

1.11 Disciplinary powers

The disciplinary Rules of the Panel in connection with breaches and alleged breaches of the Code are as follows:

1.11.1 Disciplinary action

The Executive may itself deal with a disciplinary matter where the person who is to be subject to the disciplinary action agrees the facts and the action proposed by the Executive. In any other case, where it considers that there has been a breach of the Code, the Executive may commence disciplinary proceedings before the Hearings Committee. A note setting out the factors that the Executive will take into account when deciding whether to initiate disciplinary action and in proposing the appropriate sanction to the Hearings Committee is available on the Panel's website.

1.11.2 Sanctions or other remedies for breach of the Code

If the Hearings Committee finds a breach of the Code or of a ruling of the Panel, it may:

1. issue a private statement of censure;
2. issue a public statement of censure;
3. suspend or withdraw any exemption, approval or other special status which the Panel has granted to a person, or impose conditions on the continuing enjoyment of such exemption, approval or special status, in respect of all or part of the activities to which such exemption, approval or special status relates;
4. report the offender's conduct to a UK or overseas regulatory authority or professional body (most notably the FCA) so that that authority or body can consider

whether to take disciplinary or enforcement action (for example, the FCA has power to take certain actions against an authorised person or an approved person who fails to observe proper standards of market conduct, including the power to fine); or

5. publish a Panel Statement indicating that the offender is someone who, in the Hearings Committee's opinion, is not likely to comply with the Code. The Panel Statement will normally indicate that this sanction will remain effective for only a specified period. The "cold-shouldering" Rules of the FCA and certain professional bodies would then apply such that persons authorised by the FCA and members of those professional bodies would be obliged, in certain circumstances, not to act for the person in question in a transaction subject to the Code, including any dealing in relevant securities requiring disclosure under Rule 8, for the duration of the relevant period.

1.12 Confidentiality, information sharing and co-operation

The Panel has always been scrupulous about ensuring that confidential information provided to it in the course of applying the Code is kept confidential. The Panel has a statutory duty of confidentiality so that information received by the Panel in connection with the exercise of its statutory functions may not be disclosed without the consent of the individual or business to which it relates, except as permitted by the Act.

Under the Act, the Panel must, to the extent it has power to do so, take such steps as it considers appropriate to co-operate with a number of other UK and international regulators including the FCA, the Prudential Regulation Authority, the Bank of England and other EU supervisory authorities designated for the purposes of the Directive, including by the sharing of information which the Panel is permitted to disclose under the Act. It may also exercise its powers to require documents and information for this purpose. In particular, the Panel works closely with the FCA in relation to insider dealing and market abuse.

Chapter 2

The Approach, Announcements and Independent Advice

Piers Prichard Jones
Partner
Freshfields Bruckhaus Deringer LLP

2.1   General considerations

This Chapter identifies the companies and transactions to which the Code applies. These Rules are set out in s.3 of the Introduction to the Code which was substantially revised in 2006 to reflect the implementation of the EU Directive on Takeover Bids (the "Takeover Directive"). One of the main changes to the Introduction at that time was to broaden the scope of the Panel's jurisdiction to cover a number of companies that were not previously covered by the Code. The Panel's jurisdiction will require further adjustment as a result of the UK's withdrawal from the EU, details of which are set out in the RS 2018/2 and which are discussed further below.

This Chapter also deals with Section D of the Code: Rules 1–3. These Rules are concerned with the crucial "pre-bid" period. The importance of this period cannot be over-emphasised. The commercial and tactical aspects—including the fundamental decision of whether or not to proceed with the bid—can assume paramount importance, especially following amendments to the Code which came into effect in September 2011. Once the formal "firm intention" press announcement is released the die is irretrievably cast. The Panel reiterated in its 2003 Annual Report that notwithstanding the time pressure on decisions taken in the "pre-bid" period, it is essential that the Executive is consulted under s.6(b) of the Introduction to the Code where there is any doubt whatsoever as to whether a proposed course of action is in accordance with the General Principles or the Rules of the Code.

The Panel has placed increasing emphasis on the special duty advisers have, which is to ensure that their clients are aware of their responsibilities under the Code. It is often the advisers who will be criticised by the Panel when things go wrong (for example, the criticism of the financial advisers to Transcomm Plc in the Panel's ruling in March 2004, referred to in 2.6.1 below, and the criticism of certain advisers to parties involved in a transaction by Asia Resource Minerals Plc (formerly Bumi Plc) in the Panel's ruling in November 2015). The Introduction to the Code states that financial advisers have a particular responsibility to comply with the Code and to ensure, so far as they are reasonably able, that their client and its directors are aware of their responsibilities under the Code and will comply with them, and that the Panel is consulted whenever appropriate (s.3(f)). However, it is not only financial advisers that the Panel will consider in taking responsibility for their clients' compliance with the Code.

The Panel is also determined to ensure that all members of a board of directors—not just those entrusted with the day-to-day conduct of a bid—share responsibility for compliance with the Code. Appendix 3 to the Code spells out in detail the obligation to keep all directors fully informed and the responsibility of all directors to monitor the conduct of a bid.

The Code is made up of six General Principles (the six General Principles set out in the Takeover Directive have replaced the Code's previous 10 General Principles) and 38 detailed Rules (as well as nine further Appendices). The General Principles are relevant to interpreting the Rules—they are "applied in accordance with their spirit in order to achieve their under-lying purpose" (see s.2(b) of the Introduction). The following are particularly relevant to Section D of the Code.

General Principle 4:

> "False markets must not be created in the securities of the offeree company, of the offeror company or of any other company concerned by the bid in such a way that the rise or fall of the prices of the securities becomes artificial and the normal functioning of the markets is distorted."

General Principle 5:

> "An offeror must announce a bid only after ensuring that he/she can fulfil in full any cash consideration, if such is offered, and after taking all reasonable measures to secure the implementation of any other type of consideration."

General Principle 6:

> "An offeree company must not be hindered in the conduct of its affairs for longer than is reasonable by a bid for its securities."

One more "General Principle" should be added: for all intents and purposes, a press announcement is every bit as important as the offer document itself. This Chapter will consider a variety of press announcements ranging from the "talks are in progress" or "we are considering making an offer" kind to the formal announcement of the takeover. Whatever the type, all press announcements in the takeover context are designed to achieve the same purpose: to provide information which the market is entitled to rely upon and, where appropriate, to provide information needed to avoid the creation of a false market. In either case, press announcements must be prepared to the highest standards of care and accuracy. Once statements are made in a press announcement, the Panel will invariably expect the parties to adhere to them. In effect, there is little to distinguish the press announcement from the formal offer or defence documents which follow.

2.2 Companies and transactions to which the Code applies

Section 3 of the Introduction to the Code identifies the companies and transactions to which the Code applies. As explained above, it was substantially amended in May 2006 to reflect the implementation of the Takeover Directive. The Takeover Directive determines the minimum scope of the jurisdiction of the competent authority in any EU Member State by reference to the location of the registered office of the offeree company and the regulated market on which its securities are traded. The Code's jurisdiction is, however, wider than the minimum required by the Takeover Directive.

The companies to which the Code applies will change once again as a result of the UK's withdrawal from the EU. In particular, the Panel is proposing to end the shared jurisdiction regime described in 2.2.3 below. The details are set out in RS 2018/2. At present, it is not possible to determine with certainty the date on which those changes will take effect. If the UK leaves the EU without a withdrawal agreement and associated transition period, the proposals set out in RS 2018/2 will come into effect from the date of that withdrawal. If the EU and the UK enter into a withdrawal agreement which includes a transition period, the proposals would take effect following the end of the transition period. For simplicity, the relevant date will be referred to in this Chapter as the implementation date.

References to a "Societas Europaea" in the Introduction to the Code will be replaced from the implementation date with references to a "UK Societas". This is on the basis that any UK-registered Societas Europaea will be converted automatically into a UK Societas, a new UK corporate form which the UK government has indicated will be set up to cater for the UK's withdrawal from the EU.

2.2.1 UK, Channel Islands and Isle of Man registered and traded companies

The Code applies to offers for companies and (until the implementation date) Societas Europaea whose registered offices are in the UK, the Channel Islands or the Isle of Man, and whose securities have been admitted to trading on a regulated market, (this includes the London Stock Exchange's main market, and the ISDX Main Board) in the UK or on a multilateral trading facility (the AIM and the ISDX Growth Market) in the UK or on a stock exchange in the Channel Islands or the Isle of Man (other than those companies which, up to the implementation date, are covered by shared jurisdiction arrangements, see 2.2.3 below). So, for example, if a company is registered in the UK and has its shares admitted to trading on the main market of the London Stock Exchange or admitted to trading on AIM, it is covered by the Code even if its place of central management and control is overseas.

2.2.2 Other companies

The Code also applies to all offers (not falling within 2.2.1 above or, up to the implementation date, 2.2.3 below) for other public and certain private companies and (until the implementation date) Societas Europaea that have their registered offices in the UK, the Channel Islands or the Isle of Man, but only if they are considered by the Panel to have their place of central management and control in these territories. When considering where a company is resident, the Panel will look at the structure of the board, the functions of the directors and where they are resident. Sometimes the Panel may also look at other relevant major influences on the management of the company, for example, in the case of an investment trust, the identity and location of the investment manager.

The residency test is therefore still applicable to a company that has its registered office in the UK, the Channel Islands or the Isle of Man if it is: (a) a public company whose securities are either: (i) not admitted to trading on any public market; or (ii) admitted to trading on a public market but not one that is either a regulated market (in the UK or, up to the implementation date, another EEA (European Economic Area) member state (a Member State)), a multilateral trading facility in the UK or a stock exchange in the Channel Islands or the Isle of Man—for example, a public company whose shares are only traded on the New York Stock Exchange; or (b) a private company.

Even if the directors of a target company, who do not meet the residency test, volunteer to the Panel to subject themselves to the Code or incorporate a reference to the Code in the company's articles of association, the Panel will normally refuse to accept jurisdiction.

Offers for private companies satisfying the residency test are only subject to the Code if: (a) any of their securities have been admitted to trading on any regulated market or multilateral trading facility in the UK or on any stock exchange in the Channel Islands or the Isle of Man within the past 10 years; (b) dealings and/or bid offer prices for their securities have been regularly published for at least six months within the past 10 years, whether via a newspaper, electronic price quotation system (such as the PLUS-quoted market) or otherwise; (c) any of their securities have been subject to a marketing arrangement within the past 10 years; or (d) they have filed a prospectus (and, in the case of a filing with a relevant authority outside the UK, the Channel Islands or the Isle of Man, only if such filed prospectus is public) for the issue, offer or admission to trading of securities within the past 10 years. The Introduction to the Code acknowledges that the provisions of the Code may not be appropriate to all such private companies and the Panel may therefore apply the Code with a degree of flexibility in suitable cases.

In its 2002 Annual Report, the Panel commented on the practice of re-registering a public company as a private company, with the result that the Code did not then apply to any offer for that company provided it did not fall within one of the categories described in the previous paragraph. The Panel advised that it would expect the circular convening the general meeting to effect the conversion to explain that one of the consequences of re-registration would be to take the company outside the ambit of the Code. The Panel should be consulted in advance in order to ensure that the circular contains an explanation of the Code and the implications for shareholders of re-registration. This is now reflected in s.3(e) of the Introduction to the Code, under which early consultation with the Panel is advised before re-registration, if the relevant company has more than one shareholder, so that guidance can be given by the Panel on the appropriate disclosure to be made regarding the loss of Code protection.

2.2.3   Shared jurisdiction

Section 3(a)(iii) of the Introduction to the Code deals with matters necessary to implement art.4.2(b), (c) and (e) of the Takeover Directive relating to shared jurisdiction in cases involving certain UK and other EEA registered and traded companies.

Until the implementation date, the Panel will share the regulation of an offer with a relevant competent authority in another Member State when the offeree company is:

1.   a company which has its registered office in the UK and its securities are not admitted to trading on a UK regulated market but are admitted to trading on a regulated market in one or more other Member States;
2.   a company registered in another Member State whose securities are admitted to trading only on a UK regulated market (and not, therefore, on a regulated market in any other Member State); or
3.   a company registered in another Member State whose securities are admitted to trading on regulated markets in more than one Member State including the UK (but not on a regulated market in the Member State in which it has its registered office) if:
     (a)   the company's securities were first admitted to trading on a UK regulated market;

(b) the company's securities were admitted to trading simultaneously on more than one regulated market on or after 20 May 2006 and the company notified the Panel and the other relevant regulatory authorities on the first day of trading that it had chosen the Panel to regulate it; or

(c) the company's securities were admitted to trading on more than one regulated market before 20 May 2006 and were admitted simultaneously, and either the competent authorities of the relevant Member States agreed before 19 June 2006 that the Panel should be the regulator or, failing that, the company chose on 19 June 2006 to be regulated by the Panel.

In any case falling within (3)(b) or (3)(c), the company will have to notify a Regulatory Information Service of the selection of the Panel as the relevant regulator without delay.

On the basis set out in art.4.2(e) of the Takeover Directive, the Panel will be responsible under (2) and (3) above for regulating matters relating to the consideration offered, in particular the price, and matters relating to the "bid procedure" (for example announcements of offers and the contents of the offer document) and under (1) above for matters relating to the information to be provided to employees of the offeree company and matters relating to "company law" (for example fixing the control threshold for a mandatory offer, any derogation from the obligation to launch a mandatory offer and provisions relating to frustrating action). In each case, the supervisory authority in another Member State will be responsible for those matters not regulated by the Panel.

Section 3(d) of the Introduction to the Code states that early consultation with the Panel is advised in shared jurisdiction cases so that guidance can be given on how any conflicts between the relevant Rules may be resolved and, where relevant, which provisions of the Code apply pursuant to art.4.2(e) of the Takeover Directive.

After the implementation date, the shared jurisdiction regime described above will end. This means that the Panel would no longer take jurisdiction over an offer for:

1. a company which has its registered office in a remaining Member State (i.e. not in the UK) and whose securities are admitted to trading on a UK regulated market (but not on a regulated market in that Member State); or
2. a company which has its registered office in the UK and whose securities are admitted to trading on a regulated market in a remaining Member State (and not on a UK regulated market) and which does not satisfy the "residency test" described in 2.2.2 above.

Conversely, the Code would apply (in full) to an offer for a company which has its registered office in the UK and whose securities are admitted to trading on a regulated market in a remaining Member State (but not on a UK regulated market) if the company satisfies the residency test.

As a practical matter, only a few companies are affected by these changes (RS 2019/3 contains a full list), but it will mean that takeovers for some companies will no longer be regulated by any regulatory authority, and some others will find themselves subject to dual jurisdiction—as to which see 2.2.6 below.

2.2.4   Transactions

The Code has always applied to a wider range of transactions than those covered by the Takeover Directive—the Takeover Directive applies only to public, control-seeking offers. Except in relation to cases covered by the shared jurisdiction arrangements (see 2.2.3 above), the Code applies to takeover bids and mergers however effected (including by means of statutory merger or court-approved scheme of arrangement) and also to other transactions which are used to obtain or consolidate control of a relevant company ("control" for these purposes as defined in the Code). This includes, for example, the acquisition of control pursuant to the exercise of "drag along" rights contained in a company's articles of association (see the Panel's 2001 Annual Report). The transaction in question need not involve the acquisition of a controlling interest—the Code will also apply to partial offers and offers by a parent for the minority in its subsidiary. In the case of statutory mergers under the Companies (Cross-Border Mergers) Regulations 2007, the Executive confirmed in Practice Statement No.18 that the Code will apply to a "merger by absorption" where the transferor company is a Code company and will normally apply to a "merger by formation of a new company" where one or more of the transferor companies is a Code company (unless the Panel is satisfied that the substance of the transaction is the acquisition by the Code company of a non-Code company). Note that from the implementation date, it will no longer be possible to effect a statutory merger between a UK company and a Member State company—the Companies (Cross-Border Mergers) Regulations 2007 will be revoked and Practice Statement No. 18 will be deleted.

In the case of a target company that is subject to the shared jurisdiction arrangements, the Code will apply only to offers that fall within the narrow Takeover Directive-based definition of an offer (see art.2.1(a) of the Takeover Directive), which covers only public, control-seeking offers (whether mandatory or voluntary). This would not capture, for example, a scheme of arrangement under Pt 26 of the Companies Act 2006.

For the avoidance of doubt, it is clear that the Code applies to all relevant transactions at any stage of their implementation, including, for example, when an offer is in contemplation but has not been announced.

2.2.5 *Dual holding companies and newco structures*

Since August 2002, the Code has applied to the establishment of a dual holding company structure involving a UK-resident Plc. These are corporate groups with dual holding companies, typically listed on different exchanges but having identical boards, which operate as a single economic enterprise. The Code therefore applies (subject to the considerations in the following paragraph) to a dual holding company transaction involving a UK company with shares admitted to trading on a regulated market in the UK or on a multilateral trading facility in the UK or on a stock exchange in the Channel Islands or the Isle of Man and any other public UK company (and certain private UK companies) which the Panel considers to be resident in the UK, the Channel Islands or the Isle of Man. A dual holding company transaction involving a company falling within the shared jurisdiction provisions referred to in 2.2.3 above will not, however, be subject to the Code, as these only apply to transactions falling within the narrow Takeover Directive-based definition of an offer.

Where the Code applies, the company subject to the Code will usually be treated as the offeree company and the offer regarded as a securities exchange offer for the purposes of the Code. Whilst the normal Code Rules would then apply, the Panel indicated in the consultation paper on dual listed company transactions issued in April 2002 (PCP 11), that certain Rules, principally those relating to the offer timetable and acceptances, would be applied flexibly having regard to the particular circumstances. Nevertheless, there may be cases where there is no doubt that the substance of a dual holding company transaction is the acquisition by a Code company of a non-Code company. In such circumstances, the Panel may be willing to agree that the Code should not apply. The public consultation paper referred to above also contains guidance on how the Code will be applied to newco structures (where a new holding company acquires both parties) and, as referred to above, although the Code will normally apply to a "merger by formation of a new company" under the Companies (Cross-Border Mergers) Regulations 2007 where one or more of the transferor companies is a Code company. If the Panel is satisfied that the substance of the transaction is the acquisition by the Code company of a non-Code company, it may agree that the transaction should not be subject to the Code.

2.2.6 *Dual jurisdiction*

A company which is subject to the Code may also be subject to the jurisdiction of other overseas regulators. In such circumstances, the Panel recommends early consultation so that guidance can be given on how any conflicts between the relevant requirements may be resolved.

It is now common for offers to be structured to comply with both the Code and the "tender offer" rules of the US Securities and Exchange Act of 1934. Areas of particular conflict between the US and UK rules may include market purchases, the timing of the first closing date and, in circumstances where the target is listed in the US, withdrawal rights and disclosure requirements. In addition, where share (or other security) consideration is offered, the bidder may need to comply with the registration requirements of the US Securities Act of 1933. Certain exemptions to the US tender offer rules and registration requirements are available. The extent of relief provided by these exemptions depends on the size of a non-US offeree's US shareholder base. If US-resident beneficial shareholders hold 10% or less of the shares of a non-US offeree (as calculated in accordance with the relevant Rules), the bid qualifies for the "Tier I" exemption and the bidder is able to conduct its bid in accordance with "home country" rules (i.e. the Code in the case of a bid for a company in respect of which the Panel has jurisdiction) and certain additional (largely procedural) requirements stipulated in the exemption. If US-resident beneficial shareholders hold more than 10% but not more than 40% of the shares of a non-US offeree, the bid qualifies for the "Tier II" exemption, which provides more limited exemptive relief. The cross-border exemptions do not exempt bidders from US securities law liability for misleading statements and omissions and fraudulent or manipulative acts in connection with such transactions.

Where the offeree company has a number of shareholders in any overseas jurisdiction, appropriate advice should be taken at an early stage as documentation is now required to be circulated to all shareholders unless a dispensation is available (see Rule 30.4).

2.3 The approach

Rule 1 deals with the "approach".

2.3.1 Notifying the offeree company

Rule 1(a) requires that an offeror (or its advisers) must notify a firm intention to make an offer in the first instance to the offeree board or to its advisers. The degree of contact will, in practice, vary according to the nature of the bid. Where the bid is unilateral or "hostile", pre-announcement contact is likely to be minimal. In some cases, it may take the form of a telephone call to the chairman to say that a press announcement will be released in five minutes. Many hours can be spent planning how to get hold of the chairman to receive such a call.

2.3.2 Identity

The importance of the identity of the offeror is emphasised by Rule 1(b): where an approach to the offeree company with regard to a possible offer is not made by the offeror or potential offeror, its identity must be disclosed to the board of the offeree company at the outset. This applies even in the case of a cash bid, where it might be assumed that identity is not important. The provision is reflected also in Rule 2.7(c), which requires the offeror to be identified in the formal press announcement.

Occasionally, it may not be clear who is to be regarded as the "offeror"—for example, where the offer is made by a subsidiary or a special bid vehicle, or where the bidding company is controlled by a consortium. In such circumstances, the Panel should be consulted and may be expected, in appropriate cases, to apply a "look-through" principle to the parent or "quasi" parent requiring the identity of that "parent" or controller to be disclosed.

2.4 Announcing the offer

The Code places a very strict obligation on offerors and their financial advisers to exercise due care before formally announcing an offer. This works on the basis that the announcement of a firm intention to make an offer will inevitably have a profound effect on the offeree company and the market price of its shares. While investors in a company which is the subject of an offer appreciate that it may fail due to lack of acceptances or regulatory problems, they expect that the offer will only be withdrawn for other reasons in a small minority of cases.

There are two particularly important Code provisions to note in this respect.

General Principle 5:

> "An offeror must announce a bid only after ensuring that he/she can fulfil in full any cash consideration, if such is offered, and after taking all reasonable measures to secure the implementation of any other type of consideration."

Rule 2.7(a):

> "An offeror should announce a firm intention to make an offer only after the most careful and responsible consideration and when the offeror has every reason to believe that it can and will continue to be able to implement the offer. Responsibility in this connection also rests on the financial adviser to the offeror."

General Principle 5 relates to the steps a bidder should take, before announcing the offer, to ensure that the offer consideration will be available. The announcement of an offer that includes cash must also include a confirmation by the financial adviser, or by another appropriate third party, that resources are available to the offeror sufficient to satisfy full acceptance of the offer (see Rule 2.7(d)). Rule 24.8 requires an equivalent confirmation to be given in the offer document. Although Rule

2.7(a) makes it clear that a financial adviser shares responsibility for ensuring the offeror will be able to implement the offer, under Rules 2.7(d) and 24.8 it is clear that the person giving the cash confirmation will not be expected to produce the cash itself provided "it acted responsibly and took all reasonable steps to assure itself that the cash was available".

An example of the application of these responsibilities was the proposed offer by Luirc for Merlin Properties. The offeror was a newly incorporated British Virgin Islands company with a nominal capital. When the bid was announced the offeror had received a comfort letter that funds were available, but no formal loan agreement had been negotiated or signed. The Panel ruled that no announcement of the bid should have been made before the offeror had received an irrevocable commitment to provide the funds. The Panel's ruling stated that:

> "compliance with [General Principle 5 and Rule 2.7(a)] is of great importance. The announcement of an offer is always highly significant for the offeree company and will usually affect its share price. If the offer is subsequently withdrawn, at the very least a false market in the shares in the offeree company is likely to have been created.
>
> The Executive's view is that, when a financial adviser is acting for a newly created offeror, such as an off-the-shelf overseas company, the standard of care required under [General Principle 5 and Rule 2.7(a)] clearly has an additional dimension. In short, the only way in which such an offeror and its financial adviser can be sure that funds will be available is to have an irrevocable commitment from a party upon whom reliance can reasonably be placed, for example a bank, at the time of the announcement of the offer."

As referred to above, if it did not act responsibly and take all reasonable steps as referred to in Rules 2.7(d) and 24.8, the financial adviser or other third party giving the cash confirmation may be required to come up with the cash itself. The following extract from the Panel's 1991 Annual Report is a salutary lesson:

> "In a cash offer [Rule 24.8] requires the offer document to contain confirmation, normally by the offeror's bank or financial adviser, that there are resources available to the offeror sufficient to satisfy full acceptance of the offer. If accepting shareholders are not paid and the Panel considers that the party giving the cash confirmation did not act responsibly and did not take all reasonable steps to assure itself that the cash was available, the Panel may look to the party giving the confirmation to produce the cash itself.
>
> It is a matter of judgment in each case for the party giving the cash confirmation to satisfy itself that there will be funds available to meet the offer. In making that judgment, the party giving the cash confirmation will be influenced by a variety of matters such as the standing of the offeror, the extent and nature of its relationship with the offeror and the size of the offer. In the rare event of cash not subsequently being made available to accepting shareholders, the Executive will investigate what steps were taken by the party giving the cash confirmation.
>
> In a recent case an offeror failed to pay certain of the accepting shareholders and the Executive found that the adviser that gave the cash confirmation in the offer document had not exercised adequate care in ensuring that cash would be available to the offeror. The Executive ruled that the adviser concerned should pay the consideration that was due under the offer and the outstanding payments were duly made."

In April 2005, the Executive issued Practice Statement No.10 relating to cash offers financed by the issue of offeror securities. The Executive noted that:

"if an offer, which was to be financed by the issue of offeror securities, lapses or is withdrawn owing to a failure to fulfil a condition relating to the issue, the Executive will wish to be satisfied that [General Principle 5 and Rule 2.7(a)] were complied with (so that, on announcement, the offeror and its financial adviser had had every reason to believe that the offer could and would be implemented)."

The Executive also thought that:

"in order to satisfy [General Principle 5, Rule 2.7(a) and Rule 24.8], it was the responsibility of the party giving the cash confirmation and the offeror (and, if it is not the cash confirmer, the offeror's financial adviser) to take all reasonable steps, before the announcement of the offer, to satisfy themselves that the issue of new securities will be successful, and that the offeror will have the necessary cash available to finance the full acceptance of the offer."

Rule 2.7(a) requires the offeror's pre-announcement due diligence exercise to cover all aspects of implementing the offer, not just ensuring the availability of consideration. The Panel's statement in August 1989 dealing with Wm Low's lapsed bid for Budgens is still required reading in this area. Following the announcement of its bid, Wm Low discovered details about Budgens' working capital and borrowings which led it to conclude that the offer no longer made financial sense. Since the bid was conditional on Wm Low's shareholders' approval, the Panel agreed to it being withdrawn on the basis that, with the directors of Wm Low changing their earlier recommendation to vote in favour, shareholders would inevitably withhold their approval. However, in the inquest that followed, the Panel had some strong words of criticism to say about Wm Low's financial advisers and about what was then General Principle 3 (now part of Rule 2.7(a)), including the following:

"Compliance with this principle is of great importance. The announcement of an offer inevitably has a profound effect upon the market. The share price of the offeree company will be affected and, in consequence, if the offer is subsequently withdrawn—for whatever reason—many people may have dealt on the basis of expectations which are not fulfilled. Against this background, [Rule 2.7(a)] attempts to reduce to a minimum the number of offers which are withdrawn by placing upon potential offerors and their advisers an obligation to exercise due care before making an offer. This Code duty is of a standard similar to that which the law imposes upon professional people or indeed anyone who purports to possess some special skill.

It is a duty to display that standard of skill and care which would ordinarily be expected of someone exercising or professing to exercise the particular skill in question. The Panel stresses that [Rule 2.7(a)] is designed to protect shareholders of the offeree company and those who might deal or consider dealing in the shares of the offeree company. Accordingly, to the extent that it is practically possible to exercise care, the Code duty arising under [Rule 2.7(a)] cannot be limited simply to setting out conditions to which a particular offer is subject.

The practical content of the Code duty to exercise appropriate care will inevitably depend upon all the circumstances of the case. Where there is a unilateral offer, it may be very difficult for the offeror to obtain reliable detailed information concerning the business of the offeree company. The issue of what is reasonable in each case turns in part upon the likely reaction of the offeror to unanticipated developments or revelations following the announcement of an offer. If, for example, a very large company were proposing to take over a small company just to obtain a particular product, it might be perfectly reasonable for it not to investigate the profitability or borrowings of the target, because subsequent revelations relating to those aspects of the target's business would not be relevant to the offeror. But, on the other hand, in the case of a proposed merger of companies of similar size, the offeror is likely to be much more sensitive to the precise financial position of the offeree. In such a situation, which existed in the present case, it is necessary for the offeror, where it has the opportunity to do so, to take greater care to investigate that position in advance."

In April 2005, the Executive issued Practice Statement No.11 relating to working capital requirements in cash and securities exchange offers and it stated that the Executive's practice in this area was that in the event of an offer lapsing as a result of working capital concerns, the Executive would wish to be satisfied that the offeror and its financial adviser had, at the time of announcement of the offer, complied with what are now General Principle 5 and Rule 2.7(a).

In its 1997 Annual Report, the Panel commented as follows:

"Subject to the need to maintain secrecy, parties and their advisers should … seek to address all potential concerns in relation to the offeree company before issuing an announcement of a firm intention to make an offer. To the extent that this is possible, these concerns should be identified in advance by undertaking appropriate due diligence. However, the scope for doing so will depend upon, in particular, whether or not the offeror has the co-operation of the offeree board."

A further aspect of the obligation in Rule 2.7(a) is to ensure that the offeror has obtained all necessary consents and approvals to the making of the offer before it is announced, other than those which cannot be obtained in advance and can be included as conditions or pre-conditions to the offer in accordance with Rule 13. This was illustrated in the pre-conditional, recommended offer by ONGC Videsh Ltd (OVL) for Imperial Energy Plc. After announcement of the offer and satisfaction of the stated regulatory pre-conditions, OVL sought further time before posting its offer document in order for it to be approved by the Indian Government (which controlled 74% of OVL). In dismissing OVL's appeal for an extension, the Hearings Committee of the Panel stated in Panel Statement 2008/46:

"The Committee wishes to reiterate the importance of treating a [Rule 2.7] announcement as a firm commitment to make an offer in accordance with the terms of the announcement and to follow the Code timetable unless and to the extent that the Panel modifies such obligations, something which all concerned would rightly expect to happen only in exceptional circumstances and with the consent of the offeree, at least in the event, as here, of a recommended offer. After a [Rule 2.7] announcement, to attempt to introduce unilaterally a pre-condition to the offer is manifestly unacceptable (subject to the very limited exceptions in Rule 32.4 of the Code).

The issue at the hearing seemed to the Committee ... to be not whether the Government of India had other more pressing priorities and/or was unable or unwilling until some later date to decide whether or not to approve the posting of the offer document. Rather, the prior question was whether to allow to be imposed on OVL and Imperial Energy a pre-condition enabling the Government of India to grant or withhold such approval. This is a question of principle, not one requiring detailed exploration of such matters as why the Government of India asserts such a right or of whether it has already had sufficient time to reach a decision on the point."

2.5 Secrecy

2.5.1 The basic obligation

Rule 2.1(a) imposes an obligation on all persons privy to confidential information concerning a possible offer to treat the information as secret prior to the announcement of the offer or possible offer, and requires such persons to conduct themselves so as to minimise the chances of a leak of the information. For example, confidential information should only be passed to another person if it is necessary to do so and if that person is made aware of the need for secrecy. A party to an offer and its advisers should consider at the outset what controls they are going to put in place to maintain secrecy (including by reference to the FSA's *Market Watch* issues No.21 (July 2007) and No.27 (June 2008)—"Thematic review of controls over insider information relating to public takeovers"), and this is something the Panel may well investigate if there is a leak.

These obligations are closely linked to the requirement in Rule 2.2(e) that where more than a very small number of people (essentially those who need to know in the companies concerned and their immediate advisers) are included in pre-bid discussions, the Panel should be consulted and an announcement may need to be made.

2.5.2   Financial advisers' obligations

In turn, Rule 2.1(b) places financial advisers under a specific obligation to warn clients about the requirement for secrecy and, indeed, about their responsibilities under the Code in general. In the Executive's view, it is unlikely to be sufficient simply to send a standard form memorandum to the client, so financial advisers should take steps to talk senior executives of the client through these issues in order to discharge their responsibilities under this Note.

2.5.3   Employee consultation

Although the Code never did prohibit communications with employees, in Panel Statement 2010/22 the Code Committee concluded that the Code should be amended to improve communication between the board of the offeree company and its employees and to make it clear that the Code does not prevent the passing of information in confidence during the offer period to employee representatives.

Accordingly, following the consultation in PCP 2011/1, a new Note on Rule 20.1 (now Note 3) was introduced which states that, subject to the basic secrecy obligations contained in Rule 2.1, the Code does not prevent the passing of information in confidence by an offeror or the offeree company to its own employees or employee representatives, or by an offeror to the employees or employee representatives of the offeree company (provided the employees or employee representatives are acting as such and not as shareholders). Therefore, any necessary or desired employee consultation can take place both before and during a bid, subject to the confidentiality requirements of Rule 2.1.

2.6   Pre-bid announcements

2.6.1   *When an announcement is required*

Rules 2.2–2.6 deal with the difficult issue of announcements made before the formal offer announcement (historically referred to as "possible offer announcements" or "Rule 2.4 announcements"). The first issue to consider is when a possible offer announcement must be made, and here the Panel's paramount concern is to avoid the creation of a false market: see General Principle 4. The difficulty is to strike the balance between achieving this objective and protecting the legitimate commercial interests of potential offerors (who on the whole would not want to reveal their hands until they have dotted the "i's" and crossed the "t's").

An excellent explanation of the background to this perennial of topical issues is to be found in the Panel's 1988 Annual Report. In it, the Panel dealt firmly with the reluctant offeror as follows:

> "An area that has caused the Executive some concern over the last year relates to the timing and quality of information released relating to an offer. It is amongst the more important tasks of the Panel to ensure that information is made available equally to all shareholders, and also that the parties to an offer use every endeavour to prevent the creation of a false market in the securities of the companies concerned throughout the offer. Accordingly, although this is not a new problem and was the subject of a Panel Statement last September, its importance is such that it is worth repeating here.

There has on several occasions been a considerable amount of speculation concerning a possible offer; in some cases it has been well founded but in others it has not. But, whenever there is such speculation, the companies and their advisers must consider whether an announcement is required under Rule 2.2 of the Code.

In particular, Rule 2.2(d) imposes an obligation on the potential offeror to make an announcement when, before an approach has been made, the offeree company is the subject of rumour and speculation, or there is an untoward movement in its share price, and there are reasonable grounds for concluding that it is the potential offeror's actions which have led to the situation.

The Rule can sometimes pose difficulties for an offeror, particularly when he is in the process of finalising his plans. So there may be a reluctance to make an announcement, leading the offeror to accept, perhaps too readily, alternative explanations as to why there is speculation or an untoward price movement, rather than the most likely one, which is that his security is inadequate. But the Code requires that where there is speculation or an untoward price movement, but the offeror and his advisers do not propose to make an immediate announcement, the Panel should be consulted."

The Panel further emphasised its position in its 1996 Annual Report where, having stressed the need for secrecy pre-announcement and the necessity of "prior and full consultation with [the Executive] in respect of the announcement obligations under Rule 2", the Panel went on to state:

"The Executive also wishes to emphasise that a requirement on a potential offeror to make an announcement of its interest under Rule 2.2(d) can, and often does, arise prior to any decision being made to proceed with such an offer, or prior to the funding needed for such an offer being finalised. The Executive takes the view that if there is rumour and speculation relating to a particular offeree company or there is an untoward movement in its share price and there are reasonable grounds for concluding that this is as a result of the potential offeror's actions, then, even if the potential offeror has not yet decided to proceed with an offer, an announcement of its possible interest is required."

And again, in Practice Statement No.20 (issued in March 2008, revised in March 2009, and re-issued in September 2011—and required reading on the subject of Rule 2), the Executive explained that:

"on occasion, it is argued that to require an announcement referring to the possibility of an offer when the offer preparations are at a preliminary stage might, of itself, lead to the creation of a false market in the offeree company's securities. The Executive does not find this argument persuasive. In the Executive's opinion, if it appears that details of the possible offer may have leaked, leading to rumour and speculation or an untoward movement in the offeree company's share price, the overriding requirement is that an announcement should be made immediately and the fact that the offer prepara-tions are at a preliminary stage may be made clear in the announcement."

There are a number of limbs to when an announcement may be required under Rule 2.2. Rules 2.2(a) and (b) are straightfor-ward, requiring an announcement when a firm intention to bid is notified to the offeree board by or on behalf of an offeror or when the offeror triggers a mandatory offer obligation under Rule 9.1.

Rules 2.2(c), (d) and (f)(i) all apply when there is rumour and speculation concerning the offeree company, or an "untoward" movement in its share price. Paragraph (c) covers the position after an approach by or on behalf of a potential offeror to the board of the offeree company has been made. Paragraph (d) applies after a potential offeror first actively considers an offer but before an approach if there are reasonable grounds for concluding that the rumour and speculation or movement in the share price resulted from some action of the offeror—through inadequate security or otherwise. Paragraph (f) applies when a purchaser is being sought for an interest, or interests in, shares carrying in aggregate 30% or more of the voting rights of a company, or when the board of a company is seeking potential offerors. Prior to 19 September 2011, the Panel was generally significantly less likely to require an announcement if the offeree company was already in an offer period, on the basis that after there had already been one announcement of a possible offer it would be understood that additional potential offerors may emerge. However, since that date and the introduction of Note 3 on Rule 2.2, it is now the case that if rumour and speculation specifically identifies a potential offeror whose identity has not previously been announced, the Panel will now normally require an announcement, either (according to Rule 2.4—see below) by the potential offeror or by the offeree company identifying the potential offeror, even if an offer period has already commenced.

Note 1 on Rule 2.2 makes it clear that whether or not a movement is "untoward" is for the Panel to determine, on the following basis:

> "The question will be considered in the light of all relevant facts and not solely by reference to the absolute percentage movement in the price. Facts which may be considered to be relevant in determining whether a price movement is untoward for the purposes of Rules 2.2(c), (d) and (f)(i) include general market and sector movements, publicly available information relating to the company, trading activity in the company's securities and the time period over which the price movement has occurred. This list is purely illustrative and the Panel will take account of such other factors as it considers appropriate."

After an approach to the board of the offeree company (in the case of Rule 2.2(c)), or after an offer is first actively considered by a potential offeror (in the case of Rule 2.2(d)), or after the board starts to seek one or more potential offerors (in the case of Rule 2.2(f)(i)), there is an obligation to consult the Panel at the latest when the offeree company becomes the subject of any rumour and speculation relating to a possible offer for the offeree company (regardless of whether the rumour and speculation is specific to the possible transaction under consideration or the manner in which, or medium by which, it has been disseminated) or where there is a price movement of 10% or more above the lowest share price since the time of the approach etc. An abrupt price rise of a smaller percentage (for example a rise of 5% in the course of a single day) could also be regarded as untoward and accordingly the Panel should be consulted in such circumstances.

This obligation of consultation with the Executive is viewed by it as being of crucial importance in the application of Rule 2.2 although, as the Executive was keen to stress in Practice Statement No.20, "consultation will not necessarily lead to a requirement to make an announcement; this will depend on all the relevant circumstances". That Practice Statement also gives guidance on when, for the purposes of Rule 2.2(d) and Note 1, an offer will be treated as "first actively considered". The Executive will take various factors into account when determining whether and when an offer is "first actively considered", including whether the possible offer has been considered by the board, investment committee or senior management of the offeror, whether work is being undertaken by external advisers and whether external parties (e.g. potential lenders etc) have been approached. The Panel's Annual Report for 2003 also states that notwithstanding the requirement to consult "the parties should not delay an announcement in order to consult the Panel if it is clear that an announcement is required".

Practice Statement No.31 (published in 2017) outlines how the Executive interprets Rule 2 in the context of a company announcing a strategic review of its business. Often in these circumstances an offer is one of a number of options under review and it is not always clear whether a strategic review announcement will trigger the commencement of an offer period. If the announcement does refer to an offer (or a formal sales process or a merger or the search for a buyer for the company) as being an option under consideration this will automatically start an offer period (this mirrors the definition of "offer period"). Any potential offeror with which the company is in talks, or from which it has received an approach with regard to a possible offer, must be identified in the announcement, unless the strategic review incorporates a formal sales process in accordance with Note 2 on Rule 2.6. If, at the time of the announcement, the company is not in talks with any potential offeror and is not in receipt of any approach with regard to a possible offer, this should be stated in the announcement. If the review later concludes that the offer (or a formal sales process or a merger or the search for a buyer for the company) will not be pursued then the company must make a prompt public announcement in order for the offer period to end.

If the announcement does not refer to an offer (or a formal sales process or a merger or the search for a buyer for the company), the Panel will make direct enquiries of the company's advisers as to the options being considered by the board. If an offer is one option actively under consideration, or which will actively be under consideration, and there is subsequently either rumour about the offer or an untoward movement in the company's share price, the Panel will then normally require the company to make an announcement. At this point the offer period will commence and the announcement will need to identify any potential offeror with which the company is in talks or from which it has received an approach with regard to a possible offer. If the review subsequently concludes not to pursue the offer, a further prompt public announcement is required to end the offer period. Companies are encouraged to consult with the Executive prior to making any strategic review announcements in order to avoid any misunderstanding.

An announcement may also be required under Rule 2.2(e) when more than a very restricted number of people (outside those who need to know in the parties concerned and their immediate advisers) are to be approached in relation to a possible offer. This would include potential providers of finance (whether equity or debt), shareholders in the offeror or the offeree company, the offeree company's pension fund trustees, potential management candidates, significant customers of, or suppliers to, the offeree company or potential purchasers of assets. Rule 2.2(f)(ii) has a similar requirement where para.(f) applies and the number of potential purchasers or offerors approached is about to be increased to include more than a very restricted number of people.

In the case of Rule 2.2(e), the Executive regards a "very restricted number" of people to be six. However, it may be prepared to consent to more than six external parties being approached without an announcement being made, provided it is consulted in advance. In considering whether to allow a wider group to be approached, the Executive will want to be satisfied that secrecy will be maintained and, like any other person privy to price-sensitive information concerning an offer, the external parties approached must, as required by Rule 2.1, keep the discussions secret and must not themselves approach additional third parties without consulting the Panel. As required by Note 1 on Rule 2.2, in the case of Rule 2.2(f)(ii), the consent of the Executive should be obtained before more than one potential purchaser or offeror is sought.

Rule 2.3 establishes a clear demarcation of responsibility for making pre-bid announcements. Before a potential offeror approaches the offeree board, the obligation is that of the potential offeror. As a result, and as advised in Practice Statement No.20, the offeror and its financial adviser will need to establish a system that tracks the offeree company's share price on a real-time basis and at all times during market hours in order to monitor whether there is an untoward share price movement, and will need to monitor the press, newswires, trade publications and internet bulletin boards for any rumour and speculation. The offeror is also responsible for making the announcement when an obligation to make a mandatory offer under Rule 9.1 is incurred.

Once an approach has been made to the board of the offeree company, responsibility for making any possible offer announcement will move to the offeree company, who, with its financial advisers will then need to establish the same monitoring systems. And where a purchaser is being sought for an interest in shares carrying 30% or more of the voting rights but without the involvement of the offeree company, responsibility will rest with the potential seller.

Rule 2.3(d) also includes a reminder that the potential offeror should not resort to any "strong-arm tactics" in an attempt to prevent the offeree company board from making an announcement relating to the possible offer or publicly identifying the potential offeror at any time it considers appropriate. The Panel also advised in its Annual Report for 2003 and in Practice Statement No.20 that if the offeror's approach is unequivocally rejected by the offeree company, the announcement obligation will normally revert to the offeror as only the offeror will then know whether it intends to proceed with the offer.

A key issue in applying Rule 2.3 is what amounts to an "approach", which the Executive dealt with in Practice Statement No.20 as follows:

> "For these purposes, the Executive interprets the term 'approach' broadly. Each case will turn on its own facts, but the Executive normally considers an approach to have been received when a director or representative of, or an adviser to, an offeree company is informed by, or on behalf of, a potential offeror that it is considering the possibility of making an offer for the company. This may be at a very preliminary stage in the offeror's preparations and the manner of the approach may be informal and no more than broadly indicative. For example, there is no requirement for an approach to be made in writing, or for an indicative offer price (or any terms or conditions) to be specified, and it could be made as part of a conversation on unrelated matters …

In order to avoid confusion, the parties should agree which of the offeror and the offeree company has responsibility for making an announcement at any particular time following the initial approach. If the parties are unable to reach agreement as to where the responsibility rests, or if there is any doubt as to whether there has been an unequivocal rejection of an approach, the Executive should be consulted."

Except as outlined in 2.6.2 below, once a possible offer announcement obligation has arisen under Rule 2.2, the Panel will expect that it is made within a matter of minutes. As referred to in 2.6.3 below, a brief announcement of the possibility of an offer being made and identifying the potential offeror or offerors is all that is required, and so the Panel will not be sympathetic to delays as a result of drafting changes being made or parties wishing to include additional information in the announcement (a further announcement can always be made if wanted). This will also mean that in practice, and as advised in Practice Statement No.20, an offeror or offeree company, and its financial adviser, will want to have an appropriate draft announcement prepared at an early stage in any bid preparations and have a procedure in place to ensure the prompt release of the announcement if required.

There have been many instances of parties and their advisers being criticised for a failure to make a timely announcement or to consult the Panel as to whether an announcement was required, and it is worth referring to a few to highlight the Panel's approach. In February 1992, the Panel ruled that Rule 2.2(c), (d) and (e) had been breached prior to the Petrocon bid for James Wilkes. On this occasion, the share price of Wilkes had increased by some 26% before an announcement was made. Apart from share purchases, the bidder's advisers approached institutional shareholders in confidence to establish the likely reaction to a bid without the consent of the Panel. On both counts, the advisers were criticised. The responsibility then passed to James Wilkes and its advisers when the approach was made over the weekend, and they were criticised for failing to insist on an announcement.

In February 1996, in connection with Rentokil's unilateral offer for BET, the Panel concluded that Rentokil's financial advisers should have been more alert to the need to consult the Panel under Rule 2 of the Code. In that case, there was market speculation and the Panel took the view that, given the market rumour and the fact that Rentokil was at an advanced stage of preparation for a possible offer, the Panel should have been consulted immediately upon such rumours commencing. The Panel also emphasised that, as part of such consultation, there was an obligation on the financial adviser to provide the Panel with background information in order for the Panel to make a full assessment of the situation, and went on to underline the importance of prior and full consultation with the Panel in respect of the announcement obligation under Rule 2 of the Code, particularly in the context of a possible unilateral offer. The Executive similarly criticised the financial adviser to Transcomm Plc in March 2004 for its failure to consult the Executive as required by Note 1 on Rule 2.2. Transcomm had been in discussions with British Telecommunications Plc for a number of months before making an announcement that it was in talks that might lead to an offer for the company. During the period prior to the announcement, although the share price moved from 11p per share to 14.5p per share, Transcomm's financial adviser determined, without consulting the Executive, that no announcement was required. In its statement the Executive emphasised the importance the Panel attaches to Rule 2.2 and to the making of timely announcements.

It is worth noting that failure to make an announcement where there is a regulatory obligation to do so can also amount to market abuse under the Market Abuse Regulation (which came into force in July 2016). In addition, it should be noted that for a company whose home Member State is the UK and whose shares have been admitted to a securities market in the UK, a dishonest omission from, or dishonest delay in publishing an announcement, may also give rise to liability under the issuer liability regime now contained in s.90A and Sch.10A of the Financial Services and Markets Act 2000.

2.6.2 *Avoiding a possible offer announcement*

Under Note 4 on Rule 2.2, where an obligation to make a possible offer announcement would normally arise as a result of rumour and speculation or an untoward movement in the offeree company's share price, the Panel may nevertheless agree that no announcement is required provided it is satisfied that the potential offeror has ceased to actively consider making an offer. The potential offeror will therefore normally have a choice between an announcement being made that it is considering making an offer, or privately or publicly "downing tools" and walking away from the transaction. If it chooses to down tools privately, the potential offeror will be prevented under the current version of Note 4 on Rule 2.2 (introduced by RS2014/1 following PCP 2014/1) from actively considering making an offer for the offeree company for a period of three months. In this three-month period the potential offeror will also be prevented from making an approach to the board of the offeree company or acquiring any interests in shares in the offeree company.

Other restrictions also apply in this three-month period and for a further three-month period (i.e. for a period of six months from the time the private down tools dispensation is granted). These other restrictions mirror those that apply under Rule 2.8 where a potential offeror has publicly downed tools and can be set aside in any of the following circumstances: (1) where a third party announces a firm bid (not just a possible offer announcement); (2) if the offeree company announces a whitewash or a reverse takeover; (3) if the Panel determines there has been a material change of circumstances; or (4) at the request of the offeree company (although this will not normally apply in the first three months). These are the same circumstances that allow a potential offeror to set aside a "no intention to bid" statement made in an offer period.

It is important to note that the private down tools regime is more restrictive for a potential offeror than the public down tools regime. For example, in a private down tools the potential offeror is prohibited from any active consideration of the transaction for three months. While in a public no-bid statement the potential offeror is permitted to continue preparations for an offer to be made at the end of the six-month lock-out period, provided knowledge of the possible offer is not extended outside those who need to know about it in the potential offeror and its immediate advisers. The Code Committee explained the rationale for this difference in RS 2014/1:

> "The Code Committee considers it correct that a person who has been granted a dispensation under Note 4(a) on Rule 2.2 [i.e. a private 'down tools' dispensation] should be subject to more stringent restrictions than a person who has made a no intention to bid statement [i.e. a public 'down tools' statement under Rule 2.8]. The Code Committee considers that this is a function of the significant dispensation granted to such a person."

Notwithstanding that a dispensation from making a possible offer announcement may have been granted in the case of a private down tools, an announcement may still be required by the Panel if any rumour and speculation continues or is repeated or the Panel otherwise considers it necessary to prevent the creation of a false market.

2.6.3 Possible offer announcements

When a possible offer announcement obligation is triggered by Rule 2.2, a brief announcement that talks are taking place or that a potential offeror is considering making an offer will be sufficient. However, since 19 September 2011 and the amendments to the Code following the consultation in PCP 2011/1, any possible offer announcement by the offeree company must identify any potential offeror or offerors (unless previously publicly identified) with which the offeree company is in talks or from which an approach has been received (that has not been withdrawn or unequivocally rejected)—see Rule 2.4. In addition, any subsequent announcement by the offeree company that refers to the existence of a possible white knight must identify that new potential offeror.

The only exceptions to these obligations to name potential offerors are if another offeror has already announced a firm intention to make an offer for the offeree company or if the offeree company has already announced that it is seeking one or more potential offerors by means of a formal sale process as referred to in Note 2 on Rule 2.6. Paragraph 3 of Practice Statement 31 provides further information on the announcement and conduct of formal sales processes in accordance with Note 2.

The above requirements to identify potential offerors in announcements made by the offeree company were part of a package of changes introduced following the consultation in PCP 2011/1, designed to increase the protection for offeree companies against protracted "virtual bid" periods—i.e. a lengthy period of speculation, and sometimes "assault", following a possible offer announcement and before a firm offer announcement was made or the potential offeror withdrew.

Any possible offer announcement by a potential offeror or by an offeree company which first identifies a potential offeror must include a summary of the provisions of Rule 8 and specify the "put up or shut up" deadline referred to in 2.6.4 that will apply in respect of that potential offeror.

Provided it complies with these minimum content requirements, a possible offer announcement may go further and include whatever additional information about the possible offer or situation that the potential offeror or the offeree company, as the case may be, wishes to include. Indeed, there have been examples of possible offer announcements looking as full as a firm intention offer announcement, but making clear that the actual making of the formal offer was subject to the satisfaction of certain stated pre-conditions.

Where a possible offer announcement does go further, Rule 2.5 deals with any statements as to proposed offer terms that are made in the announcement and the regime requires that the Panel be consulted in advance of any statement relating to the proposed terms of a possible offer. Where a potential offeror makes an unqualified statement about the terms of a possible offer, for example if it specifies a price or says that the terms of the possible offer are "final", it will be bound by those terms if it does proceed to make an offer, except in wholly exceptional circumstances (see in this regard Panel Statement 2011/11 relating to the possible offer for Kalahari Plc). As this applies equally to formal and informal statements there will consequently need to be strict public relations controls in place.

Proposed terms can, within limits, be expressly qualified so long as any qualification is capable of objective determination. For example, a bidder may specify a possible offer price but reserve the right to bid at a lower level of consideration in certain circumstances. A subsequent bid at a lower price will then be permitted where the specific circumstances of the particular qualification have arisen or in wholly exceptional circumstances. Qualifications that will always be permitted are a target board's recommendation and a firm offer by a third party (whereas the satisfactory outcome of a due diligence exercise will not be permitted). Where the terms refer to an anticipated price range, an approximate price, or a relative price, prior consultation with the Panel will be required.

It should be noted that, in October 2015, a new Note (Note 4) on Rule 2.5 was introduced. This provides that an offeror may reserve the right to reduce the offer consideration by the amount of all or part of a dividend subsequently paid by the offeree company and if the offeror does not reserve that right it will not normally be permitted to reduce the offer consideration by all or part of a dividend which is subsequently paid by the offeree company.

In addition, Note 4 on Rule 2.5 makes clear that an offeror which has made a "no increase statement" must reduce the value of its offer by the amount of any dividend subsequently paid by the offeree company, unless a specific reservation was included in the "no increase statement" which provided that offeree company shareholders would be entitled to receive the dividend.

With the consent of the Panel, a possible offer announcement can include pre-conditions and these can be subjective in nature (see 2.7.2 below for further details). If so, the announcement must make it clear whether these pre-conditions are waivable and must also emphasise that there is no certainty an offer will be made (even if the pre-conditions are satisfied or waived).

2.6.4 *"Put up or shut up" deadlines*

For a number of years, the Panel has operated a "put up or shut up" regime following a possible offer announcement aimed at preventing an offeree company from suffering from a protracted period of speculation before a firm offer announcement is made or a potential offeror issues a "no intention to bid" statement—and which therefore reflects General Principle 6. In its 2001 Annual Report, the Panel clarified its general approach at the time in this regard:

> "Following [a possible offer announcement] there is no fixed deadline in the Code by which a potential offeror must clarify his intentions. The timing of any subsequent announcements will depend, inter alia, on the reaction of the offeree board to the potential offeror and the state of preparedness of the potential offeror.

> Where the offeree board is prepared to enter into a dialogue with the potential offeror, many months may pass before an offer is finally made. Provided the target company is content for the uncertainty to continue, the Executive would not normally seek to intervene in the process. However, in certain circumstances, usually where the potential offeror is unwelcome, the target company may request the Executive to intervene by imposing a deadline by which the potential offeror must clarify his intentions, i.e. 'put up or shut up'.

> In this regard, 'put up' is communicated by way of a … firm offer announcement and 'shut up' by way of a no intention to bid statement.

Requests by the target company for the offeror to be required to 'put up or shut up' are generally made at the early stages of an offer period. In such cases, the Executive endeavours to balance the interests of shareholders in not being deprived of the opportunity to consider the possibility of an offer against potential damage to the target company's business arising from the uncertainty surrounding the company and the distraction for management. In this regard, the Executive's normal approach is to seek clarification by the potential offeror within six to eight weeks from the original announcement of the possible offer. If a request is made at a later stage, the Executive will consider the circumstances at that time.

If the potential offeror clarifies his intentions by way of a no intention to bid statement, this statement will be governed by Rule 2.8 and the potential offeror will normally be prevented from making an offer for the company for a period of six months (unless there is a material change of circumstances and subject to any specific reservations set out in the statement). However, if the Executive considers that the offeree company has suffered excessive siege as a result of the potential offeror's actions, it may impose the restrictions contained within Rule 35.1(b) and prevent the potential offeror from making an offer for a period of 12 months."

This concept was formally incorporated into the Code for the first time in 2004. However, the regime was substantially altered on 19 September 2011, following the consultation in PCP 2011/1, and is now contained in Rule 2.6. Under the current regime, whenever a potential offeror makes a possible offer announcement or an offeree company announces the identity of a potential offeror in accordance with the requirements of Rule 2.4 (or otherwise), an automatic 28-day "put up or shut up" deadline will apply. So, it is no longer necessary for the offeree company to request a deadline be set and the deadline is no longer a matter to be negotiated between the offeree company, the potential offeror and the Panel (and will be shorter than the six–eight weeks that previously applied).

The only exceptions to this automatic imposition of a 28-day deadline will be if a third party has already announced a firm intention to make an offer for the offeree company (or does so subsequently, in which case the deadline will cease to apply) or if the offeree company has already announced that it is seeking one or more potential offerors for the offeree company by means of a formal sales process as envisaged by Note 2 on Rule 2.6.

Where the 28-day deadline applies, the potential offeror must by 17.00 on the relevant "put up or shut up" date (or any extension to it) either announce a firm intention to make an offer for the offeree company in accordance with Rule 2.7 or announce that it does not intend to make an offer for the offeree company (a "no intention to bid statement" or "Rule 2.8 statement"), or secure the Panel's consent to an extension to the deadline. An extension to the deadline will only be granted at the request of the board of the offeree company (and normally only shortly before the deadline is due to expire). In considering whether to grant its consent, the Panel will take into account, among other matters, the status of negotiations between the parties and the anticipated timetable to reach a recommended deal. If extended, the offeree company must promptly announce the new "put up or shut up" deadline and must comment in the announcement on the above factors. Once extended, the same regime applies to the new deadline.

Where there is more than one potential offeror subject to "put up or shut up" deadlines, Note 1 on Rule 2.6 makes clear that the offeree company may request different deadline extensions for different potential offerors and may request a deadline extension for one potential offeror, but not others.

2.6.5 *"No intention to bid" statements*

Where a potential offeror "shuts up" at the end of (or before) a "put up or shut up" deadline, under Rule 2.8 it, and any concert party (and any person that subsequently acts in concert with either of them), will be prevented from, broadly, announcing an offer or possible offer for the offeree company or purchasing or agreeing to purchase assets which are significant to the offeree company, in each case for six months from the date of the statement. Note 5 on Rule 2.8 sets out the basis on which assets may be considered "significant" for these purposes and provides guidance that assets representing more than 75% of the offeree company (by reference to certain tests) will normally be regarded as being significant. However, an announcement of an offer or possible offer or a significant asset purchase can be made prior to the end of the six-month period (i.e. the Rule 2.8 restrictions will cease to apply) if the potential offeror includes certain reservations in its announcement and the relevant circumstances in a reservation arises. The reservations are : (1) the Panel determines there has been a material change of circumstances; (2) a third party announces a firm bid for the offeree company (not just a possible offer announcement); (3) the offeree company announces a whitewash or reverse takeover; or (4) the board of the offeree company agrees to the "no intention to bid" statement being set aside (although, if the statement was made after a third party had made a formal offer announcement, this limb will normally only apply if that other offer has been withdrawn or lapsed and, in the period following the making of the statement and prior to the offer being withdrawn or lapsing, neither the person who made the statement nor any of its concert parties has acquired an interest in any shares of the offeree company). If the potential offeror wishes to approach the offeree company to seek its agreement to the statement being set aside it must first get the Panel's consent to the approach being made. If no such agreement is forthcoming, no further approach is permitted within the six-month lock-out period.

Since 8 January 2018 (following RS2017/1), it is necessary to set out the above reservations in any no intention to bid statement if a potential offeror wishes to rely on any of them. Previously, following changes introduced in 2011, it was not necessary to do so.

A person may also make a Rule 2.8 announcement or statement during an offer period even though it has not been publicly identified as a potential offeror—and on occasion "no intention to bid" statements are made even though no offer period has commenced (for example by a person responding to unfounded speculation about its intentions in relation to a potential competitor). Rule 2.8 applies to such statements in the same way as if made during an offer period and in response to a "put up or shut up" deadline, except that where the "no intention to bid" statement is made in relation to a company that is not in an offer period, the person may also include in the statement other specific events (reservations) following which the restrictions in Rule 2.8 would cease to apply (in addition to those that apply automatically as above).

The Panel should be consulted before any "no intention to bid" statement is issued, particularly if it is intended to include specific reservations to set aside the statement (Note 1 on Rule 2.8).

Note that the Panel applies this Rule 2.8 not only to formal public statements, but also to informal or private comments which are subsequently publicly reported. It also takes the view that a simple denial of speculation as to the person's intention to make a bid, even though falling short of an explicit statement that the person does not intend to make a bid, will still be caught. So Rule 2.8 contains traps for the unwary.

2.6.6   Statement of interest by potential competing bidder

The Code also deals with holding statements by potential rival offerors. During the battle for control of National Westminster Bank Plc (NatWest) the Executive (and, on appeal, the Panel) refused to impose a "put up or shut up" timetable on the Royal Bank of Scotland (RBS) in the early stages of the offer period. The Bank of Scotland (BOS) had announced a firm intention to bid for NatWest and RBS had announced, following press speculation, that it had been considering and would continue to consider its position. BOS requested that the Panel impose a deadline on RBS to clarify its position as the announcement had, in BOS's view, created market uncertainty and had allowed RBS to obtain an unfair advantage over BOS. RBS submitted that it had done nothing to create or increase market uncertainty. The Panel refused to set a firm deadline for RBS to clarify its intentions but indicated that "Day 50" appeared to the Panel to be the latest day for clarification of RBS's position—although the Panel reserved the right to specify an earlier or later date depending upon developments.

This principle is now enshrined in the Code in Rules 2.6(d) and (e) and (where the offer is being implemented by a scheme of management) in s.4 of Appendix 7, albeit that a deadline of 17.00 on "Day 53" rather than on or around "Day 50" now applies following changes introduced by RS 2014/1. Rule 2.6(d) deals with a potential offeror that has made a possible offer announcement where another party has made a formal offer announcement (whether before or after the possible offer announcement) and Rule 2.6(e) deals with the situation where the potential offeror has not been identified at the time when another party has made a formal offer announcement and the offeree company subsequently refers to the existence of an unidentified potential competing offeror. Both Rules provide that, by 17.00 on the 53rd day following the publication of the first offeror's initial offer document, the potential offeror must either announce a firm offer in accordance with Rule 2.7 or make a Rule 2.8 statement. For a scheme of arrangement, s.4(a) of Appendix 7 imposes an equivalent deadline of 17.00 on the seventh day prior to the date of the shareholder meetings. However, under s.4(6) of Appendix 7, "where appropriate", the Panel may permit the potential offeror to clarify its position after the date of the shareholder meetings but before the date of the court sanction hearing.

The Panel's concern in this area is that target shareholders have sufficient time to accept the first offer if the rival bidder decides not to bid (i.e. "shuts up").

2.7 Bid announcements

2.7.1 Announcement of a firm intention to make an offer

As referred to above, the provisions of Rule 2.7(a) require that a firm intention to make a bid should only be announced when the offeror has every reason to believe that it can and will be able to implement the offer. In citing the Executive's submission in the Panel's decision on the OVL offer for Imperial Energy, the Panel noted that:

> " [The Executive] pointed to the distinction in the Code between an announcement of a firm intention to make an offer under [Rule 2.7] and an announcement of a possible offer under Rule 2.4. The former represents a formal commitment to proceed with an offer and, as such, will almost inevitably have a profound effect upon the offeree company and the market price of its shares—hence the need for care on the part of both an offeror and its financial adviser ..."

The required contents of an announcement of a firm intention to make an offer (as opposed to a Rule 2.4 announcement) are specified in Rule 2.7(c). In particular, the announcement must:

1. set out the terms of the offer—detailed terms will be included, although a number of "further terms" are postponed until the offer document;
2. identify the offeror—the questions mentioned above about who is the offeror (see 2.3.2 above) will again need to be considered;
3. include all conditions or pre-conditions to which the offer or the making of it is subject;
4. set out the intentions of the offeror with regard to the business, employees and pension scheme(s) of the offeree company;
5. give details of any agreements or arrangements to which the offeror is a party which relate to the circumstances in which it may or may not invoke or seek to invoke a

pre-condition or a condition to its offer and the conse-quences of its doing so, including details of any break fees payable as a result (see Rule 2.7(c)(v));

6. give details of any relevant securities of the offeree company in which the offeror or any person acting in concert with it has an interest or in respect of which it has a right to subscribe, in each case specifying the nature of the interests or rights concerned. Similar details of any short positions, any agreement to sell, any delivery obligation or right to require another person to purchase or take delivery, must also be stated;

7. give details of any irrevocable commitment or letter of intent procured by the offeror or any person acting in concert with it;

8. give details of any relevant securities of the offeree company which the offeror or any person acting in concert with it has borrowed or lent, save for any borrowed relevant securities which have been either on-lent or sold and details of any relevant financial collateral arrange-ments;

9. give details of any dealing arrangement of the kind referred to in Note 11 on the definition of acting in concert to which the offeror or any person acting in concert with it is a party;

10. include a summary of the provisions of Rule 8 (the Rule requiring disclosure of dealings during an offer period);

11. include a summary of any offer-related arrangement permitted under, or excluded from, Rule 21.2;

12. include a list of the documents on display in accordance with Rule 26.2 (and a website address where these documents are published); and

13. include a statement that the offeror will have the right to reduce the offer consideration by any dividend (or other distribution) which is paid or becomes payable by the offeree company to offeree company shareholders, unless and to the extent that the announcement provides that offeree company shareholders will be entitled to receive and retain all or part of a specified dividend (or other distribution) in addition to the offer consideration.

As explained in 2.4, the offer announcement must also include confirmation from the financial adviser that resources are available to the offeror sufficient to satisfy full acceptance of the offer where it is a cash offer (Rule 2.7(d)).

Note 1 on Rule 2.7, which was introduced on 8 January 2018 (following RS 2017/2), provides further detail on the requirements in paragraph 4 above relating to an offeror's intentions with regard to the business, employees and pension scheme(s) of the offeree company. It includes a requirement that the offeror makes specific statements, among other things, with regard to the offeree company's research and development functions, the balance of skills and functions of the offeree company's employees and management and the location of the offeree company's headquarters and headquarters functions. These requirements reflect a desire for the offeror to make such intention statements at an earlier stage of the offer than was previously the case (when such statements were only required to be made in the offer document).

Two other points on the Notes to Rule 2.7 are worth mentioning:

1. a reminder is given that the language used in the announcement should clearly and concisely reflect the position being described. This reflects the general requirement that press announcements be prepared with a standard of care and accuracy effectively equivalent to that imposed on the formal offer document; and
2. there is a warning that the Panel should be consulted before: (a) any condition is included which is not entirely objective; (b) any condition relating to financing is included; or (c) it is intended to make a pre-conditional Rule 2.7 announcement.

2.7.2   *Pre-conditional offer announcements*

Over the years, there have been a number of pre-conditional offers (i.e. an offer where the offer document will only be posted if certain pre-conditions are satisfied). The most common pre-conditions relate to regulatory clearances where these are unlikely to be obtained in the usual Code timetable. Some examples include Carnival Corporation's initially hostile offer for P&O Princess Cruises, the proposed merger between Granada and Carlton, E.ON's bid for Powergen, BHP Billiton's hostile bid for Rio Tinto (which was subsequently withdrawn when one of the regulatory pre-conditions was invoked), Royal Dutch Shell's bid for BG, AB InBev's bid for SABMiller and 21st Century Fox's and Comcast's respective bids for Sky. Carnival Corporation's first offer for P&O Princess Cruises was also subject to a financing pre-condition in respect of the cash element of the offer (later reformulated as a pre-condition to a partial cash alternative). Lafarge's hostile offer for Blue Circle likewise included a financing pre-condition (that funding for the offer was arranged on terms satisfactory to it).

In light of the increasing use of pre-conditions, the Code Committee of the Panel issued Consultation Paper 2004/4 and Response Statement 2004/4 in which it reviewed its previous approach to pre-conditions. Changes were made to the Code in April 2005. The Code Committee considered it necessary to look separately at pre-conditional possible offer announcements made under Rule 2.5 (as it is now) and pre-conditional firm offer announcements made under Rule 2.7 (as it is now). The inclusion of pre-conditions in either type of announcement requires prior consultation with the Panel (see Rule 2.5(c) and Note 2 on Rule 2.7 respectively). The Panel takes a strict approach to permitted pre-conditions in firm offer announcements on the basis that the announcement of a pre-conditional offer under Rule 2.7 is intended and required to provide a high level of certainty—as with any Rule 2.7 firm offer announcement.

Rule 13.3 sets out the pre-conditions that will be acceptable to the Panel in a Rule 2.7 announcement. Except with the consent of the Panel, an offer must not be announced subject to a pre-condition unless the pre-condition concerned:

1. relates to a Competition and Markets Authority clearance or (even after the implementation date) a European Commission clearance; or
2. involves another material official authorisation or regulatory clearance relating to the offer and either the offer is publicly recommended by the offeree company board or the Panel is satisfied that it is likely to prove impossible to obtain the authorisation or clearance within the Code timetable.

Also, the degree of subjectivity permitted in pre-conditions included in a Rule 2.7 announcement is now the same as that permitted for conventional offer conditions (Rule 13.1), and the test for invoking pre-conditions is now basically the same as that for conventional conditions (Rules 13.2 and 13.4(a)). The Code Committee decided against allowing greater flexibility. Although many different types of pre-conditions had been used in the past, from April 2005 an offeror has only been allowed to include the pre-conditions described above and the Panel will no longer allow wide and/or subjective pre-conditions in Rule 2.7 announcements. According to the Code Committee in RS 2004/4, the circumstances in which the Panel should be prepared to consider exercising its discretion to allow pre-conditions outside the permitted categories, are likely to be very limited, for example if it relates to a matter concerning the offeree company that is likely to be incapable of resolution within the normal offer timetable and is a matter without which it would be unreasonable to expect the offeror to make the offer at all.

As referred to above, pre-conditional Rule 2.7 announcements have sometimes contained a pre-condition in relation to financing (i.e. that the offeror will have the facilities in place to finance the cash element of a bid) or in relation to the adequacy of working capital for the enlarged group. In PCP 2004/4 and in RS 2004/4, the Code Committee proposed that the same prohibition on financing conditions in offers should normally also apply to financing pre-conditions.

However, as set out in the Note on Rules 13.1 and 13.3, in exceptional cases the Panel may be prepared to accept a pre-condition related to financing either in addition to another pre-condition permitted by Rule 13.3 or otherwise; for example where, due to the likely period required to obtain any necessary material official authorisation or regulatory clearance, it is not reasonable for the offeror to maintain committed financing throughout the offer period, in which case:

1. the financing pre-condition must be satisfied (or waived), or the offer must be withdrawn, within 21 days after the satisfaction (or waiver) of any other pre-condition(s) permitted by Rule 13.3; and
2. the offeror and its financial adviser must confirm in writing to the Panel before announcement of the offer that they are not aware of any reason why the offeror would be unable to satisfy the financing pre-condition within that 21-day period.

It is clear from PCP 2004/4 and RS 2004/4 that the Panel has adopted the same approach to working capital conditions. However, the Panel exercised its discretion to allow the pre-conditional offer by Boots for Unichem in October 2005, for example, to include a pre-condition that the two companies be reasonably satisfied for the purposes of the requirements of the FSA and the UKLA that the necessary financing facilities would be available on reasonable market terms, following completion of their merger, to provide for the working capital requirements of the group.

As regards possible offer announcements, subjective pre-conditions can be included and do not have to be confined to anti-trust clearances etc. This is on the basis that, since the making of the offer still remains within the discretion of the potential offeror even where the pre-conditions are satisfied, neither shareholders nor the market can gain any more certainty from a requirement that only objective pre-conditions will be permissible. Therefore, a possible offer can be pre-conditional on, for example, offeree board recommendation, satisfactory due diligence or arranging financing. However, in order to avoid false market concerns, it must be clear from the wording of any possible offer announcement whether or not the pre-conditions must be satisfied before an offer can be made or whether they are waivable (see Rule 2.5(c)). If a pre-condition is not stated to be waivable, the potential offeror would not normally be permitted to make an offer unless the pre-condition was clearly satisfied.

In order to ensure that shareholders and the market are not confused as to whether a potential offeror is committed to proceed if the pre-conditions are satisfied, a pre-conditional possible offer announcement should include a prominent warning to the effect that the announcement does not amount to a firm intention to make an offer and that, accordingly, there can be no certainty that any offer will be made even if the pre-conditions are satisfied or waived.

2.7.3 Disclosure in the offer announcement of side agreements relating to pre-conditions and conditions

In December 2001, the Code was amended to impose an obligation to disclose side agreements (whether formal or informal) relating to offer pre-conditions and conditions. When a firm intention to make an offer is announced, that announcement must include details of any agreements or arrangements to which the offeror is party which relate to the circumstances in which it may or may not invoke or seek to invoke a pre-condition or a condition to its offer and the consequences of its doing so, including details of any break fees payable as a result. This requirement has been incorporated as Rule 2.7(c)(v).

It should be noted that this obligation extends to agreements in relation to the acceptance condition, for example if a bidder undertakes to a lending bank that it will not declare the offer unconditional as to acceptances unless at least 75% acceptances are achieved.

This obligation should not generally extend to a disclosure letter entered into between an offeror and an offeree company where one or more of the conditions to the offer contains an explicit carve out for information disclosed in writing by the offeree company to the offeror—although this should be confirmed with the Panel on a case-by-case basis.

The Panel stated that, in exceptional circumstances, it would be prepared to grant a dispensation from this obligation in respect of agreements which are commercially sensitive and/or do not have a bearing on the offer. Furthermore, in the context of regulatory side agreements, the Panel may be prepared to grant a dispensation from the obligation of disclosure where the offeree company and its advisers confirm in writing that disclosure would be likely to prejudice negotiations with the relevant regulatory authority to an extent which is material in the context of the offer.

Under the normal principles of the Code, parties are required to behave in a manner which is consistent with what has been publicly disclosed. However, the Panel has acknowledged that where parties had good commercial reasons to amend the terms of a side agreement once they had been publicly disclosed, the Panel could grant them dispensation to do so.

2.7.4 Circulation of announcement

Under Rule 2.11, whenever an offer period commences (except where the offer period begins with a Rule 2.7 announcement), the offeree company is required to circulate the relevant announcement to its shareholders and certain other persons (including option-holders), and to make it readily available to its employee representatives (or the employees themselves) and to the trustees of its pension scheme(s). It also has to circulate any Rule 2.7 firm offer announcement. Also, both the offeror and the offeree company have to make the Rule 2.7 announcement, or a summary, readily available to their employee representatives or, where there are no such representatives, to the employees themselves, and in the case of the offeree company only, to the trustees of its pension scheme(s). This rule also imposes a requirement on the offeror and offeree company, where necessary, to explain the implications of the announcement. Also, where the offeree company is sending any announcement or summary to its employee representatives "or employees" and the trustees of its pension scheme(s), it must also inform them of the rights of the employee representatives and pension scheme trustees (as the case may be) under Rule 25.9 and the offeree company's responsibility for the costs reasonably incurred by the employee representatives in obtaining the advice under Rule 25.9. Following RS 2004/3 and RS 2008/3, there are additional requirements to include both a summary of the provisions of Rule 8 in any Rule 2.11 circular and a statement that offeree company shareholders' address details may be provided to the offeror as required under s.4 of Appendix 4 of the Code and a contact telephone number for use by recipients wishing to contact the offeree company regarding administrative matters.

When the bid is hostile, this obligation on the offeree company is often rather grudgingly discharged: a repudiatory letter from the offeree board dismissing the bid is accompanied by an Appendix with the detailed terms and conditions of the offer set out in tiny type designed to discourage all but the most persistent readers!

2.7.5 Consequences of announcement

Following an announcement of a firm intention to make an offer, the offeror must normally proceed with the offer unless, in accordance with the provisions of Rule 13, the offeror is permitted to invoke a pre-condition to the posting of the offer or would be permitted to invoke a condition to the offer if the offer were made. An exception to this obligation in Rule 2.7(b) is that with the consent of the Panel, an offeror can be released from the obligation to proceed if a competitor has already announced a firm intention to make a higher offer.

2.7.6 *Announcement of numbers of relevant securities in issue*

The Panel explained in PCP 14 issued in April 2003 that there had been cases where a party had failed to comply with the dealing disclosure obligations in Rule 8 because it had been unaware either of the exact number of relevant securities in issue or that holdings or dealings in certain lines of stock were disclosable. The sources on which firms often rely for the relevant information are not always up to date or accurate and a company's issued share capital can alter frequently. Therefore, the Panel considered it would be in the interests of the market generally for every company whose securities are subject to the dealing disclosure regime in Rule 8 to announce the exact number of the relevant securities in issue and keep the market updated of any subsequent changes.

Accordingly, in July 2003, Rule 2.9 (formerly Rule 2.10) was introduced which requires the offeree company, when an offer period begins, to announce, as soon as possible and in any case by 09.00 on the next business day, details of all classes of relevant securities issued by the offeree company, together with the numbers of such securities in issue. Following the consultation in PCP 2014/1, a new deadline of 07.15 (rather than 09.00) on the next business day was introduced by RS 2014/1. An offeror or potential offeror must also announce the same details relating to its relevant securities as soon as possible and in any case by 07.15 on the business day following any announcement identifying it as an offeror or potential offeror, unless it has stated that its offer is likely to be solely in cash. The announcement should include, where relevant, the International Securities Identification Number for each relevant security. If the information included in an announcement made under Rule 2.9 changes during the offer period, a revised announcement must be made as soon as possible. Note 1 on Rule 2.9 (introduced by RS 2005/2) states that, for the purposes of that Rule, options to subscribe for new securities in the offeree company or an offeror are not to be treated as a class of relevant securities. Note 2 on Rule 2.9 makes it clear that only relevant securities which are held and in issue outside treasury should be included in the announcement.

2.7.7 Disclosure of irrevocable commitments, letters of intent and interests in relevant securities

The Code changed in this area on 1 January 2015, following the introduction of various proposals in PCP 2014/1 by RS2014/1.

Under Rule 2.10(a) (formerly Rule 2.11(a)), any irrevocable commitment or letter of intent procured during an offer period should be disclosed by no later than 12.00 noon on the following business day.

Under Rule 2.10(b) (formerly Rule 2.11(b)), any irrevocable commitment or letter of intent procured prior to an offer period should be disclosed by no later than 12.00 noon on the business day following the identification of the offeror as such (and not in the Offeror's Opening Position Disclosure).

In each case, the announcement must include full details of the nature of the irrevocable commitment or letter of intent, as set out in Note 3 to Rule 2.10.

No separate disclosure is required when details of irrevocable commitments and letters of intent are disclosed in a firm or possible offer announcement made by no later than 12.00 noon on the business day following the date on which they are procured.

Rule 2.7(c) has reinstated the requirement, which existed prior to 2010, for an offeror to disclose details of the interests and short positions in the relevant securities of the offeree company held by it, and by persons acting in concert with it, and of any irrevocable commitments and letters of intent which it has procured, in its firm offer announcement. These details were previously required to be disclosed in the offeror's Opening Position Disclosure.

2.8   Independent advice

2.8.1   *Offeree*

Under Rule 3.1, the board of an offeree company must obtain competent independent advice as to whether the financial terms of any offer are fair and reasonable and make the substance of that advice known to its shareholders. The Panel has been at pains to stress the importance of the adviser's role in assisting the board in presenting its views, and in ensuring that full information, and the board's reasoned arguments, are circulated to shareholders.

The Notes on Rule 3.1 amplify the basic Rule, and cover:

1.   management buyouts and offers by controlling shareholders (stressing the importance of the independence of the advice obtained in these circumstances);
2.   the situation where there is uncertainty about the financial information in the offeree company's most recently published financial results—important factors must be highlighted by the board and the independent adviser; and
3.   the situation where the financial adviser is unable to express a view on the merits of an offer. In these circumstances, an explanation must be given in the offeree board circular. The Panel should also be consulted in advance about the explanation which is to be given.

2.8.2   *Offeror company*

The offeror board (where the offeror is a company which would be subject to the Code if it was the offeree company) is under a similar obligation to seek independent advice where the offer is a reverse takeover (i.e. where the offeror may need to increase its existing issued voting equity share capital by more than 100%) or where the directors have a conflict of interest. Examples of a conflict of interest given in Note 2 on Rule 3.2 include where there are significant cross-shareholdings between an offeror and the offeree company, a number of directors common to both companies or when a person has a substantial interest in both companies.

Advice obtained under Rule 3.2 should be obtained by the offeror board before the offer is made and should address the question of whether the offer is in the shareholders' interests. The offeror shareholders must be given sufficient time to consider this advice before any meeting is held at which a vote is to be taken on the offer.

2.8.3   *The financial adviser*

Rule 3.3 (and Appendix 3) reinforces the requirement that financial advice must be independent. If one part of a multi-service organisation acts for the offeror, another part of it may well not be permitted to act for the offeree company. In addition, those with a significant interest in, or financial connection with, either the offeror or offeree company will normally be disqualified. For example, if the investment management arm of a bank advises an investment trust, the corporate finance arm will not normally be able to act for that trust in a bid as an independent Rule 3 adviser.

In its 1995 Annual Report, the Panel emphasised the importance of independent advice, stating:

> "The Panel has always regarded it as of paramount importance that the adviser should be sufficiently independent so that its advice should be objective beyond question.
>
> A prospective adviser to an offeree company might not be considered sufficiently independent, for example, if it has had a recent advisory role with the offeror or has a very close advisory relationship with a large shareholder in the offeree company. The precise circumstances of every case will be different, links may be economic or advisory and sometimes quite a fine judgment will have to be made. The views of the offeree company's board will always be an important factor. The Panel strongly recommends early

consultation with the Executive in any case where the independence of an adviser could be in doubt."

This is echoed in Note 1 to Rule 3.3. An example of the application of this Note 1 was the role of Dresdner Kleinwort Benson in relation to the offer by Abbey National for Cater Allen (as reflected in Panel Statement 1997/9). In that case, the Panel upheld a ruling by the Executive that Dresdner Kleinwort Benson would not be an appropriate person under Note 1 on Rule 3.3 to give independent advice to Cater Allen in relation to the recommended offer by Abbey National. This was due to Kleinwort Benson's "close, recent and continuing" advisory relationship with Abbey National; Kleinworts had been one of Abbey's advisers since flotation. The Panel emphasised the importance of the adviser not only being independent, but also of being viewed objectively as being independent. Cater Allen therefore had to appoint another adviser to give advice under Rule 3.1.

Specifically in relation to broking relationships, in its 2002 Annual Report, in reference to Rule 3.1, the Panel stated:

"Financial advisers within groups which have an advisory relationship with an offeror are not normally regarded as appropriate persons to give advice to the offeree board on an offer. In this context, broking relationships with an offeror are considered in the same light as other types of advisory relationship. Whilst it is accepted that the strength and nature of broking relationships, and the services provided under them, vary widely, such relationships generally create a potential conflict of interest.

In one or two recent cases, groups have assumed that a potential conflict of interest arising from an offeror broking relationship can be addressed satisfactorily by the broker standing down from its role for the duration of the offer. The Executive's view is that this action will not normally be sufficient to resolve concerns as to independence. Therefore, in cases where an offeree adviser's group has an offeror broking relationship, the Executive should be consulted at an early stage."

The Executive outlined its approach to determining whether an adviser is independent for these purposes in Practice Statement No.21, which also explained something of a relaxation in its approach in recognition of the fact that relationships between companies and financial advisers are less exclusive than was previously the case. In considering whether an adviser is independent, the Executive will examine the strength of the overall relationship between the offeror and the adviser's group, including:

1. the nature of all matters in relation to which the adviser has provided the offeror with advice over the preceding 12 to 24-month period and any matters in contemplation—this is not limited to corporate finance advice, but includes other services, for example leading a debt syndication;
2. the size of past transactions on which the adviser's group has advised over the relevant period and the locations in which they were undertaken;
3. the frequency with which the adviser's group has advised the offeror and the extent to which the offeror has instructed other financial advisers during the relevant period; and
4. the fee income paid to the adviser and its group during the period, both in terms of total fees and their significance to the adviser's group.

As a result, the Executive may conclude that a recent, or even a current, advisory role for the offeror may not be material and therefore should not compromise the independence of the adviser (which is a relaxation of its previous position that advising the offeror on any matter at the same time as the proposed offer would generally mean the adviser should not be considered independent). However, the Executive continues to take the view that an adviser which is in the same group as a corporate broker to an offeror is not independent for these purposes.

Appendix 3 also deals with the problem of conflicts of interest and "material confidential information", particularly where the financial adviser has previously advised one of the other parties to the bid. This arose specifically out of the difficulties which ensued on the TKM bid for Molins, which were dealt with in Panel Statement 1987/13. The conclusion is that conflicts of interest cannot necessarily be resolved by the creation of internal Chinese walls.

The Panel has also considered whether the nature of a financial adviser's fee arrangements may give rise to a conflict of interest that would prevent it from acting as a Rule 3 adviser. In Panel Statement 1999/11, the Panel stated:

> "Arrangements which reward an adviser to the offeree dependent on failure of a hostile offer, irrespective of the offer price, give rise to, or create the perception of, an actual or potential conflict of interest. In these circumstances, the adviser will normally be disqualified from acting as independent Rule 3 adviser. Similar considerations will apply to any fee payable on failure of an offer below an unrealistically high price. The Executive should be consulted in any case of doubt. The Panel may in appropriate cases require disclosure in the offer documentation to enable the arrangements to be subjected to public scrutiny."

This followed the takeover by The Great Universal Stores of Argos. A new Note 3 on Rule 3.3 was introduced into the Code in July 2000 implementing this statement and requiring consultation with the Panel where fee arrangements might be such as to create a conflict of interest. The Note does not, however, require a success fee to be disclosed, as was envisaged in the statement.

Chapter 3

Share Dealings and Holdings: Restrictions and Disclosure Requirements

Robert Innes
Partner
Slaughter and May

Chris McGaffin
Partner
Slaughter and May

3.1   Introduction

This Chapter is principally concerned with the Rules of the Code which restrict, or require the disclosure of, dealings in shares before and during a takeover bid. However, there are additional rules that apply to dealings in shares at any time, such as the Companies Act 2006 (2006 Act), the Disclosure Guidance and Transparency Rules (DTRs), the Criminal Justice Act 1993 (CJA 1993), the Financial Services and Markets Act 2000 (FSMA), the Market Abuse Regulation (Regulation 596/2014) (MAR) and the Financial Services Act 2012 (FS Act 2012). These additional rules will also be considered in this Chapter.

It will be apparent from the above list of sources that one of the principal concerns in the takeovers field is to ensure that all the different sets of rules which apply to the transaction in hand have been identified and, where they overlap, to ensure that each is complied with. Steps taken with one set of regulations in mind may have adverse consequences under another and a balance may have to be struck. Furthermore, not all rules are absolute in their application; in particular, the Rules set out in the Code are not always strictly construed and, even where their meaning appears clear, may be relaxed or perhaps even extended by the Panel in particular circumstances. How such Rules should be applied is often a matter of judgment based on experience, but discussions with the Panel on points of difficulty will be a regular feature of major transactions.

Two sets of regulations not addressed in detail in this Chapter (although there are references where appropriate) are the FCA Listing Rules and the FCA Prospectus Rules (collectively, the Listing Regime) of the Financial Conduct Authority (FCA). This is on the basis that the Listing Regime is not normally directly relevant to dealings in shares during a takeover bid. However, it should be borne in mind that it may be relevant in certain circumstances (particularly those rules relating to the announcement of, or the obtaining of shareholder consent for, significant transactions and limiting the scope of indemnities which a listed company can give to third parties buying shares on its behalf).

3.2 Applicability of the Rules

The first question to be addressed in this area is: in what circumstances do each of the particular sets of rules or provisions apply, if at all?

3.2.1 The Code

As discussed in Chapter 2, broadly speaking, the Code applies to offers for all companies (and Societas Europaea) that have their registered offices in the UK, the Channel Islands or the Isle of Man and have securities which are (or, in certain cases, have been) admitted to trading on a regulated market or multilateral trading facility in the UK or on any stock exchange in the Channel Islands or the Isle of Man. The Code also applies to offers for public companies (and Societas Europaea) which have their registered offices in the UK, the Channel

Islands or the Isle of Man and which are considered by the Panel to have their place of central management and control in any such country/crown dependency. On 23 June 2016, the UK voted to leave the EU. On exit day Instrument 2019/3 will come into effect, removing Societas Europaea from the remit of the code but continuing to apply in relation to UK Societas.

One of the main functions of the Code is to regulate changes of "control" in companies to which it applies: thus, the Code is not generally applicable to offers relating only to non-voting or non-equity capital (except offers under Rule 15 (Appropriate offer for convertibles etc)), but it does cover transactions, not amounting to full takeover offers, in which control is obtained or consolidated. Control for Code purposes is deemed to be exercised by those with an "interest" (see 3.2.1.1 below) in 30% or more of the "voting rights" in the target either alone or as part of a "concert party" (see 3.2.1.3 below).

The Rules of the Code of most relevance to dealings in shares which might result in control being obtained or consolidated are Rules 5 and 9. Rule 5 has the effect of prohibiting, subject to certain exceptions, the acquisition by a person and its concert parties of interests in shares carrying 30% or more of the voting rights of a company or, where a person and its concert parties are already interested in shares carrying between 30% and 50% of the voting rights, the acquisition of an interest in any other shares carrying such voting rights. Rule 9 has the effect of requiring a person to make a mandatory offer when that person is able (such as through the use of exemptions to Rule 5) to acquire, and does acquire, an interest in shares which (taken together with shares in which persons acting in concert with him are interested) carry 30% or more of the voting rights of a company (or, where a person and its concert parties are already interested in shares carrying between 30% and 50% of the voting rights, the acquisition of an interest in any other shares carrying such voting rights) (see further 3.3.1.3, 3.3.1.4 and 4.2 below).

The Code also contains detailed Rules concerning the disclosure of dealings during the "offer period" (principally Rule 8, see further 3.4.3.1 and 3.4.3.2 below). These Rules are not restricted to dealings by the "parties to the offer" but extend to other parties interested in "relevant securities" of the target or offeror.

The Panel has kept the dealing disclosure requirements under review with the most recent wholesale amendments to Rule 8 coming into force on 19 April 2010 (see Code Committee Instrument 2009/6 (Instrument 2009/6)). The Panel introduced the requirement for an "opening position disclosure" and extended the requirements to disclose dealings and positions on a composite basis. These amendments continue the pattern of increased transparency in relation to the position of, and dealings by, persons involved in takeover bids with the aim of enabling the Panel and the market to develop a more comprehensive understanding of circumstances surrounding an offer. The Rules of the Code which restrict or require the disclosure of dealings make use of a number of important defined terms. Certain of these terms are explained below.

3.2.1.1   Interests in securities

When considering interests in shares or relevant securities under the Code, the focus has historically been on direct holdings of shares or relevant securities and restrictions and disclosure requirements have been applied to persons "purchasing securities". However, the growth in prominence of the derivatives market and developments in market practice since the turn of the century mean that persons with long derivative or option positions may exercise significant de facto control over the underlying securities.

In the case of a long contract for difference (CFD), the counterparty with whom the CFD holder takes out the contract will typically hedge its exposure by acquiring the shares which underlie the CFD. The counterparty will also sometimes agree (usually informally) to exercise the voting rights attaching to these shares in accordance with the wishes of the CFD holder. Therefore, while the holder of a CFD will not appear on the register of shareholders of the company in question, it may be able to control the exercise of votes in respect of a significant proportion of its shares. Furthermore, the terms of the CFD or market practice may enable the CFD holder to receive the underlying shares acquired by the counterparty in settlement of the CFD.

For example, in the case of BAE Systems' offer for Alvis during 2004, BAE Systems obtained irrevocable commitments from a number of funds which had entered into CFDs referenced to shares representing approximately 16% of the issued share capital of Alvis. Some of these funds entered into commitments with BAE Systems to:

> "request physical settlement of the CFDs in accordance with market practice ... and then to assent to the offer all shares received by them as a result of this physical settlement process."

Other CFD holders who did not give such a commitment to BAE Systems expressly consented to the counterparty with whom they had entered into a CFD giving BAE Systems a standard irrevocable commitment to accept the offer in respect of the Alvis shares held by it as a hedge against its position under the relevant CFD.

Similarly, in the same year a number of funds entered into long CFDs referenced to shares in Marks & Spencer during the period of Revival Acquisitions' interest in the company. These funds sought to put pressure on the board of Marks & Spencer to grant Revival Acquisitions access to carry out due diligence. The funds were aware that their statements of support would be made public and their intention was to influence the debate on whether due diligence access should be granted.

As a result of these developments, the Code Committee made a number of changes to the Code to ensure that it covers all relevant interests and not just traditional holdings of shares or other securities.

The resulting Code provisions are not just applicable to CFDs but also to other types of derivatives. Similarly, they are also applicable to dealings in options because, despite the differences between options and derivatives, counterparties to options may also hedge their exposure by acquiring the shares underlying the option and persons holding call options may obtain a measure of de facto control over shares in a similar way to holders of long CFDs.

It should be noted that a person with a short position in securities will not normally be treated as interested in them and will therefore not be subject to a disclosure obligation. The Panel has kept the disclosure of short positions under review and consulted on this point in 2009 (see para.5 of Public Consultation Paper PCP 2009/1 (PCP 2009/1)). The Panel's view was that an arguable case could be made for the introduction of a "short trigger" provision, whereby the Code's disclosure requirements would apply to a person who has a significant gross short position in the relevant securities of a party to an offer but who does not have a long position of 1% or more in any such securities. However, it concluded that it would not be proportionate to introduce such a new disclosure requirement for the relatively unusual cases in which short positions would not otherwise be subject to disclosure under the Code (see para.5 of Response Statement RS 2009/1: Extending the Code's Disclosure Regime (RS 2009/1)). The Code Committee has reserved its right to review the "short trigger" proposal in the future but has stated that it has no current intention of doing so.

Guidance from the Panel in its Practice Statement No.22 of 10 July 2008 (last amended 12 September 2016) indicates that where an offeror has received an irrevocable commitment to accept its offer, that will not, of itself, result in the offeror being considered to be interested in the shares to which the irrevocable commitment relates (other than for the purposes of Rule 5 of the Code). Where an irrevocable undertaking includes a voting undertaking, the question arises on whether this gives the offeror "the right ... to exercise or direct the exercise of voting rights attaching to them" for the purposes of para.2 of the definition of interest in securities. Practice Statement No.22 para.3.3 indicates the Panel would not normally consider an offeror to be interested in the shares to which the irrevocable commitment relates provided that the voting undertaking is:

1. given in the context of an irrevocable commitment to accept the offer;
2. limited to the duration of the offer or, if earlier, until the irrevocable commitment otherwise ceases to be binding; and
3. limited to matters which relate to ensuring that the offer is successful.

3.2.1.2 Dealings

The definition of "dealings" under the Code covers any action which results in an increase or decrease in the number of securities in which a person is interested or in respect of which he has a short position. The definition was extended in 2005 to transactions involving derivatives and options and, in 2010, new Notes 1 and 2 were added to clarify that the term encompasses indemnity and other dealing arrangements with concert parties, but does not include securities borrowing and lending except where Rule 4.6 applies (see Instrument 2009/6). This may change in the future as the Code Committee raised in the consultation paper PCP 2009/1 the question of whether the definition of dealings should be amended so as to treat borrowing and lending transactions as dealings. They decided not to put forward detailed proposals at that time, but the PCP did describe in substance the amendments that they believed might be made if detailed proposals were put forward in the future. On 1 January 2015 a new para.(g) was inserted into the definition of "dealings" to clarify that the redemption or purchase by the target or offeror of its own relevant securities does constitute a dealing in those relevant securities.

3.2.1.3   Concert parties

The term "concert parties", which used to describe gatherings at the end of the pier in seaside resorts, was adopted by the Panel in the early days of the Code to describe associated parties acting together. For most purposes under the Code and for disclosure purposes under the DTRs and the 2006 Act (see 3.4.1 and 3.4.2 below), the holdings or acquisitions of shares in a target by parties "acting in concert" are aggregated. The concert party concept is expressed in different ways in the Code, the DTRs and the 2006 Act and is not used as a defined term other than in the Code, but in each case concert parties are capable of being constituted even where there is no formal written concert party agreement.

The Code also previously applied to the similar category of "associates" of a party to an offer and persons falling within either or both categories were subject to disclosure requirements under the Code. Since 19 April 2010 (as a result of amendments under Instrument 2009/6) the "associate" concept has been deleted in order to simplify the application of the Code, and the provisions of the Code which previously referred to an associate of a party to an offer now refer to persons acting in concert.

For Code purposes, a concert party is a combination of persons who cooperate to achieve or consolidate control of the target or to frustrate the successful outcome of a bid (see the Definitions section of the Code). The Code definition of a concert party does not require active co-operation between the parties, is not limited to parties co-operating through the acquisition of shares by any of them and includes persons who co-operate with the target company with a view to frustrating the successful outcome of a bid. The consequences of being a member of a concert party will generally bite under Rules 5, 6, 8, 9 and 11 when any of the relevant parties acquires shares.

Furthermore, under the Code definition of acting in concert, a person and each of its affiliated persons will be deemed to be acting in concert with each other. An "affiliated person" is defined in Note 2 to the definition of acting in concert as any undertaking in respect of which any person:

1. has a majority of the shareholders' or members' voting rights;
2. is a shareholder or member and at the same time has the right to appoint or remove a majority of its board;
3. is a shareholder or member and alone controls a majority of the shareholders' or members' voting rights pursuant to an agreement with other shareholders or members; or
4. has the power to exercise, or actually exercises, dominant influence or control.

The Code definition of acting in concert also provides that certain persons, including holding companies, subsidiaries, sister subsidiaries, 20%-owned associated companies, directors, connected advisers, pension schemes and the pension schemes of associated companies are presumed to be acting in concert with a company unless the contrary is established. Likewise, investors in a bidding consortium are presumed to be acting in concert with the offeror and, if they are part of a larger organisation, the Panel should be consulted to establish which other parts of the organisation will also be regarded as acting in concert. Furthermore, the Code presumes that a person's "close relatives" (which became a defined term on 23 November 2015) are acting in concert with that person, although the Panel has stated that this presumption can be rebutted if it can be demonstrated clearly that there has been a breakdown in the relationship between that person and other members of the family (see p.3 of Panel Statement 2015/03). The Code applies the same presumption to the related trusts of a person, as well as the "close relatives" of a founder of a company (and their close relatives and related trusts). In addition, where a private company is sold to a Code company and the sellers receive new shares in the Code company as consideration, those sellers are presumed to be acting in concert. Similar presumptions apply to investors in a company before it became a Code company; for example before an IPO of that company.

The notes to the Code definition of acting in concert give additional guidance as to how the term is understood by the Panel. In relation to other parts of a financial services organisation of which a consortium investor is part, for example, the Panel will consider waiving the presumption if the investment in the consortium amounts to less than 50% of the share capital of the offeror. The Panel will normally waive the presumption in relation to other parts of the organisation if the investment in the consortium is 10% or less (Note 6 on the Code definition of acting in concert). Similarly, the Panel will normally regard the presumption of concertedness between a company and its pension scheme as having been rebutted if an independent third party has absolute discretion regarding dealing, voting and offer acceptance decisions relating to any securities in which the pension scheme is interested (Note 7 on the Code definition of acting in concert).

The presumption that advisers will act in concert with their clients (presumption 7 of the Code definition of acting in concert) was considered in the case of Songbird Acquisition Ltd's bid for Canary Wharf Group Plc (see Panel Statement 2004/12). In its statement of 23 April 2004, the Panel made it clear that the presumption does not only apply to advisers who have been engaged to act on the offer or on a transaction related to the offer; other advisers who have a relationship with the offeror or target company (or a concert party thereof) will also be presumed to be acting in concert with that party. The presumption can, however, be rebutted (as it was in the Canary Wharf case). The question of whether or not the presumption should be rebutted is determined by the Panel, taking into account all relevant factors including whether the adviser is named in the company's annual report and accounts, and whether the adviser has stood down or offered to do so and, if so, why.

A person will not normally be treated as acting in concert with an offeror or target company by reason only of giving an irrevocable commitment, but Note 9 to the Code definition of acting in concert states that the Panel will consider the position of such a person in order to determine whether he is acting in concert if either:

1. the terms of the irrevocable commitment give the offeror or target company either the right (whether conditional or absolute) to exercise or direct the exercise of the voting rights attaching to the shares or general control of them; or
2. the person acquires an interest in more shares.

The Panel should therefore be consulted before the acquisition of any further interest in shares in such circumstances.

Further guidance from the Panel in Practice Statement No.22 indicates that the Panel is of the view that, although the precise wording of a voting undertaking contained in an irrevocable commitment to accept an offer may vary, it would generally comprise an undertaking to vote the relevant shares in accordance with the instructions of the offeror in the context of both resolutions required to implement the offer and resolutions which, if passed, might result in a condition of its offer not being fulfilled or might frustrate the offer in some other way.

The Panel considers that, in entering into a voting undertaking of this type, a shareholder is doing no more than what is logically consistent with his irrevocable commitment to accept the offer, since he is undertaking to vote the shares in a manner consistent with his acceptance decision. As such the Panel has indicated it would not consider the offeror to have acquired general control of the relevant shares for the purposes of the definition of acting in concert provided the voting undertaking is:

1. given in the context of an irrevocable commitment to accept the offer;
2. limited to the duration of the offer or, if earlier, until the irrevocable commitment otherwise ceases to be binding; and

3.   limited to matters which relate to ensuring that the offer is successful.

Where the Panel agrees that the presumption is rebutted in any individual case, it may, where it considers it appropriate, require that a person who would otherwise have been treated as a person acting in concert make a private disclosure to the Panel (containing the details that would have been required under Rule 8.4) if he deals in any relevant securities during an offer period. This requirement, which was introduced by Instrument 2009/6, is set out in Note 10 to the acting in concert definition and is designed to enable the Panel to monitor whether or not the presumption of concertedness should continue to be treated as rebutted during the offer period.

In addition to the definition and the notes which follow it, there are a number of other provisions of the Code which are relevant to understanding the concept of acting in concert. These provisions include, notably, the Notes on Rule 9.1 (see further 3.3.1.4 below).

Note 2 on Rule 9.1 provides that the Panel will normally presume that shareholders who make or threaten to make a "board control-seeking proposal" at any general meeting of a company are acting in concert with each other and with their proposed directors. Parties will be presumed to be acting in concert from the time that an agreement or understanding between them is reached, so any purchase of the company's shares by any of them thereafter could give rise to a mandatory offer obligation. However, it should be noted that the Panel takes a retrospective approach to the determination of appropriate consideration in respect of bids involving concert parties: although a concert party relationship may only arise at a certain point, the dealings of the parties prior to that point may be relevant for the purposes of determining the level and nature of consideration under a subsequent offer (see further 3.3.1.5 (Rule 6) and 3.3.1.6 (Rule 11) below).Concerns were raised by various shareholders as part of the 2009 Walker Review of Corporate Governance of the UK Banking Industry that these provisions acted as a barrier to co-operative action by fund managers and institutional shareholders. In response, the Panel issued Practice Statement No.26 on 9 September 2009 which sought to provide clarification of when a mandatory offer would be triggered by activist shareholders cooperating with each other. In para.1.4, the Panel confirmed that, of themselves, the following factors would not lead to the conclusion that the parties were acting in concert:

1. discussions between shareholders about possible issues which might be raised with a company's board;
2. joint representation by shareholders to the board; and
3. the agreement by shareholders to vote in the same way on a particular resolution at a general meeting.

The Panel also notes in para.1.6 of this Practice Statement that even if a "board control-seeking" resolution were to be proposed by activist shareholders, no mandatory offer would be required if, at the time that any such agreement or understanding is reached, steps are taken to prevent the acquisition of interests in securities in the relevant company by those shareholders.

Separately, Note 5 on Rule 9.1 provides that the Panel must be consulted before the acquisition of an interest in shares where:

1. the aggregate number of shares in which the directors, any other persons acting, or presumed to be acting, in concert with the directors and the trustees of an employee benefit trust (EBT) are interested will carry 30% or more of the voting rights (or, if already carrying 30% or more, will increase further) as a result of the acquisition; or
2. a person or group of persons acting, or presumed to be acting, in concert is interested in shares carrying 30% or more (but does not hold shares carrying more than 50%) of the voting rights and it is proposed that an EBT acquires an interest in any other shares.

Note 5 goes on to provide that no presumption of concertedness will apply in respect of any shares held in an EBT that are controlled by the beneficiaries.

The Note states that the Panel will consider "all relevant factors" in concluding whether the trustees of an EBT are acting in concert with the directors and/or a controller or group of persons acting, or presumed to be acting, in concert. The Note contains a non-exhaustive list of factors which will be taken into account.

For the purposes of Rule 9.1, the Panel has traditionally treated a group of persons acting in concert as a single person. Usually, therefore, the person responsible for making the mandatory offer (the person whose acquisition triggered the mandatory bid) will extend such offer to shareholders outside the concert party but not to members of the concert party itself. Following the Panel's Annual Report for 2002/3 at p.14, however, the person responsible for making the offer may extend it to other concert party members if it wishes, although it is under no obligation to do so.

Similarly, the 2006 Act treats persons as acting together in a less formal manner than the normal, strict legal meaning of contractual agreement; for instance, ss.824 and 825 when read together treat two or more persons as one (such that each party to the agreement is interested in all the shares in which any other party to the agreement is interested) where there exists any "agreement or arrangement" between them for the acquisition of shares. Section 824 (6)(a) makes it clear that "agreement or arrangement" includes a non-legally binding agreement or arrangement, provided there exists a mutuality of undertakings, expectations or understandings.

Finally, it is worth noting that the Panel strongly recommends that parties consult the Panel whenever they have doubts about the application of the Code's definition of "acting in concert". In its statement of public censure of Credit Suisse, Freshfields Bruckhaus Deringer and Holman Fenwick Willan (Panel Statement 2015/15: Asia Resource Minerals Plc (formerly Bumi Plc)) in respect of advice given during the acquisition of the Bakrie Group and PT Bukit Mutiara, the Panel stated at para.7.1 that the need for consultation is "particularly acute" where there is uncertainty as to whether parties may be acting in concert. The Panel also reiterated that legal or other professional advice as to whether parties are acting in concert, or reliance on warranties or representations from those parties stating that they are not acting in concert, is never an alternative to such consultation.

3.2.2 The 2006 Act

The 2006 Act will be relevant in a variety of circumstances. The acquisition of any shares in a UK-incorporated public company may lead to an obligation to disclose, at the request of that company, where the acquiror is, or has within the previous three years been, interested in its shares, along with certain other details (s.793, as to which, see further 3.4.2.3 below).

The 2006 Act contains powers compulsorily to purchase minority shareholdings once an offer for shares in the target has been accepted by holders of 90% of the shares of the relevant class to which the offer relates, excluding any shares in the company held as treasury shares (s.979). Hence, any shareholder with a holding of more than 10% of the shares to which an offer relates is able to thwart the operation of this mechanism and remain an unwanted minority holder.

Finally, as became apparent in the aftermath of the takeover by Guinness of the Distillers Company, restrictions on a public company giving financial assistance in connection with the purchase of its own shares (now contained in Ch.2 of Pt 18 of the 2006 Act) may apply to a takeover, not only in connection with any purchase of shares in a target, but also in relation to indemnities given by offerors in connection with various aspects of share-for-share offers.

3.2.3 DTRs

Chapter 5 (Vote Holder and Issuer Notification Rules) of the DTRs applies to: (1) UK and overseas companies whose home state is the UK and which have shares traded on a regulated market; and (2) UK companies with shares traded on a prescribed market (for example AIM). It does not apply to non-UK issuers whose home state is not the UK. In preparation for the UK's departure from the EU, the FCA has published a consultation paper on proposed amendments to the FCA Handbook, including to the DTRs (CP18/36). One such proposal is that DTR 5 should apply to all issuers that have securities admitted to trading on a UK regulated market, removing the home state requirement.

Non-EEA companies may benefit from an exemption from the requirements of DTR 5 if they are subject to equivalent requirements under their domestic legislation. At the date of writing, the FCA has determined that the laws of the United States of America, Japan, and Switzerland impose equivalent requirements (see *https://www.fca.org.uk/markets/ukla/regulatory-disclosures/equivalence-non-eea-regimes* [Accessed 19 June 2019]). The notification obligations are discussed at 3.4.1 below.

Under DTR 5.6 at the end of each calendar month, an issuer must (assuming an increase or decrease has occurred) announce the total number of voting rights and capital in respect of each class of share which it issues, and the total number of voting rights attaching to shares held in treasury. An issuer must also disclose changes in total voting rights and capital, other than those which are immaterial, as soon as possible (and in any event no later than the end of the business day following the day on which the increase or decrease occurs). The issuer must make the decision as to what is immaterial but the FCA's guidance makes it clear that an increase or decrease of 1% or more is likely to be material. It is the responsibility of each shareholder to monitor company announcements: the number of issued shares as announced by the company is taken as the denominator for determining whether disclosure thresholds have been reached by a shareholder (even where it has not engaged in any dealings). In addition, DTR 5 contains announcement obligations on an issuer which acquires or disposes of its own shares, in cases where the percentage held reaches, exceeds or falls below 5% or 10% of the voting rights.

The DTRs also previously placed an obligation on "persons discharging managerial responsibility" (PDMRs), who include directors, to notify listed companies of share dealings, which the company must then announce. From 3 July 2016, these obligations were replaced by provisions in MAR. These obligations are not discussed in this Chapter.

3.2.4   CJA 1993, FSMA and MAR

Part V of the CJA 1993 applies to dealings in shares on a regulated market, including the Main Market of the London Stock Exchange, regardless of the place of incorporation or residence of the company whose shares are being transferred. Its primary purpose is to prohibit certain dealings by, and certain activities of, persons who have inside information. In particular, when in possession of inside information, it is an offence for an individual not only to deal or to "encourage" others—such as corporate employees or clients—to deal, but also to disclose the information other than in proper performance of the functions of his employment, office or profession.

The FSMA controls the manner in which securities may be offered and admitted to listing on the Official List. It also contains provisions relevant to all takeovers, such as restrictions on financial promotions (s.21). Prior to the regulatory changes introduced by the FS Act 2012 on 1 April 2013, the FSMA contained a provision for an offence relating to misleading statements or courses of conduct (s.397). This provision has now been repealed and replaced by three offences relating to the making of misleading statements or courses of conduct under Pt 7 of the FS Act 2012. Two of these offences largely replicate the old s.397 offences; the third covers the making of false or misleading statements, or the creation of false or misleading impressions, in relation to "relevant benchmarks" (with the London Interbank Offered Rate (LIBOR) being the only relevant benchmark specified so far).

MAR relates to the control of market abuse, replacing the previous statutory market abuse regime in July 2016 (see 3.3.4.2 below).

These provisions result in a considerable potential overlap between the jurisdiction of the FCA and the Panel. In light of this, the FCA and the Panel have agreed a set of operating guidelines (the Operating Guidelines) which are intended, inter alia, to assist in determining how each of them should exercise its functions in cases of jurisdictional overlap. The Operating Guidelines provide at para.12 that where, during a takeover bid, matters arise which may amount to market misconduct, the FCA will not exercise its powers during the bid save in exceptional circumstances (see 3.3.4.3 below).

3.2.5   Other Rules

Finally, it will always be necessary to consider whether antitrust considerations and law and regulation in specific industries and/or in other jurisdictions will be relevant to share dealings in a takeover situation. The acquisition of material minority stakes may require approvals under such provisions. Particular care will need to be taken where securities are listed on more than one market to ensure that the requirements of each stock exchange (which may conflict) are complied with.

3.3   Restrictions on the freedom to deal

We will first deal with rules prohibiting or restricting share dealings which only apply in the context of a takeover, and then turn to restrictions with general application.

3.3.1   The Code

3.3.1.1   Dealings by offerors and persons acting in concert

Before turning to the detailed Rules of the Code, it is worth recording that there was, during 1997, speculation that the Panel might change the Code to restrict the ability of a bidder and its advisers to buy shares in the market during an offer period. This was largely prompted by the takeover in December 1996 of Northern Electric by CalEnergy, the US utility. Some commentators have said that Northern Electric was acquired too cheaply because CalEnergy had an unfair advantage as it was able to buy 30% of Northern Electric's shares while the price was depressed owing to the possibility of a referral to the former Monopolies and Mergers Commission. The price recovered when the bid was cleared and the offer received only 20% acceptances. But with 30% already in hand, CalEnergy gained control by the narrowest of margins. Some have, therefore, called on the Panel to adopt the US practice where a bidder is barred from market purchases once an offer has been made. Others have asked for the 30% threshold up to which a bidder can buy under Rule 5 (see 3.3.1.3 below) to be cut to 15%, or for purchases to be prohibited at a time when there is regulatory uncertainty. However, many others take the view that there is no good public policy reason for restricting market activity during a bid. If shareholders are willing to sell out early at or below the offer price in return for certainty, then that is their prerogative (and the bidder will be barred by the insider dealing legislation from buying if it has price-sensitive information about a likely regulatory outcome that the market does not, as to which see 3.3.3.4 below). It appears that the Panel has no current plans to amend the Code in this regard, which is in keeping with its preferred approach of a generally permissive regime on dealings, focusing on consequences and disclosure.

3.3.1.2 *Rule 4: Restrictions on dealings prior to and during the offer period*

Between the time when there is reason to suppose an offer or approach is contemplated and the announcement of that offer or approach (or the termination of discussions), Rule 4.1 prohibits all dealings in the securities of the target or (on a share-for-share offer) the offeror by any person who is privy to price-sensitive information concerning the offer or possible offer, apart from dealings in target securities by the offeror itself.

One difficulty which sometimes arises in this context, normally in connection with joint or consortium offers, is the identification of the offeror (i.e. the party which is permitted to deal in target securities notwithstanding its being in possession of confidential price-sensitive information). Note 2 on Rules 4.1 and 4.2 provides that the Panel must be consulted before any acquisitions of interests in target company securities are made by members or potential members of a consortium and that it will not normally be appropriate for members of a consortium to acquire interests in such securities unless, for example, there are arrangements to ensure that such acquisitions are made proportionate to members' interests in the consortium company or under arrangements which give no profit to the party making the acquisition. These restrictions will not, of course, apply to a party which can properly be characterised as an offeror (including a joint offeror).

Note 3 provides a limited exception to the Rule 4.1 prohibition allowing a party acting in concert with the offeror to deal provided that it is done on the basis that the offeror carries the economic risk and is entitled to the rewards of the transaction. Careful consideration of the insider dealing legislation and Listing Rules provisions on indemnity arrangements (see Listing Rule 10.2.4) will, however, be required before any such transaction is implemented.

Note 4 amplifies Rule 4.1 and provides that where an announcement has been made that an offer is contemplated and discussions are then terminated or the offeror decides not to proceed with the offer, no person (including the offeror) privy to this price-sensitive information may deal until the position is publicly clarified. Note 5 further prohibits directors and financial advisers from dealing contrary to advice given by them in relation to an offer.

Once an offer has been announced, Rule 4.2 prohibits the offeror and its concert parties from selling any securities in the target except with the prior consent of the Panel and following 24 hours' public notice that such sales might be made; the Panel's consent will not be given where the offer is a mandatory offer under Rule 9, and no sales at a price below the value of the offer will, in any event, be permitted. Once notice of a possible sale has been given under this rule, neither the offeror nor its concert parties may acquire an interest in any target securities and any revision to the terms of the offer will be permitted only in exceptional circumstances. The Panel should also be consulted whenever the offeror or its concert parties proposes to enter into or close any type of transaction which may result in target securities being sold during the offer period (either by that party or by the counterparty to the transaction). The rule is designed to prevent offerors and persons acting in concert with them from misleading or manipulating the market and is also therefore a reflection of General Principle 4 of the Code which prohibits the creation of false markets.

The Panel will give dispensation in exceptional circumstances from the usual consequences of a sale under Rule 4.2 as it did in March 2003 in connection with the hostile offer by Capital Management and Investment Plc (CMI) for Six Continents Plc (Six Continents). The offer involved the issue of a very large number of CMI shares as consideration relative to the number already in issue. In order to avoid potential concerns under Rule 6 (see 3.3.1.5 below) about whether the offer could be valued at a price at or above the prices paid by CMI as part of its pre-offer stake-building, the Panel Executive agreed with CMI's proposal that it would sell those shares which had been acquired and donate the profit to charity. The Panel Executive ruled (Panel Statement 2003/7) that the disposal by CMI of its shares in Six Continents was not intended to mislead or manipulate the market but rather was a pragmatic solution to any potential concerns arising under Rule 6. The Panel Executive therefore gave its consent under Rule 4.2 to the sale by CMI of its shares in Six Continents and ruled that the usual consequences of a sale under Rule 4.2 should not apply in this case.

Panel Statement 2003/5 addressed Rule 4.2 in light of the behaviour of Indigo Capital LLC (Indigo) in relation to Regus Plc (Regus). In this case, Indigo had entered into CFDs referenced to shares in Regus. The Panel Executive considered on p.6 that the closing out of such a CFD by Indigo during the offer period should be treated as equivalent to the sale of the underlying shares represented by the CFD, and as such subject to Rule 4.2. This was on the basis, discussed above, that it will most often be the case that a party with whom a CFD is entered into will hedge its exposure by acquiring an equivalent number of shares in the target company in the market. Accordingly, when such a CFD is closed out, the party with whom the CFD was entered into can reasonably be expected to sell the shares it had acquired to hedge its exposure.

In addition, as mentioned above, Rule 4.2 requires that when a sale of relevant securities is permitted by the Panel Executive, no such sale can be made at below the prevailing offer price and thereafter neither the offeror nor any person acting in concert with it may acquire an interest in any securities of the target company. The Panel Executive said at p.7 of Panel Statement 2003/5 that in a case such as the Indigo case where the offeror had not announced the price of its offer, it would normally treat the requirement of Rule 4.2 that sales cannot be made at below the offer price as setting a ceiling on the price at which the potential offeror would subsequently be allowed to make its formal offer, that ceiling being the price at which the relevant securities were sold.

In the Indigo case itself, however, in view of the fact that the closing out of the CFD was not disclosed to the market at the time (as it should have been) such that, in fact, there was no misleading impression that could have been created and also that to set a ceiling on the price would have the undesirable effect of possibly depriving Regus shareholders of any offer being made by Indigo at above the price at which they closed out the CFD, the Panel Executive ruled (on an ex parte basis) that the closing out of the CFD should not set a ceiling on the price of any future offer for Regus by Indigo. The Panel Executive also considered it relevant in making this ruling that further CFDs in respect of the same aggregate number of underlying shares were entered into by Indigo on the same date as the closing out of the CFD and that the number of underlying shares concerned was small.

The Panel Executive, however, ruled that the restriction on future purchases of shares set out in Rule 4.2 should apply as a consequence of the closing out of the CFD, such that during the offer period neither Indigo, nor any person acting in concert with it, would be permitted to acquire any further Regus shares or to enter into any further derivatives referenced to Regus shares. Indigo accepted the ruling.

In July 1998, the Panel introduced Rule 4.4 which prohibited financial advisers and stockbrokers (and their related entities except for "exempt principal traders" and "exempt fund managers") to a target company (or any associated companies) from dealing in interests in target company securities during an offer period. Following amendments to the Code in 2006, the prohibition now prevents financial advisers and corporate brokers during an offer period from:

1. either for their own account or on behalf of discretionary clients, acquiring interests in target company shares;
2. making any loan to a person to assist them in acquiring any such interests (save for lending in the ordinary course of business to established customers); or
3. entering into any indemnity or option or other arrangements which may be an inducement for a person to retain, deal or refrain from dealing in relevant securities of the target company.

The introduction of this rule followed controversial examples of purchases by a target's advisers. A note on Rule 4.4 now makes it clear that restriction (3) above does not prevent an adviser to a target company from procuring irrevocable commitments or letters of intent not to accept an offer.

The Panel has also encountered some instances of offerors, target companies and persons associated with them borrowing or lending securities or seeking to unwind such transactions during an offer period. The Panel expressed concern that the purpose underlying the borrowing or lending may have been to secure a tactical advantage or to manipulate the price or location of securities (see PCP 2004/3) and introduced Rule 4.6 to address these concerns. Rule 4.6 prohibits the following persons from entering into or taking action to unwind a securities borrowing or lending transaction in respect of relevant securities of the target during an offer period without first obtaining the consent of the Panel:

1.   an offeror;
2.   the target; and
3.   any person acting in concert with an offeror or with the target.

Consent of the Panel was previously also required in relation to entering into or taking action to unwind securities borrowing or lending transactions in respect of relevant securities of an offeror but, as from 19 April 2010, such consent has only been required in respect of relevant securities of the target.

Rule 4.6(b) requires persons who are subject to Rule 4.6(a) and who enter into or take action to unwind a securities borrowing or lending transaction in respect of relevant securities of an offeror (other than a cash offeror) or, with the consent of the Panel under Rule 4.6(a), the target to disclose details of the transaction in accordance with Rule 8 (see Note 5(l) on Rule 8).

In addition, Rule 4.6 also applies to the entry into of certain financial collateral arrangements in relation to a target's relevant securities (see Note 4 to Rule 4.6).

It is worth noting that persons who have borrowed or lent shares will be treated for the purposes of Rule 9 as if they are interested in such shares provided that they have not been on-lent or sold. Note 17 to Rule 9.1 states that the Panel must be consulted where such action may result in an obligation to make a mandatory offer. Note 17 was amended on 19 April 2010 to clarify that intra-day securities borrowing and lending will only be relevant to whether a mandatory offer has been triggered if these transactions would result in an increase to the person's "net borrowing position" in a company's shares at midnight on the day in question.

On 8 January 2018, the newly introduced Rule 4.7 came into effect as part of a number of measures to regulate a structure where an asset sale directly competed with offers. These rules were largely introduced in response to two such transactions in 2016 in which the target had received an offer, but decided that better value could be delivered to shareholders by selling all of its assets to a third party and returning the proceeds to shareholders (in circumstances were that third party buyer were prohibited from increasing a previously made offer).

Rule 4.7 prevents a purchaser or potential purchaser of all or substantially all of the offeree's assets from acquiring interests in shares in the offeree during the offer period unless the offeree board has made a statement quantifying the amount per share expected to be paid to shareholders, and then only to the extent that the price paid does not exceed the amount stated. The Code Committee considered this rule necessary to avoid the situation where an offeror that was acquiring shares in a target company may be disadvantaged by the consequences of Rules 6 and 11, whereas an asset purchaser that was acquiring shares would not have similar consequences.

Rule 4.7 applies not only in relation to an asset purchaser but also to any person whose relationship with the asset purchaser is such that, if the asset purchaser were an offeror, that person would be treated as acting in concert with the asset purchaser.

3.3.1.3   *Rule 5: Timing restrictions on acquisitions*

Subject to certain exceptions, Rule 5.1 prohibits the acquisition by any person of interests in shares if the result of such acquisition would be: (i) to increase the number of shares in which that person is interested (when aggregated with the holdings of that person's concert parties) to a number of shares carrying 30% or more of the target's voting rights; or (ii) to increase (by any amount) a similarly aggregated interest in 30% or more of the target's voting rights. The rule ceases to apply once a person acquires interests in shares carrying more than 50% of a company's voting rights. The primary purpose of Rule 5, as will be seen by the permitted exceptions, is to ensure the target board has the opportunity to make its case to its shareholders in an unrecommended situation before the bidder has acquired control.

The preamble to Rule 5 specifies that, for the purposes of Rule 5 only, "the number of shares in which a person will be treated as having an interest includes any shares in respect of which he has received an irrevocable commitment". The definition of "irrevocable commitments" in the Code includes both commitments to accept and commitments not to accept an offer, and both therefore count towards the relevant threshold.

As will be seen below, one of the exceptions to Rule 5.1 is that the relevant acquisition immediately precedes the announcement of a recommended offer (Rule 5.2(b)). Accordingly, although the restrictions in Rule 5 are capable of applying to irrevocable commitments, they can be avoided if the irrevocable commitments are executed immediately before the announcement of a firm intention to make an offer, provided the offer is to be recommended. This is another reason why it is often appropriate for irrevocable commitments to be executed on the evening prior to any announcement of an offer.

It should be noted that Rule 5 differs from the mandatory offer provisions in Rule 9 (see 3.3.1.4 below) in that receipt of an irrevocable commitment only constitutes an interest in securities for the purposes of Rule 5, and not for Rule 9. This means that a bidder can obtain irrevocable commitments over 30% or more of the target's voting shares where permitted by Rule 5 (most significantly where the offer is recommended) without triggering the mandatory offer provisions in Rule 9. However, Rule 5 would preclude a bidder from obtaining irrevocable commitments over 30% or more of the target's voting shares in the context of a hostile bid (unless it fell within the "single shareholder" exemption in Rule 5.2(a), as to which see further below). It should further be noted that, even if the offeror does not mind incurring a Rule 9 obligation, they may be prevented from doing so by Rule 5.

The main exceptions to Rule 5.1 (set out in Rule 5.2) are acquisitions of interests in shares carrying voting rights:

1. from a single shareholder where it is the only acquisition within a period of seven days (although this exception is not available in respect of an acquisition made after the announcement of a firm intention to make an offer where posting of the offer document is not subject to a pre-condition, nor where the acquisition is from a principal trader or a fund manager managing investment accounts on behalf of more than one underlying client, regardless of whether or not on a discretionary basis);
2. which immediately precede and are conditional upon the announcement of a recommended offer (or, if the offer is not recommended, the acquisition is made with the consent of the board of the target);
3. made after the announcement of a firm (unconditional) intention to make an offer:
    (a) with the agreement of the target's board;
    (b) where either that or any competing offer is or has been recommended;
    (c) where the first closing date of that or any competing offer has passed; or
    (d) where the offer has become unconditional in all respects;
4. by way of acceptance of an offer; or
5. if the acquisition is permitted by Note 11 on Rule 9.1 or Note 5 on the Notes on Dispensations from Rule 9.

There are a number of Notes to Rule 5.1 which clarify its scope. For example, Note 5 states that Rule 5.1 does not apply to acquisitions of interests in shares which do not increase the percentage of shares carrying voting rights in which that person is interested (for example if a shareholder takes up his entitlement under a fully underwritten rights issue or if a person acquires shares on exercise of a call option). Similarly,

Note 2 provides that the Rule does not cover acquisitions of new shares, securities convertible into new shares, rights to subscribe for new shares (other than pursuant to a rights issue) or new or existing shares under a share option scheme (albeit that the acquisition of new shares as a result of the exercise of conversion or subscription rights or options must be treated as an acquisition from a single shareholder falling within exception (1) above).

Acquisitions of interests in shares under exception (1) above must be notified by noon the following business day to the target, a Regulatory Information Service (RIS) and the Panel under Rule 5.4. Rule 5.3 states that any such acquisition of interests in shares will preclude the possibility of making further acquisitions under that exception unless the acquiror makes an offer for all the shares in the target and that offer subsequently lapses.

It should be noted, however, that any acquisition made under one of the exceptions to Rule 5 will almost inevitably bind the acquiror to make an offer under Rule 9, as referred to below.

The Panel stated in para.1.4 of PCP 2009/3 of 9 December 2009 that it is proposing in due course to undertake a general review of Rule 5 in order to establish whether there might be a case for amending or deleting certain (or even all) of the provisions of the Rule. However, the Panel noted in para.3.6 of RS 2009/3 of 5 March 2010 that it is not clear when such review might be undertaken.

The Code Committee considered Rule 5.1 and the exemption summarised in para.3(c) above when it amended Rule 24.1(1) with effect from 8 January 2018. Rule 24.1(a) now prohibits an offeror from publishing an offer document for 14 days from the announcement of its firm intention to make an offer, unless it has the consent of the offeree board. In the context of a unilateral offer, the ability of the offeree board to withhold its consent provides it with certainty that it will have at least 28 days from the date of the firm offer announcement until it has to publish its initial circular under Rule 25.1(a). The Code

Committee noted that the offeree board will now have certainty that the restriction in Rule 5.1 will continue to apply for a minimum period of 35 days from the date of the firm offer announcement (being the 14 days during which the offer document cannot be published, and the minimum 21 days set out in Rule 31.1 for which the offer must remain open until the first closing date).

3.3.1.4   *Rule 9: The mandatory offer*

Rule 9 was amended in May 2006 in light of the requirements of the European Directive on Takeover Bids (Directive 2004/25) (the Takeover Directive) and to reflect the broader concept of interests in securities which is now used in the Code. The Rule now states that, where a person acquires an interest in target shares which (taken together with shares in which he and persons acting in concert with him are interested) carry 30% or more of the voting rights in the target, the acquiror and (depending on the circumstances) its concert parties are required (except with the consent of the Panel) to make a cash offer for the outstanding shares in the target (although the offer need not extend to shares held in treasury) at a price not less than the highest price paid for target shares by the acquiror or its concert parties during the 12 months prior to the announcement of that offer. This requirement is also triggered by any acquisition of an interest in shares by a person who, together with his concert parties, is interested in shares carrying not less than 30% of the voting rights in the target if such person does not hold shares carrying more than 50% of such voting rights and if the effect of such acquisition is to increase the percentage of the shares carrying voting rights in which that person is interested.

The changes made to the Code in light of the Takeover Directive make it explicit in Rule 9.5(b) that if the offeror or its concert parties acquire any interest in target shares after the announcement of an offer under Rule 9 and before the offer closes for acceptance, the offer price must be increased to not less than the highest price paid for those target shares. It was also clarified in Rule 9.1 that an offer will not be required where control of the target is acquired as a result of a voluntary offer.

Subject to the terms of any withdrawal agreement between the UK and the EU, the Takeovers Directive will cease to apply in the UK on the UK's withdrawal from the EU. On 11 February 2019, the Takeovers (Amendment) EU Exit) Regulations 2019 were published, which provides for the transposition of these requirements of the Takeover Directive into UK law in the event that no agreement is reached.

A mandatory offer made pursuant to Rule 9 may not be subject to any conditions other than a 50% acceptance condition (which will be satisfied upon the offeror having received acceptances in respect of shares which, together with shares acquired or agreed to be acquired before or during the offer, will result in the offeror and concert parties holding shares carrying more than 50% of the voting rights in the target (Rule 9.3(a))). Pursuant to Note 2 to Rule 9.3, the Panel must be consulted if an offeror, or a person acting in concert with it, has borrowed or lent target shares so that the Panel can consider how such shares should be treated for the purpose of the acceptance condition. Rule 9.3(a) is reinforced by Rule 9.3(b) which provides that no acquisition of any interest in shares which would trigger a mandatory offer obligation may be made if the making or implementation of such an offer would or might be dependent on the passing of a resolution at any meeting of shareholders of the offeror or upon any other conditions, consents or arrangements.

In addition, any offer made under Rule 9 must (if the relevant jurisdictional criteria are met) contain a term that it will lapse if, before the first closing date of the offer or the date when the offer becomes unconditional (whichever is the later), it is referred to the Competition and Markets Authority under Sch.4 to the Enterprise and Regulatory Reform Act 2013 (defined in the Code as a "Phase 2 CMA reference"), or the European Commission initiates Phase 2 proceedings under art.6(1)(c) of Council Regulation 139/2004 (Rules 9.4, 12.1(a) and 12.1(b)).

Section 2 of the Schemes Appendix to the Code (Appendix 7), which was adopted on 14 January 2008, clarifies that an obligation to make a mandatory offer under Rule 9 may not be satisfied by an offer structured as a scheme of arrangement unless the Panel consents and Note 1 sets out the factors that the Panel will take into account when considering whether to so consent. Note 2 provides that an offeror using a scheme should not trigger a mandatory offer under Rule 9 without the Panel's prior consent to either satisfy its mandatory offer obligation by way of a scheme or to switch the transaction to a contractual offer structure.

One issue which has recently been resolved is the definition of "voting rights". On 23 November 2015, the definition of "voting rights" was amended to clarify that shares (other than treasury shares) which are subject to a restriction on the exercise of voting rights, or to a suspension of voting rights, will still normally be regarded as having voting rights exercisable at a general meeting for the purposes of the Code. This change removes the ability of a company to issue suspended voting shares (i.e. shares which carry little or no voting rights) as a means to avoid the application of Rule 9 (including the requirement for a whitewash). The change was made to codify the Bumi Plc decision (Panel Statement 2013/2). In this case, Borneo Bumi Energi & Metal Pte Ltd had sought to argue that "voting rights" must be interpreted by reference to the reduced number of voting rights they were able to exercise in practice due to the restrictions imposed by the Panel; the Panel disagreed, but it was acknowledged that the drafting of the definition of "voting rights" "could have been clearer".

Most of the difficult issues which arise in the context of Rule 9 concern whether or not particular persons are "acting in concert". Such issues are the subject of 3.2.1.3 above and Chapter 4. Issues do also arise, however, in relation to whether or not particular acquisitions of interests in shares or securities should have the effect of triggering the mandatory offer obligation.

In this connection, Note 11 on Rule 9.1 previously stated that normally, where shareholdings in a company are reduced by sales or diluted as a result of an issue of new shares, the provisions of Rule 9 will apply to the reduced or diluted holding. As a result, controlling shareholders were not able to restore their holdings to original levels by the acquisition of shares without incurring an obligation to make a general offer. In July 1999, the Panel considered the position of controlling shareholders and concluded that it was appropriate to permit controlling shareholders some ability to purchase further shares, notwithstanding that they (or the concert party of which they formed part) held 30% or more of the voting rights in a company. Accordingly (and after further amendment in May 2006), Note 11 now provides that if a person or group of persons acting in concert reduces its interest in shares, but without reducing its interest to less than 30%, such person or persons may subsequently acquire an interest in further shares without incurring an obligation to make a Rule 9 offer, provided that: (i) the total number of shares in which interests are acquired on this basis in any period of 12 months does not exceed 1% of the voting share capital for the time being; and (ii) the percentage of shares in which the relevant person or persons acting in concert are interested following any such acquisition does not exceed the highest percentage of shares in which such person or persons were interested in the previous 12 months. Parties with a controlling interest will not, as a result, be permitted to increase the percentage of shares in which they are interested progressively from one year to the next. A reduction of the percentage of shares in which a person or concert party is interested by dilution will be treated in the same way as a sale for these purposes.

Similarly, Rule 37.1 provides that when a company redeems or purchases its own voting shares, any resulting increase in the percentage of shares carrying voting rights in which a person is, or a group of persons acting in concert are, interested will be treated as an acquisition for the purposes of Rule 9. Note 1 on Rule 37.1, however, provides that a person so interested who comes to exceed the limits in Rule 9.1 as a result of a company's redemption or purchase of its own shares will not normally incur an obligation to make a mandatory offer unless that person is a director, or the relationship of the person with any one or more of the directors is such that the person is, or is presumed to be, acting in concert with any of the directors. For this purpose, a person who has appointed a representative to the board of the company is treated as a director. Note 1 goes on to provide that there is no presumption that any or all of the directors are acting in concert solely by reason of a proposed redemption or repurchase or by reason of a decision to seek shareholder authority for a redemption or repurchase.

It is worth noting that the exception provided for in Note 1 on Rule 37.1 will not apply if a person (or any relevant member of a group of persons acting in concert) who is interested in shares has acquired an interest at a time when he had reason to believe that a redemption or purchase by the company of its own shares would take place (Note 2). In any event, the Panel must be consulted in advance in any case where Rule 9 might be relevant (Note 4). This will include any case where a person or group of persons acting in concert is interested in shares carrying 30% or more of the voting rights of a company, but does not hold shares carrying more than 50% of such voting rights, or where such person(s) may become interested in shares carrying 30% or more of such voting rights on full implementation of the proposed redemption or purchase of own shares. Further, the Panel must be consulted if the aggregate interests of the directors and any other persons acting in concert, or presumed to be acting in concert, with any of the directors amount to 30% or more of such shares, or may be increased to 30% or more on full implementation of the proposed redemption or purchase of own shares.

Notwithstanding the foregoing, there are certain circumstances in which the Panel will be prepared to waive an obligation which would otherwise arise under Rule 9 including, for example, where there is an independent vote at a shareholders' meeting (see Note 1 of the Notes on Dispensations from Rule 9). Rule 37.1 (see above) contains a similar provision regarding the waiver of a mandatory offer obligation which would otherwise arise following the redemption or purchase by a company of its own shares. Detailed Rules concerning the obtaining of a waiver are set out in Appendix 1 to the Code (the Whitewash Guidance Note).

It should be noted, however, that the Panel will not (as specified in Note 1 of the Notes on Dispensations from Rule 9) normally grant a waiver if the person to whom the new securities are to be issued or any persons acting in concert with him have purchased shares in the company in the 12 months prior to posting of the shareholder circular relating to the proposals but subsequent to negotiations, discussions or the reaching of understandings or agreements with the directors of the company in relation to the proposals. Similarly, any waiver will be invalidated if there are any such purchases between the posting of the circular and the holding of the meeting of independent shareholders.

On 16 August 2002 (in Panel Statement 2002/17), the Panel announced that it had dismissed an appeal against the decision of the Panel Executive to grant a waiver from the obligation that would otherwise have arisen under Rule 9.1 in connection with a proposed issue of shares in Alexanders Holdings Plc (Alexanders) to Orb Estates Plc (Orb Estates) as consideration for the acquisition by Alexanders of certain subsidiaries of Orb Estates. The shares proposed to be issued to Orb Estates amounted to approximately 75.1% of Alexanders' enlarged share capital. On 19 August 2002 (in Panel Statement 2002/18), the Panel gave the reasons for its decision. The decision of the Panel considered, inter alia, disqualifying transactions, put options and equality of treatment. The Panel Executive confirmed in para.6(g) that the provision regarding disqualifying transactions (referred to above) was introduced to ensure equality of treatment for all shareholders and to prevent some shareholders being allowed a cash exit from the company while the remaining body of shareholders was not afforded that option. Accordingly, this safeguard should not apply when an acquisition of shares is made at a time when a proposed transaction which will give rise to a change in control is not in contemplation. It is only where the transaction and the purchase of target company shares can be regarded in some way as part of the same overall transaction that there can be equality concerns (para.44).

Similarly, the Panel held that the relevant date for determining whether the constituent elements of a disqualifying transaction are present in relation to the entry into of a put option is the date on which the put option agreement is executed. This is when the acquiror incurs the potential obligation to acquire the shares and, therefore, when equal treatment of all holders of target securities under General Principle 1 should be considered (para.54).

Rule 9 was amended on 30 March 2009 to remove the requirement to seek the consent of the Panel to board appointments of nominees of Rule 9 offerors. Rule 9.7 was also introduced with the aim of clarifying both the requirements relating to the disposal of interests in shares by persons who have triggered a mandatory bid obligation and the application of restrictions on the exercise of voting rights attaching to shares in which such persons are interested. The principal purpose of these restrictions is to prevent a potential offeror acquiring shares that would trigger a Rule 9 offer, exercising rights attaching to the shares and then disposing of the shares as an alternative to making an offer pursuant to Rule 9.1.

On 22 December 2017 the Outer House of the Court of Session ruled in the case of the *Panel on Takeovers and Mergers v King* [2017] CSOH 156; 2018 S.L.T. 79 in the context of Rule 9 offers. This is the first case in which the Panel has applied to Court for an enforcement order pursuant to its rights under s.955 of the Companies Act 2006. The Takeover Appeal Board had ruled on 13 March 2017 that Mr King had acted in concert with others to acquire more than 30% of the voting rights in Rangers Football Club, and he thus was obliged under Rule 9 of the Code to make a mandatory offer for all shares not held by him and his concert parties. King failed to comply, and the Takeover Appeal Board commenced proceedings on 13 April 2017.

The Court of Session rejected the argument from King that he should not be required to make a Rule 9 offer due to his inability to access the funds, because the funds he had used to purchase the shares were held on trust. As a matter of fact, the Court was satisfied that King had control over the trust funds. To ensure the proper administration of the Code, the Court considered that the Panel should be able to pierce through trust structures to discover the person actually in control of an offer to acquire shares.

The Court stated that "in nearly all cases, if asked by the Panel to enforce its decision by granting an order", it would do so, nonetheless confirming that the Companies Act allowed it discretion to refuse to grant an order in rare cases. The Court found in favour of the Panel, noting that "the Panel is the body which is charged with the duty of evaluating the evidence and making findings of fact", confirming that the court is reluctant to act as a court of appeal against decisions of the Panel.

3.3.1.5 Rule 6: Minimum level of consideration

Under Rule 6.1, an offer may not be made on less favourable terms (but need not necessarily be in cash, even if the acquisitions were for cash (although see 3.3.1.6 below)) than the highest price paid by the offeror or its concert parties (as to which see 3.2.1.3 above) for interests in target shares during the three months prior to the commencement of the offer period or during the period between commencement of the offer period and formal announcement of the offer. This obligation may also arise in respect of acquisitions made prior to this three-month period if the Panel considers there are circumstances which render this necessary to give effect to the general principle that all holders of securities be treated equally. The Panel will not normally exercise this discretion unless the sellers, or other parties to the transactions giving rise to the interests, are directors of, or other persons closely connected with, the offeror or target (Note 2).

Note 4 on Rule 6 explains how to calculate the highest price paid. The price paid for purchases of shares is simply the price agreed between the purchaser and the vendor. In the case of an unexercised call option, the price paid will normally be treated as the middle market price of the relevant shares at the time the option is entered into. In the case of a call option which has been exercised, the price paid will normally be treated as the amount paid on exercise of the option together with any amount paid by the option-holder on entering into the option. In the case of a written put option (whether exercised or not), the price paid will normally be treated as the amount paid or payable on exercise of the option less any amount paid by the option-holder on entering into the option. In the case of a derivative, the price paid will normally be treated as the initial reference price of the underlying derivative together with any fee paid on entering into the derivative. However, if any of the option exercise prices or derivative reference prices are calculated by reference to the average price of a number of acquisitions by the counterparty of interests in underlying securities, the price paid will normally be determined to be the highest price at which such acquisitions are actually made. The Note also indicates that when calculating the figure any stamp duty or broker's commission payable should be excluded.

Note 1 on Rule 6 provides that the Panel will, "in exceptional circumstances", permit offers at a price which does not match one paid less than three months earlier. The factors which the Panel will take into account in determining whether to exercise this discretion include whether the relevant acquisition was made on terms then prevailing in the market, changes in the market price of the shares since the relevant acquisition and whether interests in shares have been acquired at high prices from directors or other persons closely connected with the offeror or target.

If, following the formal announcement of an offer, any interest in target shares is acquired at a price exceeding the offer price, the offer must be revised immediately to reflect the terms of such purchase (Rule 6.2).

Both Rules 6.1 and 6.2 acknowledge that acquisitions of interests in shares giving rise to obligations under those Rules may also give rise to obligations under Rule 11 (see 3.3.1.6 below). Compliance with Rule 11 will normally be regarded as satisfying Rule 6.

Note 3 on Rule 6 applies where interests in shares in a target have been acquired at a relevant time and the offer includes securities as consideration. The Note makes clear that the securities offered as consideration must, at the date of announcement of the firm intention to make the offer, have a value at least equal to the highest relevant price paid. The Note goes on to say that if there is a restricted market in the securities of the offeror, or if the amount of securities to be issued is large in relation to the amount already issued, the Panel may require justification of prices used to determine the value of the offer. Note 3 was discussed in Panel Statement 2003/7 published in March 2003 in connection with the hostile offer by CMI for Six Continents, referred to at 3.3.1.2 above.

CMI was an AIM-listed cash shell with a net asset value of about £41 million. Six Continents was a FTSE 100 company. Prior to announcement of its offer, CMI acquired shares representing about 0.3% of Six Continents' issued share capital. CMI's basic offer was on a share-for-share basis with a partial cash alternative. The Panel Executive stated on p.3 that, given the very great number of new CMI shares that were being offered as consideration, Note 3 was applicable in establishing whether the value of the offer was at least equal to the highest price paid by CMI in buying Six Continents shares in the market. The Panel Executive said that Note 3 recognised that, in cases where the amount of listed securities to be issued was large in relation to the amount already issued, the market price of the offeror's shares at the time of announcement of the offer might not be capable of providing an accurate yardstick against which to determine whether the offeror had satisfied its Rule 6 obligation. As discussed earlier, the Panel Executive went on to explain that it had accepted CMI's proposal that it should sell the Six Continents shares it had acquired and donate the profits to charity in order to solve any potential concerns under Rule 6. This ruling by the Panel Executive makes it clear that a listed bid vehicle which is proposing a reverse takeover containing a share-for-share element and which has recently acquired target shares in the market may find it very difficult to justify to the Panel its valuation of the offer for Rule 6 purposes. The Panel Executive also ruled on p.4 that the sale by CMI of the shares it had acquired in Six Continents would not give rise to any consequences under Rule 4.2 (see 3.3.1.2 above)

3.3.1.6   *Rule 11: Mandatory cash offers and mandatory securities offers*

Under Rule 11.1, which was amended on 23 November 2015, acquisitions for cash by an offeror or its concert parties (as to which see 3.2.1.3 above):

1.   during the offer period, and within 12 months prior to its commencement, of any interests in shares of any class under offer representing 10% or more of the shares of that class in issue; or
2.   during the offer period, of any interests in shares of any class under offer,

will require the offeror to make its offer for that class in cash, or to make a cash alternative available, at not less than the highest price paid for the relevant interest in shares during those 12 months or during the offer period, as appropriate. Note 1 on Rule 11.1 explains how to calculate the highest price paid for different types of interest in shares in these circumstances. The process is exactly the same as that set out in Note 4 on Rule 6 (see 3.3.1.5 above).

Interests acquired in exchange for securities will normally be deemed to be acquired for cash unless the seller, or other party to the transaction giving rise to the interest, is required to hold the securities received or receivable in exchange until either the offer has lapsed or the offer consideration has been posted to accepting shareholders (Note 5 on Rule 11.1). This Rule was amended in July 1998 to include the requirement to make a cash alternative available where any target shares of the class under offer are purchased by the offeror or its concert parties during the offer period. This amendment followed criticism of offerors using the 10% threshold as a loophole to allow them to make cash purchases during the offer period favouring a minority of shareholders.

Rule 11.2 requires the making of a securities offer in similar circumstances to those in which a cash offer is required by Rule 11.1. The effect of Rule 11.2 is to require a securities exchange offer if, during or within three months prior to the commencement of the offer period, the offeror and persons acting in concert with it have acquired, in exchange for securities, interests in shares of the class under offer representing 10% or more of the shares of that class in issue. An obligation to make a cash offer under Rule 11.1 will also arise in these circumstances, unless there is an obligation on the vendor to hold on to the securities received or receivable until the offer has lapsed or consideration has been posted.

There are a number of important Notes on Rule 11.2:

1. Note 1 provides that the securities offered pursuant to Rule 11.2 must be offered on the basis of the number of consideration securities received or receivable by the relevant sellers, or other parties to the transactions giving rise to the interests, for each target company share rather than on the basis of securities equivalent to the value of the securities received or receivable by the sellers or other parties at the time of the relevant purchases. The Panel clarified in para.4.1 of Response Statement RS 6 that, in considering the required level of an offer, it will take into account a corporate action (such as a rights issue or a share split) if as a result shareholders would not be treated equally and will also require any special features attached to securities offered to a seller (such as contingent value rights) to be attached to the securities to be made available under any offer.
2. Note 2 provides a discretion to the Panel to require a securities offer to be offered to all other holders of shares of that class even where the 10% threshold has not been reached, or where the relevant purchase took place more

than three months prior to the commencement of the offer period. Exercise of the discretion will normally be limited to situations where the sellers of the relevant shares or other parties to the transactions giving rise to the interests are directors of, or other persons closely connected with, the offeror or target company.

3. Note 3 makes clear that where an offeror acquires target shares in exchange for securities and the offeror has arranged for these securities to be immediately placed for cash on the seller's behalf (a vendor placing), then there should be no obligation to provide a securities offer to all shareholders.

Finally, Note 12 on Rule 11.1 clarifies that where a new offer is announced in accordance with Rule 12.2(b)(ii) (i.e. following anti-trust clearance from the Competition and Markets Authority or the European Commission), acquisitions of interests in target company shares made for cash during the competition reference period will be deemed to be acquisitions during the new offer period for the purposes of Rule 11.1(b). Note 7 on Rule 11.2 makes clear that acquisitions during the competition reference period will also be deemed to be acquisitions during the new offer period for the purposes of Rule 11.2 (and so may trigger an obligation to make a securities exchange offer available to all shareholders).

3.3.1.7 *Rule 16: Special deals and management incentivisation*

When an offer is in progress or is reasonably in contemplation, Rule 16.1 prohibits (without the consent of the Panel) the offeror or its concert parties from dealing in target shares or entering into arrangements which involve acceptance of the offer, if there are favourable conditions attached which are not available to all target shareholders. Irrevocable undertakings to accept an offer should not, therefore, confer any valuable benefit on the person giving the undertaking—a point also of importance in ensuring that the shares which are the subject of such an undertaking count for the purposes of the squeeze-out provisions of the 2006 Act.

In addition, an arrangement made with a person who, while not a shareholder, is interested in shares carrying voting rights in a target (such as options or derivatives holders), is also prohibited under Rule 16.1 if favourable conditions are attached which have not been extended to the shareholders. However, there is no requirement to extend any offer, or any "special deal" falling within Rule 16.1, to persons who are interested in shares but are not shareholders.

Note 1 on Rule 16.1 specifies that arrangements where there is a promise to make good to a seller of shares any difference between the sale price and the price of any subsequent successful offer are arrangements to which Rule 16.1 applies. Similarly, an irrevocable undertaking, combined with an option to put if the offer fails, will be prohibited by Rule 16.1.

The Panel has over time developed a flexible approach to interpreting Rule 16.1 where one or more shareholders in the target company participate in a vehicle making the offer. Otherwise, management buy-outs would effectively be prohibited, to the potential detriment of existing target shareholders, as well as offers by one or more such shareholders. The Panel has therefore usually ruled that when two or more persons form a consortium whereby each can properly be considered to be a joint offeror, Rule 16.1 is not contravened if one or more of them is already a shareholder in the target company. Subject to that, joint offerors may make arrangements between themselves concerning the future membership, control and management of the business being acquired.

In the context of what constitutes a joint offeror, the Panel issued Panel Statement 2003/25 on 21 November 2003 concerning Brascan Corporation's appeal against an earlier Panel ruling that arrangements between the members of a consortium, formed with a view to the potential acquisition of Canary Wharf Group Plc, did not contravene Rule 16. The Panel stated in para.16 that the criteria for assessing whether or not a person was a joint offeror were as follows.

1. What proportion of the equity share capital of the bid vehicle will the person own after completion of the acquisition?
2. Will the person be able to exert a significant influence over the future management and direction of the bid vehicle?
3. What contribution is the person making to the consortium?
4. Will the person be able to influence significantly the conduct of the bid?
5. Are there arrangements in place to enable the person to exit from his investment in the bid vehicle within a short time or at a time when other equity investors cannot?

In dismissing the appeal, the Panel stressed at para.17 that each case must be decided upon its own facts and that earlier decisions on different facts are of little precedent value.

Rule 16.2 aims to simplify the manner in which the Code applies to management incentive arrangements and reduce the range of circumstances in which consultation is required (see Code Committee Instrument 2009/5). Rule 16.2(a) provides that (absent consent from the Panel) where an offeror has entered into or reached an advanced stage of discussions on proposals to enter into incentivisation arrangements with members of the target's management who are interested in target shares, relevant details of the arrangements or proposals must be disclosed and the independent adviser to the target must state publicly that in its opinion the arrangements are fair and reasonable. Where the value of the arrangements entered into or proposed to be entered into is significant and/or the nature of the arrangements is unusual either in the context of the relevant industry or good practice, the Panel must be consulted and its consent to the arrangements obtained (Rule 16.2(b)). The Panel may also require, as a condition to its consent, that the arrangements be approved at a general meeting of the target's independent shareholders.

Where the members of the management are shareholders in the target, and, as a result of the incentivisation arrangements, they will become shareholders in the offeror on a basis that is not being made available to all other target shareholders, Rule 16.2(c) requires that such arrangements be approved at a general meeting of the target's independent shareholders.

Note 1 on Rule 16.2 provides that where members of the target are to receive offeror securities pursuant to an appropriate offer or proposal made in accordance with Rule 15, Rule 16.2(a) and (b) will apply, but shareholder approval will not normally be required in respect of such offer or proposal.

If the only target shareholders who receive offeror securities are members of the target's management, Note 2 sets out that the Panel will not, so long as the requirements of Rule 16.2 are complied with, require all target shareholders to be offered offeror securities pursuant to Rule 11.2, even though such members of management propose to sell, in exchange for offeror securities, more than 10% of the target shares.

3.3.1.8 *Competitive bid processes*

The Panel raised concerns in a consultation paper issued in October 2001 (PCP 7) about the ability of the then framework of the Code to resolve competitive situations in an orderly fashion and create as little uncertainty for the shareholders of the target as possible.

With these concerns in mind the Panel adopted a number of changes to the Code which, it was hoped, would limit the times when the Code fails to resolve a competitive situation in an orderly and timely manner. In terms of the subject matter of this Chapter, the introduction of Rule 35.4 is particularly relevant. This states that, except with the consent of the Panel, where an offer has been one of two or more competing offers and has lapsed, neither that offeror, nor any concert party of that offeror, may acquire any interest in shares in the target company on more favourable terms than those made available under its lapsed offer until each of the competing offers has either been declared unconditional in all respects or has itself lapsed. This amendment has closed the loophole which previously allowed lapsed competitive bidders the possibility of frustrating another offeror's bid.

3.3.1.9 *Disenfranchisement of shares acquired during an offer period*

Following the Panel's June 2010 review of certain elements of the Takeover Code, respondents suggested that the Code be amended to remove the ability of shareholders to vote shares acquired after the commencement of an offer period. Another suggestion was the creation of "qualifying periods" which would similarly govern when votes attaching to shares could be exercised. The respondents suggesting such amendments were keen to counter perceived short-termism, exemplified by investors who may be acquiring shares following the announcement of a possible offer in the expectation that the offer price would exceed their acquisition cost. Following a consultation, the Code Committee affirmed that such changes would offend General Principle 1 of treating all shareholders equally and the generally accepted position of "one share, one vote". The Code Committee stated that it would not propose such changes without an equivalent change in company law (see Panel Statement 2010/22).

3.3.2 *The 2006 Act*

Although the 2006 Act does not expressly prohibit or restrict dealings in shares during a takeover, there are certain aspects of the compulsory acquisition procedure (set out in ss.979–982 of the 2006 Act) which may impact on the desirability of such dealings by an offeror or its associates.

Under s.979 of the 2006 Act, in order to exercise the right to purchase compulsorily outstanding minority shareholdings following a bid, an offeror must have acquired or unconditionally contracted to acquire "by virtue of acceptances of the offer": (i) not less than 90% in value of the shares of the class "to which the offer relates"; and (ii) 90% of the voting rights attaching to those shares. The definition of "shares" for these purposes excludes treasury shares.

In considering these tests, shares in the target purchased by an offeror after the offer has been made (i.e. after the posting of the offer document) may also be treated as acquired by virtue of an acceptance of the offer (s.979(8) and (10) of the 2006 Act) if:

1. the value of the consideration for which they are acquired or contracted to be acquired (the "acquisition consideration") does not at that time exceed the value of the consideration specified in the terms of the offer; or
2. those terms are subsequently revised so that, when the revision is announced, the value of the acquisition consideration (calculated at the time of the acquisition) no longer exceeds the value of the consideration specified in those terms.

Shares in the target purchased after the offer has been made by those who are "associates" of the offeror for the purposes of these provisions (including group companies, companies in which the offeror is substantially interested, nominees and concert parties (s.988(1)) may be "shares to which the offer relates" if their purchase fulfils either condition (1) or (2) above (s.979(9)). If the purchasing associates then assent such shares to the offer, they may thus be counted towards the 90% threshold for the exercise of compulsory purchase rights. However, any shares owned by associates before the offer is made by the posting of the offer document are ignored in calculating whether the 90% level has been attained (s.977(2)).

Purchases of target company shares by an offeror or its associates after the making of an offer (i.e. after the posting of the formal offer document) should, therefore, have no adverse effect on the offeror's ability to reach a position where it can exercise compulsory acquisition rights over minority shareholdings. However, where shares are purchased either by the offeror or an associate before the offer is formally made, the level of acceptances required for the exercise of compulsory purchase rights will be 90% of a correspondingly smaller proportion of the target's total share capital (and, therefore, potentially more difficult to achieve).

Another point to note relates to the drafting of irrevocable commitments to accept an offer. A "takeover offer" is defined in s.974 of the 2006 Act as "an offer to acquire all the shares … other than shares that at the date of the offer are already held by the offeror" being an offer in respect of which the terms are the same "in relation to all the shares to which the offer relates".

Section 975(2) provides that:

> "the reference in Section 974(2) to shares already held by the offeror does not include a reference to shares that are the subject of a contract … entered into by deed and for no consideration, for consideration of negligible value or for consideration consisting of a promise by the offeror to make the offer."

It follows from this that irrevocable commitments should:

1. be drafted so as to be for no consideration and executed as a deed;
2. contain negligible consideration; or
3. contain as their sole consideration a promise by the offeror to make the offer.

Otherwise, the shares which are the subject of irrevocable commitments are excluded for compulsory acquisition purposes (in the same way that a market purchase of shares made before the offer would be excluded) counting neither towards the numerator nor towards the denominator in determining whether the 90% threshold has been reached and thus making it more difficult to apply the compulsory acquisition procedure.

3.3.3   CJA 1993

3.3.3.1   CJA 1993 offences

Part V of the CJA 1993 came into force on 1 March 1994 and was designed to bring English law into line with the EC Insider Dealing Directive (89/592). The CJA 1993 renders it an offence for an individual to:

1. deal in price-affected securities if he has inside information relating thereto which they hold as an "insider" (i.e. by virtue of his or her directorship, employment, shareholding, office or profession or which they have obtained from an inside source (s.57)) (s.52(1));
2. encourage any other person (which would include a company) to deal in securities which he himself is prohibited from dealing in (s.52(2)(a)); or
3. disclose the inside information to another person other than in the proper performance of the functions of his employment, office or profession (s.52(2)(b)).

It should be noted that, as referred to above, these offences can only be committed by individuals (and not by companies). However, the scope of the offence provided for in s.52(1) extends to catch individuals who procure dealings by other persons, including companies (s.55).

3.3.3.2   Relationship with the Market Abuse Regulation

There are certain aspects of the insider dealing prohibition provided for in CJA 1993 which are similar in application and scope to the market abuse regime. Market abuse is addressed further in 3.3.4.2 below.

3.3.3.3   Contravention

A contravention of Part V of the CJA 1993 results in exposure to the risk of a fine or imprisonment under s.61(1). However, s.63(2) makes it clear that no contract is void or unenforceable merely because it is made in contravention of the Act. In March

2013, Richard Joseph, formerly a futures trader, was found guilty of six counts of conspiracy to deal as an insider and sentenced to four years on each count, to be served concurrently. To date, the FCA, and previously the FSA, have secured 32 convictions in relation to insider dealing, with the two most recent convictions having been secured in relation to the takeover of Logica Plc by CGI Holdings (Europe) Ltd (see the FCA's press release at *https://www.fca.org.uk/news/press-releases/ two-sentenced-insider-dealing-case* [Accessed 19 June 2019]).

3.3.3.4 Consequences for takeovers

The insider dealing legislation will normally have the effect of preventing share dealing in price-affected securities by a potential offeror who, as part of pre-bid due diligence, has been given price-sensitive information by the target. This is because the individuals in receipt of the price-sensitive information are likely to be taken to have procured or encouraged any such dealings in contravention of s.52(1) or 52(2)(a). Similarly, such individuals, the directors of the offeror and others in the know will be prohibited from dealing in price-affected securities on their own account and, even in the absence of receipt of confidential information, they will be prevented from dealing on their own account by their knowledge that a bid is in contemplation.

However, most of the prohibitions in the Act do not apply where the only relevant inside information is that the acquiring party is contemplating a takeover offer and the dealings are made to facilitate the offer—the "market information" defence (s.53(4), giving effect to Sch.1 of the CJA 1993). It is, therefore, not an offence for directors or employees of a potential offeror to procure purchases of the shares of a target by the offeror or others in the knowledge that a full scale bid is in contemplation, if the dealing is to facilitate the completion or carrying out of the bid, provided they have no other relevant inside information.

It is important to consider the implications of undertaking due diligence prior to the announcement of an offer, as this may affect the availability of the market information defence. Even where pre-bid due diligence is proposed, it may be possible to avoid insider dealing concerns by setting up an information barrier arrangement within the financial adviser to the offeror. Under such an arrangement, information provided by the target would be vetted for price-sensitivity by employees of the offeror's financial adviser who were not engaged in providing advice to the offeror. Only information which was not price-sensitive would be passed to the offeror and the offeror's advisory team. It is worth noting that, for CJA 1993 purposes, there is no reason why the information barrier arrangement should not be set up within the offeror rather than within its financial adviser. However, this would give rise to market abuse concerns (as a result of the fact that both companies and individuals can commit market abuse) (see further 3.3.4.2 below).

In general, the CJA 1993 should not normally inhibit purchases of target shares following an announcement of a bid. This is because, if the bid is hostile, then the offeror is unlikely to have received confidential information and, if recommended, it is unlikely that any information will remain price-sensitive following announcement of the bid, since the target will have taken all information into account in recommending the offer. This point is not, however, beyond doubt and the offeror will need to be satisfied that there is no expectation of profit attributable to the price-sensitive information, because the information is reflected in the offer price. Offerors tend not to take comfort solely in the fact that if a target has chosen not to disclose information, then there is good argument that the information is not price sensitive—this is for a number of reasons, including the possibility that the target has not conducted its analysis correctly and/or the target may have concluded it has a legitimate basis for delaying disclosure (see 3.3.4.2 below).

3.3.3.5 *Appointment of investigating inspectors*

Section 168 of the FSMA confers power on the Secretary of State, FCA and the PRA to appoint inspectors to investigate whether any offence under Pt V of the CJA 1993 has been committed. Section 177 of the FSMA then lays down penalties for refusal to comply with these investigations. Although a refusal to answer any questions put by the inspectors will entitle the inspectors to bring the case before the court, the court may only punish a reluctant interviewee if it is satisfied that he has acted without reasonable excuse in refusing to reply.

3.3.3.6 *CFDs: No longer a loophole*

It is generally not possible to offset the expenses of a bid by the use of cash-settled derivatives (including CFDs) linked to the share price of the target or the share prices of companies in the same business sector as the target. Such contracts were controversially used in the bid by Trafalgar House for Northern Electric. Trafalgar House effectively bet that the share price of a number of electricity distribution companies (including Northern Electric) would rise as a result of its offer by striking a series of CFDs with its investment bank, Swiss Bank Corporation. After consultation with the Panel (which had initially concluded that Trafalgar House's strategy was legitimate), the Securities and Investment Board (later the FSA and, now, the FCA) effectively prohibited the use of derivative contracts for the purpose of offsetting the expenses of a bid by issuing a guidance document in December 1996 (under s.206 of the Financial Services Act 1986) which stated that such contracts should not be entered into on the basis of inside information (including information that a bid may be made) where they would provide only a cash benefit and would not constitute a step towards the accomplishment of the takeover. The guidance reflected legal advice received by the Securities and Investment Board to the effect that cash-settled derivatives do not facilitate the accomplishment of takeovers and that the parties to them cannot therefore rely on the CJA 1993 "market information" defence. Although the Securities and Investment Board guidance no longer has any statutory underpinning (the Financial Services Act 1986 having been repealed in its entirety by FSMA), it is nevertheless still considered to reflect best practice and to be an accurate statement of the law. The Section on Market Abuse in the FCA Handbook, MAR 1, reinforces the position by stating that an example of market abuse would be:

> "an offeror or potential offeror entering into a transaction in a financial instrument, using inside information concerning the proposed bid, that provides merely an economic exposure to movements in the price of the target company's shares (for example, a spread bet on the target company's share price) (MAR 1.3.2(G)(3))."

It should be noted, however, that neither CJA 1993 nor the Securities and Investment Board's guidance (nor, indeed, the market abuse regime) has the effect of completely prohibiting the use of derivative contracts in the context of takeovers (particularly where such contracts provide for physical settlement). Indeed, there have been a number of recent examples of their use or attempted use as part of pre-bid stake-building efforts. As will be evident, however, the legal and regulatory consequences of their use are not wholly straightforward.

3.3.4 FSMA, the FS Act 2012 and the Market Abuse Regulation

3.3.4.1 Sections 89–91 of the FS Act 2012: Misleading statements and practices

Section 90(1) of the FS Act 2012 may be particularly significant in the context of takeovers. As part of the changes introduced by the FS Act 2012, Pt 7 of the Act repealed s.397 of the FSMA, which had prohibited the making of misleading statements and market manipulation, and replaced it with ss.89–91 of the FS Act 2012, which makes it a criminal offence to:

(i)   make false or misleading statements (s.89);
(ii) create false or misleading impressions (s.90); and
(iii) make false or misleading statements or create a false or misleading impression in relation to the setting of relevant benchmarks (s.91).

Sections 89 and 90 largely replicate the effect of s.397 of the FSMA. The only "relevant" benchmark under s.91 will be LIBOR and the provision is a reaction to recent global investigations into LIBOR's alleged manipulation by a number of banks.

Section 90 of the FS Act 2012 makes it an offence to do any act or engage in a course of conduct which creates a false or misleading impression as to the market value of any investments if this is done for the purpose of creating that impression and of thereby: (i) inducing a person to deal, or refrain from dealing, in those investments; and/or (ii) obtaining a profit or avoiding a loss. It is a defence under s.90(9)(a) to show that a person reasonably believed their act or conduct would not create a false or misleading impression.

If associates of a target purchase shares as a defensive tactic against a dawn raid, the clear aim is to create a misleading impression as to the value of the target's shares. However, it seems (at least, it is the Department for Business, Energy and Industrial Strategy's view) that if all relevant facts are disclosed, no such impression will be created. Hence, if the associate puts his or her motives on the screen at the time of their bid for the stock, it seems that no offence would be committed. Of course, this suggested course is unlikely to arouse much enthusiasm among the broking community and, if he or she immediately discloses their dealing under Rule 8 of the Code (see 3.4.3.1 below), probably there would be little risk of prosecution. The position would be similar in respect of agreements with the target to sell its shares.

Liability may also be incurred by the offeror and its associates. Purchases of the offeror's shares by associates in takeovers where the consideration includes shares in the offeror could amount to a breach of s.90(1). Much will depend upon the purpose of such acquisition: if it is genuinely for a long-term investment, it is hard to see how the section is contravened, but if the main purpose is merely to inflate the value of the offeror's share price, there may be a breach. A share support operation, of the type carried out on the Guinness bid for

Distillers, would therefore be a criminal offence under s.90(1) (at the time of these events the relevant statutory provision was s.13(1)(a)(i) of the Prevention of Fraud (Investments) Act 1958).

Further criminal liability may be incurred if purchases of offeror shares are carried out by an associate with the benefit of an indemnity from the offeror as this may also involve unlawful financial assistance by the offeror for the purpose of the acquisition of its own shares, which is an offence under ss.678 and 680 of the 2006 Act. In this area it should be noted that, if a false market in any listed securities arises, then the relevant listed company must consider whether it is required by the DTRs to release information to the public. Where a company is under such an obligation, a failure to comply with it can, arguably, amount to a course of conduct for s.90 purposes.

3.3.4.2 The market abuse regime

The Market Abuse Regulation (Regulation 596/2014) (MAR) and its associated technical standards (as contained in various Delegated and Implementing Regulations and Directives made under MAR) repealed and replaced the Market Abuse Directive (2003/6/EC) (MAD) and its implementing legislation with effect from 3 July 2016, establishing an updated EU market abuse regime. Although MAR has direct application in the UK, implementation required a number of amendments to primary and secondary legislation, including to Part VIII of the FSMA. These amendments were made by means of a statutory instrument, the Financial Services and Markets Act 2000 (Market Abuse) Regulations 2016 (MAR Regulations). Much of the FCA's Code of Market Conduct has been replaced with signposts to the relevant provisions of MAR and associated technical standards. The new regime introduced a series of offences which are very similar to the old civil law offences under the FSMA. The new regime is described below.

Despite the UK's vote to leave the EU, on 24 June 2016 the FCA confirmed that EU financial regulation "will remain applicable until any changes are made, which will be a matter for

Government and Parliament" (see *https://www.fca.org.uk/news/ european-union-referendum-result-statement* [Accessed 19 June 2019]). It is expected that MAR will continue to apply in the UK under the Great Repeal Bill, subject to any further action taken by the Government or Parliament in relation to the UK's membership of the EU. In the event that the UK leaves the EU without a deal, the Market Abuse (Amendment) (EU Exit) Regulations 2018 will take effect on exit day. This instrument shall not alter the policy approach to the market abuse regime, other than to reflect the UK's position outside the EU by, among other things, transferring regulatory functions to the appropriate UK bodies.

3.3.4.2.1 Categories of abusive behaviour

The categories of market abuse are set out in arts 14 and 15 of the MAR. Instead of the six categories of abusive behaviour which existed under the old FSMA regime (insider dealing; improper disclosure of inside information; manipulating trans-actions; manipulating devices; dissemination of inside infor-mation; and misleading behaviour and market distortion), there are now four categories. These categories are:

1. engaging or attempting to engage in insider dealing;
2. recommending that another person engage in insider dealing or inducing another person to engage in insider dealing;
3. unlawfully disclosing inside information; and
4. engaging in or attempting to engage in "market manipula-tion".

Generally speaking, the scope of MAR is broader than that of MAD in that it covers new markets, additional financial instruments and trading strategies.

Article 2 of the MAR states that the behaviours listed in MAR must occur in relation to "financial instruments", as defined by para.(15) of art.4(1) and s.C of Annex 1 of the MiFID II Directive (2014/65). This definition includes, among others, transferable securities (such as shares), units in collective investment undertakings, money-market instruments and various options, futures and swaps.

3.3.4.2.2   Regulated markets, MTFs and OTFs

The old regime only applied to FSMA s.118 behaviours which occurred in relation to qualifying investments admitted to trading (or in respect of which a request for admission to trading has been made) on a "prescribed market". This included all regulated markets in the EEA.

Article 2 of the MAR now extends the scope of the market abuse regime to cover financial instruments admitted to trading (or in respect of which a request for admission to trading has been made) on multilateral trading facilities (MTFs) and financial instruments admitted to trading on organised trading facilities (OTFs). Article 2 also includes certain over-the-counter trading (such as derivatives and credit default swaps) within its scope.

Provisions in MAR referring to concepts that were introduced by MiFID II, including OTFs, apply from the MiFID II application date, 3 January 2018.

3.3.4.2.3   Insiders

An "insider" is defined in art.8(4) of the MAR (previously s.118B of the FSMA) as any person who has inside information:

1. as a result of his or her membership of an administrative, management or supervisory body of an issuer of financial instruments;
2. as a result of his or her holding in the capital of an issuer of qualifying investments;
3. as a result of his or her having access to the information through the exercise of their employment, profession or duties; or
4. as a result of his or her criminal activities.

Under art.8(4) of the MAR, an "insider" also includes any person who has inside information which he or she has obtained by other means and which they know, or "ought" to know, is inside information (s.118 of the FSMA contained a similar provision, whereby a person who had inside information which he or she could "reasonably be expected" to know was inside information was an "insider").

3.3.4.2.4 Inside information

MAD defined "inside information" as precise and non-public information that, if made public, would be likely to have a significant effect on the prices of financial instruments. The essential elements of this definition have been retained under MAR, though the concept has been amended and broadened in certain respects. "Inside information" is now defined in art.7 of the MAR as information:

1. of a precise nature;
2. which has not been made public; and
3. would, if it were made public, be likely to have a significant effect on the prices of the relevant financial instruments.

3.3.4.2.5 Consequences of market abuse

Part VIII of the FSMA, including in relation to penalties for market abuse, was extensively amended by the MAR Regulations. New sections were inserted relating to the FCA's power to prohibit individuals from managing or dealing (s.123A), suspend permission to carry on regulated activities (s.123B) and exercise administrative sanctions (s.123C). The FCA is also able to impose an unlimited fine (s.123(2) refers to "a penalty of such amount as it considers appropriate") and has the option of electing not to impose a fine but to issue a public censure (s.123(3)).

The largest fine levied for market abuse by the FSA or FCA under FSMA was imposed in 2004 on Shell Transport and Trading Company, Royal Dutch Petroleum Company and the

Royal Dutch/Shell Group of Companies (Shell), who were fined £17 million for market abuse and breach of the Listing Rules without admitting or denying culpability. The market abuse occurred in relation to the misstatement of its proved reserves, which led to Shell being investigated for the old "misleading conduct" limb of market abuse.

Individuals have also received large fines: on 9 November 2011, Mr Rameshkumar Goenka, a Dubai-based private investor, was fined US $9,621,240 for manipulating the closing share price of Reliance Industries Ltd in order to avoid a loss under an over-the-counter structured product. This is the largest fine by the FSA or FCA against an individual for market abuse to date (see FSA press notice 94/2011).

As referred to above (see 3.3.3.2), much of the behaviour prohibited by the market abuse regime bears some resemblance to the offence of insider dealing provided for in CJA 1993 and many of the cases brought by the FSA since the market abuse regime first came into force on 1 December 2001 were for the misuse of information. For example, on 25 January 2012, Mr David Einhorn, owner of the US hedge fund Greenlight Capital (Greenlight), was fined £3,368,000 for allegedly using inside information about an upcoming rights issue to order the sale of part of Greenlight's stake in Punch Taverns Plc (Punch), thereby avoiding a significant loss when Punch's share price subsequently dropped by around 30%. In July 2016, the FCA imposed a public censure, ordered restitution costs and issued a fine of £59,557 to Mr Gavin Breeze in respect of shares in MoPowered Group Plc which he sold, on the basis of inside information, to avoid making a loss.

3.3.4.2.6 Exemptions and defences

Under the old regime, FSMA established numerous exemptions and defences to market abuse. For example, under s.118A(5) of the FSMA, behaviour did not amount to market abuse if:

1. it conformed with a Rule which included a provision to the effect that behaviour conforming with the Rule did not amount to market abuse;
2. it conformed with Regulation 2273/2003 of 22 December 2003 regarding exemptions for buy-back programmes and stabilisation of financial instruments; or
3. it was done by a person acting on behalf of a public authority in pursuit of monetary policies with respect to exchange rates or the management of public debt or foreign exchange reserves.

Furthermore, the FCA was not able to impose a penalty where there are reasonable grounds for it to be satisfied that the relevant person believed, on reasonable grounds, that his behaviour did not amount to market abuse and took all reasonable precautions and exercised all due diligence to avoid engaging in market abuse (FSMA s.123(2)). This was a defence only against a penalty and not against a finding of market abuse.

Finally, the FCA was required by s.119(1) of the FSMA to produce a Code of Market Conduct (the Code of Market Conduct was set out in MAR 1 of the FCA Handbook) which, inter alia, outlined behaviour that would not amount to market abuse. Most notably in the context of takeovers, the Code of Market Conduct included provisions which are similar in effect to the market information defence provided for in CJA 1993 (see 3.3.3.4 above).

Under the new regime, ss.118A(5) and 119(1) of the FSMA have been repealed, and the defence in s.123(2) of the FSMA has been removed. Much of the old content still remains: for example, similar MAR provisions exist in relation to s.118A(5)'s exemptions for buy-backs (MAR art.5, and accompanying technical standards on buybacks) and transactions by a Member State in the pursuit of monetary policy (MAR art.6). MAR also identifies other categories of behaviour which will not give rise to a presumption of insider dealing (known as "legitimate behaviour" and outlined in MAR art.9) which mirror the old MAD provisions. Similarly, art.13 of the MAR allows national regulators to establish "accepted market practices" (provided certain criteria and conditions in MAR and accompanying technical standards in Delegated Regulation 2016/908 are met), which also reflects the position under MAD (although the UK had not previously established any accepted market practices under the MAD regime). Similarly, the FCA is no longer obliged to produce a Code of Market Conduct under s.119(1) of the FSMA, and the Code of Market Conduct was removed on 3 July 2016 by MAR Instrument 2016 (FCA 2016/31). MAR 1 has however been amended to contain where possible, and as far as legally permitted, guidance where this is possible as well as signposting to relevant MAR provisions where this is not possible.

Furthermore, in the context of takeovers, a significant new "market soundings" safe harbour has been introduced to the offence of unlawfully disclosing inside information (MAR art.11). A "market sounding" is defined as the communication of information to potential investors before the announcement of a transaction, to gauge their possible interest in that transaction and the conditions relating to it (e.g. size and price). A safe harbour will apply to market soundings provided that certain pre-disclosure, disclosure and record-keeping obligations (outlined in MAR with accompanying technical standards in Delegated Regulation 2016/960) are complied with.

3.3.4.3 *The effect of the FSMA and the Market Abuse Regime on the Panel*

As a result of the market abuse regime, there is a significant potential overlap between the jurisdiction of the Panel and that of the FCA in relation to takeovers. Under the old FSA regime, there was some initial concern that this overlap might result in hostile participants dragging the FSA into contested bids as a tactic. In order to allay these fears, the Government introduced a provision into the FSMA to enable the FSA, and then FCA, to establish a safe harbour for behaviour which complied with the Code (s.120). The FCA did this at MAR 1.10.3G–1.10.6C of its

Code of Market Conduct (these provisions stated that compliance with certain, specified, Rules of the Code would not constitute a breach of the market abuse regime). Nevertheless, s.120 of the FSMA has now been repealed and the guidance contained in MAR and its accompanying technical standards will now prevail over the FCA's Code of Market Conduct. MAR 1 states that compliance with these Takeover Code provisions is "unlikely to", of itself, amount to market abuse (the Code of Market Conduct previously stated that compliance "does not", of itself, amount to market abuse).

In addition (and as mentioned in 3.2.4 above), the Panel and the FCA have agreed a set of Operating Guidelines which are intended, inter alia, to assist in determining how each of them should exercise its functions in cases of jurisdictional overlap. The Operating Guidelines provide that where, during a takeover bid, matters arise which may amount to market misconduct, the FCA will not exercise its powers during the bid save in exceptional circumstances. The exceptional circumstances referred to in para.12.2 of the Operating Guidelines are:

1. where the Panel asks the FCA to use its power to impose penalties or its powers to seek injunctive or restitutionary relief from the courts;
2. where the suspected misconduct contravenes arts 14 or 15 of the MAR or Pt V of the CJA 1993 (insider dealing);
3. where the suspected misconduct extends to securities or a class of securities which may be outside the Panel's jurisdiction; or
4. where the suspected misconduct threatens or has threatened the stability of the financial system.

In any event, the FCA will consult with the Panel before taking any action which may affect the timetable or outcome of a takeover bid (para.12.3). The Operating Guidelines also contain similar principles relevant to situations where there is jurisdictional overlap between the Panel and the FCA but no takeover bid is actually in progress (see para.1 of the Operating Guidelines dated 8 July 2016).

3.4 Disclosure of share dealings

This section will address the subject of disclosure of share dealings. Although disclosure should be no more than a mechanical exercise, it may be important in the early, planning stages of a transaction and is easy to overlook once a bid is underway, when information may be difficult to collect in the time required. Further, the disclosure requirements of the Code have been considerably extended over time, most recently in April 2010.

3.4.1 DTRs

The obligations under DTR 5 relate to: (i) shares of UK and non-UK issuers whose home state is the UK and which are admitted to trading on a regulated market in the UK; and (ii) shares of UK issuers which are admitted to trading on a prescribed market (such as AIM). DTR 5.1.2 provides that a person (which includes a natural person, a legal person or an unincorporated body such as a partnership) must notify an issuer of shares, in accordance with prescribed procedures and including prescribed information, of certain voting rights which it holds as shareholder (including direct and indirect holdings of shares and depository receipts, and including discretionary proxies), or which it holds through a direct or indirect holding of certain financial instruments with a right under a legally binding agreement to call for existing issued shares carrying voting rights. The relevant financial instruments include transferable securities, options, futures, swaps, forward rate agreements and some other derivatives. Changes were made on 26 November 2015 to implement Directive 2013/50/EU amending the Transparency Directive (known as the Amending Directive). Following these changes, holdings of financial instruments relating to unissued shares are no longer notifiable. These instruments, which include convertible bonds and nil paid rights, were previously notifiable as financial instruments with "similar economic effects", but will now only be notifiable if relating to existing issued shares.

The FSA previously estimated that approximately 30% of equity trades were in some way driven by CFD transactions referenced to underlying shares and, as these positions did not previously have to be disclosed under DTR 5, it used to be impossible to determine who had significant economic exposure to an issuer's shares. In June 2009 the FSA therefore amended DTR 5 to introduce a general disclosure regime of long positions in CFDs and other derivative instruments that may have a similar effect with the aim of achieving greater disclosure (see PS09/3).

Notifications required by DTR 5 must be made as soon as possible and in any case not later than two trading days (or four trading days for non-UK issuers) after the date on which the notifying person learns—or should have learnt—of the event that has given rise to the requirement to make the disclosure. Even if the disclosing person does not learn of the event, he or she will in general be deemed to have knowledge of the event two trading days after the event has taken place (DTR 5.8.3R). When disclosure is made to an issuer whose shares are traded on a regulated market, a copy of the notification must also be filed electronically with the FCA (DTR 5.9.1R(1) and DTR 5.10.1R). The issuer must as soon as possible make the disclosure public.

Under DTR 5.1.2R, notification must be made if the percentage of voting rights held reaches, exceeds or falls below 3% or any subsequent 1%. These thresholds for notification are the same as was the case under the Companies Act 1985. Higher thresholds apply to non-UK issuers (thresholds at each 5% interval, up to 30%, and then at 50% and 75%). The DTR 5 notification requirements also apply where a holding changes as a result of changes to the structure of the share capital of an issuer, and where information announced by the issuer in respect of the total number of voting rights and capital in respect of each share class would cause a holding to be re-calculated.

DTR 5.1.3 provides that a notification need never be made in respect of:

1. shares acquired or shares underlying financial instruments within DTR 5.3.1R(1) to the extent that such financial instruments are acquired for clearing and settlement purposes within a four-day settlement cycle;
2. shares held or shares underlying financial instruments within DTR 5.3.1R(1) to the extent that such financial instruments are held by a custodian or nominee (in its capacity as such), provided that the custodian or nominee receives its instructions in written or electronic form;
3. shares held or shares underlying financial instruments within DTR 5.3.1R(1) to the extent that such financial instruments are held by a market maker in its capacity as such, up to a 10% holding and subject to certain conditions;
4. shares held or shares underlying financial instruments within DTR 5.3.1R(1) to the extent that such financial instruments are held by a credit institution or investment firm, provided they are held on the trading book, they do not exceed a 5% holding, and the voting rights are not used "to intervene in the management of the issuer"; and
5. shares held under a collateral transaction, provided voting rights are not exercised.

DTR 5.3.1R details the financial instruments holdings of which may trigger the notification obligation under DTR 5.1.2R.

DTR 5.1.5R provides that a notification need only be made at 5%, 10% and higher thresholds in respect of:

1. an FCA-authorised manager's interest in voting rights attaching to shares managed for the shareholder under a written agreement;
2. voting rights exercisable by the operator of an authorised unit trust scheme, an authorised contractual scheme, a recognised scheme or a UCITS (Undertakings for Collective Investment in Transferable Securities) scheme; or
3. voting rights exercisable by an ICVC (Investment Company with Variable Capital).

Under DTR 5.2.1R(e) and 5.2.2G(1), a parent company must generally aggregate its holdings with those of its "controlled undertakings" (this term, as defined in the FCA Handbook Glossary, includes most entities that would fall within the definition of subsidiary undertaking for the purposes of the 2006 Act). In certain circumstances, holdings of an asset manager and its parent may be required to be aggregated (see DTR 5.4). To avoid the requirement for such aggregation, a parent undertaking must ensure that it does not, and must be able to demonstrate to the FCA that it does not, interfere with the exercise of voting rights by the asset manager.

3.4.2   The 2006 Act

3.4.2.1   An "interest" for the purposes of the 2006 Act

For the purposes of disclosure of interests, when required, under the 2006 Act (see 3.4.2.2 and 3.4.2.3), an "interest" includes any interest in shares, including where a person has entered into a contract to acquire shares, or, not being the registered holder, is entitled to exercise any right conferred by holding the shares (or control the exercise of that right by another) (s.820(4)).

An option constitutes a disclosable interest. For the purposes of s.793 only (see further below), a right to subscribe for shares is also disclosable (s.821). A person is also deemed to be "interested" in shares (under s.823(1)) if a body corporate is interested in them and the directors of that body corporate are accustomed to act on the first person's instructions, or the first person is entitled to exercise or control the exercise of one-third of the voting rights of the body corporate in a general meeting. Similarly, shares of spouses, civil partners, infant children and step-children are aggregated for the purposes of these provisions under s.822.

3.4.2.2 Concert parties

Section 824 of the 2006 Act requires the disclosure of interests arising under concert party arrangements, where such disclosure is required pursuant to a s.793 notice (see 3.4.2.3 below). "Concert party arrangements" are not defined, but the arrangements covered include a non-legally binding arrangement where the parties have mutuality of undertakings, expectations or understandings, but exclude underwriting and sub-underwriting agreements (s.824(6)(b)). The concept of an "arrangement" would probably catch circumstances where parties merely communicate in some way without necessarily any express oral or written statement, and thereby create expectations in each other of how each will behave in the future. Hence, potentially, the ambit of these provisions, like those under the Companies Act 1985 that these provisions replace, is very wide. However, the concert party agreements and arrangements concerned are only those which include provision for the acquisition by one or more of the parties of interests in the shares of a target company and which impose obligations with respect to "their use, retention or disposal" (s.824(2)(a)).

The consequence of such an agreement or arrangement is that, under s.825, each of the parties to it is deemed to be interested in all the shares in which each of the other parties is interested. It is, therefore, not possible secretly to build a significant stake in a target company by means of splitting holdings between numerous concert parties. In discharging notification obligations under these provisions, concert parties are required to specify in which shares they have interests by virtue of them being deemed to have interests in shares in which other parties are interested (s.825(4)); in addition, they must state the names and (so far as known to them) addresses of the other concert parties.

3.4.2.3 Section 793 notices

Section 793 notices were previously known as s.212 notices, in reference to the relevant provision of the Companies Act 1985.

Pursuant to s.793 a public company may require any person whom the company "knows or has reasonable cause to believe" to be, or to have been at any time during the three immediately preceding years, interested in any of its shares (whether or not the number of shares exceeds the 3% level):

1. to confirm or deny that fact;
2. to give particulars of any interests he has or has had during the previous three years;
3. if any other person is or has been interested in the same shares, to give "so far as lies within his knowledge" particulars with respect to that other interest; and
4. if he is no longer interested in shares in the target, to give "so far as lies within his knowledge" particulars of the identity of the person who acquired their interest.

It is worth noting that, at least on one view, a potential offeror will have an interest in the relevant share capital of the target company if it obtains an irrevocable commitment from a shareholder to accept the offer when made. Accordingly, a target company would, on this basis, be entitled to serve a s.793 notice on a potential offeror to ascertain details of any irrevocable commitments received. There is, therefore, a clear advantage for the offeror in irrevocable commitments not normally being entered into until the evening prior to the announcement of an offer or possible offer.

A reply to any notice given by a company under s.793 must be given within any "reasonable time as may be specified in the notice" (s.793(7)). In cases of urgency (for example during the closing stages of a contested bid) a "reasonable time" would not generally be more than two days (see *Lonrho Plc v Edelman* (1989) 5 B.C.C. 68; [1989] B.C.L.C. 309 Ch D (Companies Ct), which was decided under the equivalent provisions in the Companies Act 1985) and may be 24 hours, or even less. Here, too, a person is deemed to be interested in shares if he or she is a party to a concert party arrangement (s.793(5)).

For the purposes of s.793, references to "shares" are to the relevant company's issued shares with voting rights, including treasury shares. Temporary suspension of voting rights does not cause shares to be excluded from this definition.

For the purposes of s.793, a person is deemed to be interested in shares even if he is interested only as a nominee. Thus a nominee can be required to give details, so far as known to him or her, of the true owner of the shares; clearly this is the most sensible approach since the section aims at ensuring the fullest information possible is available to a company. Where, however, the true owner is not required by the DTRs himself to give notice of their interest (by virtue of that interest not being a notifiable interest, for example if they are a nominee), it may be possible to extend the period during which a target company is unable to ascertain the true owner of some of its shares by the device of giving instructions for the acquisition of shares through a chain of nominees each of whom is unaware of the identity of any others in the chain apart from those immediately next to them. The target company would then be obliged to send out a series of notices before identifying the person at the end of the chain.

It is worth noting that Swiss banks, for example, have regarded themselves as bound by secrecy laws which prevent them from answering s.793 notices. There are, however, doubts, both (it appears) under Swiss law and (certainly) in relation to the obligations under English law as to whether reliance on such grounds for refusing to answer a s.793 notice may be regarded as excusing the recipient from the consequences of such refusal (see *Re Geers Gross Plc* [1987] 1 W.L.R. 1649; (1987) 3 B.C.C. 528 CA (Civ Div)).

3.4.2.4 *Consequences of contravention of the 2006 Act*

The failure of a person to respond to a notice under s.793, or responding in a manner which a person knows to be false or reckless, is an offence which may be punished by imprisonment or a fine (s.795(3)). In addition, the shares in question may be disenfranchised; disenfranchisement may be effected by the target under powers in its articles of association or by the court at the instigation of the target company under s.794

(in the case of failure to answer a s.793 notice). The basic approach of the courts in this area has been that the company has an unqualified right to know who owns its shares (see *Re Geers Gross Plc*). However, problems may arise in an interlocutory application in deciding whether there has genuinely been an untruthful answer to the notice. It should be noted that a person does not commit an offence by failing to respond to a s.793 notice if he or she can prove that the request in the notice was frivolous or vexatious (s.795(2)).

Companies are required to maintain registers of notices given and replies received under s.793 (s.808). Obviously, these registers may contain information useful to any person contemplating a bid for the company concerned and the registers are required to be made available for inspection. But although s.793 gives a company extensive powers in relation to its shareholders, it is perhaps worth mentioning that many companies continue to be ignorant of the identity of their shareholders because they do not exercise their rights. In many instances, therefore, there is no register from which information may be gleaned. Even where companies do have such registers, attempts have been made to avoid publicising the information which a s.793 notice may reveal by sending out notices which appear to be given under that section, but which (arguably) are not; replies are then not registered. The effectiveness of such ploys must be open to doubt.

3.4.3 The Code

The provisions of the Code relating to disclosure of holdings and dealings normally only apply during an offer period (i.e. after the time when an announcement has been made of a proposed or possible offer).

3.4.3.1 Disclosure of opening positions

Prior to 19 April 2010, the disclosure regime under Rule 8 of the Code only related to dealings in relevant securities during the offer period. However, in May 2009 the Code Committee issued PCP 2009/1: Extending the Code's Disclosure Regime, which put forward proposals regarding, inter alia, a requirement for various persons to publicly disclose their holdings of relevant securities following the commencement of an offer period, regardless of whether or not a dealing had taken place. The purpose of this change was to increase transparency as to where voting control of securities lay: the Code Committee was of the view that the Code's disclosure regime did not fully achieve this objective as persons were not required to disclose their holdings of relevant securities unless and until they dealt in them.

With effect from 19 April 2010, Rule 8 therefore requires those subject to the Code's disclosure regime (as described below) to disclose their positions in relevant securities of the target and (in the case of a securities exchange offer) the offeror, regardless of whether they have dealt in relevant securities of the company concerned, by way of an "opening position disclosure".

Certain definitional changes have also been introduced:

1. A definition of "cash offeror" has been included in the Code which includes an offeror (or potential offeror) which has announced, or in respect of which the target has announced, that its offer is, or is likely to be, solely in cash.
2. "Parties to the offer" is now a defined term and covers the target, the offeror and any competing offeror whose identity has been publicly announced (including a potential target or offeror).
3. The Code Committee concluded that reference to "associates" of the offeror and target in Rule 8 (and elsewhere in the Code) should be replaced with references to persons acting in concert and the definition in the Code of associates has therefore been deleted.
4. For the purposes of Rule 8 only, the term "relevant securities" does not include securities of a cash offeror (Rule 8, Note 1).

An opening position disclosure (as described below) is required to be made by the following persons:

1. the offeror (after its identity is first publicly announced) (Rule 8.1(a));
2. the target (Rule 8.2(a));
3. any person who is interested in 1% or more of any class of relevant securities of any party to the offer (other than a cash offeror) at the time of the announcement that commences the offer period or the time of announcement that identifies an offeror (as the case may be) (Rule 8.3(a) and Note 7); and
4. exempt principal traders connected with an offeror or the target who do not have recognised intermediary status (who were previously subject to Rule 38.5(b)) or who do have such status but who hold any interest or short position in or right to subscribe for any relevant securities of any party to the offer (other than a cash offeror) in a proprietary capacity (Rules 8.5(a) and (b)).

As noted above, if a potential offeror has not yet been identified as such, it will not need to make an opening position disclosure under Rule 8.1(a) (which applies only to the offeror) until after the announcement that first identifies it publicly as an offeror (Note 12). However, a potential offeror will still need to make an opening position disclosure in accordance with Rule 8.3 (which applies to persons with interests in securities representing 1% or more) if applicable, but it is not required to disclose the fact that it is a potential offeror.

The regime does not require that persons acting in concert with a party to the offer make an opening position disclosure since the details of their holdings, if any, are required to be included in the opening position disclosure made by the party to the offer with whom he is acting in concert (Notes 2(c) and 5(a)(iv)).

If members of a consortium that has not been publicly identified as such may be required to issue an opening position disclosure under Rule 8.3(c), they will not normally be required to make a joint opening position disclosure which could identify them as such, although any member of the consortium who is interested in 1% or more of a class of relevant securities of the target would be required to make an individual opening position disclosure under Rule 8.3(a) (Note 12(b)). In any such situation, the Panel must be consulted.

The opening position disclosure must be made no later than 12.00 (or, in the case of persons disclosing under (3) above, 15.30) on the tenth business day after the commencement of the offer period or the announcement that first identifies a paper offeror as such (Note 2). The Code Committee gave careful consideration to the appropriate deadline for opening position disclosures and this period has been adopted to enable the offeror and the target to collect and collate accurate details of the positions not only held by themselves but also their concert parties. This is likely to be less time consuming for other market participants (who will generally be required to ascertain details of their own positions only); however, the Code Committee rejected the idea of setting different deadline dates for different classes of person.

If a person is required to make an opening position disclosure and it deals in relevant securities of any party to the offer (other than a cash offeror) before midnight on the day before the deadline for releasing the opening position disclosure, that person (other than in the case of a party to the offer) is not required to release an opening position disclosure as it is required instead to make a dealing disclosure (as to which see 3.4.3.2 below) (Notes 2(b)(i) and 2(d)(i)). In the case of a party to the offer, such dealing disclosure would only be in respect of its own positions and holdings and, as such, a separate opening position disclosure is still required, which would include the information in respect of any persons acting in concert with it (Note 2(a)(i)).

Notes 4 and 5 on Rule 8 set out the information that must be contained in an opening position disclosure and specimen disclosure forms are available online or may be obtained from the Panel. One point to note in this regard is that the opening position disclosure must be made on the basis of "composite disclosure", which means that the person who is required to make an opening position disclosure due to the size of his holding of relevant securities in one party to the offer, is required also to disclose all holdings of relevant securities in all parties to the offer (other than a cash offeror).

3.4.3.2 *Disclosure of dealings*

Rule 8 continues, as it did prior to 19 April 2010, to require various persons to publicly disclose their dealings in relevant securities of any party to the offer, other than a cash offeror. The persons who are required to make dealing disclosures are the same as those required to make an opening position disclosure (see 3.4.3.1 above) plus any person acting in concert with a party to the offer (Rules 8.1(b), 8.2(b), 8.3(b), 8.4 and 8.5(c)). The obligation in respect of the parties to the offer and their concert parties only applies to dealings on their own account or for discretionary clients.

The dealings disclosure must be made by 12.00 (or, in the case of a person disclosing due to having an interest in relevant securities of 1% or more, 15.30) on the business day following the dealing (Note 2).

The Rule 8.1(b) obligation to disclose dealings extends to cover a potential offeror (and persons acting in concert with it) which has been referred to in an announcement but not publicly named, or which is a participant in a formal sale process announced by the target (regardless of whether it was a participant at the time of the announcement). A potential offeror (and its concert parties) is therefore required to make a dealing disclosure in respect of any dealings in relevant securities of the target after the time of that announcement (or, if later, after the time at which it becomes a participant in the formal sale process) and is also required to make an announcement that it is considering making an offer via a RIS (under Rule 30.1). Of course, the circumstances in which this obligation will be relevant from a practical perspective are now more limited following the introduction of amended Rules in relation to the identification of potential offerors (see further Chapter 2).

A party to the offer and its concert parties must also announce the procuring of irrevocable commitments or letters of intent in accordance with Rule 2.10, which replaced Rule 8.4 with effect from 19 April 2010 (see 3.4.3.3 below).

The Panel has stated that it attaches great importance to compliance with Rule 8.3 on the basis that "disclosure underpins market transparency which, in turn, constitutes a fundamental protection for shareholders and others who deal in the United Kingdom securities markets" (p.3 of Panel Statement 2003/16). Where people act pursuant to any sort of understanding to acquire or control an interest in relevant securities, they will normally be deemed to be a single person for the purposes of this Rule (Rule 8.3(c)); and where relevant securities are managed on a discretionary basis by an investment management group then (unless the Panel agrees) all funds under management will be treated as the investments of a single person (Rule 8.3(d)).

The Code Committee proposed in PCP 2010/2 that the threshold for disclosure in Rule 8.3 should be reduced from 1% to 0.5%. However following a consultation, on 21 October 2010 the Code Committee concluded that in light of the relatively recent overhaul of Rule 8, the appropriateness of the disclosure threshold should be monitored and the change was rejected (see Panel Statement 2010/22).

Rule 8.3 applies equally to exempt fund managers (whether or not connected with the offeror or target) as to any other 1% holder. It does not, however, apply to a recognised intermediary acting in a client-serving capacity unless the recognised intermediary is an exempt principal trader connected with the offeror or target (Rule 8.3(e) and Note 9) (see 3.5.1 below), or is a concert party of the offeror or target (in which case disclosure under Rule 8.4 is required). See 3.5.2 below for further information about recognised intermediary status.

Rule 8.3 was considered by the Panel in connection with BC Capital Partners' proposed offer for Mitchells & Butlers Plc (M&B) (Panel Statement 2003/9). M&B was to become one of two successor companies to Six Continents following the latter's demerger. This prompted the question of how to determine a 1% holder in relation to M&B, prior to the time of the demerger becoming effective and dealings in shares in M&B commencing. The Panel Executive ruled that a relevant person's percentage holding in the When Issued shares of M&B should be aggregated with that person's percentage holding in Six Continents' shares since a holding in Six Continents' shares would, at the time the demerger became effective, translate into an equivalent holding in M&B shares. Therefore, a person that held 0.5% of Six Continents' shares and acquired 0.8% of the When Issued shares of M&B was treated as being a 1% holder in relation to M&B (although not Six Continents, see below), notwithstanding that he or she did not hold 1% in either stock individually.

Six Continents itself was already in an offer period following an announcement made by Sun Capital Partners Ltd. However, as a holding of When Issued shares in M&B would not translate into an effective holding in Six Continents, there was no need to aggregate shareholdings in M&B and Six Continents when calculating percentage interests in Six Continents.

Rule 8 was substantially modified in the wake of the Guinness affair. In particular, Note 10 now states that intermediaries are expected to co-operate with the Panel in its enquiries, including by identifying clients. The requirement for co-operation with the Panel is now reinforced by provisions set out in the MAR volume of the FCA Handbook. These state, in broad terms, that a firm which acts for any person in connection with a transaction to which the Code applies must cease to act for that person if it has reasonable grounds for believing that the person in question, or his principal, is not complying or is not likely to comply with the Code; and provide such information and assistance as the Panel may reasonably require to perform its functions (MAR art.4.3).

In order to assist the Panel's monitoring of compliance with Rule 8.3, Rule 22 has been amended with effect from 19 April 2010 to oblige the offeror and the target to assist the Panel in identifying persons who are interested in 1% or more of any class of relevant securities of that party and, in particular, to provide the Panel promptly after commencement of the offer period with details of all persons who are reasonably considered to be so interested. As an additional obligation, at the same time as the information is provided to the Panel, the offeror and the target are required to send all such persons an explanation of their disclosure obligations under Rule 8. However, if the target has sent those persons a copy of an announcement or circular in accordance with Rule 2.11 (and these would summarise the requirements of Rule 8), then there is no requirement to separately notify them of their Rule 8 obligations.

The Code Committee originally proposed in PCP 2009/2 that Rule 22 be amended to require that offerors and targets take all reasonable steps to identify persons who are interested in 1% or more of any class of relevant security, including requiring the issue of s.793 notices (as to which see 3.4.2.3 above). However, following consultation, the Code Committee accepted that this would be unduly onerous and that boards should only be required to provide information that is readily available. In para.2.47 of RS 2009/1 the Code Committee has therefore clarified that in complying with the requirements of amended Rule 22, it would expect boards to normally provide the Panel with details from the following sources:

1. the company's shareholder register;
2. notifications received pursuant to the DTRs and responses to s.793 notices (to the extent that the company has issued such notices); and
3. analysis previously received, or readily available, from the company's brokers or other advisers.

Dealing disclosures under Rule 8 must contain the information set out in Note 5 and as detailed in the Panel's specimen disclosure forms (which are available online or may be obtained from the Panel).

As is the case for opening position disclosures, dealing disclosures must be made on a composite disclosure basis. This is reflected in Note 5 and requires that:

1.   any person who has a gross long interest of 1% or more in a class of relevant securities of any party to the offer (other than a cash offeror) is required to disclose any dealings in relevant securities not only of that party but of any other party to the offer (other than a cash offeror); and
2.   any person who is required to make a dealing disclosure is required to disclose details of his interests and short positions in the relevant securities of both the party to the offer in whose relevant securities the dealing occurred and any other party to the offer (other than a cash offeror).

If a person is disclosing details in respect of more than one party to the offer at the same time, a separate disclosure form must be used for each such party.

The Panel Executive considers it best practice for incorrect details to be corrected in a separate disclosure rather than in a disclosure containing details of previously undisclosed dealings. Note 13 on Rule 8 requires that any incorrect details included in a dealing disclosure should be corrected as soon as practicable in a subsequent disclosure and that such disclosure should:

1.   state clearly that it corrects details previously disclosed;
2.   identify the disclosure or disclosures being corrected; and
3.   provide sufficient detail for the reader to understand the nature of the correction.

In the case of any doubt, the Note suggests the Panel be consulted. Private dealing disclosures are required to be made to the Panel:

1.   by a party to the offer and any person acting in concert with that party if it deals for the account of non-discretionary investment clients in any relevant securities

of any party to the offer (other than a cash offeror) during an offer period (Rule 8.7); and

2. in certain circumstances by exempt fund managers (Rule 8.6) (see 3.5.3.2).

3.4.3.3 *Disclosure of irrevocable commitments and letters of intent*

Rule 2.10 requires a party to the offer or any concert party thereof who procures an irrevocable commitment or letter of intent during the course of an offer period to announce the details publicly by no later than 12.00 noon the following business day (Rule 2.10(a)). By virtue of amendments following RS 2014/1, which came into effect on 1 January 2015, a party to the offer or any concert party thereof who has procured an irrevocable commitment or letter of intent prior to the commencement of the offer period must publicly disclose the details by no later than 12.00 noon on the business day following either the commencement of the offer period or (in the case of an offeror) the date of the announcement that first identifies it. However, no separate announcement is required where these details are set out in either a Rule 2.7 announcement or an announcement of a possible offer which is published no later than noon on the business day following such procurement (Note 1).

Rule 2.10(c) states that if a person who has given an irrevocable commitment or letter of intent either becomes aware that he will not be able to comply with the terms of that commitment or letter or no longer intends to do so, that person must promptly announce the updated position or so notify the relevant party to the offer and the Panel. Upon receipt of such notification, the relevant party to the offer must then promptly announce such information.

In a situation where a party to the offer has procured a letter of intent prior to the commencement of the offer period, the relevant party should ensure that the letter of intent continues to represent up-to-date intentions of the shareholder or other person concerned (Note 4 on Rule 2.10). This requirement is similar to the requirement in the Note on Rule 19.3 for a party to an offer to verify the up-to-date intentions of the shareholders or other person before making a "statement of support".

3.4.3.4   *Other disclosure obligations under the Code*

Rule 7.1 requires an immediate public announcement to be made whenever there is an acquisition of an interest in shares which triggers an obligation to increase an offer under Rule 6, to make a mandatory offer under Rule 9 or to make a mandatory cash or securities offer under Rule 11. Such an announcement should, whenever practicable, state the nature of the interest, the number of shares concerned and the price paid.

Following an acquisition of an interest in shares from a single shareholder permitted by Rule 5.2(a), a public announcement is required not later than 12.00 on the following business day (Rule 5.4); normally, however, such an announcement will be preceded by the announcement of a Rule 9 offer.

Disclosures of shareholding interests and of dealings are also required when an announcement is issued on a bid closing date, or on an offer being declared unconditional as to acceptances, or on an offer being revised (Rule 17), and must be included in offer and defence documents (Rules 24.4 and 25.4). Following the June 2010 review of certain aspects of the Takeover Code, the Code Committee explained that some respondents to the consultation had suggested that offeree company shareholders should be compelled to disclose either their acceptance of an offer or their vote in favour of a scheme. The perceived benefit to this arrangement would be greater accountability and transparency as regards institutional investors. The Code Committee rejected these proposals and in Panel Statement 2010/22 explained that it perceived little practical benefit from such disclosures.

A Rule 17 announcement, and offer and defence documents, are required to include the full extent of the relevant securities of the target in which the offeror (or persons acting in concert with it) is interested or in which it has a short position (Rule

17.1(b)). In addition, a Rule 17 announcement requires details of acceptances, including the extent to which acceptances have been received from persons acting in concert with the offeror or in respect of shares which were the subject of an irrevocable commitment or letter of intent; and details of any relevant securities of the target in respect of which the offeror (or any person acting in concert with it) has an outstanding irrevocable commitment or letter of intent (Rule 17.1(a)). In addition, a Rule 17 announcement and offer and defence documents must detail securities borrowed or lent by the offeror (or persons acting in concert with it (Rule 17.1(d))) in order to facilitate a full understanding of the extent to which the voting rights attached to the relevant securities of the parties to the offer are currently controlled by such persons.

Following RS 8, the Panel amended what is now Note 2 on Rule 24.4 (previously Note 4 on Rule 24.3) on 21 February 2002. This amendment had the effect of relaxing the restrictions on disclosing dealings in shares before or during the offer period on an aggregated basis (subject to the requirement that no significant dealings are thereby concealed). The Code Committee was of the opinion that there are occasions when there is little benefit in listing a large number of transactions during or shortly before the offer period. It therefore decided that all purchases and sales during the offer period can be aggregated. Furthermore, the Code Committee decided:

1. to extend to three months the period prior to the offer period during which dealings may be aggregated on a monthly basis; and
2. to permit dealings in the nine months prior to that period to be aggregated on a quarterly basis.

The Note requires that acquisitions and disposals should not be netted off, that the highest and lowest prices should be stated and that disclosure should distinguish between different categories of interest in relevant securities and short positions. The entirety of the provisions in Note 2 on Rule 24.4 are now subject to a full list of all dealings (together with a draft of the proposed aggregate disclosure) being sent to the Panel for approval prior to the posting of the offer documentation, and being available for inspection. It is also worth noting that Note 4 on Rule 24.4 and Note 2 on Rule 25.4 now require details of securities of competing offerors to also be included in the relevant documents.

3.5 Miscellaneous

We will now deal briefly with some miscellaneous topics concerning share dealings of which advisers on a takeover will need to have some understanding.

3.5.1 *Dealings by principal traders and fund managers*

There has historically been a good deal of confusion about how the Code treats dealings by connected principal traders and fund managers. On 25 April 2005, following the consultation on market-related issues, the Code was amended, mainly to clarify and codify elements of the Panel's practice which had developed over time. It is, perhaps, simplest to address the provisions which apply to both principal traders and fund managers before looking at the Code provisions which are specific to one or the other.

The term "market maker" was previously used in the Code, but was replaced with the term "Principal trader" on 25 April 2005, as the Panel had adopted this term following the introduction of SETS (see 3.5.4 below), after which there were no recognised market makers in SETS-traded securities. It also reflects the policy which has been adopted by the Panel for some time that all principal trading activities (not just market making activities) should be eligible for exempt status (see below).

The amendments made on 25 April 2005 also introduced a new defined term, that of "connected adviser". Connected advisers normally include only:

1. in relation to the offeror or target—an organisation which is advising that party in relation to the offer and a corporate broker to that party; and
2. in relation to a person who is acting in concert with the offeror or the target—an organisation which is advising that person either in relation to the offer or in relation to the matter which is the reason for that person being a member of the relevant concert party.

The Code definition of acting in concert contains a presumption (presumption 7) that a connected adviser acts in concert with its client and, if its client is acting in concert with the offeror or the target, the connected adviser is also presumed to act in concert with the offeror or target, in respect of the interests in shares of that adviser and the persons controlling, controlled by or under the same control as, that adviser. Hence, when the adviser is part of a larger financial services organisation, the presumption of concertedness extends to all entities within that group.

However, principal traders and fund managers who can demonstrate to the Panel's satisfaction their independence from corporate advisory and corporate broking operations in their group are granted exempt status. Exempt status is obtained by application to the Panel. The Panel will consider all relevant factors in deciding any applications including group structure, separate physical location, the history of the organisation as a whole (including past records of cooperative or independent action), the extent of the use of common services, common directorships, financial interests of the relevant executives in the group as a whole and the existence of an effective compliance department. The effect of exempt status is to remove the principal trader or fund manager from the presumption of concertedness that would otherwise apply. However, the principal trader or fund manager will still be regarded as connected with the offeror or target company, as appropriate (see Note 3 on the definitions of exempt fund manager and exempt principal trader).

It should be noted that exempt status is not relevant unless the sole reason for the connection is that the principal trader or fund manager is controlled by, controls or is under the same control as a connected adviser to the offeror, target, or person acting in concert with the offeror or target (Note 2 on the Code definitions of exempt fund manager and exempt principal trader). If a fund manager or principal trader's exempt status is not relevant, or if they do not have exempt status, Rule 7.2 applies. Connected fund managers and principal traders will not normally be presumed to be acting in concert with an offeror or potential offeror until that party's identity as an offeror or potential offeror is publicly announced, or (if earlier) the time at which the fund manager or principal trader had actual knowledge of the possibility of an offer being made by a person with whom it is connected (Rule 7.2(a)). When this is the case, Rules 4.2, 4.6, 5, 6, 9, 11 and 36 will be relevant. Similarly, under Rule 7.2(b), connected fund managers and principal traders will not normally be presumed to be acting in concert with the target until the commencement of the offer period, or (if earlier) the time at which the fund manager or principal trader had actual knowledge of the possibility of an offer being made. Rules 4.4, 4.6, 5 and 9 may then be relevant.

The Code reflects the Panel's practice of permitting a connected non-exempt principal trader or fund manager, after it is presumed to be acting in concert, to acquire or sell interests in target shares so as to flatten its book position within a short period (usually 24–48 hours) of being presumed to be acting in concert. The Panel will then not apply the usual Code consequences to dealings undertaken with its consent in this way (see Notes 3 and 4 to Rule 7.2).

3.5.2 *Recognised intermediary status*

As part of the amendments made to the Code in relation to dealings in derivatives and options, the Code Committee reviewed the status of investment institutions under the Code. The product of this review was the creation of a new "recognised intermediary status" for trading desks which trade as principal for client-serving purposes. This status allows the interests of the recognised intermediary in shares as a result of positions in derivatives and options not to be taken into account in establishing whether the trading desk (or the organisation of which it forms part) is interested in 30% or more of a company's shares carrying voting rights for the purposes of Rule 9.

The rationale behind the introduction of recognised intermediary status is that certain investment institutions, especially client-serving desks of investment banks, are likely to have substantial derivatives and options positions in the ordinary course of their business and this should not require them to make mandatory offers under Rule 9.1.

To obtain recognised intermediary status, the desk must apply to the Panel and satisfy a number of suitability conditions regarding the nature of its activities and the organisation of which it forms part.

It should be noted that recognised intermediary status is an entirely separate regime from the exempt status regime. Hence, where a recognised intermediary is (or is part of) an exempt principal trader connected with an offeror or target company, the position under the Code remains unchanged.

3.5.3   Fund managers

3.5.3.1   Restrictions on dealings

Although Rules 38.1–38.4 (see 3.5.4.1 below) do not specifically apply to exempt fund managers, the Panel has stated that it "would not expect such a fund manager to take any action with the intention of assisting the group's corporate finance clients because this would undermine the basis on which exempt status was granted to it" (PCP 2004/3, para.1.8).

3.5.3.2   Disclosure: Rule 8

An exempt fund manager who is connected with the offeror or target, and who deals in relevant securities for the account of discretionary investment clients, is required to make private disclosure of such dealings to the Panel (Rule 8.6(a)). If, however, a connected exempt fund manager holds a greater than 1% interest in the relevant securities, then it will have to make the usual public disclosure under Rule 8.3 (in which case, private disclosure will not normally be required in addition (Rule 8.6(b)). The latter is also true, of course, of non-connected fund managers holding a 1% (or greater) interest, but non-connected principal traders are under no such obligation.

Connected fund managers which do not enjoy exempt status must make public disclosure of their dealings in the normal way.

3.5.4   Principal traders

3.5.4.1   Restrictions on dealings

Granting exempt status to principal traders left a risk of concerted action, which was considered by the Panel to be more acute in respect of market making, involving the use of the organisation's own capital, than in respect of discretionary fund management, where managers owe fiduciary duties to their investment clients and are therefore less likely to take action to assist the organisation's corporate finance clients. Accordingly, Rule 38.1 prohibits an exempt connected principal trader from dealing with the purpose of assisting the offeror or target; Rule 38.2 also prohibits the offeror and its concert parties from dealing as principal, during the offer period, with an exempt principal trader connected with the offeror in shares of the target; Rule 38.3 states that such a principal trader may not assent its shares to the offer or purchase such shares in assented form until after the offer is unconditional as to acceptances; and Rule 38.4 prohibits shares owned by an exempt connected principal trader from being voted in the context of an offer. In order to ensure compliance with Rules 38.1 and 38.2, the Code now states that during an offer period, an offeror and persons acting in concert with it must not acquire an interest in any securities of the target company through any anonymous order book system, or through any other means, unless it can be established that the seller (or other party to the transaction in question) is not an exempt principal trader connected with the offeror (Rule 4.2(b)).

Dealings by exempt principal traders are also relevant for the purposes of Rule 9. The Panel Executive has adopted a standard approach to aggregation which requires compliance officers of multi-service financial organisations to monitor closely the aggregate holdings of the group so as to ensure that Rule 9 is not breached. This is now reflected in Note 16 on Rule 9.1 (as amended by Instrument 2014/2), which states that Rule 9 will be relevant if the aggregate number of shares in which all persons under the same control (including any exempt fund manager or exempt principal trader) are interested carry 30% or more of the voting rights of the relevant company. However, if recognised intermediary status has not fallen away under Note 3 of the definition of recognised intermediary, a recognised intermediary acting in a client-serving capacity will not be treated as interested in any securities, unless they are held in a proprietary capacity and fall within paragraphs 3 or 4 of the definition of interests in securities. Note 16 also provides that if such a group of persons includes a principal trader and the aggregate number of shares in a company in which the group is interested approaches or exceeds 30% of the voting rights, the Panel may consent to the principal trader continuing to acquire shares in the company without consequence under Rule 9.1, provided that the company is not in an offer period, the shares are acquired in a client serving capacity and the number of shares which the principal trader holds in a client serving capacity does not at any relevant time exceed 3% of the voting rights of the company.

3.5.4.2 Disclosure

Before the Code Committee amended the Code to take into account dealings in derivatives and options, an unconnected principal trader who dealt in that capacity did not have to make disclosure under Rule 8.3 when their holding rose above 1% (in contrast to the position for an unconnected fund manager and all other shareholders). As part of its review of the status of investment institutions under the Code, the Code Committee has developed further the Code's long-standing disclosure exception for recognised market makers and other intermediaries. Under the amended regime, the exception from disclosure under Rule 8.3(d) applies to all investment desks enjoying recognised intermediary status. In practice, this exception is more widely available than previously, when it was only available to unconnected principal traders. For example, a trading desk not registered as a market maker with the LSE or an LSE-registered member firm dealing as principal in order book securities could potentially apply for recognised intermediary status but would not constitute a principal trader. Some commentators assume that connected principal traders have a similar immunity from disclosure so that market-making arms of investment banks are able secretly to build up stakes in the target while another part of the organisation is advising the bidder. In fact, this is not the case. Exempt connected principal traders (i.e. within the same group as the financial adviser or broker) are already required to disclose all dealings (although in aggregated form) under Rule 8.5 (which replaced old Rule 38.5 with effect from 19 April 2010) (see Note 9 on Rule 8) via a RIS by 12.00 on the business day following the dealing, while connected principal traders which are not exempt will have disclosure obligations under Rules 8.3 and 8.4.

Chapter 4

Mandatory and Voluntary Offers and Their Terms

Nick Adams
Partner
Norton Rose Fulbright LLP

Paul Whitelock
Partner
Norton Rose Fulbright LLP

4.1 Introduction

Rules 9–13 restrict the freedom which a party has at common law in his or her decision whether or not to bid for control of a company to which the Code applies and, where he or she does make a bid, to choose the consideration he or she offers and the conditions which he or she attaches to his or her bid.

They do this in a number of ways:

1. Rule 9 obliges a person (or persons acting in concert) to make a bid in certain circumstances, specifies the minimum consideration to be offered and limits the conditions which can be attached to the bid.
2. Rule 10 requires a bid to contain a minimum acceptance condition.
3. Rule 11 requires a voluntary offeror in certain situations to offer a minimum cash price, a cash alternative or to make a securities offer.
4. Rule 12 requires a particular term to be included in an offer which could trigger an in-depth (Phase 2) investigation by the UK or EU competition authorities.

5.   Rule 13 prohibits certain types of condition and restricts the ability of an offeror to invoke a condition to lapse an offer.

Different principles apply to partial offers, which are governed by Rule 36 and are covered in Ch.5.

Many of the Rules referred to in this Chapter are qualified by wording "except with the consent of the Panel". It is therefore important to understand the philosophy of the Panel in these matters.

Except as mentioned, the Rules referred to in this Chapter apply equally to contractual offers and to offers implemented by way of a scheme of arrangement.

4.2   The mandatory offer and its terms

Rule 9 provides that where:

1.   any person (which can be an individual as well as a company);
2.   acquires (whether by one transaction or a series of transactions over a period of time) an interest in shares in a company;
3.   which in itself, or when aggregated with shares in which the person and persons acting in concert with it are already interested;
4.   carries 30% or more of the voting rights of the company,

then such person must make an offer:

1.   to acquire all other equity shares in the company (whether voting or non-voting, but excluding any shares held in treasury); and
2.   to acquire any other class of transferable securities in the company carrying voting rights (again, excluding any shares held in treasury),

on the terms and conditions required by Rule 9.

The Rule also requires such a bid where any person who (together with any persons acting in concert with it) is already interested in shares carrying 30% or more of the voting rights of a company, but does not hold shares carrying more than 50% of such voting rights, acquires (or any person acting in concert with it acquires) an interest in any other shares which increases the percentage of shares carrying voting rights in which it is interested.

"Voting rights" are defined as all the voting rights attributable to the share capital of a company which are currently exercisable at a general meeting. Except for treasury shares, any shares which are subject to: (a) a restriction on the exercise of voting rights (in an undertaking or agreement by or between a shareholder and the company or a third party or arising by law or regulation); or (b) a suspension of voting rights (whether implemented by means of the company's articles of association or otherwise), will normally be regarded as having voting rights which are currently exercisable at a general meeting.

A person will be treated as having an "interest in shares" if he or she has a long economic exposure, whether absolute or conditional, to changes in the price of shares and in particular if:

1. he or she owns the shares;
2. he or she has the right (whether conditional or absolute) to exercise or direct the exercise of the voting rights attaching to them or has general control of them;
3. by virtue of any agreement to purchase, option or derivative, he or she has the right or option to acquire them or call for their delivery or is under an obligation to take delivery of them (whether such right, option or obligation is conditional or absolute and whether it is in the money or otherwise); or

4.   he or she is party to any derivative whose value is determined by reference to their price and which results, or may result, in his or her having a long position in them.[1]

Consequently, the thresholds for the triggering of a mandatory offer obligation pursuant to Rule 9.1 are not limited by reference to holdings of shares carrying voting rights but will also take into account other interests in shares acquired by virtue of long derivatives, call options and written put options. A person will not normally be treated as having acquired an interest in further shares just because the nature of his or her interest has changed (for example, where a person acquires shares upon the exercise of a call option over existing shares), provided that the aggregate number of shares in which the person is interested remains the same (Note 18 on Rule 9.1).

Rule 9 is based on General Principle 1, which provides, inter alia, that where a person acquires control of a company, the other holders of securities must be protected.

"Control" is defined in the Definitions section of the Code as an interest, or interests, in shares carrying in aggregate 30% or more of the voting rights of a company, irrespective of whether such interest or interests give de facto control.

From time to time there have been suggestions that the 30% figure should be reduced. Article 5 of the Takeover Directive requires Member States to introduce Rules relating to mandatory bids but does not specify the threshold at which a mandatory bid has to be made: this is left to individual Member States to determine. In the UK, the 30% threshold is thought to strike an appropriate balance between protecting minority shareholders and not unduly restricting takeover activity.

---

[1]   For the purposes of Rule 5 only, a person will also be treated as interested in shares if he or she has received an irrevocable commitment in respect of them. Rule 5 is discussed in further detail in Ch.3.

The 1991 Annual Report of the Panel contained the following helpful explanation of the philosophy underlying Rule 9:

> "The philosophy underlying this Rule is that, if effective control of a company is obtained by the acquisition of shares, the principle of equality of treatment for shareholders requires that all shareholders should have the opportunity to obtain the price per share paid for that control (it will usually be a premium price) and that they should have the opportunity to get out of the company if they do not like what has happened."

An important bolstering of this principle is contained in Rule 9.6, which requires directors (and their close relatives[2] and the related trusts of any of them) who sell shares to a person (or enter into options, derivatives or other transactions with a person) which would trigger a Rule 9 obligation to make it a condition of the sale (or other relevant transaction) that the person will make a Rule 9 bid. In addition, such directors should (except with the consent of the Panel) remain on the board until the later of the first closing date or the date on which the offer becomes wholly unconditional so as to ensure proper conduct of the bid. This important provision should not be overlooked; it imposes an obligation on the seller of the shares and its significance is indicated by the fact that an equivalent of Rule 9.6 appeared in the Code before the remainder of Rule 9.

In practice, Rule 9 mandatory offers are contractual rather than effected by way of a scheme of arrangement, although s.2 of Appendix 7 to the Code does allow a mandatory offer under Rule 9 to be implemented by way of a scheme of arrangement with the Panel's prior consent. Note 1 on s.2 refers to the views of the offeree board and its independent adviser and the likely timetable of the scheme as being factors that the Panel will take into account in considering whether or not to permit a

---

[2] A person's close relatives will normally include: (1) the person's spouse, civil partner or cohabitant; (2) the person's children, parents, brothers, sisters, grandchildren and grandparents, and those of any person described in (1); and (3) the spouse, civil partner or cohabitant of any person described in (2).

mandatory offer to be made by way of a scheme. Note 1 also states that, if the Panel does consent to a mandatory offer being effected by way of a scheme of arrangement and the scheme lapses for a reason that would not have caused a contractual offer to lapse (for example, the court does not sanction the scheme), the offeror must immediately make a contractual offer in compliance with Rule 9 (and the scheme circular must include a statement to that effect).

4.2.1 The terms and conditions of mandatory bids

4.2.1.1 Price

Rule 9.5(a) requires that a mandatory offer must be in cash (or be accompanied by a cash alternative) at not less than the highest price paid by the offeror or any person acting in concert with it for any interest in shares of the relevant class during the 12 months prior to the announcement of that offer. The Panel should be consulted where there is more than one class of share capital involved. Rule 9.5(b) also states that if, after a Rule 9 offer has been made for a class of shares but before it closes for acceptance, the offeror or anyone acting in concert with it acquires a further interest in shares of that class at above the offer price, it must increase its offer price for that class of shares to not less than the highest price paid for the interest so acquired.

Note 1 on Rule 9.5 explains that sometimes, where a significant number of acquisitions which have to be taken into account for the purposes of the Rule have been securities exchange transactions, the principle of equality of treatment may make it undesirable that the offer be a cash only offer, and that the same securities, but with a cash alternative, may be required to be offered. The Panel should be consulted in such cases.

Rule 9.5(c) grants the Panel a discretion to adjust the highest price calculated under Rules 9.5(a) and 9.5(b). Note 3 on Rule 9.5 identifies some of the considerations which the Panel might take into account in deciding whether to make such an adjustment; one situation might be where the mandatory bid is being made as part of a rescue operation. The price payable in any of the situations set out in Note 3 will be the price that is fair and reasonable taking into account all the factors that are relevant to the circumstances. In any case where the highest price is adjusted, the Panel will publish its decision.

The other Notes on Rule 9.5 give further guidance on calculation of the price to be offered, including where dealings in options and derivatives are relevant.

4.2.1.2   Competition references[3]

Rule 9.4 requires any mandatory bid to which Rule 12 applies (see 4.4 below) to contain the term required by Rule 12.1 providing that the offer will lapse in the event it is referred for a Phase 2 investigation by either the UK or EU competition authorities. If a mandatory bid lapses pursuant to Rule 12.1 and competition clearance is then obtained, the offer must be re-made on the same terms as soon as practicable. The Panel would normally expect an offeror whose offer has lapsed pursuant to Rule 12.1 to proceed with all due diligence before the Competition and Markets Authority (CMA) or European Commission, although Note 1 on Rule 9.4 envisages situations where intervening action taken with the consent of the Panel may make this unnecessary. However, it cannot be a condition of a mandatory bid that there is no referral for a Phase 2 investigation or that clearance is received from the competition authorities.

4.2.1.3   Acceptance condition

Rule 9.3 requires that, except with the consent of the Panel, a mandatory bid must be conditional only upon acceptances being received in respect of shares which (together with shares acquired or agreed to be acquired before or during the offer) will result in the offeror and its concert parties holding shares carrying more than 50% of the voting rights. Note 1 on Rule 9.3 recognises that there will be no such condition where more

---

[3]   For minor changes to be made to Rule 12 in the event of Brexit, see RS 2018/2—also see further 4.4 below.

than 50% of the voting rights are already held before the offer is made. Although the Code has not formally disapplied Rule 9.3 in the case of a mandatory offer implemented by way of a scheme of arrangement, in practice this provision can only apply to a contractual offer as an offer by way of a scheme requires approval by the relevant majority of shareholders in a court convened shareholder meeting (as well as court sanction) rather than acceptance by individual shareholders.

4.2.1.4 *Other conditions*

Rule 9.3(a) prohibits other conditions being attached to mandatory bids and Rule 9.3(b) prohibits the making of an acquisition that would trigger a mandatory bid where the making or implementation of the bid would (or might) be dependent on the passing of a resolution by offeror shareholders or upon any other conditions, consents or arrangements. As a consequence, it is not possible to include in mandatory offers the detailed protective conditions customarily included in voluntary offers (see 4.3.3 below) regarding material adverse change, or consents of shareholders, or clearances by third parties.

As far as material adverse changes are concerned, these are treated as entirely the risk of the person whose acquisition has triggered the obligation to make a mandatory bid.

As far as consents of an offeror's shareholders or other conditions, consents or arrangements are concerned, again this is generally treated as something the offeror should have dealt with before triggering the bid. Note 3 on Rule 9.3 does provide that the Panel may consider a request for dispensation but notes that this will only be granted in exceptional circumstances—examples given in the Note include (in each case subject to various provisos and limitations) when the necessary cash is to be provided (wholly or in part) by an issue of new securities or when any official authorisation or regulatory clearance is required before the offer document is published. Where a dispensation is granted, the offeror must endeavour to fulfil all the other conditions with all due diligence. If it is intended to seek a dispensation, early stage consultation with the Panel will be critical.

4.2.2   Who are deemed to be "persons acting in concert"?

This question is a crucial one, since the aggregation of the interests in shares of people who are deemed to be acting in concert may result in an obligation to make a bid. The opening sentence in the Notes on Rule 9.1 states: "The majority of questions which arise in the context of Rule 9 relate to persons acting in concert."

The Definitions section of the Code defines the term as follows:

> "Persons acting in concert comprise persons who, pursuant to an agreement or understanding (whether formal or informal), co-operate to obtain or consolidate control ... of a company or to frustrate the successful outcome of an offer for a company ...".

There is a deeming provision in the definition which states that a person and each of its "affiliated persons" will be deemed to be acting in concert all with each other.[4]

The definition of "acting in concert" then continues with a series of presumptions as to those persons who are in concert. These fall into nine self-contained categories; someone in one of these categories is presumed to be in concert only with those in the same category and not with those in another category. However, the presumptions are rebuttable, and they are not meant to be exhaustive. They are followed by a series of Notes

---

[4]   For these purposes affiliated persons are undertakings in respect of which any person: (a) has a majority of the shareholders' or members' voting rights; (b) is a shareholder or member and at the same time has the right to appoint or remove a majority of the members of its board of directors; (c) is a shareholder or member and alone controls a majority of the shareholders' or members' voting rights pursuant to an agreement entered into with other shareholders or members; or (d) has the power to exercise, or actually exercises, dominant influence or control. For these purposes, a person's rights as regards voting, appointment or removal shall include the rights of any other affiliated person and those of any person or entity acting in his or her own name but on behalf of that person or of any other affiliated person.

discussed in other contexts in this Guide. In addition, the presumptions are supplemented in some cases by guidance issued by the Panel on how the presumptions are applied (see for instance, Practice Statement No.12 on the application of presumption (4)). This Chapter will concentrate on the guidance given in those Notes and in the Notes on Rule 9.1 which is of particular relevance to Rule 9.

4.2.2.1 *Persons coming together to act in concert or shareholders voting together*

If persons already interested in shares carrying 30% or more of the voting rights in a company but not previously acting in concert merely decide to co-operate to obtain or consolidate control of a company, this will not normally trigger a bid (provided that acquisitions made prior to coming together were made without the knowledge of the other concert parties). However, once they have come together, the acquisition by one of them of any further interest in shares carrying voting rights in that company could trigger a mandatory offer (Note 1 on Rule 9.1), with purchases made over the previous 12 months then becoming relevant for the purpose of determining the price to be offered even if such purchases had been made without the concert parties' knowledge and prior to coming together (Rule 9.5).

The Panel does not normally regard the action of shareholders voting together on particular resolutions, discussing possible issues which might be raised with a company's Board or making joint representations to a company as indicative of a group acting in concert. An exception to this general principle is contained in Note 2 on Rule 9.1. Practice Statement No.26 on shareholder activism contains guidance on the application of Note 2. In summary, the Panel will normally presume shareholders who requisition or threaten to requisition the consideration of a "board control-seeking proposal" at a shareholders' meeting, together with their supporters as at the date of the requisition or threat, to be acting in concert with each other and with the proposed directors, with the result that subsequent acquisitions of interests in shares after an agreement or understanding is reached to propose a board control-seeking proposal could trigger a mandatory offer. In determining if a proposal is board control-seeking, the Panel will have regard to a number of factors, including the specific factors listed in Note 2. The most important factor is whether there is a relationship (other than an insignificant relationship) between any of the proposed directors and any of the shareholders proposing them or their supporters. If such a relationship exists then the other factors set out in Note 2 will also need to be considered to determine whether the proposal is board control-seeking, including the number of directors to be appointed or replaced compared with the total size of the board and the board positions held by the directors being replaced and to be held by the proposed directors. In practice, board control-seeking resolutions are relatively rare and, in the majority of normal collective shareholder actions, no mandatory offer issues would therefore arise.

4.2.2.2 Break-up of concert parties

Note 1 on the definition of "acting in concert" indicates that the Panel needs clear evidence before it will accept that parties, once held to be in concert, are no longer in concert. This will be particularly relevant where, the original objective of the concert party having been achieved and co-operation having ceased, one of its members wishes to make a further acquisition without triggering a mandatory offer.

The composition of concert parties can also change. The sale of its interest in shares by an outgoing member of the concert party to a continuing member (or the transfer of interests in shares between members of the concert party) may, in certain circumstances, trigger an obligation on the part of the purchaser to make a mandatory bid. Note 4 on Rule 9.1 describes these circumstances.

4.2.2.3 *Acquisition of part only of an interest in shares*

Difficult questions arise when a shareholder who holds more than 30% sells less than 30% to a single purchaser or two or more purchasers who are acting in concert. One may see a sale of 29.99% in these circumstances, obviously designed to protect the purchaser from Rule 9. In such circumstances the Panel are rightly concerned as to whether seller and purchaser are effectively acting in concert in respect of all their shares, or the seller has allowed the purchaser to acquire a significant degree of control over the retained shares, so that a mandatory offer should be made.

The Panel will take account of such factors as whether the seller is an "insider", whether the price paid effectively contained a control premium, whether there are any arrangements (however informal) between seller and purchaser regarding the seller's retained shares or whether the retained shares are, in themselves, a significant part of the company's capital. Obviously fine judgments will be involved and the fact that the seller retains a substantial number of shares in respect of which it intends to act independently will be helpful in rebutting any presumption of concerted behaviour. Similar considerations will arise where the seller remains interested in shares but without itself owning any of such shares, or where the acquisition is not of the shares themselves but of another type of interest in shares. Note 6 on Rule 9.1 provides guidance on the point, but each case is inevitably different and the Panel should always be consulted.

4.2.2.4 *Employee benefit trusts*

Note 5 on Rule 9.1 concerns trustees of employee benefit trusts (EBTs) as potential concert parties. The Panel must be consulted in advance when an acquisition is proposed and the aggregate number of shares in which the directors, those persons acting in concert with them and the trustees of an EBT are interested would as a result carry 30% or more of the voting rights or, if already carrying 30% or more, would increase further. Similarly, the Panel must be consulted where a person or a group of persons acting in concert is interested in shares carrying 30% or more (but does not hold shares carrying more than 50%) of the voting rights of a company, and it is proposed that an EBT acquires an interest in shares. The mere establishment and operation of an EBT will not by itself give rise to a presumption that the trustees are acting in concert with the directors and/or a controller (or group of persons acting in concert). However, the Panel will consider all relevant factors in making their determination, including the non-exhaustive list contained in Note 5 on Rule 9.1. No presumption of concertedness will apply in respect of shares held within the EBT but controlled by the beneficiaries.

4.2.3   Dispensations from Rule 9

The Code acknowledges that in certain circumstances it would be inequitable, and therefore unnecessary in order to satisfy the equality of treatment principle, to require a mandatory bid to be made.

There is a specific dispensation at the end of Rule 9.1 for control achieved through a voluntary bid. In addition, there are a series of Notes (Dispensation Notes) at the end of Rule 9 which list six situations in which the Panel may, or will, dispense with the need to make an offer. These are as follows.

4.2.3.1   The "Whitewash" procedure

The Whitewash dispensation is available on the issue of new securities, either as consideration for an acquisition or on a cash subscription. Where such an issue is of such a size that it would otherwise trigger a Rule 9 bid, the Panel will normally waive the obligation to make the bid if the requirements of Dispensation Note 1 and of Appendix 1 to the Code are complied with. Particular features of these requirements are:

1.   the issue must be approved at a shareholders' meeting of the company issuing the securities, the vote must be conducted by poll rather than a show of hands, and only independent shareholders may vote;

2.   the circular to shareholders convening the meeting must give full details of the transaction, comply with the detailed requirements of para.4 of Appendix 1 as to its contents, contain a number of warnings, contain (unless the relevant person(s) have entered into an agreement with the company not to make an offer or have stated in the circular that they do not intend to make an offer) a statement that the relevant person(s) will not be restricted from making an offer in the event that the proposals are approved and include competent independent advice on the proposals. It is noteworthy that a Whitewash circular is one of the few documents that the Panel insists it must approve before it is sent to shareholders; and

3.   the Whitewash dispensation is not normally available if there have been "disqualifying" acquisitions of interests in shares of the company during the preceding 12 months by the person or persons to whom the new securities are to be issued (or persons acting in concert with it or them) and those dealings occurred after discussions on the transaction to be approved by the Whitewash had begun (see para.3 of Appendix 1).

The philosophy behind this dispensation is that the vote gives independent shareholders the opportunity to veto the change of control before it takes place. Further, if there is a premium for control involved it accrues to the company, and therefore to all shareholders, rather than to a selling shareholder.

Consistent with this philosophy, the persons to whom the new shares are to be issued (and persons acting in concert with them) may not otherwise acquire any interest in shares in the company during the period between publication of the circular and the time shareholders' approval is obtained. Once approval has been obtained, there is no restriction (apart from those restrictions applying generally by virtue of Rules 5 and 9) on such persons acquiring any interest in other shares in the company (save that where shareholders approve the issue of convertible securities, options or warrants where no immediate voting rights are obtained, any further acquisition of shares should be discussed with the Panel to establish the number of shares to which the waiver will be deemed to apply (see para.7 of Appendix 1)).

See also 4.2.3.5 below in relation to the "accelerated white-wash" procedure.

4.2.3.2 *Enforcement of security for a loan*

Where shares or other securities are charged as security for a loan and the lender enforces as a result of the borrower's default, the lender may find itself (either alone or with persons with whom it is in concert) holding an interest in shares carrying more than 30% of the voting rights. Where the threshold is crossed purely as a result of such an enforcement, the Panel will not normally require the lender to make a mandatory offer provided that a sufficient number of the shares over which it has an interest are sold within a limited period to persons unconnected with the lender. In order to prevent the lender exercising control, it must consult with the Panel as to the ability to exercise its voting rights prior to such a sale (see Rule 9.7 which is discussed in further detail in 4.2.5.4 below). Where arrangements are to be made involving a transfer of voting rights to the lender, but which do not amount to enforcement of the security, the Panel will wish to be convinced that such arrangements are necessary to preserve the lender's security and that the security was not given at a time when the lender had reason to believe enforcement was likely. Where a lender sells all or part of a shareholding following enforcement, the purchaser will be subject to the provisions of Rule 9 if the acquisition results in them crossing a relevant threshold.

Although a receiver, liquidator or administrator of a company is not required to make an offer under Rule 9 when he or she acquires an interest in shares carrying 30% or more of the voting rights in another company, any purchaser from such a person will be subject to the provisions of Rule 9 if they cross a relevant threshold.

4.2.3.3   Rescue operations

Where a company is insolvent or prospectively insolvent because it is undercapitalised, the directors will obviously wish to restore it to solvency, either by issuing new shares in exchange for new cash or by arranging with certain of its loan creditors to exchange their debt for shares. Its financial difficulties may be such that its existing equity shares are worth little, so that meaningful new capital is likely to represent more than 30% of the voting share capital after the rescue.

However, sometimes the financial crisis may be such that the only way the company can be saved is by an urgent rescue operation involving the issue of new shares without the prior approval of independent shareholders or an acquisition of existing shares by the rescuer which would otherwise fall within the provisions of Rule 9. Dispensation Note 3 indicates that in such circumstances the Panel may waive the need for a mandatory bid provided that independent shareholder approval for the rescue operation is obtained as soon as possible after it has happened or the Panel is satisfied that some other provision is made for the protection of independent shareholders. If neither of these solutions is available, the rescuer will be required to make a mandatory offer, although the Panel may consider an adjustment to the highest price required for such offer pursuant to Note 3 on Rule 9.5.

4.2.3.4   Inadvertent mistake

Dispensation Note 4 acknowledges that sometimes there may be a crossing of a relevant threshold as a result of an innocent mistake. In that event the Panel will not normally require a mandatory offer if the holding is within a limited period reduced to below 30% by sales to persons unconnected with the purchaser. In order to prevent any such person exercising control in the meantime, the Panel must be consulted as to the ability to exercise voting rights prior to such sales (see Rule 9.7 which is discussed in further detail in 4.2.5.4 below).

It should be noted that a dispensation is not necessarily available if a purchaser knowingly acquires an interest in shares carrying more than 30% of the voting rights on the basis that it will place out a sufficient percentage of this interest to reduce its holding to below 30%. Note 7 on Rule 9.1 envisages situations in which dispensation may be given in such circumstances.

4.2.3.5 *Shares carrying 50% or more of the voting rights*

Dispensation Note 5 acknowledges that the Panel will consider waiving the requirement to make a mandatory offer if:

1. persons holding shares carrying 50% or more of the voting rights state in writing that they will not accept it (this is because it is pointless to make the offer if the acceptance condition will not be satisfied);
2. shares carrying 50% or more of the voting rights are already held by one person; or
3. in the case of an issue of new securities, independent shareholders holding shares carrying more than 50% of the voting rights of the company which would be capable of being cast on a "whitewash" resolution (see 4.2.3.1 above) confirm in writing that they approve the proposed waiver and would vote in favour of any resolution to that effect at a general meeting (commonly referred to as the "accelerated whitewash" procedure).

4.2.3.6 *Enfranchisement of non-voting shares*

If a person crosses a Rule 9 threshold as a result of non-voting shares in which it is already interested being enfranchised, Dispensation Note 6 provides that it will not be required to make a mandatory offer unless shares or interests in shares have been acquired at a time when the person had reason to believe that enfranchisement would take place. This dispensation reflects the fact that the person has not crossed the threshold by a voluntary act.

4.2.4 Redemption or purchase by a company of its own shares

The position where a person's interest in shares is caused to cross the threshold by reason of a redemption or purchase of its own shares by the company itself is covered by Rule 37.1 rather than a Dispensation Note on Rule 9. Rule 37.1 states that a person who crosses a Rule 9 threshold as a result of a company's redemption or purchase of its own shares will not normally incur an obligation to make a mandatory offer unless that person is a director or is acting in concert with any of the directors (see Note 1 on Rule 37.1 for further details). It should be noted that a person who has appointed a representative to the board of the company, and investment managers of investment trusts, will be treated as a "director" for these purposes. Subject to prior consultation, the Panel will normally waive an obligation to make a mandatory offer arising by a person's interest in shares crossing the relevant mandatory offer threshold by reason of a redemption or purchase of own shares, provided that there is a vote of independent shareholders and a procedure similar to that of the Whitewash procedure (see 4.2.3.1 above) is followed. In fact, where the directors are aware that a mandatory bid obligation might be incurred as a result of a purchase by a company of its own shares, they should ensure an appropriate resolution to approve a waiver of the mandatory bid obligation is put to independent shareholders (see Note 3 on Rule 37.1).

4.2.5 Other points in relation to Rule 9

4.2.5.1 Who must make the offer

The person whose acquisition causes the 30% threshold to be crossed or who acquires an interest in further shares triggering a Rule 9 obligation has primary responsibility to make the bid (Rule 9.1). However, Rule 9.2 provides that where there is a concert party the principal members of the party may also be obliged to make the offer depending on the circumstances of the case. The Note on Rule 9.2 provides some guidance, but consultation with the Panel as to who should make the bid where there is a concert party is highly desirable. The person required to make a mandatory offer may extend the offer to other concert parties, but will not normally be required to do so.

4.2.5.2   *The chain principle*

If a person or group of persons acting in concert acquires shares resulting in a holding of over 50% of the voting rights of any company (which need not be a company to which the Code applies) which is interested, either directly or through intermediate companies, in shares of a second company, the Panel may require a mandatory bid if such a bid would have been triggered if that person or group of persons had directly acquired the interest in the shares of the second company owned by the first company. Generally speaking, however, the Panel will not apply this principle (which is set out in Note 8 on Rule 9.1) unless either the interest in shares which the first company has in the second company is significant in relation to the first company (taking account of a number of factors including, as appropriate, the assets, profits and market values of the respective companies, with relative values of 50% or more normally regarded as significant), or unless securing control of the second company might reasonably be considered to be a significant purpose of acquiring control of the first company. The Panel should be consulted in all cases which may come within the scope of the chain principle in order to establish whether a mandatory bid is required. Recent examples of the chain principle include the 2014 offer for Songbird Estates which then triggered a mandatory offer for the shares in Canary Wharf Group not already held by Songbird Estates and the ruling by the Panel in April 2018 that the proposed acquisition by The Walt Disney Company of Twenty-First Century Fox would result in Disney being required to make a mandatory offer for the shares in Sky not already held by Fox.[5]

---

[5]   In relation to Sky, the Panel also set out how pricing a chain principle offer may be approached (see Statement 2018/4 issued by the Takeover Appeal Board and Panel Statement 2018/14).

4.2.5.3   *Triggering Rule 9 during the course of a voluntary offer*

Rule 5.2 may in certain circumstances, subject as set out in the next paragraph in the case of a scheme, permit a voluntary offeror to take its interest in shares in the offeree above the 30% threshold during an offer period (although Note 4 on Rule 32.1, which only applies to contractual offers, may preclude it from doing so unless the offer can remain open for acceptance for at least 14 further days following the date on which the amended offer document is posted). The obvious situation in which an offeror might want to trigger a Rule 9 bid would be one where it felt obliged to pick up a parcel of shares overhanging the market. If it does so, it must waive all conditions other than those permitted by Rule 9 and announce the mandatory offer immediately. If a voluntary offeror (or any person acting in concert with it) wishes to make such an acquisition, Note 9 on Rule 9.1 requires the Panel to be consulted in advance.

Note 2 on Section 2 of Appendix 7 of the Code provides that, where a voluntary offer is proceeding by way of a scheme of arrangement, the offeror (and persons acting in concert with it) must not acquire an interest in shares in the offeree company which would trigger a mandatory offer under Rule 9 unless it has first obtained the Panel's consent either to satisfy its obligation under Rule 9 by way of a scheme or to switch to a contractual offer. This reflects the requirement referred to above that a mandatory offer cannot be made by way of a scheme of arrangement without the prior consent of the Panel.

4.2.5.4   *Voting restrictions and disposal of interests*

Rule 9.7 provides that where the Panel has agreed to a person who has triggered a Rule 9 obligation disposing of interests in shares as an alternative to making a mandatory offer, and in certain other specified circumstances, the Panel must be consulted as to the application, pending completion of the disposal, of restrictions on the exercise of voting rights (or the procurement of the exercise of voting rights) attaching to the shares in which that person and its concert parties are interested. Note 2 on Rule 9.7 provides guidance on the number of shares to which voting restrictions will normally be applied.

4.2.5.5 *Convertible securities, warrants and options*

Generally speaking, the acquisition of securities convertible into, warrants in respect of, or options or other rights to subscribe for, new shares does not give rise to an obligation to make a general offer under Rule 9, although the subsequent exercise of the conversion or subscription rights or options will be treated as an acquisition of an interest in the shares for the purposes of the Rule. Even then the exercise of those conversion or subscription rights will not usually be regarded as triggering a general offer if the issue of the convertible securities or subscription rights was approved by a Whitewash procedure (however the Panel must be consulted if there have been intervening acquisitions of further interests in voting shares, in order to establish the number of shares to which the Whitewash waiver will be deemed to apply). If a person acquires subscription rights, options etc. and does not seek a whitewash at the time of entry into those arrangements, it will not generally be permitted to seek a whitewash for the subsequent exercise of such options or subscription rights.

If a fund management organisation (or persons under the same control as it) holds options, warrants or other rights to subscribe for shares carrying voting rights in an investment company or investment trust (or securities convertible into such shares) at the time of its IPO, which on exercise or conversion (as appropriate) would otherwise result in a mandatory offer obligation being triggered, no such obligation will normally arise provided that the terms have been disclosed in the prospectus or other public offering documen-tation (and the form of such disclosure has been approved by the Panel before publication) (see Panel Practice Statement No.12).

Any holder of conversion or subscription rights who intends to exercise such rights and will, as a result, become interested in shares carrying 30% or more of the voting rights of a company must consult the Panel before doing so to determine whether a mandatory offer obligation would arise under Rule 9 and if so at what price.

4.2.5.6   The "bounceback" principle

A person's interest in shares can be reduced by a number of events, such as a sale by it or an issue of further shares by the company itself or a transfer by the company of shares out of treasury. If the effect of this event is to reduce its interest in shares to below 30% of the voting rights, it will still have to make a mandatory offer if it subsequently makes a further acquisition and as a result the number of shares in which it is interested would, once again, carry more than 30% of the voting rights (unless it qualifies for one of the dispensations). It is treated for all purposes as starting from the base of its reduced percentage and subsequently crossing the 30% threshold by voluntary action.

Note 11 on Rule 9.1 permits, in limited circumstances, acquisitions by persons (or groups of persons acting in concert) who are interested in shares carrying more than 30% of the voting rights of a company. If such a person or group of persons reduces its interest but not to less than 30%, then they may subsequently acquire an interest in further shares, subject to the following restrictions, without incurring an obligation to make a general offer:

1. the total number of shares in which interests may be acquired in any period of 12 months must not exceed 1% of the voting share capital for the time being (and reductions cannot be netted off against acquisitions for these purposes); and
2. the percentage of shares in which the relevant person or group of persons acting in concert is interested following any acquisition must not exceed the highest percentage of shares in which such person or group of persons was interested in the previous 12 months.

The Panel will also regard a reduction of the percentage of shares in which the person or group is interested as a result of dilution following the new issue of shares as being relevant for these purposes. However, where an existing shareholder participates in a placing then the Panel will look at the shareholder's percentage interest following completion of the placing, rather than treating it as a reduction in percentage interest followed by a subsequent increase.

4.2.5.7   Gifts

Note 12 on Rule 9.1 requires the Panel to be consulted if a person receives a gift of shares or an interest in shares which takes the aggregate number of shares in which he or she is interested to 30% or more.

4.2.6   Practical effects of Rule 9

Rule 9 has three important effects in practice:

1. it discourages a holding of interests in shares which carry more than 29.99% of the voting rights of a company;
2. it discourages a voluntary offeror from making market purchases permitted by Rule 5.2 if it wants to maintain a full set of conditions to its offer; and
3. it encourages persons who might be in concert and who are close to (or over) the 30% threshold to consult the Panel.

4.3   The voluntary offer and its terms

In accordance with Rule 2.7(c)(iii), an offeror is required to announce all the conditions to which an offer is subject at the time that a firm intention to make a bid is announced. Generally speaking, the conditions attaching to an offer are a matter for the offeror. However, the Code does impose certain restrictions so as to ensure that its General Principles are honoured.

4.3.1 *When a particular form of consideration is required*

Rule 11.1 requires an offer to be in cash, or have a cash alternative, if:

1. the offeror and its concert parties have acquired interests in shares of any class under offer in the offeree company during the offer period or within the preceding 12 months for cash, and the interests so acquired represent 10% or more of the shares of that class in issue (in which case the cash price offered for that class must be not less than the highest price paid during such period);
2. any interest in shares of any class under offer in the offeree company is acquired for cash by an offeror or any person acting in concert with it during the offer period (in which case the cash price offered for that class must be not less than the highest price paid during such period); or
3. in the view of the Panel there are circumstances which render such a course necessary in order to give effect to General Principle 1.

This requirement is additional to the minimum value requirement contained in Rule 6 (see Ch.3).

The Notes on the Rule contain guidance on how the price paid for any acquisition of an interest in shares (either through the direct purchase of shares or through entering into an option or derivative) will be determined. There is also particular guidance in relation to the conversion or exercise of securities convertible into, warrants in respect of, or options or other rights to subscribe for, new shares.

There are a number of other important points contained in the Notes on Rule 11.1. Note 2 provides that the Panel will not normally allow sales to be netted off against acquisitions in calculating the 10% limit. Note 5 indicates that acquisitions of interests in shares in exchange for securities will normally be deemed to be acquisitions for cash on the basis of the value of the securities at the time of the acquisition (unless the recipient is required to hold the securities received or receivable until either the offer has lapsed or consideration has been posted to accepting shareholders). Note 8 provides that the Panel should be consulted if shares in the company have been allotted (even if provisionally) but not yet issued—for example where there is a rights issue in progress.

It is important to note that Rule 11.1 can be triggered after the offer period commences, although the Notes on Rule 32.1 contain restrictions on this in the 14 days before the last date on which the offer can become unconditional as to acceptances (and, in the case of a scheme of arrangement, Section 7 of Appendix 7 contains a similar restriction, requiring Panel consent before any revision can be made in the 14 days prior to the date of the shareholder meetings to implement the scheme). If an acquisition of an interest in shares is made which triggers Rule 11.1 at a time when there is a cash alternative which is not lower than the acquisition price, there is no problem. If there is no cash alternative, Note 6 requires an immediate announcement of the necessary revision of the offer to include a cash alternative at not less than the transaction price. Similarly there must be a revision and an immediate announcement if the transaction price exceeds the present offer price. Difficulties can arise if it is a person deemed to be in concert with the offeror, rather than the offeror itself, which makes an acquisition which triggers the Rule; in the Guinness/Distillers bid a purchase of shares in Distillers at above the bid price was made by a party which the Panel ruled, after completion of the bid, to have been in concert with Guinness; the Panel ruled (Panel Statement 1989/13) that Guinness should top up, by payments to Distillers' former shareholders, its purchase price to the level to which it would have been required to revise its offer by Rule 11.1.

The Rule is effectively an (albeit limited) exemption from General Principle 1, in that it enables an offeror to acquire an interest in shares for cash without making a cash alternative available to other shareholders provided that the aggregate interest acquired within the preceding 12 months represents less than 10% and no interest in shares is acquired for cash during the offer period. It is for this reason that Rule 11.1(c) envisages that there may be circumstances in which General Principle 1 requires there to be a cash alternative even if the 10% threshold is not crossed. Note 4 indicates that this discretion will not normally be exercised unless the vendors or the parties to the transactions giving rise to the interests are directors of, or otherwise closely connected with, the offeror or the offeree company. It also notes that Rule 11(c) may be relevant where interests in shares representing 10% or more of a class have been acquired in the previous 12 months for a mixture of securities and cash and provides that the Panel should be consulted in all relevant cases.

Rule 11.2 requires that, where interests in shares of any class of the offeree company representing 10% or more of the shares of that class in issue have been acquired by an offeror and any person acting in concert with it in exchange for securities in the three months prior to the commencement of and during the offer period, such securities will normally be required to be offered to all other holders of shares of that class. Note 1 on Rule 11.2 provides that any securities required to be offered must be offered on the basis of the same number of consideration securities received or receivable by the vendor or other party to the transaction for each offeree company share rather than on the basis of securities equivalent to the value of the securities received or receivable at the time of the relevant acquisition.

Rule 11.3 enables an offeror to seek dispensation from the obligation to pay the highest price given during the relevant period and the Note on that Rule sets out the factors which the Panel might take into account when considering such an application. These factors are not expressed to be exhaustive; for example the Panel may take into account a substantial collapse in the offeree company's share price after the acquisitions were made as a result of new information about its business becoming publicly available where the acquisition had been made before these events.

4.3.2 *The acceptance condition*

In any contractual offer (as opposed to an offer effected by way of a scheme of arrangement) for voting equity share capital or for other transferable securities carrying voting rights, Rule 10 requires there to be an unwaivable condition that the offer will not become or be declared unconditional as to acceptances unless the offeror has acquired or agreed to acquire (either under the offer or otherwise) shares carrying over 50% of the voting rights.

The rationale for the 50% threshold for contractual offers is that the offeror will control the board of the offeree company, and thus have management control. The Panel normally regards 50% plus one share control as determinative. In PCP 2010/2, the Panel consulted, amongst other things, on raising the minimum acceptance condition threshold. In Panel Statement 2010/22, the Panel confirmed that respondents were almost unanimously opposed to raising the minimum acceptance threshold on the basis that it is inextricably linked to the threshold for passing an ordinary resolution (which itself would enable Board changes to be made).

Note 1 on Rule 10 envisages that there can be certain exceptional circumstances where Rule 10 can be waived, but it would be important to consult the Panel at the earliest stage in such a situation. If an offeror wished to acquire less than 50% it might consider the alternative of making a partial offer under Rule 36 (see Ch.5).

For the purposes of the acceptance condition, Note 2 on Rule 10 requires the offeror to take account of all shares carrying voting rights which are unconditionally allotted or issued before the offer becomes or is declared unconditional as to acceptances. By implication it does not allow the condition to take into account shares which can be issued as a result of conversion rights or options being exercised after the offer closes. It is a common feature of conversion rights and share option schemes that they can be exercised in connection with a takeover and normally these rights will persist for a period after the offer closes.

The difficulties which this can cause were illustrated in the Boots offer for Ward White in 1989. Ward White had a class of convertible preference shares which, if fully converted, would have increased the ordinary share capital of Ward White by more than 40%. Boots made offers, each subject to a separate acceptance condition, for both the convertible preference shares and the ordinary shares. The last date for lodging conversion notices was the day before the last day on which Boots could (by virtue of Rule 31.6) declare its offers unconditional as to acceptances (failing which declaration its bids would have to lapse). The question arose as to whether ordinary shares which would in due course be allotted on conversion, but which could not yet be allotted, should or should not be taken into account in deciding whether the acceptance condition in the offer for the ordinary shares was satisfied. A decision either way could have produced a bizarre result, depending upon patterns of exercise of the conversion rights which could not be known when the Panel had to make its decision. The difficulties inherent in deciding which approach was preferable were indicated by the fact that the Panel Executive's ruling was reversed by the full Panel on appeal, who decided that the literal interpretation of Note 2 on Rule 10 should be followed and that only ordinary shares actually allotted could be taken into account.

This ruling (Panel Statement 1989/15) means it is important that offerors carefully consider all potential subscription and conversion rights when framing and deciding upon the timing of their offers. In order to ensure that an offeror has sufficient information for this purpose, Note 3 on Rule 10 requires the offeree company to provide all such information to an offeror on request.

Given the number of respects in which a 50% plus one share level of acceptances triggers actions under the Code, and also the psychological effect of an offeror announcing that it has achieved over 50% acceptances, the Panel attaches considerable importance to the verification of acceptances. In 1988, Blue Circle declared its bid for Birmid Qualcast unconditional as to acceptances when it thought it had attained that level, but in fact had not done so because of a mistaken double counting. In the aftermath of that bid the Panel introduced a number of detailed provisions relating to the verification of acceptances, which are set out in the Notes on Rule 10 and in the Receiving Agents' Code of Practice set out in Appendix 4 to the Code.

One feature of these provisions is that an offeror's receiving agent can only treat an acceptance in respect of certificated shares as valid if it is accompanied by the relevant share certificate, or in the absence of such a certificate, specified confirmatory documentation. This Rule reflects the basic equitable principle that a vendor's inability to produce his or her share certificate puts his or her purchaser on notice that there might be inconsistent proprietary rights. In the case of shares held through CREST, proof of ownership of shares in dematerialised form is provided electronically to the offeror's receiving agent.

Notwithstanding that Rule 10 only requires a 50% acceptance condition, it is usual for offer documents to specify a level of 90% of the shares to which the offer relates in the acceptance condition. This level is chosen because it is the threshold at which the compulsory purchase provisions of Ch.3, Pt 28 of the Companies Act 2006 can apply. Attainment of that level also facilitates the conversion of the offeree company to a private company, able to take advantage of the more liberal regime in UK companies legislation for private companies, following completion of the takeover. However, such conditions retain to the offeror the right to waive that condition down to a lower level, subject to the Rule 10 minimum of over 50%. An offeror may choose to declare the offer unconditional as to acceptances once the 50% plus one share level has been obtained so as to accelerate further acceptances, although this is very much a tactical consideration. For example, financiers of a bid (particularly where the bid is highly leveraged, such as in most MBOs) may require a guarantee and supporting charges from the offeree company; this can only be given after the offeree has become a private company and is no longer subject to the financial assistance prohibition applicable to public companies under the Companies Act 2006. Generally speaking, it is necessary to be certain that the compulsory purchase provisions can be activated to achieve this, and in such cases it may not be possible to waive the 90% level (this is because the holders of 5% or more of the offeree company could in theory apply to the court for cancellation of any special resolution passed to convert the offeree into a private company). Another possibility might be where the offeree company is in financial or other difficulty and unfettered control is considered necessary.

Where an offer includes shares held by the offeree company in treasury, the offeree company is not permitted to accept the offer until after it has become unconditional as to acceptances (Rule 4.5), so treasury shares cannot be used to meet the acceptance condition.

Rule 10 does not apply to an offer effected by way of a scheme of arrangement. This is because schemes of arrangement do not involve approval by individual shareholders; instead they require approval by offeree shareholders being a majority in number of those voting, representing at least 75% in nominal value of shares voted, at a shareholders' meeting at which only independent shareholders may vote, with subsequent sanction by the court. Once a scheme has obtained shareholder approval and court sanction and has become effective, all offeree shareholders are bound so that the issues referred to above relating to non-accepting shareholders do not apply.

4.3.3 Other conditions

Offer documents in voluntary bids usually contain very detailed conditions. They need to be identified at the earliest stage, since Rule 2.7(c)(iii) requires all conditions to be specified when a firm intention to make an offer is announced.

These conditions generally fall into three categories, namely those:

1. requiring specific action in order to enable the offer to proceed;
2. concerning possible governmental action or regulatory action which might be triggered by the offer; and
3. giving the offeror the opportunity to withdraw if there is material adverse change in relation to the offeree company.

4.3.3.1 *Conditions requiring specific action*

If the takeover is a Class 1 transaction for the offeror, or if an offeror is offering shares and its directors' share issuing powers are insufficient to implement the offer, the offeror will have to make its offer conditional upon the necessary resolutions of its own shareholders.

It is standard practice for offeror shareholder resolutions to approve not only the offer but also any increased or revised offer approved by the offeror's board. This is both to give the offeror flexibility and because the Code timetable might render it impracticable to convene another general meeting to seek further shareholder approval. However, under the UKLA's Listing Rules, a further shareholder authority will be required where the takeover constitutes a Class 1 transaction for the offeror and it proposes to increase the consideration payable under the offer by 10% or more or make any other material change to the terms of the transaction.

Where listed offeror shares are to be issued by way of consideration, a condition relating to their admission to listing will have to be included. Where a cash bid is being financed by the issue of offeror securities, the bid must only be conditional on matters that are necessary, as a matter of law or regulatory requirement, to issue those securities (Rule 13.4). Generally the only permissible conditions will be the passing of any necessary shareholder resolution and listing of the securities. It will not be appropriate, therefore, for the offer to be conditional upon any placing, underpinning or underwriting agreement in relation to the issue of the new securities becoming unconditional and/or not being terminated. A condition of this nature is not necessary as a matter of law or regulatory requirement in order to issue the new securities or, therefore, to implement the offer. Panel Practice Statement 10 notes that, where an offer (which was to be financed by the issue of offeror securities) lapses or is withdrawn as a result of a failure to fulfil a condition relating to the issue of securities, the Panel will want to be satisfied that on announcement, the offeror and its financial adviser had every reason to believe that it could, and would continue to be able to, implement the offer (in accordance with Rule 2.7(a)). The Panel will also want to be satisfied that the offeror used all reasonable efforts to ensure the satisfaction of the condition as required by Rule 13.5(b).

When the offer is conditional on an offeror shareholder approval, as a result of a change in circumstances the offeror directors may determine that they are no longer able to recommend that shareholders approve the necessary resolution. In those circumstances the Panel will be concerned to ensure that, in making the bid, the offeror complied with the provisions of General Principle 5 and Rule 2.7(a) and had given the proposed offer careful and responsible consideration before announcement and having done so had no reason to believe it would not be able to implement it. Subject to this, the Panel may, in appropriate circumstances, agree to the bid being withdrawn (such as in AbbVie's offer for Shire which lapsed in 2014 or Hammerson's offer for Intu Properties which lapsed in 2018) or, with the consent of the target, to a revised and lower bid (such as in the 2008 bid by Lloyds TSB for HBOS).

If the offeree company has already put proposals to its own shareholders to approve another transaction, it is permissible to make it a condition of the bid that the proposals are approved, or alternatively voted down. If such a transaction is proposed by the offeree company's board to its shareholders after the bid is announced, this situation will normally be covered by one of the conditions referred to in 4.3.3.3 below.

If the offeree company's Articles of Association contain restrictions on the ownership of shares, these will need to be amended before the bid can be completed.

4.3.3.2 *Regulatory matters*

Where some form of licence is fundamental to the offeree company's business, the confirmation of the relevant regulatory authority's approval to the change of control is usually made a specific condition.

Bids will usually contain a condition about merger clearance from the UK or, where relevant, EU competition authorities (a condition which supplements the Rule 12 term referred to in 4.4 below) and those involving an important US dimension will refer to the expiry of all US antitrust waiting periods.

Such specific provisions are usually backed up by more general provisions referring to all necessary official authorisations being obtained and no adverse regulatory action being taken (noting more than 140 jurisdictions now have some form of merger control regime). Such regulatory action, particularly when taken overseas, is in many ways analogous to the situation which can arise in relation to a UK or EU reference for an in-depth competition investigation. There is, however, an important difference between what happens to a bid if there is a reference to competition authorities of the kind envisaged in Rule 12 and what happens if there is a reference to a regulatory authority only covered by the more general condition. This is because, if a bid lapses as a result of a "Rule 12 reference", the offeror must normally clarify its intentions (by either announcing a firm intention to make an offer or making a no bid statement) within 21 days of obtaining merger clearance from the UK or EU competition authorities, whereas if an offeror lapses its offer because of another type of regulatory reference it is precluded by Rule 35.1 from (amongst other things) re-bidding within 12 months unless the Panel gives it dispensation.

This distinction did not make any difference in the 1989 Hoylake bid for BAT. BAT had an insurance subsidiary in the US and various US regulatory reviews were instituted, as a result of which Hoylake had to lapse its bid. The regulatory procedures having been completed, Hoylake requested Rule 35.1 dispensation in order to re-bid. This was given (Panel Statements 1989/20 and 1989/21) on the basis that the new bid would have to follow exactly the same shortened timetable as applies when a bid which has lapsed under Rule 12 is remade. The analogy with the Rule 12 situation was clear in this bid, but may not always be so; Note (b) on Rules 35.1 and 35.2 encourages reference to the Panel as soon as possible where there may be delays in obtaining material official authorisations or regulatory clearances relating to an offer.

Another important distinction is that, under Rule 13.2, the restrictions on invoking conditions referred to in 4.3.4 below will not apply to UK or EU competition conditions (and this is not proposed to change following Brexit – see RS 2018/2). This means that a bidder may invoke such a condition without restriction, whereas in invoking a regulatory condition a bidder will have to comply with the materiality test contained in Rule 13.5. In light of this, it is not unusual for target companies to seek to agree the terms of what might be satisfactory clearance with the bidder such that the bidder will effectively be obliged to proceed or otherwise face paying a break fee to the target.

4.3.3.3 *Material change in circumstances conditions*

Such conditions perform a very important function, at least in theory, because (if the offeror cannot lapse its bid under the acceptance condition or Rule 12) they give the offeror its only opportunity to walk away from the bid if it finds something seriously amiss with the offeree company's business in the course of the takeover. It has no opportunity to extract warranties, and where the bid is not recommended will have had no opportunity to conduct a due diligence exercise other than on the basis of publicly available information. Further, an offeree company is likely to publish more information during the course of a takeover bid than it would normally do—indeed it is obliged by General Principle 2 and Rule 23 to give shareholders sufficient information to enable them to reach a properly informed decision on the bid and not to withhold relevant information from them. Apart from this, offeree companies can become subjected to heavy press scrutiny. Much about the offeree's business will therefore become public knowledge during the course of the bid, and if the information is bad news the offeror will want the opportunity to withdraw.

Material change conditions will usually cover a number of situations, including transactions outside the ordinary course of business, litigation, the discovery of provisions of loan documents or contractual obligations which would restrict completion of the bid or affect the offeree company's business and compliance with environmental laws.

The words "material" and "adverse" appear with some regularity in these conditions, as they do in certain regulatory conditions. This, and indeed the general approach to regulatory and material change conditions, is governed by two requirements of Rule 13. The first of these requirements is that an offer must not normally be subject to conditions which depend solely on subjective judgments by the offeror or its directors or the fulfilment of which is in their hands (Rule 13.1). It is acknowledged in the Rule that elements of subjectivity are unavoidable in certain circumstances (for instance, in connection with regulatory clearances), but it is clear that the Panel will expect to be consulted unless such conditions follow the usual form. The second requirement is covered in 4.3.4 below.

4.3.4 *Invoking conditions*

Rule 13.5 provides that an offeror should not invoke a condition (other than an acceptance condition or a condition included pursuant to Rule 12) so as to cause its offer to lapse or to be withdrawn unless the circumstances which give rise to a right to invoke the condition are of material significance to the offeror in the context of the offer.

211

The issue was considered in detail by the Panel in connection with the offer by WPP for Tempus (Panel Statement 2001/15). The Panel met on 31 October 2001 to hear an appeal by WPP against the Panel Executive's refusal to allow WPP to invoke the material adverse change condition in relation to its offer for Tempus. WPP was of the view that there had been a material adverse change in the prospects of Tempus after the announcement of WPP's offer and, in particular, following the events in the US on 11 September 2001.

It was agreed between the parties that the issue for the Panel was whether WPP had established that there had been a material adverse change in the prospects of Tempus which was of material significance to WPP in the context of its offer for Tempus. There was disagreement, however, about the definition of "material" for these purposes.

The Panel received submissions in relation to the various commercial issues, including in relation to the prospects of Tempus and its profitability. The Panel also had regard to the rationale for the acquisition as expressed in the WPP offering documentation.

As regards "materiality" the Panel took the view that meeting the test specified in the Code requires an adverse change of very considerable significance striking at the heart of the purpose of the transaction in question, analogous to something that would justify frustration of a legal contract. The Panel took the view that to accept a lower test would allow an offeror to use a material adverse change condition to defeat the object of the Code Rules and previously expressed Panel policy. The Panel, accordingly, did not accept the test proposed by WPP that it is sufficient if there has been "a change which undermines, from the offeror's perspective, the rationale for having made the offer at the price and on the terms specified".

The Panel did consider that a change in general economic circumstances may legitimately be relied upon when seeking to invoke the relevant condition, but only if and to the extent that the requirements mentioned above are met.

The Panel's conclusion is worth noting:

> "For an offeror to invoke a material adverse change condition and so withdraw its offer requires, in the opinion of the Panel, the offeror to demonstrate to the Panel that exceptional circumstances have arisen affecting the offeree company which could not have reasonably been foreseen at the time of the announcement of the offer. The effect of the circumstances in point must be sufficiently adverse to meet the high test of materiality [mentioned above] and judged, at least in the present type of case, not in terms of short-term profitability but on their effect on the longer-term prospects of the offeree company. Indeed, as WPP made clear it was the longer-term prospects of Tempus which had provided the strategic rationale for the offer and this seemed to the Panel to be central to the value which WPP placed on Tempus at that time.
>
> The Panel considered the submissions of the parties and the arguments they made at the time of the hearing, including but not limited to the basis of the attempts to predict the future profits of Tempus, the longer term effects of the events of September 11 on Tempus, the general economic decline affecting the advertising industry before and after the posting of the offer and the strategic reasons for WPP's offer for Tempus. The Panel came to the conclusion, on the evidence before it, that WPP had failed to demonstrate that … there was a material adverse change in the context of the bid such as to entitle them to invoke the material adverse change condition, and had so failed by a considerable margin. The appeal, therefore, failed."

WPP's arguments would not have been assisted by the market purchases of Tempus shares which it made on 17 September. However, the Panel's ruling is not based on those purchases.

The Panel Executive issued Practice Statement No.5 in April 2004 which clarified the statement it had made that the test of "material significance" required an adverse change that was "analogous ... to something that would justify frustration of a legal contract". Some practitioners had interpreted this to mean that an offeror would need to demonstrate legal frustration in order to be able to invoke a condition to an offer. The Panel Executive subsequently confirmed that although the standard required is high, it does not require the offeror to demonstrate frustration in the legal sense.

In August 2004 the Code Committee issued Panel Consultation Paper 2004/4 which contained a number of proposed changes to the Code relating to conditions. In this paper the Code Committee considered whether the strict test for invoking conditions contained in Note 2 on Rule 13 (now Rule 13.5) should apply to bespoke conditions, which may have been heavily negotiated between the offeror and the offeree. Although the Code Committee concluded that Note 2 on Rule 13 should apply in all cases, a new Note on Rule 13 was proposed which would make it clear that in determining whether a condition can be invoked the Panel should be able to take account of whether or not the condition was the subject of negotiation, whether the condition was expressly drawn to the offeree company shareholders' attention in the offer document and its consequences clearly explained and whether the condition was included to take account of the particular nature of the business of the offeree company. This proposal was, however, withdrawn by the Code Committee following consultation, largely on the basis that inclusion of a list of specific factors to be taken into account might result in undue weight being given to those factors. Nevertheless, the Committee reiterated that the factors listed above remain of general relevance.

An example of where the Panel did allow an offeror to invoke a condition under Rule 13.5(a) so as to lapse its offer was the Pension Corporation's bid for Telent which was announced in September 2007. In this case the offeror included in its offer a condition that no changes had been made to any relevant pension schemes. As well as being included with the other conditions in an appendix to the offer document, the condition (unlike any of the other conditions) was expressly referred to and brought to offeree shareholders' attention in the main body of the offer document. In the event, the Pensions Regulator replaced the trustees to the offeree's pension scheme with three of its own choice who could not be removed for six months. The replacement of the trustees could have been an obstacle to restructuring the pension scheme, which included a significant sum in an escrow account (more than the total value of the bid) and in these circumstances the Panel permitted the offeror to withdraw its offer (although in fact the offer was not ultimately withdrawn). Such examples are very rare and are likely to depend on the extent to which the factors referred to above are met in the particular circumstances.

An offeror is obliged to use all reasonable efforts to ensure the satisfaction of the conditions to its offer (Rule 13.5(b)). This is to prevent an offeror seeking to cause a condition which is not subject to a materiality threshold (such as a condition included pursuant to Rule 12) not to be satisfied in order to lapse a bid where the offeror would be unable to rely on a material adverse change condition or other protective condition to do so.

The Panel Executive issued a further practice statement in April 2005 (Practice Statement No.11) regarding the acceptability of offer conditions relating to the working capital requirements of the enlarged offeror group after the completion of an offer. The Executive clarified that an offeror will not, other than in exceptional circumstances (such as those described in Rule 13.4(c) of the Code in relation to financing pre-conditions), be permitted to include such a condition to its offer and, if working capital concerns arise after announcement of the offer, the offeror will only be able to allow its offer to lapse if it is able to invoke one of the conditions to the offer in accordance with the application of Rule 13.5(a).

In some circumstances an offer will include conditions relating to the offeror which benefit the offeree company (known as "offeree protection conditions"), as well as standard conditions which benefit the offeror. Offeree protection conditions are generally only found in securities exchange offers, particularly where the offeror and offeree company are of a similar size. Under Rule 13.1, such conditions will not normally be permitted where they depend solely on subjective judgments by the offeree or its directors or where the fulfilment of such conditions is in their hands. Rule 13.6 provides that an offeree company should not invoke (or cause or permit the offeror to invoke) any condition to an offer unless the circumstances which give rise to the right to invoke the condition are of material significance to the shareholders of the offeree company in the context of the offer. Note 1 on that Rule makes it clear, however, that the circumstances in which the Panel may permit an offeree company to invoke (or cause or permit the offeror to invoke) a condition are not necessarily the same as those in which an offeror would be permitted to invoke a condition. The Panel retains flexibility to consider each case on its merits, taking into account the circumstances. Rather than simply having to decide whether an offer should lapse or not, Note 2 on Rule 13.6 (which does not apply to an offer implemented by way of a scheme of arrangement) provides that the Panel should also have the flexibility to require, as an alternative, the introduction of withdrawal rights, so that shareholders who had accepted the relevant offer would be given a period of time to withdraw their acceptance.

Rule 35.1 reinforces Rule 13, in that an offeror which lapses its offer will, subject to certain exceptions set out in the Notes on Rule 35, have to wait a year before (amongst other things) bidding again.

As an illustrative example of the Panel's attitude to such situations, in 1995 the Panel was asked to permit Trafalgar House to make a new bid for Northern Electric following its decision to lapse its offer following a substantial fall in the market value of the Regional Electricity Companies as a result of a statement by Professor Littlechild, the Director General of the Office of Electricity Regulation. At the time it decided to lapse Trafalgar House held 76% acceptances.

Trafalgar House submitted that the circumstances were so exceptional as to justify the Panel permitting a new offer. It contended that shareholder interests would best be served by a new offer. There was substantial shareholder support for a new offer. The Northern Electric Board stated it would not agree to a new offer until the regulatory uncertainty was removed. The Panel refused to consent to Trafalgar launching a new bid. Although unusual, the circumstances did not justify the granting of a dispensation under Rule 35.

4.4 Competition law issues

Offerors also have to consider the possible application of competition laws—in particular, UK merger control under the Enterprise Act 2002 and EU merger control under the EU Merger Regulation, Regulation 139/2004.[6] The application of any merger control rules will at the very least have an impact on the timetable, especially if a Phase 2 investigation is opened by the UK or EU competition authorities.[7]

There are specific jurisdictional tests for determining whether these merger control rules apply. The UK test is based on the UK turnover of the offeree company or the parties' shares of supply of a particular good or service in, or in a substantial part of, the UK. The EU test is based on the parties' turnovers derived worldwide, within the EU and within the individual EU Member States. A transaction may fall under either set of rules (and in limited circumstances under both[8]). Generally, if the transaction falls within the scope of the EU merger control

---

[6] OJ [2004] L24/1.

[7] The Code only specifically deals with UK and EU merger control (competition/antitrust) regimes which are dealt with under Rule 12 as discussed below. If such regimes in other jurisdictions are relevant, these will be dealt with in separate condition(s) which will be subject to the provisions of Rule 13. See further 4.3.3.2 above.

[8] In the event of Brexit, there will be much greater scope for transactions to be subject to parallel reviews by both the CMA in the UK under the UK merger control rules and the European Commission under the EU rules given the EU Merger Regulation will no longer apply to the UK (although the exact timing of this change may depend on any applicable implementation period).

217

rules, the European Commission is granted exclusive jurisdiction over the transaction, thereby precluding examination by the national competition authorities in the individual EU Member States. However, there are two exceptions, one of which allows the merger to be referred back to the national competition authorities and the other of which enables them to take parallel jurisdiction over certain aspects of the transaction. In limited circumstances, the European Commission may also be requested to review a transaction over which it does not otherwise have jurisdiction, instead of the national competition authorities.

Rule 12 requires every offer to which either of these competition regimes might be relevant to contain a term whereby it will lapse if, before the first closing date or the date when the offer becomes or is declared unconditional as to acceptances, whichever is the later (or, in the case of an offer implemented by way of a scheme of arrangement, before the shareholder meeting or meetings which will need to be held to approve the scheme):

1. the merger is referred to a Phase 2 investigation by the CMA in the UK; or
2. the European Commission initiates Phase 2 proceedings under the EU Merger Regulation, or refers the merger back to the UK and it is then referred to a Phase 2 investigation by the CMA.[9]

Both UK and EU competition authorities are subject to timetables within which decisions on whether an in-depth competition investigation is to be opened must be taken. These timetables do not necessarily tie in with the first closing date. Both authorities are well aware of the timetabling constraints

---

[9] For minor changes to be made to Rule 12 in the event of Brexit, see RS 2018/2. These changes are intended to reflect the fact that, once the UK has withdrawn from the EU and is outside the EU Merger Regulation regime, the European Commission will no longer be able to refer a matter back to the CMA pursuant to the EU Merger Regulation as is currently contemplated by Rules 12.1(b) and (c). As a result, references to such a referral will be deleted and the rule will simply refer to there being a Phase 2 CMA reference or the initiation of Phase 2 proceedings by the European Commission.

of the Code, but cannot always meet them. If there is a delay the Panel will usually "freeze" the bid timetable at the request of either the offeror or the offeree company (Rule 31.6(a)(iii)). If the competition authority concerned subsequently decides not to refer the transaction for a Phase 2 investigation, Note 5 on Rule 31.6 provides that the bid timetable will normally start again on the second day following the announcement of such decision.

If there is a Phase 2 investigation by either the UK or EU competition authorities, the offer must lapse (unless announced subject to a pre-condition relating to merger control clearance—see below) and there will usually be a lengthy period whilst the competition determination is being made (Rule 12.2(a)). The underlying aims of the Code in such circumstances are to acknowledge that an offeror subject to such an investigation is in a similar position to a "potential offeror", to prevent a continuation of an offer campaign during this period and to ensure equality of information amongst competing offerors. During this period Rule 21.1 continues to apply, with limited exceptions (Note 4 on Rule 21.1). The requirements of the Code relating to the release of information by either the offeror or the offeree do not normally continue to apply, but Rule 19.7 provides that the Panel may require any statements made during the competition reference period to be substantiated or, if this is not possible, withdrawn if the merger is subsequently cleared by the competition authorities and a further offer is made. Note 2 on Rule 12.2 sets out the other provisions of the Code which remain relevant, in most cases with some specific modifications. Where an offer was announced subject to a pre-condition relating to merger control clearance, the offer period will generally continue if there is a Phase 2 competition investigation, with the Code applying in the usual way, although Note 3 on Rule 12.2 provides that the Panel may grant dispensations from the applicable Rules if it would be proportionate in the circumstances to do so.

If the offer period ends under Rule 12.2(a) but the merger is cleared at the end of the in-depth competition investigation, Rule 12.2(b)(ii) provides that the offeror may make a new offer provided that it does so within 21 days after the announcement of the clearance decision. If the merger is prohibited, Rule 12.2(b)(iii) will prevent the offeror, together with any person acting in concert with it, from, inter alia, making a new offer for six months from the date of the decision except with the Panel's consent.

Chapter 5

Provisions Applicable to all Offers, Partial Offers and Redemption or Purchase by a Company of its Own Securities

Seth Jones
Partner
Allen & Overy LLP

5.1 Introduction

This Chapter deals with three sections of the Takeover Code:

1. provisions applicable to all offers (Section H);
2. partial offers (Section P); and
3. redemption or purchase by a company of its own securities (Section Q).

The Rules of the Code, like the General Principles, are applied by the Panel in accordance with their spirit to achieve their underlying purpose. In order to understand the practical application of the Rules, it is therefore important to appreciate the spirit or philosophy underlying the particular Rules, and not just the precise wording used. A common purpose of the three sections covered by this Chapter is to ensure that the offeree company shareholders are treated fairly and that shareholders of the same class are afforded equivalent treatment. This reflects General Principle 1 and is one of the principal purposes of the Code.

5.2 Provisions applicable to all offers

Section H of the Code falls into two parts:

1. a substantive part, comprising Rules to ensure equivalent treatment (Rules 14–16); and
2. an administrative part, comprising Rules on the timing and content of announcements of acceptance levels and provisions relating to proxy forms (Rules 17 and 18).

5.2.1 Equivalent treatment

Rule 14 contains requirements for comparable offers where there is more than one class of equity share capital. Rule 15 requires an appropriate offer to be made for convertible securities (including warrants and options). Rule 16 prohibits special deals being made with certain shareholders (or other persons interested in shares carrying voting rights) which offer them favourable conditions. Rule 16 also contains requirements relating to management incentive arrangements.

5.2.1.1 Rule 14: Comparable offers for different classes of equity

Rule 14.1 provides that, where an offeree company has more than one class of equity share capital, the offeror must make a comparable offer for each class, whether such class carries voting rights or not. If, however, an offer is made for non-voting shares only, it is not necessary to make an offer also for the voting class. This reflects the fact that the Code is principally concerned with the acquisition of voting control. The Panel requires prior consultation in all Rule 14 cases.

5.2.1.1.1 The meaning of "equity share capital"

If shares have uncapped rights to either dividends or capital, they will be equity share capital for the purposes of s.548 of the Companies Act 2006. The Code acknowledges, however, that the requirement to make a comparable offer need not apply to shares which are equity only on technical grounds. For instance, some shares which are designed to be equity share capital under the Companies Act may have very limited equity rights. Unless a company is in financial difficulties, and there is a real possibility of a winding up, the existence or otherwise of uncapped rights to dividends (as opposed to capital) is likely to be the most relevant factor. If, for example, these rights are subject to the company first having to make an unrealistic level of profits (making the shares so-called "technical equity" only), the Panel may decide not to regard the shares as equity for the purposes of Rule 14.1.

5.2.1.1.2   Conditionality

In order to save holders of non-voting (or limited voting) equity shares from being "stranded" because of low acceptances for that class, Rule 14.1 states that an offer for such shares should not be conditional upon any particular level of acceptances in respect of the class in question, or on the approval of that class, unless the offer for the voting equity is also conditional on the success of the offer for the non-voting (or limited voting) equity. Therefore, an offeror will often wish to include an acceptance condition for the non-voting equity in the conditions of the offer for the voting equity. The Code does not expressly prevent the offer for the non-voting equity share capital from being made subject to other conditions which are different and independent from those in the voting equity offer. Rule 14.2 provides that separate offers must be made for each class of shares.

5.2.1.1.3   Different classes of equity

In the case of certain companies, there may be one class of voting equity shares and another class of non-voting equity shares, or only limited voting, or perhaps weighted voting, equity shares.

There are a number of companies whose shares are admitted to trading on a UK regulated market (such as the Main Market of the London Stock Exchange) or multilateral trading facility (such as AIM) and which have two or more classes of publicly quoted equity shares. However, the Code applies more broadly to all public companies (including those without securities admitted to trading on a relevant public market), as well as to certain private companies where there has been certain public involvement in the previous 10 years, if they are registered in the UK, the Channel Islands, or the Isle of Man and have their place of central management and control in one of those jurisdictions—see s.3(a) of the Introduction to the Code, and also Response Statement 2012/3 for a synopsis of the types of company which are subject to the Code. There is, therefore, considerable scope for the potential application of Rule 14.

Over the years, there have been a number of offers for companies with two or more classes of equity shares. Recent examples include the competing offers by Severn Trent and Ancala for Dee Valley Group in November 2016, where offers were made for both the ordinary voting shares and the ordinary non-voting shares.

The question of whether separate classes of share existed arose in connection with the Eurotunnel restructuring in 2007. In that case, the same offer was made to those Eurotunnel shareholders who were entitled to travel privileges on Eurotunnel as was made to shareholders who did not have any travel privileges. The shareholders who had travel privileges argued that this amounted to a breach of General Principle 1 (on the basis that they would lose their privileges if they accepted the offer, whereas other shareholders would not be so affected) and also Rule 14 (on the basis that their shares were a separate class for this purpose and should therefore have received a separate offer). Both the Panel Executive and the Hearings Committee rejected these arguments, and certain of the shareholders appealed to the Takeover Appeal Board. The Board rejected the appeal on the basis that the travel privileges were personal rights and were not attached to or an integral part of the share rights. Accordingly, there was found to be no separate class and therefore no requirement for separate offers (see Takeover Appeal Board Statement 2007/2).

5.2.1.1.4   What is a "comparable" offer?

Where an offeree company does have more than one class of equity shares, it will be necessary to determine what is a "comparable" offer for the purposes of Rule 14.1. A number of questions will arise. For instance, where there are differing voting rights, should the offeror give a premium for voting control and, if so, how much? Can it offer a different type of consideration, such as shares or other paper for one class and cash for the other?

The Code sets down a method of assessing the comparability of offers involving two or more classes of equity share capital where the prices for all the classes involved are published in the Daily Official List. It states that the ratio of the offer values for the different classes should normally be equal to the average of the ratios of the middle market quotations taken from the Daily Official List over the course of the six months preceding commencement of the offer period. The Panel will not normally allow any other ratio to be used unless the advisers to the offeror and the offeree company are jointly able to justify it. Thus, in practice, an alternative ratio is likely to be difficult to apply other than in the context of a recommended bid.

If prices for one or more of the classes are not published in the Daily Official List, no specific guidance is given. Instead, the Code requires that the ratio of the offer values must be justified to the Panel in advance. This is what happened, for example, in the recommended offers by American Express for Sharepeople Group (an unlisted company), made in December 2000, where the offeror was able to justify to the Panel the proposed ratio of the offer values as between the offeree company's ordinary shares and two classes of preference shares, which were both treated as equity. It is no doubt easier to justify a ratio to the Panel where the offers are recommended by the offeree company's directors, and supported by its independent financial adviser, than where they are hostile.

The Code also does not provide any guidance on the question of comparability in the type of consideration under offer, save to say that a comparable offer need not necessarily be an identical offer. In practice, an offeror may find it difficult to persuade the Panel that one type of consideration (for example cash) can be offered to the holders of one class of equity and another type of consideration (for example securities) be offered to the holders of another class.

5.2.1.1.5 Interaction with other Rules

Finally, it should be noted that, although Rule 14 does not require comparable offers to be made for non-voting, non-equity share capital, offers for non-equity securities may be required under Rule 15 (see 5.2.1.2 below) if, for example, they are convertible into equity shares.

5.2.1.2 *Rule 15: Appropriate offers for convertibles, options etc*

If an offer is made for voting equity share capital or for other transferable securities carrying voting rights (the voting equity offer) and the offeree company also has in issue securities which are convertible into, or which comprise options or other rights to subscribe for, securities to which the voting equity offer relates (Rule 15 securities), Rule 15 requires an appropriate offer (or proposal) to be made for those Rule 15 securities. The purpose of Rule 15 is to safeguard the interests of the holders of Rule 15 securities in their capacity as potential holders of the shares to which the voting equity offer relates. The Executive's interpretation and application of certain of the provisions of Rule 15 is the subject of a practice statement (see Practice Statement No.24 in relation to appropriate offers and proposals under Rule 15).

5.2.1.2.1 What is an "appropriate" offer or proposal?

The Code does not elaborate on what is meant by "appropriate" but informal guidance is contained in Practice Statement No.24. In order to be "appropriate", the Executive considers that a Rule 15 offer or proposal should be for no less than the "see through" price—i.e. the price which would be payable under the main voting equity offer for any shares which would arise from the exercise of the conversion, option or subscription rights, less a deduction for any price payable on the exercise of such rights.

As convertible securities do not have an exercise price, their see through value will always be positive. Therefore, an offer or proposal at no less than the see through value will always be required for convertible securities, even if it would be below their market price. Where the market price (if any) of any Rule 15 securities is higher than their see through value (for example, where a convertible security may be trading as a fixed income security), the Executive does not require the Rule 15 offer or proposal to be at market price or above.

As with Rule 15 offers and proposals generally, the terms offered or proposed in relation to convertible securities may nonetheless be more generous than simple see through. For example, where the conversion terms are less attractive to holders than redeeming the convertible bonds at par, the Panel will usually agree that a proposal to redeem the convertible bonds in accordance with their terms is sufficient for Rule 15 purposes and that no separate offer or proposal is necessary.

In the case of Vista Funds' recommended acquisition of Misys in April 2012, the conversion terms in relation to Misys' convertible bonds were more attractive to holders than a redemption of their bonds at par (plus accrued interest) and the offeror therefore made a separate cash offer for the bonds in accordance with Rule 15. Under the convertible bond offer, bondholders were entitled to receive a cash payment equivalent to the amount a converting bondholder would have received if the bondholder had converted its bonds at the enhanced conversion price applicable on a change of control (under the terms of the bonds) and been entitled to the same cash consideration for the resulting shares under the terms of the main voting equity offer.

Similarly, in May 2019, Connect Bidco (being a consortium vehicle owned by funds advised by Apax and other investors) made a Rule 15 proposal to holders of convertible bonds in connection with Connect Bidco's recommended offer for Inmarsat. Under the terms of the Rule 15 proposal, accepting bondholders would receive US$305,215.35 in cash for each US$200,000 in principal amount of Inmarsat convertible bonds, which was equal to the amount a bondholder would receive if the holder converted its bonds at the change of control conversion price under the terms of the bonds and received: (i) the cash to which such holder would be entitled upon conversion; and (ii) an amount equal to the cash consideration under the main equity offer.

In the case of Vodafone's recommended acquisition of Cable & Wireless Worldwide in May 2012, Vodafone also made a separate cash offer for C&W's convertible bonds in accordance with Rule 15. Under Vodafone's convertible bond offer, C&W bondholders were entitled to receive an amount equal to the value of all remaining payments of principal and interest on their bonds up to and including the scheduled maturity date of the bonds, discounted to the settlement date. Bondholders could also exercise their conversion rights and accept the Vodafone offer for their resulting shares, but they were advised that the consideration payable to them under the main voting equity offer was expected to be lower than the consideration which would be payable under the separate convertible bond offer.

So far as other types of Rule 15 security are concerned, if the see through value is zero or would leave a negative figure (for example options that are "out of the money"), no Rule 15 offer or proposal will normally be required so far as the Panel is concerned. See, for example, ESWC's offer for Prologic in March 2012, where no Rule 15 offer or proposal was made in respect of employee share options or warrants to subscribe for Prologic shares as they were all "out of the money". In other cases, however, even if the rights are "out of the money", an offeror may nonetheless want to make an offer in order to encourage holders of the securities to sell out, particularly if their conversion or subscription rights do not lapse at some stage following the voting equity offer. Furthermore, if a takeover offer is made for convertibles or warrants, as a separate class, non-assented securities may be subject to the statutory squeeze-out provisions if sufficient acceptances are received (see 5.2.1.2.3 below).

The Executive does not require any particular form of consideration to be offered to holders of Rule 15 securities, and there is no requirement for them to be offered the same form of consideration as offered under the voting equity offer. One way of making an appropriate offer for Rule 15 securities could be, for example, to offer an equivalent convertible or option in the offeror company.

Equality of treatment is required as between holders of the same class of Rule 15 security (for example option holders in the same scheme), but it is acceptable for there to be different treatment as between holders of different classes and as between such holders and the offeree company shareholders (unless the different treatment is to give particular sharehold-ers a special deal which would contravene Rule 16—see 5.2.1.3 below).

Where the voting equity offer is a securities exchange offer but offeror securities are not being offered to the holders of the Rule 15 securities, the see through value of the Rule 15 securities should normally be calculated by reference to the value of the voting equity offer on the latest practicable date prior to the despatch of the Rule 15 offer or proposal. If offeror securities are also being offered to the holders of Rule 15 securities, the exchange ratio offered to such holders should be no less favourable than that offered under the voting equity offer.

5.2.1.2.2 "Exercise and accept" proposals

If the holders of Rule 15 securities are able to exercise their rights prior to (or on) the voting equity offer becoming wholly unconditional, a proposal that such holders exercise their rights so as to be able to accept the voting equity offer (an "exercise and accept" proposal) is normally regarded as sufficient for Rule 15 purposes.

In the case of Electrabel's recommended offer for International Power (IPR) in May 2012, for example, conversion rights in respect of IPR's three outstanding series of convertible bonds were all currently exercisable and bondholders also benefited from enhanced conversion terms for a limited period after the main voting equity offer (which was implemented by a scheme of arrangement) became effective. Accordingly, Electrabel's basic proposal for Rule 15 purposes was "exercise and accept", and bondholders were also recommended to convert by no later than the end of the special conversion period in order to receive the enhanced conversion terms. As is usual with schemes of arrangement, if conversion rights were exercised after the record time for the scheme, changes to the offeree company's articles of association, which were approved by offeree shareholders at the same time as the scheme, ensured that the resulting shares were automatically transferred to the offeror in exchange for the offer consideration. The terms of the IPR bonds also gave the bondholders a right of redemption (although this was less favourable than "exercise and accept" in the circumstances) and the issuer a squeeze-out right once 85% of the bonds had been converted or purchased and cancelled.

Consideration should be given to the tax consequences, especially for option holders, of exercising their rights and accepting the offer as compared with other forms of proposal, for example cash payments for releasing their rights or the grant of equivalent rights in the offeror. If the rights do not lapse (but will continue to be exercisable in the future), it may be in the interests of the offeror, just as much as the holders of the rights, for proposals to be made to get rid of those rights.

5.2.1.2.3 Timing of a Rule 15 offer or proposal and conditionality

All relevant documents, announcements and other information sent to offeree company shareholders and other persons with information rights in connection with an offer must also, where practicable, be sent at the same time (for information) to the holders of Rule 15 securities. If the terms of the Rule 15 securities enable the holders to exercise their conversion, option or subscription rights during the course of the voting equity offer and to accept the offer following any such exercise, that fact must also be made clear in the relevant documents, announcements and other information.

Rule 15 requires that, wherever practicable, the offer or proposal for the Rule 15 securities should also be despatched at the same time as the main voting equity offer. If this is not practicable (and often it is not in the case of employee share options, particularly in hostile offers where the offeror is unlikely to have full details of the options outstanding), the Panel must be consulted. The Executive will normally expect the Rule 15 offer or proposal to be despatched, at the latest, as soon as possible after the voting equity offer is declared wholly unconditional. In practice, at least so far as employee share options are concerned, the offer document will usually state that proposals will be made to option holders in due course. In the case of a recommended offer, the proposals will typically be made at such time which enables option holders to choose between any alternatives which may be made available under the equity offer and so as to receive any consideration at around the same time as the offer consideration is paid to shareholders under the equity offer. If the offer is hostile, it may be the case that the proposals will be made at or around the time the offer becomes wholly unconditional (see Melrose's proposals to holders of awards under share incentive schemes in connection with its hostile offer for GKN in 2018).

Where the voting equity offer is being implemented by scheme of arrangement, option holder proposals will typically be made at or around the same time that the scheme document is posted to shareholders. This enables the effect of the proposals on the interests of the offeree company directors to be addressed in the explanatory statement sent to shareholders in the scheme document, which is a statutory requirement (see s.897(2) of the Companies Act 2006). It also makes it possible to satisfy the court that option holders' interests have been dealt with, when the court is asked to sanction the scheme, and allows the option holders themselves to exercise their options promptly on the scheme becoming effective.

Rule 15 provides that the offeree company's board must obtain independent advice on the offer or proposal (including if it is simply "exercise and accept"). The substance of this advice must be made known to the holders of the securities in question, together with the board's view. If a number of alternative courses of action are available to the holders of the Rule 15 securities, the Panel expects the board's view to extend to advising on which course of action is recommended. It will sometimes be necessary for at least some of the offeree company's directors to remain in office for a short period after the main voting equity offer is declared wholly unconditional, assuming the offer is successful, so as to give an independent board view on any subsequent Rule 15 offer or proposal. In any event, care should be taken to ensure that the mandate of the independent adviser for Rule 3 purposes extends to advising on any Rule 15 offer or proposal.

To protect individual holders of Rule 15 securities from being "stranded" against their will, the Code provides that the offer or proposal to them should not normally be made conditional on any particular level of acceptances. It is permissible, however, to include a condition in the main voting equity offer requiring a particular level of acceptances under the Rule 15 offer. For example, in the offer for Essar Energy in March 2014, the shares offer was made conditional upon, amongst other things, acceptances being received in respect of not less than 90% of Essar's outstanding convertible bonds pursuant to a separate bonds offer which was itself conditional on the shares offer becoming or being declared unconditional in all respects. The 90% threshold was set on the basis that the offeror could utilise the statutory squeeze-out provisions in Ch.3 of Pt 28 of the Companies Act 2006 in respect of the convertible bonds.

Depending on the terms of the Rule 15 securities in question, it may also be possible to make the Rule 15 proposal by way of a scheme of arrangement to be considered at a meeting of the relevant holders—where the resolution to approve the scheme will require approval by a majority in number of holders present (in person or by proxy) representing 75% or more in value of the relevant securities voted. Normally such a proposal, once approved by the relevant holders and sanctioned by the court, is binding on all the holders of the rights in question. If, however, a Rule 15 proposal put by way of a scheme is not so approved, or not sanctioned by the court, the offeror will be required to make a further Rule 15 offer which is not conditional on any level of acceptances or approval.

A Rule 15 offer or proposal is normally required to be kept open for at least 21 days following the date on which the relevant documentation is sent to the holders of the Rule 15 securities. However, if the only Rule 15 offer or proposal is "exercise and accept", the Executive's normal practice is to require the voting equity offer to remain open for not less than 21 days after the later of the date on which the documentation containing the "exercise and accept" proposal is despatched and the date on which the voting equity offer becomes or is declared wholly unconditional.

5.2.1.2.4   Interaction with other Rules

If an offer for convertible securities is required by Rule 9 or Rule 14, compliance with the relevant Rule will be regarded as satisfying the obligation to make an appropriate offer or proposal under Rule 15.

It is possible for a particular type of share to be both equity, at least in the technical sense, and also convertible (for example a convertible preference share will be treated as equity share capital, for the purposes of s.548 of the Companies Act 2006, if it includes a right to participate in any dividends paid to ordinary shareholders in addition to any preferential dividend right it may also enjoy). In these circumstances, the question arises whether there should be a "comparable" offer under Rule 14 or an "appropriate" offer under Rule 15. This can lead to a significant difference in the required offer value.

A Rule 15 offer or proposal can, as noted above, be made on more favourable terms than the see through value. However, where certain holders of Rule 15 securities are also offeree company shareholders (for example directors or a significant shareholder perhaps), and the proposed Rule 15 offer or proposal is to be made on more generous terms than the see through value, the Executive will be concerned to ensure that the Rule 15 offer or proposal does not have the effect of indirectly giving such holders more favourable treatment than other shareholders in a manner prohibited by Rule 16 (see below).

5.2.1.3 *Rule 16: Special deals and management incentivisation*

Rule 16.1 is founded in General Principle 1 of the Code which provides that all holders of securities of the same class in an offeree company must be afforded equivalent treatment.

Rule 16.1 prohibits an offeror (or persons acting in concert with it) from making arrangements with shareholders or dealing in shares in the offeree company if there are favourable conditions attached which are not extended to all offeree company shareholders. The prohibition applies both during an offer and when one is reasonably in contemplation, and it also extends to entering into arrangements to deal in shares or arrangements which involve acceptance of an offer. It also applies in the six months following a successful offer, during which period Rule 35.3 prohibits a successful offeror from acquiring further shares in the offeree company at a price higher than that available under the offer.

Rule 16.1 also prohibits any arrangement with a person who is interested in shares carrying voting rights in the offeree company (for example a person with a long derivative or option position, who is not necessarily a shareholder) if favourable conditions are attached which are not being extended to all shareholders. There is, however, no requirement for an offeror to extend any offer, or any "special deal" falling within Rule 16.1, to persons who are not shareholders of the offeree company but who have another interest in offeree company shares.

The prohibition on special deals imposed by Rule 16.1 frequently raises difficult issues for both practitioners and the Panel. The Code sets out specific rules and guidance regarding four circumstances which have commonly or historically required consideration under this Rule: top-ups, disposals of offeree company assets and finders' fees (which are expressly dealt with in Notes 1, 2 and 3 respectively on Rule 16.1); and management incentive arrangements (which are dealt with in Rule 16.2).

The Panel Executive has also published a Practice Statement in relation to debt syndication during offer periods which describes, amongst other things, how the provisions of Rule 16 (and Rule 20) may be applicable in this context and the steps that may be taken to avoid breaching the rule in relevant cases (see Practice Statement No.25).

5.2.1.3.1   Top-ups

One sort of special deal which is expressly prohibited is where the offeror buys shares outright but the seller says that he or she wants a top-up if the offeror subsequently pays more under a general offer for the target. Top-ups of this nature were quite common at one time, but now they are prohibited (see Panel Statement 1988/11 for an example of a case where the question of whether such a top-up arrangement existed was under consideration). To enable certain shareholders to be able to hedge their bets (i.e. to realise a cash exit whether or not an offer is made or succeeds but also to get the maximum paid under any offer) would not be treating all shareholders equally. Similarly, the Rule also prohibits shareholders entering into an irrevocable commitment to accept an offer if it is combined with a put option exercisable if the offer fails. However, an offeror may obtain an irrevocable commitment combined with a call option over the shares in question, as the shareholder is not then given a definite exit.

Arrangements made by an offeror with a person acting in concert with it, whereby that person acquires an interest in offeree company shares, are not prohibited provided that the offeror bears all the risks and receives all the benefits and the concert party receives no other benefit (or potential benefit), for example a fee for undertaking the acquisition, beyond normal expenses and carrying costs. In cases of doubt, the Panel should be consulted. Rule 4, which contains certain restrictions on dealings, will also be relevant in these circumstances (see Note 3 on Rules 4.1 and 4.2).

5.2.1.3.2 Disposal of assets

Another way of giving a special deal to a person interested in shares in the offeree company would be to enter into a transaction to dispose of some of the offeree company's assets to such person at a favourable price. To guard against this, Note 2 on Rule 16.1 provides that the Panel will normally consent to these arrangements provided that:

1. the independent adviser to the offeree company publicly states that the terms of the transaction are fair and reasonable; and
2. the offeree company's shareholders give their approval at a general meeting (at this meeting the vote must be a separate vote of independent shareholders and the vote must be taken on a poll).

Accordingly, a disposal of assets in these circumstances is normally only possible in a recommended offer situation.

As stated at the end of Note 2 on Rule 16.1, the Panel will consider allowing such a procedure in respect of other transactions where the issues are similar. An example of this is provided by the offer by Headway Investment Partners for

Ludgate Environmental Fund in December 2016. In connection with the offer, Headway proposed certain amendments to the investment management agreement which was in place between Ludgate and Ludgate Investments (the investment adviser to Ludgate). Since Ludgate Investments (and certain of its related persons) held shares in the offeree company, the Panel required the proposed amendments to be approved by a simple majority of independent Ludgate shareholders. In addition, Ludgate's independent financial adviser stated that it had advised the Ludgate directors that the terms of the proposed amendments were fair and reasonable. Headway made its offer conditional on the approval of the proposed amendments by the independent shareholders under Rule 16, and the resolution was duly passed.

A further example arose on Asia Coal Energy Ventures Ltd's (ACE) offer for Asia Resource Minerals Plc (ARMS) in 2015. Raiffeisen Bank International AG (RBI), the holder of a 23.8% stake in ARMS, entered into an irrevocable undertaking to accept ACE's offer. At the same time, RBI entered into an agreement with ACE to transfer certain loans and security interests to ACE which were unrelated to ARMS. The Panel Executive permitted the arrangement to be entered into provided that the independent financial adviser to ARMS publicly stated that the terms of the transaction were fair and reasonable and that the independent ARMS shareholders approved the transaction at a general meeting, which in the event they did.

In relation to Blackstone's offer for Taliesin Property Fund, announced in December 2017, an agreement was entered into between the offeror and certain offeree company shareholders relating to the transfer to the offeror of entities which provide investment management services to the offeree company. The Panel Executive permitted the arrangement under Rule 16 on the basis that the offeree company's financial adviser publicly stated that, in its opinion, the terms of the transaction were fair and reasonable so far as independent shareholders were concerned and independent shareholders approved the transaction.

A further example arose in relation to the offer by CYBG for Virgin Money in 2018. Virgin Group (the holder of approximately 35% of the shares in Virgin Money) agreed with the bidder to make certain amendments to the trade mark licence between Virgin Group and Virgin Money in relation to the use of the Virgin brand. The Panel permitted this arrangement under Rule 16 subject to a fairness opinion from Virgin Money's financial adviser and the approval of the independent shareholders of Virgin Money.

If a transaction with an offeree company shareholder is agreed after an offer has become unconditional, the Panel may look into it and will want to be satisfied that there was in fact no pre-arrangement. The Panel will be similarly concerned if, for example, more favourable trading arrangements are entered into with shareholders after an offer has become unconditional.

A disposal of certain of the offeror's assets to an offeree shareholder would also need to be considered in terms of Rule 16.

5.2.1.3.3 Finders' fees

If a person interested in shares in the offeree company is paid a finder's fee for the part he or she has played in promoting an offer, this may be a special deal. The Panel will, however, normally permit a finder's fee if the finder's interest in the offeree shares is not substantial (less than 1%, say) and the amount of the fee is not abnormal—that is, it is not more than would have been paid to the finder if he or she was not interested in the offeree company's shares. Finders' fees are now rarely encountered in practice.

5.2.1.3.4 Management incentive arrangements

An offeror will often wish to incentivise the management of the offeree company so that they remain with the enlarged group. This is likely to arise, in particular, in connection with so-called "public to private" transactions involving private equity and other financial investors, as well as management buy-outs

(MBOs) and similar types of transaction, as seen on transactions such as Toscafund and Penta Capital's offer for Daisy Group in 2014 and Carlyle's offer for Nationwide Accident Repair Services in 2015. It can, however, arise in any type of transaction wherever the offeror wishes to retain and incentivise particular members of the offeree company's existing management.

Management incentive arrangements can take a number of different forms. In "public to private", MBOs and similar types of transaction, it will often be desirable to allow certain members of management to exchange (i.e. "roll over") their shares in the offeree company for securities in the offeror bid vehicle, whereas non-management shareholders will not be given the same opportunity. In other cases, management may be financially incentivised by reference to underlying profitability and/or share price performance without acquiring an interest in any offeror securities. An offeror may also wish to offer particular members of the offeree company's management enhanced remuneration packages, which may take the form of new or improved service contracts or bonus arrangements or the opportunity to participate in the offeror's own employee share plans (which would confer a right to receive shares in the offeror at some future point in time).

Where the management concerned also holds shares in the offeree company, incentive arrangements can give rise to concerns relating to General Principle 1 (which requires offeree company shareholders to be afforded equivalent treatment). They can also give rise to concerns as to their effect on the offeree board's assessment of a proposed offer and/or the amount of consideration that might be left for non-management shareholders. Accordingly, Rule 16.2 of the Code provides various procedural safeguards to ensure that the philosophy underlying General Principle 1 and Rule 16.1 is respected whilst enabling management to participate in the ongoing business through different types of incentive arrangement which, by definition, cannot be extended to all other offeree company shareholders.

Under Rule 16.2, where an offeror enters into (or reaches an advanced stage of discussions or proposals to enter into) any form of incentivisation arrangements with members of the offeree company's management who are interested in shares of the offeree, the relevant details of the arrangements (or proposals) must be disclosed and the independent adviser to the offeree company must state publicly that in its opinion the arrangements are fair and reasonable. When forming its opinion, the independent adviser is expected to consider whether the incentives being offered to management are fair and reasonable in the context of the managers acting in their capacity as such (which is acceptable) or whether, implicitly, the arrangements also include additional benefits and incentives which are being made available to them because they are interested in shares (which is not acceptable). The independent adviser will be expected to have regard to the whole of the incentive arrangements being offered (including any enhanced remuneration package). The independent adviser will also be expected to take into account all relevant circumstances, including for example the particular skills of the individual concerned, the circumstances of the company in question and/or comparable remuneration packages provided to management of peer group companies.

The question also arises whether independent shareholder approval will be required, in addition to the "fair and reasonable" opinion required of the independent adviser to the offeree company. Where managers who are also shareholders in the offeree company are being offered shares in the offeror on a basis that is not being made available to all other offeree company shareholders then, in order to comply with the requirement of the Takeover Directive that any derogation from the Rules must "respect" the General Principles (see arts 3(1)(a) and 4(5) of the Takeover Directive), independent shareholder approval must always now be obtained (Rule 16.2(c)). See, for example, the offer by Carlyle for Nationwide Accident Repair Services in April 2015, in which members of the Nationwide management team were entitled to subscribe for "sweet equity" and additional shares and loan notes in the bid vehicle, an arrangement which was not made available to other shareholders in the offeree. Similarly, independent shareholder approval was required in relation to the management incentive arrangements entered into on Bain Capital's offer for esure Group plc in 2018 and the offer by CVC and Blackstone for Paysafe Group Plc in 2017.

Rule 16.2 is focused on members of management who are interested in shares of the offeree company. The Panel believes, however, that management incentive arrangements can still be relevant to offeree company shareholders even where members of management are not interested in shares (and thus independent shareholder approval is not required in order to comply with the Takeover Directive). This may be the case, for example, by virtue of the influence which such arrangements might have on the board's recommendation or on the amount of consideration made available for shareholders. The Panel therefore requires to be consulted in cases where significant and/or unusual incentive arrangements are proposed in relation to members of the management of the offeree company, regardless of whether they are interested in shares of the offeree company.

It will be a question of judgement whether the value of incentive arrangements for members of management who are not interested in shares is significant and/or the nature of the arrangements is unusual, and this needs to be assessed both in the context of the relevant industry in which the companies operate and by reference to good practice. In certain circumstances, in addition to requiring a "fair and reasonable" opinion from the independent adviser to the offeree company, the Panel may make its consent to such arrangements conditional on independent shareholder approval (Rule 16.2(b)). This is what happened, for example, in the case of the offer by Tracsis for Sky High in March 2013, where the proposed cash bonus incentivisation arrangement between Tracsis and two executive directors of Sky High (one of whom was not an offeree company shareholder) was made subject to independent shareholder approval.

Some limited guidance is provided in Response Statement 2009/2 on the question of whether independent shareholder approval is likely to be required in relation to new remuneration packages. It is said that, where these simply reflect the existing remuneration policy of the offeror, they would not normally be viewed as significant and/or unusual in which case they would not need to be approved by shareholders. The independent adviser to the offeree company will, however, still be required to state publicly that any such enhanced remuneration packages are, in its opinion, fair and reasonable.

Where shareholder approval is required, it must be provided by way of a separate vote of independent shareholders, taken on a poll. It is not therefore possible to include such an approval as part of a composite resolution to approve other matters in relation to an offer, for example a resolution of offeree company shareholders to approve a scheme of arrangement to implement the acquisition by the offeror. The Panel may, however, allow the offer to be made conditional on the passing of any resolution required to approve the management incentive arrangements, with the result that the offer may lapse if the resolution is not approved. In the case of the recommended merger between Glencore and Xstrata in 2012, Glencore's initial offer was made conditional, amongst other things, upon independent Xstrata shareholders approving certain management incentive arrangements for Xstrata management and senior employees. In its revised offer for Xstrata, however, the offer was no longer made conditional upon the approval of revised management incentive arrangements. Xstrata shareholders duly approved the revised offer, subject to the resolution to approve the revised management incentive arrangements not being passed, and the merger proceeded on that basis.

The term "management" is not defined for the purposes of Rule 16.2 and the Executive adopts a flexible approach. In practice, the Executive usually interprets "management" to comprise those directors and senior executives of the offeree who have the power to make managerial decisions affecting the future development and business prospects of the company concerned. The Executive may also be prepared to allow the holdings of those directors' immediate families to be included in the management arrangements, if otherwise permitted. In addition, the Executive may be prepared to allow management below offeree company board level to participate in the arrangements, provided they are sufficiently key personnel (for example they are directors of a principal operating subsidiary): see, for example, the recommended proposals for the acquisition of the Peacock Group by Henson No.1 Ltd in November 2005, where the holdings of the spouse of one of the executive directors and of two members of management below board level were included in the share exchange proposals. The holdings of self-invested personal pensions (SIPPs) and fund managers linked to members of management may also be included: see, for example, the management incentive arrangements associated with Sanlam's offer for Merchant Securities in November 2011. The Executive expects to be consulted on all situations where it is unclear which individuals may be viewed as part of "management" for these purposes.

Rule 16.2 also includes a requirement to consult the Panel if any changes to the status of management incentive arrangements are made after the offer document has been published. If the changes are material, disclosure of the relevant details and a statement by the offeree company's independent adviser that the arrangements are fair and reasonable will be required and, if merited on the facts, independent shareholder approval may also need to be obtained.

In many cases, an offeror may choose to refrain from holding any incentivisation discussions with the offeree company management until after the offer has completed. However, it should be noted that, if it is intended to put incentivisation arrangements in place after completion of an offer, but either no discussions or only limited discussions have taken place, this fact must be publicly stated and relevant details of any discussions which have taken place must be disclosed. Where no incentivisation arrangements are proposed, this must also be publicly stated.

Rule 16.2 is also capable of applying in whitewash transactions, where some form of incentivisation arrangement is being provided to the management of the company which is treated as the "offeree company" in these circumstances (i.e. the company issuing the new securities and seeking the whitewash) by any member of the "offeror" camp (i.e. any potential controlling shareholder receiving new shares in the offeree)—see s.4(g) in Appendix 1 to the Code. An example of this occurred in connection with the potential acquisition by Bidtimes of PowerHouse Energy in April 2011. The acquisition constituted a reverse takeover for Bidtimes, given that it needed to increase its share capital by well over 100% to satisfy the share consideration being offered to PowerHouse shareholders, and a whitewash vote of independent Bidtimes shareholders was required in order to exempt certain of the selling PowerHouse shareholders (who were treated as acting in concert) from having to make a general offer for Bidtimes under Rule 9 by virtue of receiving in excess of 30% of Bidtimes as a result of the acquisition. The approval of independent Bidtimes shareholders was also required under Rule 16.2 in relation to a success fee which was payable by one of the principal members of the concert party to a company advising it on the transaction, given that a director and controlling shareholder of the corporate adviser was also a director and shareholder in Bidtimes.

5.2.1.3.5 Joint offerors

In the same way that Rule 16 does not apply to a genuine offeror who already holds shares in the offeree company, in respect of any arrangements it may make regarding its own shares in the offeree company or otherwise, the Panel acknowledges that Rule 16 is not relevant where two or more persons come together to form a consortium on such terms and in such circumstances that each of them can properly be considered to be a joint offeror.

Rule 16 will not, therefore, apply where an offeree company shareholder can properly be characterised as acting as joint offeror. Consortium members (including members of management) who are treated by the Panel as joint offerors will be free to enter into their own arrangements without the need for those arrangements to require a fair and reasonable opinion from an independent adviser or independent shareholder approval. By way of example, when Chain Bidco (a consortium vehicle owned by Toscafund, Penta Capital and Matthew Riley, the chief executive of Daisy Group) made a cash offer for Daisy Group in October 2014, Matthew Riley was treated as a joint offeror with the result that Rule 16 did not apply to the arrangements whereby Matthew Riley exchanged his stake in Daisy Group for shares in the bidding vehicle. This may be contrasted with the offer by Al Mirqab Capital for Heritage Oil in May 2014, where the arrangements for Tony Buckingham, the founder and a major shareholder in Heritage Oil, to roll-over part of his Heritage shareholding for a stake in the bid vehicle (amongst other arrangements) required independent shareholder approval under Rule 16.2. This indicated that Mr Buckingham was not regarded as acting as a joint offeror alongside Al Mirqab Capital.

The distinction between receiving a special deal as offeree company shareholder (which is subject to the prohibitions and restrictions in General Principle 1 and Rule 16) and acting as joint offeror (where it is not) can be a fine one. All potential joint offeror cases require early consultation with the Panel, who, in addition to considering the arguments put forward by the proposed joint offerors, may seek the views of the offeree company and its advisers.

A genuine offeror is seen as a person who, alone or with others, seeks to obtain control of an offeree company and have a meaningful role in the conduct of the bid and who, following the acquisition of control, can expect to exert a significant influence over the offeree company, to participate in distributions of profits and surplus capital and to benefit from any increase in the value of the offeree company, while at the same time bearing the risk of a fall in its value resulting from the poor performance of the company's business or adverse market conditions.

In determining whether a person can properly be considered to be an offeror (or joint offeror), rather than simply acting in concert with the offeror, the Panel Executive will consider the following factors.

1. What proportion of the equity share capital of the bid vehicle will the person own after completion of the acquisition?
2. Will the person be able to exert a significant influence over the future management and direction of the bid vehicle?
3. What contribution is the person making to the consortium?
4. Will the person be able to influence significantly the conduct of the bid?
5. Are there arrangements in place to enable the person to exit from his or her investment in the bid vehicle within a short time or at a time when other equity investors cannot?

The appropriateness of these factors was endorsed by the Panel in the case concerning Canary Wharf Group (see Panel Statement 2003/25). The Panel did, however, stress that the above factors should not be regarded as exhaustive, and that it is also necessary to ensure that, even if the criteria seem to be satisfied to a degree sufficient to justify treating the person in question as an offeror, the arrangements looked at as a whole are consistent with General Principle 1 and Rule 16. The Panel also said that no single factor should be regarded as determinative, nor is it necessary that a person satisfies each factor.

In the Canary Wharf case, the Panel was satisfied that a particular offeree company shareholder should be treated as a joint offeror and that, accordingly, the terms of the consortium arrangements in which he was involved did not infringe General Principle 1 or Rule 16. It was found, in that case, that the shareholder concerned would have in excess of 30% of the equity in the bid vehicle, making him the largest single shareholder, and that the consortium arrangements gave him significant influence over the direction of the bid vehicle and the future management of the business. It was also found that the shareholder was making a substantial contribution to the consortium, both in financial and managerial terms, and that he was exposed to substantial risks and had no arrangements for a short-term exit. The Panel did, however, also stress that each case must be decided upon its own facts and that therefore previous decisions arrived at on different facts are likely to be of little help in determining the acceptability of consortium arrangements in other cases.

A recent example of a bid by joint offerors was the offer for Chime Communications in August 2015 by Bell Bidder Limited, a bid vehicle formed for the purpose of making the offer by Providence and WPP. WPP held approximately 20% of Chime's issued ordinary share capital and, upon completion of the offer, WPP exchanged these shares for a stake in Bell Bidder Ltd. Both shareholders had rights to decide on key matters relating to the conduct of the bid as well as the ongoing governance, management and business of Bell Bidder Ltd and Chime following completion of the transaction.

Another example was the offer by Pollen Street Capital and BC Partners for Shawbrook Group Plc (March 2017), where Pollen Street Capital, as a joint offeror, was permitted to exchange its 38% stake in Shawbrook for shares in the bid vehicle in circumstances where all other shareholders were only entitled to the cash offer.

It follows that, where an offeree company shareholder cannot be characterised as a joint offeror, and is not a manager of the offeree company as referred to in 5.2.1.3.4 above, a special deal involving a "roll over" into shares in the bidding vehicle (when all other shareholders would not be given the same opportunity) is not generally permissible, even with the benefit of a fair and reasonable statement from the offeree company's independent financial adviser and an independent shareholder vote, and will be prohibited by the overriding requirement for shareholders of the same class to be afforded equivalent treatment as set out in General Principle 1 and Rule 16. In these cases, any roll-over must be offered to all shareholders on equal terms.

5.2.1.3.6 Debt syndication

Practice Statement No.25 describes the way in which the Executive normally interprets and applies certain provisions of the Code, including Rule 16, in the context of the primary syndication of debt financing for an offer during offer periods. Rule 16 may be in point where a debt finance provider who is allocated a debt participation following the completion of the syndication process, or a potential debt finance provider who is approached to take part in a proposed debt syndication, (in either case, a "syndicate") also holds shares in the offeree company, or acquires such shares during the offer period. The Executive's concern in this context is primarily based on the possibility that favourable debt terms might be used as a means of providing additional value to a syndicatee in its capacity as an offeree company shareholder. This would be the case if, for example, a syndicatee's equity department agreed that it would accept a lower offer for its shares in the offeree company than would otherwise have been the case because the syndicatee's debt department was allocated a participation in the syndicate, perhaps on attractive terms. In addition, the Executive is concerned to ensure that the decision of a syndicatee's equity department as to whether or not it should accept the offer should not otherwise be influenced by the participation of the syndicatee's debt department in the syndicate.

The Executive believes that the knowledge that a syndicatee's equity department has about the participation of its debt department in a debt syndication, and the terms of that participation, is critical in determining the application of Rule 16. This is because the Executive considers that, without this knowledge, it would be unlikely that value would be transferred between the equity and debt components of the transaction or that the decision of the equity department as to whether or not it should accept an offer would be influenced.

In view of this, the Executive normally takes the view that, in relation to a syndicatee which holds shares in the offeree company or which acquires shares during the offer period, no problems would arise under Rule 16 provided effective information barriers are in place between its equity and debt departments. Paragraph 6 of Practice Statement 25 sets out the minimum standards which the Executive has identified for an information barrier to be effective in preventing issues arising under Rule 16 in this context.

If, however, an effective information barrier has not been established then the Executive will want to establish whether or not the debt being syndicated is on "market terms":

1. if the offeror is able to demonstrate to the Executive's satisfaction that the debt being syndicated is on "market terms", the Executive would not normally consider there to be an issue under Rule 16. This is on the basis that, if an offeror is able to prove that a syndicatee has been allocated "plain vanilla" debt with no special features which is on similar terms to debt issued in comparable transactions, the Executive would consider the scope for a transfer of value to occur as between the equity and debt components of the transaction, or for the decision of the syndicatee's equity department to be influenced, would be minimised;
2. if, on the other hand, the debt being syndicated is not on "market terms", the Executive will normally require further information in order to determine whether there is an issue under Rule 16. For example, the Executive would seek to gain an understanding of the identity of the syndicatees, the reasons why the syndicatees were invited to participate in the syndicate, the basis and terms on which the debt was allocated to syndicatees, and the extent to which syndicatees hold shares in the offeree company.

5.2.1.3.7   Other cases

Rule 16 is concerned with special deals for particular shareholders which are (or may be) on favourable terms. It follows, therefore, that Rule 16 (and General Principle 1) will not be relevant where a particular shareholder voluntarily accepts a less favourable deal than other shareholders. Rule 16 will also not be relevant where all offeree company shareholders are being offered the same opportunity to exchange their shares in the offeree company for securities in the offeror, even if it is clear that the opportunity provided will not be attractive to all of them. For example, in the offer by Anheuser-Busch Inbev for SABMiller announced in 2015, all shareholders were to be offered cash for their SABMiller shares and, alternatively, shares in AB Inbev at a discount at the time of announcement to the cash value of the offer and subject to a lock-up. The share alternative was designed primarily for the two major share-holders in SABMiller to continue to have an equity participa-tion post-completion and to minimise certain tax costs, whilst affording all other shareholders the same opportunity in compliance with General Principle 1.

A similar situation arose in the buyout offer by RAB Capital Holdings for RAB Capital in July 2011, where the offeree company directors leading the buyout elected to receive an unlisted share alternative which was also made available to all other shareholders but which was not recommended to them by the offeree company's independent directors or adviser. See also the offer for Theo Fennell in August 2013 which included an unlisted share alternative comprising shares in the bid vehicle which was made available to all offeree shareholders but which was not recommended. In that case, various other arrangements involving one or more offeree company director shareholders also required a "fair and reasonable" statement from the offeree company's independent adviser as well as independent shareholder approval: these comprised a "sweet equity" arrangement by way of management incentivisation, new director service agreements, a so-called "brand repatria-tion" agreement and a separate purchase agreement relating to shares in an associated company.

5.2.1.3.8   Interaction with other Rules

Where members of the management of the offeree company are to receive offeror securities pursuant to an appropriate offer or proposal made in accordance with Rule 15, relevant details of the arrangement must be disclosed and the independent adviser of the offeree must give a fair and reasonable opinion in accordance with Rule 16.2(a), but shareholder approval will not normally be required.

If the only shareholders in the offeree company who receive offeror securities are members of the management of the offeree company, the Panel will not, so long as the requirements of Rule 16.2 are complied with, require all offeree company shareholders to be offered offeror securities pursuant to Rule 11.2, even though such management members propose to sell more than 10% of the offeree company's shares in exchange for offeror securities.

In addition to the requirement to disclose relevant details of any management incentive arrangements or proposals under Rule 16.2(b), it is also worth noting that full particulars of any special arrangements between the offeror or any person acting in concert with it and any of the directors, shareholders or recent shareholders of the offeree company, having any connection with or dependence upon the offer, also need to be disclosed in the offer document under Rule 24.6.

5.2.1.4 *Compensation rulings*

Section 10(c) of the Introduction to the Code provides that, where a person has breached the requirements of (amongst others) Rules 14, 15 or 16.1 of the Code, the Panel may rule that the person concerned must make a payment to the shareholders, or former shareholders, in the offeree company which ensures that such holders receive what they would have been entitled to receive if the relevant Rule had been complied with. The ruling may also require interest to be paid up to the date of payment.

5.2.2 *Administrative provisions*

Rules 17 and 18 contain certain administrative provisions relating to all offers. Rule 17 deals with announcements of acceptance levels and Rule 18 with certain provisions in forms of acceptance.

5.2.2.1   Rule 17: Announcements of acceptance levels

5.2.2.1.1   Timing and contents

Rule 17.1 requires an announcement of the level of acceptances to be made after the occurrence of certain events, namely:

1.   any expiry date—that is, any date on which the offeror could allow the bid to lapse if insufficient acceptances have been received. This will obviously include the first closing date of an offer, usually the minimum period of 21 days after the despatch of the offer document; it will also include any subsequent closing date if the offer is extended; the Code also states that a date on which any alternative form of consideration available under the offer expires is also to be treated as an expiry date, even if the offer itself is not due to expire at that time;
2.   when the offer becomes or is declared unconditional as to acceptances—which may of course also be an expiry date, though not necessarily, and it could be before or after the first closing date;
3.   whenever the offer is revised—including where a revision is required as a result of a purchase of offeree company shares above the then current offer value, if otherwise permitted, in which case the announcement required by Rule 7.1 should also include the information required under Rule 17.1; and
4.   whenever the offer is extended—that may also be an expiry date, though not necessarily.

The deadline for announcements required by Rule 17.1 is 08.00 on the first business day following the relevant event. However, on the final day of the offer (i.e. the day beyond which the offer cannot be extended if not unconditional as to acceptances, which is normally the 60th day after posting unless the offeror has made a "no extension" statement for an earlier date or the Panel has consented to a later date which it may do in certain circumstances), the announcement must normally be made by 17.00 on that day—not 08.00 on the following business day. If an offer is likely to reach the final day, the offeror and its advisers should consider Rule 31.6 closely in advance as it has a number of detailed requirements about timing.

Rule 17.1 also specifies that the following must be included in the announcement:

1. the number of shares for which acceptances of the offer have been received, specifying the extent to which acceptances have been received from persons acting in concert with the offeror or in respect of shares which were subject to an irrevocable commitment or a letter of intent procured by the offeror or any person acting in concert with the offeror;
2. details of any relevant securities of the offeree company in which the offeror or any person acting in concert with it has an interest or in respect of which he or she has a right to subscribe, in each case specifying the nature of the interests or rights concerned (similar details of any short positions, whether conditional or absolute and whether in the money or otherwise, including any short position under a derivative, any agreement to sell or any delivery obligation or right to require another person to purchase or take delivery, must also be stated);
3. details of any relevant securities of the offeree company in respect of which the offeror or any person acting in concert with it has an outstanding irrevocable commitment or letter of intent; and
4. details of any relevant securities of the offeree company which the offeror or any person acting in concert with it has borrowed or lent, save for any borrowed shares which have been either on-lent or sold,

and the announcement must specify the percentages of each class of relevant securities represented by these figures.

A Rule 17 announcement must also include a prominent statement of the total number of shares which can be counted towards satisfaction of the acceptance condition and must specify the percentages of each class of relevant securities represented by these figures. The Code has strict Rules for determining what acceptances and share purchases may be counted towards fulfilling an acceptance condition (see Rule 10 including, in particular, Notes 4 and 5). Accordingly, an acceptance of the offer may only be counted for this purpose if (in cases where the acceptance is effected by means of CREST without an acceptance form) the transfer to the relevant member's escrow account has settled in respect of the relevant number of shares on or before the last time for acceptance or (where the acceptance is effected by means of an acceptance form) the acceptance is received by the offeror's receiving agent on or before such time, the form is completed to a suitable standard and:

1. the form is accompanied by the relevant share certificates and, where necessary, any other documents required to show title;
2. in the case of a holding in CREST, it is covered by a transfer to the relevant member's escrow account, details of which are provided in the form;
3. the acceptor is registered in the register of members as the holder of the shares in question as at the final time for acceptance and those shares are not included as acceptances in any other respect; or
4. the acceptance form is certified by the offeree company's registrar.

Similarly, share purchases may only be counted if:

1. the offeror (or its nominee or, in a Rule 9 offer, a person acting in concert with it) is the registered holder of the shares; or
2. a duly executed transfer in favour of the offeror (or its nominee or, in a Rule 9 offer, concert party) has been received and is accompanied by the relevant share certificates or is certified by the target's registrar.

The Panel should be consulted if the offeror wishes to make any other statement about acceptance levels in a Rule 17 announcement.

If an offer is to become or be declared unconditional as to acceptances before the final closing date, the criteria for determining which acceptances and purchases can be counted towards fulfilling the acceptance condition (although not necessarily for the purposes of a Rule 17 announcement) are stricter in one particular respect (see Rule 10, Note 6). In these circumstances, it is not possible to take account of acceptances solely on the grounds that they are from a registered holder, unless they are also accompanied by share certificates or (in the case of a holding in CREST) covered by a transfer to the relevant member's escrow account or (in any case) certified by the target's registrar.

In addition, before the offer becomes or is declared unconditional as to acceptances, the offeror's receiving agent must have issued a certificate which states the number of acceptances and purchases which comply with the above requirements. A copy of that certificate must be sent to the Panel and the offeree company's financial adviser as soon as possible.

The above requirements were introduced into the Code following the situation which arose in the Blue Circle offer for Birmid in 1988. In that case there was an announcement that there were sufficient acceptances and purchases for the bid to become unconditional. It was, however, subsequently found that some incomplete purchases had been included and a further announcement had to be made that the bid had in fact lapsed (see Panel Statements 1988/4 and 1988/22).

Rule 24.7 of the Code requires an offer document to state that the offeror will make announcements on the required occasions and what will be included within those announcements.

5.2.2.1.2   Failure to announce

If the offeror, having announced the offer to be unconditional as to acceptances, fails to announce the details required by Rule 17.1 by 15.30 on the following business day, then automatically every acceptor has the right to withdraw his or her acceptance. Subject to Rule 31.6, that right to withdraw cannot be terminated for at least eight days and then it can only be terminated by the offeror reconfirming that the bid is still unconditional as to acceptances, assuming of course that by the end of that eight days it is still unconditional as to acceptances. If too many people have withdrawn, the bid may no longer be capable of being reconfirmed as unconditional as to acceptances.

On the final day, however, when Rule 31.6 applies, an offer must either become or be declared unconditional as to acceptances or lapse. If it becomes or is declared unconditional as to acceptances, it is generally not then capable of becoming conditional as to acceptances again. It follows that any withdrawal rights which may have arisen will cease to be exercisable beyond the final time for lodging acceptances which can be taken into account for the purposes of Rule 31.6. This is also consistent with when the general right of withdrawal ceases to be exercisable under Rule 34.1.

5.2.2.1.3 General statements about acceptances and withdrawals

During an offer, particularly in a competitive situation, an offeror or its advisers may be tempted to make general statements about the level of acceptances received, or the number or percentage of shareholders who have accepted the offer. In these circumstances, the Panel will require an immediate announcement to be made in conformity with Rule 17. As noted above, a formal Rule 17 announcement will need to make clear which acceptances can be counted towards fulfilling the acceptance condition.

Conversely, in the case of a hostile offer, an offeree company may wish to draw attention to withdrawals of acceptances. In this case, the Panel requires prior consultation before any announcement is made. The Panel is usually concerned to ensure, in particular, that the market is not misled by conflicting announcements of withdrawals and acceptances.

Rule 19.3 may also be relevant: an offeror or offeree company should not make statements about levels of support from shareholders unless their up-to-date intentions have been clearly stated to the company or its advisers and satisfactory verification (which usually means written) can be provided to the Panel. If such evidence cannot be provided, the Executive will usually require a statement of retraction or clarification to be made. There have been many recent examples of such statements, for example in relation to the offers by Abbvie for Shire (2014), Anheuser-Busch Inbev for SABMiller (2015), Sainsbury for Home Retail (2016), and Melrose for GKN (2018).

5.2.2.1.4   Schemes of arrangement

Rule 17 is not applicable in the case of schemes of arrangement. In its place, the provisions of s.5 of Appendix 7 of the Code provide that an announcement should be made as soon as practicable after the results of the shareholder meetings are known, stating whether or not the resolutions were passed by the requisite majorities and giving details of the voting results in relation to the meetings including (where applicable) the number of votes cast for and against the resolutions and the number of shareholders who voted for and against them. Announcements are also required as soon as practicable following the court sanction hearing and, assuming the scheme proceeds to that stage, the scheme effective date.

5.2.2.2   *Rule 18: The use of proxies in relation to acceptances*

Rule 18 relates to the appointment of proxies to exercise voting rights and other sorts of rights. The offeror will usually include, as part of the terms of acceptance, a provision by which an accepting shareholder appoints the offeror, or someone nominated by him or her, as the acceptor's proxy and authorises that person to exercise rights on his or her behalf. The purpose of this is normally to enable the offeror to exercise the rights attached to the acceptor's shares in the offeree company between the time when the offer goes wholly unconditional and the time when the offeror is registered on

the register of members. In the absence of any other arrangement, until the offeror becomes the registered holder of the
shares, the rights attached to them would continue to be
exercisable by the accepting shareholder.

Rule 18 states that the appointment as proxy should be
expressed in terms that it will become effective only if the offer
has become wholly unconditional or (in the case of voting by
the proxy) if the resolution in question concerns the last
remaining condition of the offer (other than any admission to
listing or admission to trading condition) and the offer would
either become wholly unconditional (save for satisfaction of
any such condition) or lapse depending upon the outcome of
the resolution in question. This exception is to enable votes to
be cast at a general meeting of the offeree company if one is
needed for the purposes of the offer. In order for an offeror to
benefit from the appointment, it may be necessary for it to
waive any outstanding, waivable conditions save for the
admission to listing or admission to trading condition which, if
applicable, will always be the last condition to be satisfied.

One other circumstance in which the Panel is likely, in practice,
to permit the offeror to use proxies acquired as a result of the
acceptance process, before the offer has become wholly
unconditional, is where the offeree company proposes to
dispose of certain assets for which shareholder approval is
required and the offer is conditional on the proposed sale not
being approved at the offeree company's general meeting.

The Code goes on to say that the offeror can only use the votes
to satisfy the conditions of the offer. In other words, it would
not be possible for the offeror (for example if it had cold feet
about the offer) to exercise voting rights over shares in the
offeree company to defeat the conditions of its offer. In these
circumstances, however, an offeror may be able to lapse its
offer on an expiry date if it has failed to satisfy the 90%
acceptance condition which is often inserted for compulsory
acquisition purposes (although this "get out" would not be
available where the offeror has chosen to implement its offer by
means of a scheme of arrangement).

The proxy form must also make it clear that the appointment ceases to be valid if the acceptor withdraws his or her acceptance.

Finally, it has to be made clear that the appointment relates only to the shares which are the subject of the acceptance. In other words, if (for example) Barclays Bank has several million shares in the offeree company registered in its name, all as nominee, and it is instructed by one person to accept the offer, an appointment of the offeror as a proxy in relation to those shares may not be taken as an appointment in relation to all the other shares in the offeree company held by Barclays.

Rule 18 does not restrict the terms on which a proxy may be obtained, or other shareholder rights acquired, otherwise than as a term of acceptance (for example, as part of a separate proxy solicitation exercise).

Rule 18 is not applicable in the case of schemes of arrangement and is disapplied by virtue of s.16 of Appendix 7 to the Code.

5.3   Partial offers

The provisions of the Code on partial offers (Section P, Rule 36) are also concerned with the application of General Principle 1 regarding equivalent treatment.

A partial offer is an offer for less than 100% of the voting share capital of a company, taking into account any shares already owned by the offeror and persons acting in concert with it. In other words, a partial offer is one which is not capable of resulting in the offeror and its concert parties being interested in 100% of the voting rights of a company.

Partial offers are relatively uncommon for the simple reason that offerors usually wish to acquire 100% control, which avoids the need to take account of the interests of minority shareholders longer term, whilst offeree company shareholders are usually reluctant to cede control without the ability to get out for 100% of their holdings. Nonetheless, partial offers may prove attractive in certain circumstances.

Some examples of partial offers include the offer by Zoo Hotels to acquire up to 29% of the Groucho Club London in April 2001, the offer by Carnival Corporation to acquire up to 20% of P&O Princess Cruises in March 2003 (in connection with the proposed combination of Carnival and P&O Princess under a dual listed company structure), the hostile offer by GPG Group to acquire an additional 25% of De Vere in March 2004, the offer by Leander Group to acquire 74.9% of Real Office Group in October 2008, the offer by Energees Investments to acquire approximately 70% of Regal Petroleum in 2010, the hostile offer by Thalassa to acquire an additional 25.89% of Rock Solid Images in April 2012, and the offer by FB Investors LLP to acquire 70% of Sutton Harbour Holdings Plc in November 2017.

Panel consent is always required for a partial offer. This consent is normally granted if it would not result in the offeror and its concert parties being interested in shares carrying 30% or more of the votes. A person can, of course, buy shares to give himself up to 29.9% without incurring a mandatory bid obligation under Rule 9 of the Takeover Code.

There are three ways in which a person is able to acquire shares (or interests in shares) of up to 29.9% of a company to which the Code applies:

1. by stakebuilding through the purchase of individual holdings;
2. by means of a tender offer (the Rules for which are contained in Appendix 5 of the Code); or
3. by means of a partial offer.

Share purchases may, for example, be made from particular shareholders or as part of a market operation conducted by the purchaser's broker. However, if the purchaser wishes to make an offer to all shareholders, he or she will need to do a tender or partial offer. A tender offer is made by means of a simple advertisement which must be published in two national newspapers (although a circular in the same form as the advertisement may also be posted to shareholders) and it need only be open for a minimum period of seven days. A tender offer provides a more straightforward procedure than a partial offer, which is subject to the other provisions of the Code in the normal way and is therefore a lengthier and more costly process. A tender offer may also be particularly relevant in the context of companies whose shares are not admitted to trading (where it is not therefore possible to acquire shares in the market).

A tender offer must, however, be for cash only and cannot be made subject to any conditions, other than receipt of acceptances amounting to at least 1%. Thus, where the offer consideration is to include securities or conditions need to be attached to the acquisition of shares (for example the approval of the purchaser's own shareholders or, possibly, regulatory conditions), a purchaser will have to resort to a partial offer regulated under the Code.

The amount of information which can be imparted during a tender offer is also strictly limited; in particular, no form of argument or persuasion is allowed, whereas a partial offer under the Code is not so restricted. Zoo Hotels, for example, had to proceed by way of partial offer rather than tender offer, in its attempt to acquire up to 29% of the Groucho Club, both because its offer consideration comprised Zoo shares and because its offer was unsolicited and competitive with another, general offer which meant it needed to be able to argue the relative merits of its partial offer. Zoo Hotels' partial offer was not, however, subject to any conditions: partial offers which cannot result in the offeror holding 30% or more need not be subject to any acceptance condition although an offeror may choose to include one. Thalassa's hostile partial offer for Rock Solid Images, for example, which included a share alternative and, if accepted in full, would have given the offeror 29.99% of the offeree company, also included a minimum acceptance condition.

A tender offer would also not be an option for an offeror who wants to acquire shares carrying 30% or more of the votes, unless the offeror already controls the majority of the votes (i.e. over 50%) and the Panel believes the circumstances justify the use of a tender offer.

Where a partial offer is made which could result in the offeror and its concert parties being interested in shares carrying 30% or more of the voting rights, the Panel will normally grant its consent, but only on the following conditions:

1. the holders of over 50% of the voting rights in the offeree company (excluding those held by the offeror and its concert parties) must approve the offer, even though they do not necessarily accept the offer; the way in which such approval would normally be sought is that, in the acceptance form sent out with the partial offer document, there will be a box for shareholders to tick to indicate their approval of the partial offer (this is what was required, for example, in the partial offer by FB Investors to acquire 70% of Sutton Harbour in 2017; and

2. where the offer could not result in the offeror holding more than 50% of the voting rights of the offeree company, the offer must not be declared unconditional as to acceptances unless acceptances are received for not less than the number of shares offered for—that number must be stated precisely in the offer document (see the partial offers by GPG Group for De Vere and Jardine Matheson Holdings for Jardine Lloyd Thompson Group).

The purpose of the first condition is to ensure that "over 50%" approve the making of a partial offer which, if successful, will result in the offeror and its concert parties acquiring "control" of the offeree company without all shareholders being given the opportunity to exit for 100% of their shareholdings. Rule 36.5 makes clear that the "over 50%" approval requirement applies to over 50% of the voting rights held by shareholders who are "independent" of the offeror and persons acting in concert with it, rather than over 50% of the voting rights not held by the offeror concert party.

The purpose of the second condition above is to prevent an offeror acquiring what is effective control without paying the full price—that is the offer must be fully successful. It also gives shareholders certainty that the offeror will not obtain control of the company unless the offeror receives acceptances in respect of at least the number of shares stated in the offer document, so shareholders can make their acceptance decisions on this basis. Normally, an offeror under a partial offer will permit shareholders to accept an offer for as many shares as they like, guaranteeing that their acceptances will be accepted only to the extent of their proportionate holdings. Thus, if a significant number of shareholders accept for amounts substantially in excess of their proportionate holdings, the offeror may well receive acceptances for more than the total number of shares it has offered for. In view of this, it is not normally difficult to satisfy the second condition if the price is attractive enough.

Partial offers which could result in the offeror and its concert parties being interested in shares carrying 30% or more (but less than 100%) of the voting rights of a company will not normally be permitted if there have been selective or significant acquisitions by the offeror or its concert parties in the previous 12 months or if interests in shares were acquired by any of them after the offer was reasonably in contemplation. The reason for this is, again, so as not to favour certain shareholders (i.e. those who were able to sell out in full as a result of one of the offeror's earlier acquisitions) over other shareholders who would only receive the possibility of a partial exit under the partial offer.

For the same reason, Rule 36.3 prohibits the acquisition of any interest in offeree company shares being made either:

1. during the partial offer (and this applies even for offers for less than 30%); or
2. in the 12 months after the end of the offer period if the offer was successful, unless the Panel consents.

The 12-month moratorium on acquisitions also applies following an unsuccessful partial offer for 30% or more of the voting rights of the offeree company (see Rule 35.2).

These Rules apply to concert parties (including any connected but non-exempt discretionary fund managers or principal traders who will be presumed to be acting in concert with the offeror or potential offeror once its identity has been publicly announced or is otherwise known to them) just as much as they do to the offeror.

The Panel is likely to grant its consent only if:

1. the successful offer results in less than 30% being owned by the offeror and its concert parties; or
2. there are circumstances in which, under Rule 35, an offeror would be allowed to renew a full offer within 12 months of its lapsing (for example, if the offeree company's board recommends it or if a rival offer is made by a third party).

The Code does not expressly deal with the situation where a partial offer is made which could only result in the offeror and persons acting in concert with it being interested in shares carrying less than 30% of the voting rights of the offeree company, and that offer is unsuccessful. It seems clear, however, that in these circumstances the failed offeror should be free to acquire shares immediately following the lapse of its offer without the 12-month moratorium applying. This is what happened, for example, following Thalassa's partial offer for less than 30% of Rock Solid Images. Thalassa had chosen to include a minimum acceptance condition in its offer and, following the lapse of its offer for non-satisfaction of this condition, Thalassa was nonetheless allowed to acquire shares from certain of the shareholders who had previously accepted its offer.

In the case of a partial offer which could result in the offeror holding shares carrying over 50% of the voting rights of the offeree company, Rule 36.6 requires the offer document to contain specific and prominent reference to this and to the fact that, if the offer succeeds, the offeror and its concert parties will be free (subject to Rule 36.3 and, where relevant, Note 4 on Rule 9.1) to acquire further shares without incurring any obligation under Rule 9 to make a general offer (i.e. it will have what is known as "buying freedom"; Note 4 on Rule 9.1 will be relevant where, as a result of the partial offer, the offeror does not itself hold shares carrying over 50% of the voting rights).

Rule 36.7 specifies how scaling down of acceptances is to be effected. All shareholders' acceptances up to the relevant percentage of their holdings offered for must be accepted in full. Where shares in excess of that percentage have been tendered by shareholders, the same proportion of such excess shares to the number tendered must be accepted from each shareholder.

Rule 36.8 states that, if a partial offer is made for a company with more than one class of equity share capital which could result in the offeror and its concert parties being interested in shares carrying 30% or more of the voting rights, comparable offers must be made for each class (see Rule 14). Although the Code is silent on the point, the question also arises whether an appropriate offer or proposal needs to be made for any convertible securities (see Rule 15) and, if so, whether for all such securities or only on a partial basis.

Generally speaking, the other provisions of the Code (for example as to disclosure) apply to a partial offer regulated by the Code, in the same way as they do to a general offer, except to the extent the context otherwise requires. Where it is proposed to implement a partial offer by way of a scheme of arrangement, the Panel requires prior consultation.

5.4 Redemption or purchase of own securities

Section Q (Rule 37) of the Code deals with the redemption or purchase by a company of its own securities. Such purchases can, of course, effectively be a backdoor method of obtaining control. If a director or a person acting in concert with him or her was to hold a substantial block of voting shares, any purchase of other voting shares by the company concerned would reduce the number of shares in issue (outside of treasury, where relevant) and increase the percentage which the existing block represents. It would, therefore, give that person greater control.

To protect the minority and to preserve the principle that a person may not obtain or consolidate effective control of a Code company without making an offer to all shareholders, Rule 37.1 provides that a mandatory offer obligation (under Rule 9) will arise in certain circumstances if the percentage of shares carrying voting rights in which a person or group of persons acting in concert is interested increases beyond the limits provided for in Rule 9 as a result of the redemption or purchase by a company of its own shares.

A company which is subject to the Companies Act and which purchases its own shares can choose whether to cancel them immediately or to hold them in treasury. Treasury shares can be used to satisfy awards under a company's employee share plans, resold for cash or cancelled at some future date, or they can simply continue to be held in treasury. Shares held in treasury continue to form part of the company's issued share capital but, for so long as they are held in treasury, the voting rights in respect of them are suspended. Accordingly, for the purposes of the Code (including, for example, the calculation of percentages for Rule 9 and Rule 37 purposes), it is only shares which are in issue outside of treasury which are relevant (see Panel Statement 2003/26 and the definition of "treasury shares" in the Definitions section of the Code).

Rule 37.1 is applied on the following basis:

1. a director or a person acting in concert with him or her will normally incur an obligation to make a mandatory offer under Rule 9 (unless a whitewash is obtained as referred to in point 4 below) if, as a result of a redemption or purchase by a company of its own shares, that director and any concert party comes to be interested in 30% or

more of the voting rights of the company in question or, if already interested in between 30% and 50%, his or her percentage interest is increased (however note that the directors as a whole are not presumed to be acting in concert with each other solely by reason of the proposed redemption or purchase);

2. a person who has appointed a representative to the board of the company, and managers of investment trusts, will be treated on the same basis as directors and may incur a mandatory offer obligation under Rule 9 in the circumstances described in point 1 above;

3. any other person (i.e. one who is not a director, nor acting in concert with any director, nor represented on the board, nor a manager of an investment trust) will not normally incur an obligation to make a mandatory offer under Rule 9 provided that he or she has not purchased any shares in the company at a time when he or she had reason to believe that a redemption or purchase for which requisite shareholder authority existed was being, or was likely to be, implemented in whole or in part (see, for example, the buy-back authority sought by Stobart Group in March 2014 which made clear that a 35.9% shareholder, who was neither represented on the board nor acting in concert with any director, would not be subject to any obligation to make a mandatory offer in the event that its interest increased as a result of the buy-back authority being utilised); and

4. the Panel will usually waive any mandatory offer obligation resulting from a redemption or purchase by a company of its own shares provided there have been no disqualifying transactions (see Note 5 on Rule 37.1) and there is a vote of independent shareholders and the other procedures set out in Appendix 1 to the Code are followed before the implementation of any redemption or purchase. Any such waiver, or "whitewash", is typically renewed at the same time as the relevant shareholders' authority for the purchase of shares is renewed under Ch.4, Pt 18 of the Companies Act 2006. There are numerous examples of such waivers being sought in any given year.

Each individual director is required to draw the attention of the board to any interest in relevant securities of that director and any person acting in concert with him or her at the time any redemption or purchase of the company's own shares is proposed, and whenever shareholders' authority for any such redemption or purchase is to be sought. The Panel requires prior consultation in any case where Rule 9 might be relevant. In appropriate cases, the Panel may require inclusion in the circular to shareholders of confirmation by the directors that they are not aware of any agreements or understandings between directors or persons acting in concert with them.

When is Rule 37 likely to be relevant? It is likely that the maximum number of shares which a company admitted to the Official List will propose to buyback will normally be less than 15% of its equity, in view of the additional requirements imposed by the Listing Rules where 15% or more is to be bought back (see para.12.4 of the Listing Rules). If, for example, there is a buyback of 15%, an interest in 25.5% before the buyback will become an interest in 30% afterwards. In other words, in these circumstances, any director (and persons acting in concert with him) would have to be interested in at least 25.5% of the voting rights before a whitewash is needed. Thus, if a director and his or her concert parties are interested in 25.5% or more of the voting rights, they should stop all purchases of voting shares as soon as the board starts contemplating proposals for the company to buy back its own shares. Even if they are interested in less than 25.5% of the voting rights, they may be prohibited from purchasing shares for other reasons (for example because of the insider dealing or market abuse legislation). If they are already interested in between 30% and 50%, they should of course not make any further purchases in any event if, absent some other dispensation, they wish to avoid a mandatory offer obligation.

There are certain cases when a buyback may not be permitted at all, even if a whitewash had previously been obtained, without a further, specific shareholders' approval. Normally a buyback will not be allowed (without such further approval) during an offer or if the target company's board has reason to believe that an offer might be "imminent" (Rule 21.1(a)(i)). The notice of the shareholders' meeting called to approve a buyback in such circumstances must contain information about the offer or anticipated offer. The Panel may, however, consent to the buyback without a further shareholders' approval if it is in pursuance of a contract entered into earlier or another pre-existing obligation or if a decision to take the proposed action had been taken earlier which has been partly or fully implemented (see Rule 21.1(c)(v)(A), and also art.9 of the Takeover Directive). If it is felt that these circumstances exist, the Panel must be consulted and its consent to proceed without a shareholders' meeting obtained.

An interesting question arises where a company already has a buyback programme in place which is managed by an independent third party (for example its broker) and the board subsequently has reason to believe that an offer for the company might be imminent: would the company need to obtain a further, specific shareholders' approval to continue with the buyback programme in these circumstances? It is suggested that, in these circumstances, it should be possible for such a buyback programme to continue provided that the original instruction to the company's broker was given before Rule 21.1 came into play, it is irrevocable and the broker does not know of any approach to the company concerned. The Panel should be consulted in cases where this might be an issue.

In practice, a company seeking to defend itself against an unwelcome bidder may not wish to buy back its own shares during the course of the offer if that would increase the percentage of shares which any unwelcome bidder (or stake-builder) may be interested in. Where a buyback forms part of an offeree company's defence strategy, it will therefore usually propose the buyback subject to the hostile offer lapsing (i.e. being defeated). This is what Blue Circle did, for example, as part of its successful defence against an offer from Lafarge in the first half of 2000. This case also provides an example of the rule, referred to above, that a mandatory offer obligation will not be imposed on an unwelcome shareholder in such circumstances. During the course of its offer, Lafarge had purchased 19.99%, and its financial adviser had purchased 9.61%, of Blue Circle. As part of its defence, Blue Circle promised to return capital to its shareholders, in part through a purchase of its own shares, if Lafarge's offer did not succeed. Blue Circle duly followed up with a share buyback in May 2000, after the lapse of Lafarge's offer. On the basis that Lafarge was not represented on the board of Blue Circle and that both Lafarge and its financial adviser agreed not to vote on the shareholder resolution to authorise the share buyback, the Panel agreed that any increase in their combined holding to 30% or more, as a result of the buyback, would not give rise to a mandatory bid obligation under Rule 9.

If, unusually, a buyback is effected by the offeree company during an offer, it will constitute a dealing for the purposes of Rule 8 and there will also be an obligation to disclose it in the offeree company's circular to its shareholders under Rule 25.4(c). Similarly, if the offeror purchases its own shares during the course of a securities exchange offer, that counts as a dealing in relevant securities for the purposes of Rule 8 and it will also have to be disclosed in the offer document under Rule 24.4(c). Rule 24.4(c) also provides that, in the case of a securities exchange offer, if the offeror or any person acting in concert with it has dealt in relevant securities of the offeror during the period beginning 12 months prior to the offer period and ending with the latest practicable date prior to the publication of the offer document, the details (including dates) must be disclosed: this would include any of its own shares which it has redeemed or purchased.

In practice, where an offeree company or an offeror redeems or purchases its own securities, no separate dealing disclosure will be required under Rule 8 provided that it includes in the announcement it is required to make under Rule 2.9 details of the total number of relevant securities redeemed or purchased and the prices paid.

As is made clear by Rule 37.2, after the redemption or purchase by a company of its own voting shares, all persons will be subject, in acquiring further interests in shares in the company concerned, to the provisions of Rule 9.1 (when a mandatory offer is required).

The redemption or purchase of non-voting shares (for example, most preference shares) will not be relevant for the purposes of Rule 37 which (like Rule 9) is concerned with voting rights.

Before a company starts a buyback programme, it is always worth considering if there are any Code implications, in addition to the usual tax, financial and corporate law considerations.

Chapter 6

Documents from the Offeror and the Offeree

Carlton Evans
Partner
Linklaters LLP

6.1   Introduction

Takeover documentation, particularly in contested offers, may often appear at first sight to be subject to few guiding principles. However, the content of takeover documentation is closely controlled in respect of both general approach and detailed contents, principally by the Code and, to a lesser extent, by a number of other sources of regulation, such as the Companies Act 2006, the Listing Rules, the Prospectus Rules and the Disclosure Guidance and Transparency Rules (the Disclosure Rules) of the UK Financial Conduct Authority (FCA), the Financial Services Act 2012 and the EU Market Abuse Regulation.

Over the years there has been an increase in the detailed information required by the Code in offer documentation and in the precision with which the more technical elements are drafted. This is partly due to the fact that the Code has become a document drafted in increasingly legal terms which requires close study in order that all of its provisions can be properly reflected in offer documents. In addition, the offer document is a legal document constituting an offer which, on acceptance, establishes a contractual relationship between the offeror and the offeree's shareholders. Equally, a takeover implemented by a scheme of arrangement is a Court-approved process governed by the Companies Act 2006. In addition, the offer document and related documents may also have other legal consequences (for example, if they contain misrepresentations or defamatory statements) and their drafting therefore needs to reflect this.

On 19 September 2011, significant reforms to the Code were adopted in order to better protect offerees (the 2011 Amendments). These resulted in a number of important changes to UK takeover practice, especially in relation to inducement fees, the announcement process during the early stages of a potential offer and statements by offerors about their intentions concerning the offeree's business and employees. The 2011 Amendments arose primarily from issues which occurred in the bid by Kraft for Cadbury, notably concerns over the following issues:

1. offerees feeling compelled to enter into inducement fees and similar arrangements;
2. the length of time between a possible offer announcement and a firm offer being announced; and
3. the fact that, after Kraft had announced during the offer that it thought it would be able to continue to operate a UK Cadbury facility (which Cadbury had announced would be subject to a phased closure), it changed its mind after the offer had become wholly unconditional. Kraft was publicly criticised for doing so—for breaching Rule 19.1 in not satisfying Code standards as to the accuracy of statements made during offers.

6.2 General obligations in respect of documents

6.2.1 *The spirit of the Code*

The Introduction to the Code identifies the difference between its General Principles and its Rules. The General Principles are expressed in broad terms and are "essentially statements of standards of commercial behaviour". The Rules fall into two categories: some of them expand on the General Principles and others are provisions governing specific aspects of takeover procedure. Neither the General Principles nor the Rules are framed in technical language and both are to be interpreted so as to achieve their underlying purpose. Thus, the Code is to be interpreted in accordance with its spirit rather than its letter—although its letter, in giving detailed guidance as to procedure, must not be ignored.

This approach applies as much to documentation as to any other aspect of a takeover. The documents issued by a company to its shareholders, or to the shareholders of another company, have to be drafted in a way which both complies with the detailed requirements of the Code and also enables shareholders and other persons interested in the offer to consider and evaluate fairly the arguments put forward in the course of a takeover.

6.2.2 General responsibilities in respect of offer documentation

In the context of documentation, the General Principle of the Code that is particularly relevant is General Principle 2, which requires that:

> "The holders of the securities of an offeree must have sufficient time and information to enable them to reach a properly informed decision on the bid; where it advises the holders of securities, the board of the offeree must give its view on the effects of implementation of the bid on employment, conditions of employment and the locations of the company's places of business."

This Principle (which is likely to be amended in minor respects following Brexit) is, to a large extent, repeated in Rule 19.1 and is supplemented by Rule 23.1. These Rules state:

> "19.1 Standards of care
>
> Each document, announcement or other information published, or statement made, during the course of an offer must be prepared with the highest standards of care

and accuracy. The language used must clearly and concisely reflect the position being described and the information given must be adequately and fairly presented. These requirements apply whether the document, announcement or other information is published, or the statement is made, by the party concerned or by an adviser on its behalf."

"23.1 Sufficient information

Shareholders must be given sufficient information and advice to enable them to reach a properly informed decision as to the merits or demerits of an offer. Such information must be available to shareholders early enough to enable them to make a decision in good time. No relevant information should be withheld from them. The obligation of the offeror in these respects towards the shareholders of the offeree is no less than an offeror's obligation towards its own shareholders."

As Note 1 on Rule 19.1 makes clear, it is important to note that the Panel regards financial advisers as being responsible for guiding their clients and any relevant public relations advisers with regard to information published during the course of an offer (including pursuant to social media, following amendments to the Rules that took effect in 2018).

Whatever the detailed information, comment or advice contained in offer documentation, the correct approach is that of common sense and commerciality—namely, do the documents say what they are intended to say, do they give fair and adequate information and are they likely to be understood by the persons who are to receive them, not all of whom will have the same level of commercial knowledge and sophistication?

6.2.3 *Specific standards of care: The Notes on Rule 19.1*

Rule 19.1 contains a number of notes intended to emphasise and enlarge upon the obligations of that Rule. Accordingly, the source for any fact that is material to an argument must be clearly stated, together with sufficient detail to enable the significance of the fact to be assessed. Quotations must not be taken out of context, details of their origin must be given and the board of the company using the quotation must be prepared to substantiate or corroborate comments quoted.

Pictorial representations and diagrams must be presented without distortion, and charts, graphs and other similar diagrams must be to scale. The parties to a takeover will often want to use performance figures in a way which bolsters their respective arguments—this is not forbidden, but graphs and charts used must give a fair view and the basis for them should be justifiable.

6.2.4 Directors' responsibility statements: Rule 19.2

The above provisions are buttressed by the requirement in Rule 19.2 that the directors of the relevant company should expressly accept responsibility as individuals for the information contained in each document published in connection with an offer (including any expressions of opinion) and should confirm that, to the best of their knowledge and belief (having taken all reasonable care to ensure that such is the case), the information contained in the document is in accordance with the facts and that it does not omit anything likely to affect the import of the information.

This Rule is applied slightly differently depending on the nature of the offer.

In a hostile offer, the directors of the company issuing the document generally have to accept responsibility for everything in it. However, a modified form of responsibility statement is permitted when information about another company contained in a document has been compiled from published sources (such as its report and accounts). In that case, responsibility need only be taken for "the correctness and fairness of its reproduction or presentation" (see Note 2 on

Rule 19.2). Accordingly, on a hostile bid, any factual information set out in the offer document relating to the offeree will be covered by such a qualified form of responsibility statement.

In a recommended offer, responsibility for information will generally be split between the offeror and offeree directors. The board of the offeree will be required to take full responsibility for information relating to the offeree (including the recommendation) and the board of the offeror will accept responsibility for the rest of the document.

In a securities exchange offer, where an offer document constitutes, or is accompanied by, a prospectus (or a document containing information which is regarded by the FCA as being equivalent to that of a prospectus), under the Prospectus Rules the offeror directors may be required to take responsibility for the whole of the prospectus or equivalent document, notwithstanding the ability under the Code to split responsibility between offeror and offeree directors.

In "public to private" takeovers (P2Ps), in accordance with Note 3 on Rule 19.2, the persons within a private equity house required by the Panel to take personal responsibility will often be extended to include the investment committee and/or senior employees working on the transaction, as well as the directors of the actual bidco.

In exceptional circumstances, the Panel may be willing to consent to the exclusion of a director from the responsibility statement, and sometimes agrees to this in the case of overseas offerors with large numbers of non-executive directors or with a two-tier board structure. In such cases, the exclusion and the reasons for it must be stated in the document (Rule 19.2(b)).

Separate opinions of the offeree's employee representatives and its pension scheme trustees on the effects of the offer do not need to carry a responsibility statement (see Note 4 on Rule 19.2). In addition, where investment analysts' forecasts are published by the offeree or a securities exchange offeror on its website, it must be prominently stated that the forecasts are not endorsed by the company and that they have not been reviewed or reported on in accordance with the Code (see Rule 28.7(v)).

6.2.5 *Appointment of board committees and verification*

Since many boards of directors are too large to be a viable body for preparing documentation (and most executive directors will continue to spend the majority of their time running the business), it is common practice for a board of directors to delegate day-to-day conduct of the offer to a committee, including the detailed consideration of documentation. The directors must believe that the members of the committee are competent to do the work and must disclose all relevant facts relating to themselves or otherwise relating to the documentation. Notwithstanding any delegation, however, all the directors retain ultimate responsibility, as is made clear by s.1 of Appendix 3 to the Code. This requires the circulation of papers and information to the board (including all non-routine agreements and other obligations entered into by a company in the context of the offer) and the holding of board meetings, as necessary, throughout the offer period. By this means, no director is likely to be able to claim that he or she has been relieved from his or her responsibility for ensuring the accuracy of the contents of documentation.

6.3 Early stage documents

6.3.1 *Initial offer announcements*

In the early stages of a bid, a number of documents may be issued by or on behalf of the parties.

The first of these documents will be either an announcement of a possible offer under Rule 2.4 or an announcement of a firm intention to make an offer under Rule 2.7. Practice Statement No.20 sets out the ways in which the Panel will normally interpret certain provisions of Rule 2, including when a possible offer announcement may be required and the contents of such an announcement.

The first of these announcements to be issued in any bid will start an offer period in respect of the offeree. This is important since various Rules in the Code then begin to apply.

As soon as possible thereafter, and at latest by 07.15 on the following business day, the offeree (and the offeror, or publicly identified potential offeror, in the case of a securities exchange offer) must announce details of its issued share capital (Rule 2.9). In practice, this information is often included in the main first announcement.

Thereafter, the offeree (and, in the case of a securities exchange offer, the offeror or publicly identified potential offeror) must then provide the Panel with details of persons reasonably considered to be interested in 1% or more of their share capital (Rule 22). These provisions are supported by Rule 8 which requires offerors, offerees and persons with 1% interests to announce their interests publicly—by no later than 12.00 noon on the 10th business day after the commencement of the offer period or the announcement first identifying the offeror. The Rule also requires disclosure of dealings during the offer period. Amendments made in 2014 changed these disclosure requirements slightly, accelerating the requirements to disclose irrevocable commitments and letters of intent (see Rule 2.10).

6.3.2 *The "put up or shut up" (or PUSU) regime*

As discussed above, the 2011 Amendments implemented significant new requirements in relation to possible offer announcements under Rule 2.4. These changes were driven by the overall approach of the 2011 Amendments to strengthen the position of offerees. In particular, the Rules were revised so as to reduce the period of time following a possible offer announcement during which an offeree might be under siege from a potential offeror, without that potential offeror being required to either launch a formal offer or announce that it has no intention of doing so.

Under Rule 2.4(a), a possible offer announcement by an offeree must identify any potential offeror with which it is in talks or from which an approach has been received (and not unequivocally rejected), irrespective of which potential offeror was the subject of the rumour and speculation which gave rise to an announcement obligation under Rule 2.2. As mentioned above, the first of any such announcements will commence an offer period.

In addition, such an announcement (and any subsequent announcement which first identifies a potential offeror) will also trigger an automatic, compulsory 28-day "put up or shut up" or "PUSU" deadline within which any named potential offeror will be required either to announce a firm intention to make an offer or to state that it has no intention to do so. The announcement must specify the date on which the 28-day deadline will expire and include a summary of the provisions of Rule 8 in relation to disclosure of dealings and positions.

In the case of multiple competing offerors, each potential offeror is subject to its own 28-day deadline from the date on which it is publicly identified—there is no common deadline for all, allowing any new potential offeror at least the same amount of time to consider its bid as any initial potential offeror.

6.3.2.1 *PUSU extensions*

Under Rule 2.6(c), extensions can be granted to the 28-day period. Extensions have occurred in many possible offers and are typically only granted towards the end of the 28-day, or previously extended, deadline to avoid the prospect that, otherwise, extension requests at the start of the 28-day period would become standard practice.

Extensions will normally be permitted with the consent of the Panel—but only at the request of the offeree, and after taking into account "all relevant factors", including the status and anticipated timetable for completion of negotiations. In theory at least, the offeree therefore has the ability to request: (i) different extensions to a put up or shut up deadline; and/or (ii) an extension for a preferred potential offeror and not, if it so chooses, an unwelcome potential offeror. However, this is unlikely to occur in practice.

Put up or shut up periods can be subsequently re-extended multiple times. Any extension, together with the status and timing of negotiations, must be promptly announced by the offeree.

6.3.2.2   White knights

After an offer period has begun, the offeree is not required to announce the existence of a new potential offeror with which it has thereafter begun talks or from which it receives an approach. This is an important exception since it provides an offeree with the freedom to approach a potential white knight without triggering an announcement obligation and, therefore, the automatic put up or shut up deadline. An announcement may, however, be required if "rumour and speculation accurately and specifically identifies a potential offeror which has not previously been identified in any announcement" (Note 3 on Rule 2.2). In practice, however, this is unusual. If required, any such announcement must identify that potential offeror (Rule 2.4(b)). The Rules do not expand on the "accurately and specifically identified" test but, in practice, this is likely to require more than speculation in the form of an educated guess as to who else might be interested in making an offer.

6.3.2.3   Formal sale processes and strategic reviews

Note 2 on Rule 2.6 provides a further exception to the naming and compulsory put up or shut up deadline for potential offerors—it applies in the case of a formal sale process that is initiated by the offeree. For these purposes, the Panel has stated that an announcement by an offeree of a strategic review of its business will not be sufficient to trigger this exemption, even if it refers to a possible offer, since, inter alia, such an announcement must include the phrase "formal sale process" in its heading in order to do so (see Practice Statement 31). It would, however, commence an offer period if it referred to a possible offer.

The announcement of a strategic review which does not refer to a possible offer will not trigger an offer period. However, the Panel may well investigate and may require a subsequent announcement if: (a) an offer is or will be actively considered; and (b) there is rumour and speculation about a possible offer or an untoward share price rise. Any such subsequent announcement would commence an offer period (see Practice Statement 31).

6.3.2.4 Avoiding a PUSU period by "downing tools"

The Panel may also grant a dispensation from the requirement to make an announcement which would start a PUSU period, if it is satisfied that the potential offeror has ceased active consideration of an offer. In this event, the Panel will impose on the former potential offeror the provisions of Rule 2.8 which restrict actions following a "no intention to bid" statements.

Under Rule 2.8, except with the consent of the Panel, persons who make a "no intention to bid" statement (and their concert parties) are then prohibited from taking any of the following steps in the six-month period after making such a statement:

(a) announcing an offer or possible offer;
(b) acquiring any interest in shares of the offeree if it would then require the person to make an offer;
(c) acquiring any interest in, or obtaining an irrevocable commitment in respect of, offeree shares if it would result in the former potential offeror acquiring in aggregate 30% or more of the voting rights of the offeree;

(d) making any statement which raises or confirms the possibility of an offer;

(e) taking any steps in connection with a possible offer where knowledge is extended outside of those who need to know in the potential offer and its immediate advisers; or

(f) purchasing, agreeing to purchase, or making any statement which raises or confirms the possibility that the former potential offeror is interested in purchasing, assets which are significant in relation to the offeree. Note 5 on Rule 2.8 sets out a list of factors the Panel will normally consider when assessing whether an asset is significant.

Note 2 on Rule 2.8 then sets out various circumstances in which a person is permitted to set aside a "no intention to bid" statement—as long as it specifies these circumstances in such statement—namely:

(i) the board of the offeree so agreeing (subject as set out below);

(ii) a third party (including another publicly identified potential offeror) announcing a firm intention to make an offer;

(iii) the offeree announcing a "whitewash" proposal or a reverse takeover;

(iv) the Panel determining that there has been a material change of circumstances; or

(v) where a statement is made outside an offer period, such other circumstances as the person may, with the Panel's prior consent, specify.

Where the "no intention to bid" statement specifies that it may be set aside with the agreement of the offeree board under (i) above, there are limitations on the ability to rely on this, since if the statement is made:

(i) after a third party has announced a firm intention to make an offer:

(a) the "no intention to bid" statement may only specify the agreement of the offeree board as a circumstance in which the statement may be set aside to the extent that such agreement is given *after* that third-party offer has been withdrawn or lapsed;

(b) if the person who made the "no intention to bid" statement, or any person acting in concert with it, acquires an interest in any shares in the offeree in the period following the making of the statement and prior to the third-party offer being withdrawn or lapsing, the agreement of the board of the offeree may *not* be relied on as a reason to set aside the statement *even after* the third-party offer has been withdrawn or lapsed; and

(ii) by a potential offeror which has made a statement to which Rule 2.5(a)(i) or (ii) applies (i.e. concerning the price or exchange ratio of a possible offer or that a possible offer's terms would not be increased) and which did not reserve the right not to be bound by that statement with the agreement of the board of the offeree, the board of the offeree may not, except with the consent of the Panel, agree to the restrictions on purchasing offeree assets (as described above) being set aside for three months following the date on which the statement is made.

The Panel Executive regards making an approach to the offeree as falling within Rule 2.8(e)—i.e. as a step extending knowledge of a possible offer outside those who need to know in the potential offeror and its immediate advisers. However, subject to the limitations described in subparas (i) and (ii) above, if a "no intention to bid" statement reserves the right for it to be set aside with the agreement of the offeree board, the Panel Executive will normally relax this restriction to allow a single confidential approach to the offeree board to ascertain if they would be interested in commencing talks on a possible offer (see Practice Statement 28).

The Panel applies the above general Rules to a potential offeror, which would otherwise need to be named and subject to a PUSU period in a possible offer announcement, if it is satisfied that the potential offeror has "downed tools"—i.e. ceased active consideration of an offer (see Note 4 on Rule 2.2). In this situation:

(i)   the Panel may grant a dispensation from the requirement for a possible offer announcement (although it reserves the right to require such an announcement where any rumour or speculation is ongoing and it is necessary to prevent the creation of a false market); and

(ii) if it does grant a dispensation, the above restrictions under Rule 2.8 then apply to the former potential offeror for a period of six months thereafter.

In addition, during the three-month period after the dispensation is granted, the former potential offeror is also prohibited from actively considering making an offer for the offeree, making an approach to the offeree board or acquiring any interests in shares in the offeree (Note 4(a)(ii) on Rule 2.2). It should be noted that, during this three-month period, there is therefore a stricter regime than would generally apply following making a general "no intention to bid" statement (if the relevant exceptions were specified in such a general statement).

In the second three-month period after the above restrictions are imposed on a former potential offeror, it may be allowed by the Panel to make a single confidential approach to the offeree (subject as set out above if the statement is made after a third party has announced a firm intention to make an offer)—i.e. similarly to the position following a general "no intention to bid" statement which specifies that the statement can be set aside with the agreement of the offeree board.

In each of these cases where an approach to the offeree board is permitted, if the approach is then rejected by the board of the offeree, the potential offeror will not normally be permitted to make any further approach to the board of the offeree for the remainder of the six-month period. Only the board of the offeree will be permitted to initiate further contact during this period (see Practice Statement 28).

If, however, the offeree responds by entering into talks, the normal Rules of the Code will then apply. If, as a result, a possible offer announcement is made thereafter (but within six months after the restrictions under Rule 2.8 were imposed), the

PUSU regime may be relaxed by the Panel so that it only commences at the expiry of such six-month period. The relevant announcement required in this situation should explain why a "PUSU" deadline is not required to be specified and state the date upon which the six-month restricted period will end (see Practice Statement No.28).

After such an announcement, the Rule 2.8 restrictions will not apply for the period of time that such talks continue. If talks are terminated after such an announcement but before expiry of the six-month period, the offeree must announce this and the restrictions under Rule 2.8 will then re-apply to the potential offeror for the remainder of the six-month period. If talks continue after expiry of the six-month period, the offeree will be required to announce a 28-day PUSU period in the normal way at the expiry of such period.

6.3.2.5   End of PUSU Periods

As mentioned above, prior to the expiry of the PUSU period, each identified potential offeror must either announce a firm intention to make an offer or announce that it has no intention of doing so, in which case the restrictions in Rule 2.8 described above will apply to it. If all identified potential offerors announce that they have no intention to make a firm offer, the offer period will end, notwithstanding that, at that time, the board of the offeree may still be in discussions with a white knight or other potential offeror whose existence is not known to the market. In such a situation, the offeree would, however, at least need to consider whether it should issue an announcement to avoid more general false market concerns.

If a potential offeror announces a firm intention to make an offer, the relevant put up or shut up period will no longer apply to any other potential competing offerors (Rule 2.6(b)). Instead, the provisions of Rules 2.6(d) and (e) will apply (see at 6.3.4 below). In addition, as mentioned above, any party that previously: (i) announced that it had no intention to make a firm offer; and (ii) specified that such statement could be set aside in the event that a third-party offeror announced a firm intention to make an offer will no longer be bound by such a statement and may also make a competing offer (Note 2(a)(ii) on Rule 2.8). In that case, the offeror which actually announced a firm intention to make an offer need not make the offer if any subsequent competing offeror announces an intention to make a higher offer (Rule 2.7(b)).

6.3.3 Misleading statements of intention

Rule 19.3 requires that parties to an offer (and their advisers) must take care not to issue statements which, whilst not factually inaccurate, may be misleading or may create uncertainty. This may arise in the early stages of an offer (for example, when more than one potential offeror is named by the offeree) or, after an offer is launched, when a possible competing bidder may wish to alert the market to the fact it is considering a bid—for example, with a view to reducing the chances of the initial bidder being able to purchase shares in the market in the meantime. Equally, however, it may be relevant later on in an offer.

This general obligation is supplemented in Rule 19.3 by one specific example of an unacceptable statement, namely a statement by an offeror "to the effect that it may improve its offer, or that it may make a change to the structure, conditionality or the non-financial terms of an offer, without committing itself to doing so and specifying the improvement or change". This therefore includes statements about switching from an offer to a scheme of arrangement or vice versa (see Panel Statement 2007/35 concerning the breach of this Rule by Standard Life in its bid for Resolution).

This Rule is a reflection of General Principle 4 (which requires parties to endeavour to avoid the creation of a false market) and is designed to prevent an offeror indicating that it might increase, or otherwise alter the terms of, its offer before it is able to commit itself to doing so.

Practice Statement No.19 illustrates the Panel Executive's approach in this area. It advises that, during the course of an offer, any suggestion of an improvement or change to an offer will be of particular sensitivity since it could lead to a false market being created in the securities of the offeree. It adds that, if an offeror wishes to make a holding statement in order to publicise its initial reaction to a particular development (such as an increase in a competing offeror's offer), it may state, for example, that it is "considering its position" or that it is "considering its options". It should not, however, use language which implies that it might improve or change the terms of its offer.

6.3.4 Clarification of possible offer announcements

The general obligations in Rule 19.3 are also supplemented by a specific requirement to clarify possible offer announcements which are still outstanding in the later stages of an offer (see Rule 2.6(d) and (e)).

As mentioned in 6.3.2 above, in the case of multiple competing potential offerors, once one potential offeror has announced a firm intention to make an offer, any existing or new potential competing offeror is no longer subject to any put up or shut up deadline. However, in light of the potential uncertainty which could otherwise be caused by the continued presence of a potential competing offeror at the end of an offer, Rules 2.6(d) and (e) impose a deadline by when any announced potential offeror must clarify its intentions.

Under Rule 2.6(d), where an "offeror" has announced a firm intention to make an offer and it has been announced that a publicly identified potential offeror might make a competing offer, whether or not such statement was made before or after the announcement of a firm intention to make an offer, it must clarify such statement by 17.00 on the 53rd day following the publication of the first offeror's initial offer document, by announcing either a firm intention to make an offer or that it has no intention of doing so.

Similarly, under Rule 2.6(e), once an offeror has announced a firm intention to make an offer and the offeree then refers to the existence of another potential offeror without publicly identifying it, such potential competing offeror must, by 17.00 on the 53rd day following the publication of the first offeror's initial offer document, either announce a firm intention to make an offer or confirm to the offeree that it has no intention to do so, which must then be promptly announced by the offeree.

In relation to schemes of arrangement, the date will normally be by 17.00 on the 7th day prior to the date of the shareholder meetings. However, the Panel may permit the offeror to clarify its position after the date of the shareholder meetings but before the date of the court sanction hearing (see s.4 of Appendix 7 to the Code).

In the case of multiple actual and/or potential competing offers, the Panel has sought in practice to apply the above Rule both to establish an orderly framework for their conduct and to limit, so far as practicable, the period of time for which they might extend.

The case of multiple offers was considered by the Takeover Appeal Board in relation to offers for Xchanging (see Statement 2016/1). In that ruling the Takeover Appeal Board upheld the decision of the Hearings Committee and confirmed that where, after a firm intention to make an offer has been announced: (i) a potential competing offeror (the first competing offeror) later announces a firm intention to make an offer; and (ii) it has also been announced that a publicly identified second potential offeror might also make a competing offer, the second potential competing offeror must clarify its bidding intentions in accordance with the new timetable established by the date of the offer document of the first competing offeror.

More recently, this situation was considered in competing potential and actual offers for Fidessa Group Plc (Fidessa). In that case, after Temenos Group AG and Fidessa had announced a recommended offer for Fidessa (by way of scheme), Fidessa announced that it had received approaches from Ion Investment Group (ION) and SS&C Technologies Holdings, Inc

(SS&C). The Panel initially applied Rule 2.6(d) in the normal way by imposing a deadline for clarification of seven days prior to the shareholder meetings. However, when ION announced a higher recommended offer on 20 April 2018, the Panel ruled that SS&C should clarify its intentions within 14 days thereafter (i.e. by at latest 4 May 2018), rather than the 53rd day after ION's offer document was to be published.

Finally, Note 4 on Rule 31.6 states that, if a potential competing offer is announced after an offeror has made an offer, the Panel will also normally grant the first offeror an extension to Day 60 (i.e. the last day generally allowed to satisfy the acceptance condition) with the consent of the offeree board. In such circumstances, the Panel will normally grant a corresponding extension to, or re-set, Day 46 at the request of the first offeror and with the consent of the board of the offeree.

6.3.5 *Post-offer undertakings and post-offer intention statements: Rules 19.5 and 19.6*

Based on the principles underlying Rule 19.3, specific requirements governing certain statements about the future are now contained in Rules 19.5 and 19.6.

As mentioned above, amendments were made to the Code following the statements made by Kraft, during its offer for Cadbury, about it maintaining a Cadbury facility and subsequently changing this intention after the offer had become wholly unconditional. These Rules have subsequently been reconsidered by the Panel following various high-profile situations, including long-term commitments given by Pfizer about the operations of AstraZeneca in the event of its possible offer for that company succeeding and commitments given in Softbank's offer for Arm.

They are therefore an aspect of any offer that regularly results in extremely close scrutiny by the Panel.

The Code now distinguishes between "post-offer undertakings" (in Rule 19.5) and "post-offer intention statements" (in Rule 19.6).

Post-offer undertakings are defined as statements made by a party to an offer relating to any particular course of action that the party *commits* to take, or not take, after the end of the offer period and which is described by that party as a post-offer undertaking. A party wishing to make such an undertaking must: (i) state that it is a post-offer undertaking; (ii) specify the period of time for which the undertaking is made or the date by which the course of action committed to will be completed; and (iii) prominently state any qualifications or conditions to which the undertaking is subject. The undertaking must be specific and precise, readily understandable and capable of objective assessment and not depend on subjective judgements of the party to the offer or its directors.

A party to an offer must comply with the terms of any post-offer undertaking it makes for the period of time specified in the undertaking and must complete any course of action committed to by the date specified in the undertaking. It may be excused compliance with this only if a qualification or condition set out in the undertaking applies. However, if it wishes to rely on such a qualification or condition, it must consult the Panel in advance and obtain the Panel's consent to rely on that qualification or condition. It must then generally promptly announce the course of action it has taken, or not taken, and explain how and why the relevant qualification or condition applies.

The Code also contains provisions requiring a party which has made a post-offer undertaking to submit reports to the Panel to allow the Panel to check compliance and the Panel is also entitled to require such a party to appoint a supervisor to check this.

A "post-offer intention statement" is defined as a statement made by a party to an offer relating to a particular course of action that the party *intends* to take, or not take, after the end of an offer period, other than a post-offer undertaking. In contrast to post-offer undertakings, which are normally made voluntarily by offerors, post-offer intention statements may be required to be made by an offeror—e.g. in respect of its intentions in relation to the offeree's business and employees (see at 6.4.3 below).

A post-offer intention statement must be both an accurate statement of that party's intention at the time and made on reasonable grounds (Rule 19.6). If a party makes such a statement and, during the 12-month period from the date on which the offer period ends, or such other period of time as specified in the statement, that party decides either to take a course of action different from its stated intentions or not to take a course of action which it had stated it intended to take, it must consult the Panel. That party must then generally make an announcement describing the course of action it has taken, or not taken, and explaining the reasons for doing so.

In addition, following recent Code amendments, Rule 19.6(c) now requires a party which has made a post-offer intention statement to confirm in writing to the Panel whether it has taken, or not taken, the course of action stated in the post-offer intention statement at the end of the period of 12 months from the date on which the offer period ended, or such other period as specified in the statement, and publish that confirmation in accordance with Rule 30.1.

6.4 Offer document contents: Rule 24

6.4.1 *General requirements*

The offer document is the main document in any offer. Except with the consent of the Panel, it must be sent to shareholders of the offeree and others entitled to receive it within 28 days of the announcement of a firm intention to make the offer. Following amendments in 2018, the offeror may only publish an offer document within the 14 days following the announcement of its firm intention to make an offer with the consent of the board of the offeree (Rule 24.1(a)).

See Panel Statement 2018/8 concerning Rangers International Football Club, where the Chairman of the Hearings Committee stated that Mr David King's request for an extension of the time to publish an offer document would not stand any reasonable prospect of success (presumably given, inter alia, the Panel Executive's various communications with him concerning the need for confirmation of the cash finance for the offer to be included in the offer document (see 6.4.8 below)).

The following analysis of the contents of the documentation to be issued by the respective parties to a takeover assumes that an offer is not recommended. In general, however, the Rules apply equally to a recommended offer, in which case the contents requirements in respect of offeree circulars will also apply to the recommended offer document and whatever else the offeror and offeree publish jointly (see 6.5 below).

It should also be noted as a general matter that certain information can be incorporated into offer documentation by reference and that there are alternative methods of communicating Code information to shareholders (see 6.11 below).

6.4.2 Commercial issues, terms and conditions

First and foremost, the offer document will deal with the main commercial terms and arguments for the offer—the price, the commercial logic and general "puff" for the offeror, its management and its expertise. It will also set out in full all the terms and conditions attached to the offer. These terms will include:

1. information about the consideration (for example the type of consideration, any alternative consideration, whether consideration shares carry the right to the next dividend, and the rights attached to consideration preference shares or loan stock);

2. detailed information on the circumstances in which an offer can be revised (see 6.4.7 below regarding the effect of offeree dividends on the offer price);
3. the timetable for announcements and when rights of withdrawal arise;
4. detailed information about acceptances; and
5. the warranties, undertakings and authorities given by an accepting shareholder by virtue of his or her execution of a form of acceptance.

All terms and conditions of an offer must be set out in full, without merely cross-referencing to Rules of the Code (although this requirement has been mitigated in one respect (see 6.4.6 below)). The requirement that all the conditions be comprehensive is illustrated by Rules 31.5 and 32.2 which, subject to certain exceptions, prohibit extensions to, or increases in, the offer in cases where the offeror has indicated that the offer will not be extended or, as the case may be, increased (unless the right to do so has been specifically reserved, with precise details being required of the circumstances which would trigger a right to extend or increase, although in such circumstances the Panel must be consulted).

The specific Code requirements for an offeror to satisfy concerning the contents of an offer document are to be found in Rules 24.2–24.17. These requirements may also extend to documents that are not technically offer documents, such as circulars sent to shareholders by a potential offeror which has announced an offer but subject to a pre-condition.

6.4.3 *Intentions regarding the offeree, offeror and their employees: Rule 24.2*

Under Rule 24.2(a), an offeror must explain the long term commercial justification for the offer in the offer document and cover the following points:

1. its intentions with regard to the future business of the offeree, including its intentions for any research and development functions of the offeree;

2. its intentions with regard to the continued employment of the employees and management of the offeree and its subsidiaries, including any material change in the conditions of employment or in the balance of the skills and functions of the employees and management;
3. its strategic plans for the offeree and their likely repercussions on employment and on the locations of the offeree's places of business, including on the location of the offeree's headquarters and headquarters functions;
4. its intentions with regard to employer contributions into the offeree's pension scheme(s) (including with regard to current arrangements for the funding of any scheme deficit), the accrual of benefits for existing members and the admission of new members;
5. its intentions with regard to any redeployment of the fixed assets of the offeree; and
6. its intentions with regard to the maintenance of any existing trading facilities for the offeree's relevant securities.

Where the offeror is a company, and insofar as it is affected by the offer, the offeror must also state its intentions with regard to its future business and disclose information for subparas (2) and (3) above with regard to itself (Rule 24.2(c)).

In relation to subpara.(2), prior to 20 May 2006 the offeror was merely required to describe its intentions with regard to the continued employment of the employees and the practice evolved that this requirement would be met with the rather anodyne statement that the employment and other rights of employees would be "safeguarded".

Such a statement is still typically included in offer documents. However, following the events in the Kraft bid for Cadbury and subsequent offers, recent Code amendments have deliberately aimed to improve the quality of disclosure by offerors and offerees in relation to the offeror's intentions regarding the offeree's business and its employees, in order to provide meaningful information to the offeree's shareholders and employees (see also 6.3.5 above). To that end, Rule 24.2(b) requires the offeror to make a negative statement in the offer document if it has no plans to make any changes in relation to the matters referred to in Rule 24.2(a) as summarised above. In addition, if it considers that its strategic plans for the offeree will have no repercussions on employment or the location of the offeree's place of business, the offeror must make a statement to that effect. Finally, given the significance which the Panel now places on these disclosures, it may, on occasion, pre-vet relevant sections of the offer announcement and/or offer document.

6.4.4   *Financial and other information: Rule 24.3*

Prior to the 2011 Amendments, the Code contained different disclosure requirements in respect of financial and some other information depending on: (i) the nature of the offeror, with less information being required in the case of UK listed offerors (on the basis that more extensive public information was easily available on such companies if persons wished to review it); and (ii) the nature of the offer, with more information being required if the offer included offeror securities, rather than a pure cash offer (on the basis that, in a cash offer, with the exception of any minority shareholders, offeree shareholders would not need to assess the future financial performance of the offeror).

However, the 2011 Amendments introduced a radical change of approach to the disclosure of financial information on the offeror. The rationale for this was that persons other than offeree shareholders (for example, employees) have an interest in understanding the financial strength of the offeror. Accordingly, subject to certain exceptions, detailed financial information must now be provided in relation to an offeror and the financing of an offer irrespective of the nature of the offer (i.e. even in the case of a pure cash offer by a UK listed company). However, the impact of this is almost entirely mitigated by other Rules designed to allow financial information in particular to simply be incorporated by reference (see below).

6.4.4.1   UK listed offerors

Under Rule 24.3(a), where the offeror is a company incorporated under the Companies Act 2006 (or its predecessors) and
its shares are admitted to trading on a UK regulated market or
the Alternative Investment Market (AIM) or the NEX Exchange
Growth Market, the offeror must include in the offer document:

1.   the names of its directors;
2.   the nature of its business and its financial and trading
     prospects;
3.   details of website addresses where its audited consoli-
     dated accounts for the last two financial years and any
     preliminary statement of annual results, half-yearly finan-
     cial report or interim financial information published since
     the date of its last published accounts can be found,
     together with a statement that such statement, report or
     information has been incorporated into the offer document
     by reference to the relevant website in accordance with
     Rule 24.15;
4.   in the case of a securities exchange offer, any known
     significant changes in its financial or trading position since
     the end of the last financial period for which audited
     accounts, a preliminary statement of annual results, a
     half-yearly financial report or interim financial informa-
     tion has been published (or a negative statement);
5.   a statement of the effect of full acceptance of the offer upon
     its earnings and assets and liabilities; and
6.   a summary of the principal contents of each material
     contract (not being a contract entered into in the ordinary
     course of business) entered into by the offeror or any
     subsidiary in the two years before the commencement of
     the offer period.

Under Rule 24.3(e), the information summarised under subparas (1)–(4) above must also be given in respect of the offeree
(save in respect of (4) above in a recommended offer document
(see 6.5.2 below)).

6.4.4.2   *Non–UK listed offerors and their participants*

Where the offeror is not a Companies Act 2006 company or its shares are not admitted to trading on a UK regulated market, AIM or the NEX Exchange Growth Market, it must disclose as much of the information set out in Rule 24.3(a) as is appropriate and such further information as the Panel may require (Rule 24.3(b)(i)).

The Code also requires additional information about persons who are participating in an offeror whose shares are not admitted to trading on a UK regulated market, AIM or the NEX Exchange Growth Market (for example, a private equity house in a P2P or shareholders in a consortium company formed for the purposes of the offer). The identity of such persons and details of their interests must be disclosed as well as such other information as the Panel may require (Rule 24.3(b)(ii) and (iii)). The ability of the Panel to require additional information means that in appropriate cases the Panel should be consulted in advance, so that the offer document can be properly prepared.

Similarly, where an offeror whose shares are not admitted to trading on a UK regulated market, AIM or the NEX Exchange Growth Market is the subsidiary of another company, the Panel will normally look through the offeror and require information on the ultimate holding company in the form of group accounts (Note 1 on Rule 24.3).

6.4.4.3   *Other information*

Rule 24.3 sets out further content requirements for the offer document. These include:

1.   a heading stating: "If you are in any doubt about this offer you should consult an independent financial adviser authorised under the FSMA";

2. the date when the document is published, the name and address of the offeror (including, where the offeror is a company, the type of company and the address of its registered office);
3. the identity of any person acting in concert with the offeror and, to the extent that it is known, the offeree, including, in the case of a company, its type, registered office and relationship with the offeror and, where possible, the offeree;
4. details of each class of security for which the offer is made (including the maximum and minimum percentages of those securities which the offeror undertakes to acquire);
5. the terms of the offer, including the consideration offered for each class of security, the total consideration offered and particulars of the way in which the consideration is to be paid in accordance with Rule 31.8;
6. all conditions to which the offer is subject;
7. particulars of all documents required, and procedures to be followed, for acceptance of the offer;
8. market prices for the securities to be acquired and, in the case of a securities exchange offer, securities to be offered;
9. details of any agreements or arrangements to which the offeror is a party which relate to the circumstances in which it may or may not invoke or seek to invoke a condition to its offer and the consequences of doing so including, to the extent permitted by the Code require-ments, details of any inducement fees payable as a result (see 6.8.2 below);
10. details of any irrevocable commitment or letter of intent which the offeror or any of its associates has procured in relation to relevant securities of the offeree (or, if appropri-ate, the offeror);
11. in a securities exchange offer, full particulars of the terms of the securities being offered including the rights attach-ing to them;
12. a summary of the provisions of Rule 8 (which governs the disclosure of dealings during the course of an offer);
13. the national law that will govern contracts concluded between the offeror and the holders of the offeree's securities as a result of the offer and the competent courts;

14. the compensation (if any) offered for the removal of "breakthrough" rights pursuant to art.11 of the European Directive on Takeover Bids (2004/25) (the Directive) (or, following Brexit, compensation for the removal of rights which might arise as a result of any opting-in resolution under Ch.2 of Pt 28 of the Companies Act 2006) together with particulars of the way in which the compensation is to be paid and the method employed in determining it;

15. any post-offer undertaking made by the offeror (see 6.3.5 above);

16. details of any offer-related arrangement permitted under Rule 21.2 (see further 6.8.2 below);

17. a list of the documents which the offeror has published on a website in accordance with Rules 26.1, 26.2 and 26.3 (which set out the requirements for documents to be published on a website following the announcement of an offer or the making of an offer, respectively) and the address of the website on which the documents are published (see 6.11.5 below);

18. any profit forecast or quantified financial benefits statement, and any related reports and confirmations, required by Rule 28;

19. if any document published by the offeror contains a comparison of the value of the offer with previous prices of the offeree's shares, a comparison of the current value of the offer and the price of the offeree's shares on the last business day prior to the beginning of the offer period, no matter what other comparisons are made; and

20. a summary of the ratings and outlooks provided by rating agencies in respect of the offeror and offeree prior to the beginning of the offer period, together with any changes made to those ratings or outlooks during the offer period and a summary of any reasons given for any such changes.

6.4.4.4 Sources of finance to an offeror

Following the 2011 Amendments, under Rule 24.3(f), the offer document must contain: (i) a description of how the offer is to be financed (both debt and equity) and the source(s) of the finance; and (ii) in relation to debt finance, details of the debt facilities or other instruments entered into in order to finance the offer and to refinance the existing debt or working capital facilities of the offeree, other than hedging arrangements, and in particular:

1. the amount of each facility or instrument;
2. the repayment terms;
3. interest rates;
4. any security provided;
5. a summary of the key covenants;
6. the names of the principal financing banks; and
7. if applicable, details of the time by which the offeror will be required to refinance the acquisition facilities and of the consequences if that is not done by the relevant time.

In addition, all documents relating to the financing of an offer must be put on display, along with any refinancing documents when they are entered into (see also 6.11.5 below). On occasion, however, the Panel has allowed the display of market flex provisions to be delayed with a view to assisting syndication of the debt, but generally only until posting of the offer document.

6.4.5   *Shareholdings and dealings: Rule 24.4*

Rule 24.4 contains a list of information required in the offer document concerning shareholdings and dealings of the offeror (and its directors) in the shares of the offeree and, if the offer is a securities exchange offer, the offeror. This includes details of any shares of the offeree in which, inter alia, the offeror, its concert parties and certain other connected persons have an interest or right to subscribe or which they have borrowed or lent. "Interest" is defined as "a long economic exposure whether absolute or conditional to changes in the price of securities" and a person is treated as having an interest in shares if, inter alia, he or she owns them, has the right to direct voting rights, has the right or obligation to take delivery of the shares or if he or she is a party to any derivative whose value is determined by reference to the price of the underlying shares. Rule 24.4 also requires short positions in relation to shares and derivatives referenced to those shares to be disclosed.

Under Rule 24.4(c), dealings by any person whose interests have to be disclosed under Rule 24.4(a) are required to be disclosed for the period beginning 12 months prior to the commencement of the offer period and ending with the latest practicable date before printing of the offer document. "Dealings" is construed widely and again extends to financial products referenced to offeree shares.

In the case of a securities exchange offer, equivalent information generally has to be given by the persons required to disclose their interests and dealings in offeree shares in relation to any interests and dealings they might have in offeror shares. In the case of competing offers, certain of these disclosures also extend to the competing bidder's securities.

Note 2 on Rule 24.4 states that, provided that, inter alia, no significant dealings are thereby concealed, disclosure of:

1. dealings during the offer period can be aggregated;
2. dealings in the three months prior to that period can be aggregated on a monthly basis; and
3. dealings in the nine months prior to that period can be aggregated on a quarterly basis.

6.4.6   Disclosure of fees and expenses: Rule 24.16

A new Rule was introduced as part of the 2011 Amendments requiring the detailed disclosure of the fees of any advisers to the offeror (see Rule 24.16).

The offer document must contain an estimate of the aggregate fees and expenses expected to be incurred by the offeror in connection with the offer, with separate estimates in respect of: financial and corporate broking advice; financing arrangements (including full details of any commitment or drawdown fees, which may be cross-referred to the information required under Rule 24.3(f)); legal, accounting or public relations advice; and any other professional services (such as management consultants, actuaries or specialist valuers). There is, however, no requirement to disclose an estimate of any fees expected to be incurred in relation to a supervisor appointed pursuant to Rule 19.5 (see Note 3 on Rule 24.16).

If a fee is variable, the offer document must disclose the minimum and maximum amounts payable. Where a fee is not subject to a maximum amount, that must be made clear and the arrangement explained (for instance, whether the fee is discretionary or relates to the final value of the offer or is calculated on a "time cost" basis). If a category of fees and expenses includes a variable or uncapped element, the figure or range given must reflect a reasonable estimate of the fees likely to be paid on the basis of the current offer. If the fee arrangement provides for circumstances where the fee may increase, for example where the offer is revised or a competitive situation arises, the higher amount is not required to be disclosed until such circumstances arise.

If any fee or expense within a particular category is likely at any time to exceed the estimated maximum previously disclosed by 10% or more, or if the final fees and expenses actually paid within a particular category exceed the disclosed estimated maximum by 10% or more, the offeror must promptly disclose the revised estimates, or final amounts paid, privately to the Panel, which may then require such revised estimates or final amounts paid to be announced.

Rule 25.8 also requires any such fees and expenses incurred by the offeree, if applicable, to be detailed in the offeree circular (see 6.5 below).

6.4.7 *Offeree dividends: Note 4 on Rule 2.5, Rule 2.7(c)(xiii) and Rule 24.17*

In 2015, new Rules regarding offeree dividends and other distributions were introduced.

Under these Rules, an offeror is able to reduce the offer consideration by the amount of any dividend (or other distribution) which is paid or becomes payable by the offeree to the offeree's shareholders, provided that the offeror makes an express statement that it wishes to reserve the right to reduce the offer consideration in this way. It must state whether it wishes to reserve this right in each of any possible offer announcement including possible terms, the announcement of a firm intention to make an offer and the offer document (see Note 4 on Rule 2.5, Rule 2.7(c)(xiii) and Rule 24.17).

It must also be a term of the offer that, if the offeror exercises its right to reduce the offer consideration by the amount of a dividend (or other distribution) that has not yet been paid, offeree shareholders will be entitled to retain that dividend (or other distribution).

In addition, if a "no increase" statement is made at any time and a dividend (or other distribution) is subsequently paid or becomes payable by the offeree, the offeror will normally be *required* to reduce the offer consideration by an equal amount unless, and to the extent that, the offeror has stated that offeree shareholders will be entitled to receive all or part of a specified dividend (or other distribution) in addition to their offer consideration (see Note 4(b) on Rule 2.5 and Rule 32.2).

6.4.8   Other information required by Rule 24

Other information required by Rules 24.5–24.14 includes:

1. in the case of a securities exchange offer, whether and in what manner the emoluments of the directors of the offeror will be affected by the acquisition of the offeree or any associated transaction, or an appropriate negative statement (Rule 24.5);
2. details of any agreement, arrangement or understanding (including any compensation arrangement) between the offeror or any concert party and any of the directors, recent directors, shareholders or recent shareholders of the

offeree having any connection with or dependence upon the offer (Rule 24.6). This Rule also cross-refers to Rule 16.2 which requires any management or incentivisation arrangements or proposals (or discussions) to be publicly disclosed and, depending on the facts, this may need to be supported by an opinion from the offeree's financial advisor and an independent shareholder vote;

3.   a repetition of the confirmation required to be included in the announcement of a firm intention to make an offer from the offeror's bank or financial adviser of the existence of financial resources to satisfy any cash payable under an offer, although this confirmation does not operate as a guarantee that funds will be available (Rule 24.8). A conditional confirmation is not permitted. Where an offeror proposes to finance a cash offer (or a cash alternative to a securities exchange offer) by an issue of new securities, the Panel will not regard this as "exceptional circumstances" and, accordingly, will not allow the cash confirmation given to be conditional upon the success of the issue of the new offeror securities (Practice Statement No.10), although certain necessary conditionality will be permitted—for example any required shareholder approval and/or admission of any new securities to listing.

The offeror must also promptly notify the Panel if it becomes aware or considers it likely that it will not be able to satisfy a financing condition (Rule 13.4(d)). See Panel Statement 2018/8, concerning Rangers International Football Club, where in the circumstances of that case (i.e. the Panel having previously required a mandatory offer to be made under Rule 9), the Chairman of the Hearings Committee stated that the Panel Executive had said that a sterling bank account in South Africa would not suffice for cash confirmation purposes. It is specifically worth noting that, subsequently, it was reported to the Panel Executive that transfer of the funds from South Africa to a bank account in the UK would require exchange control approval which may provide part of the reasoning underlying the Executive's decision. See also Panel Statement 2018/19 (also relating to Rangers International

Football Club), where the requirement for the cash confirmation statement to cover any shares legitimately issued by an offeree during an offer period was confirmed;
4. a statement as to the ultimate ownership of any securities acquired in pursuance of the offer (Rule 24.9);
5. a statement that, where securities offered as consideration are to be listed on the Official List or admitted to trading on AIM, the relevant listing or admission to trading condition will only be satisfied when the announcement of admission has been made. Where securities are offered as consideration and it is intended that they should be admitted to listing or to trading on any other investment exchange, the Panel should be consulted (Rule 24.10);
6. an estimate by an appropriate adviser of the value of any class of securities proposed to be issued as consideration which is not admitted to trading (Rule 24.11). In such an offer, however, it will not normally be possible for the offeror to satisfy the Panel that the value of its offer exceeds the price of any purchases of offeree shares that might have been made to which Rule 6 applies;
7. a statement to the effect that, except with the consent of the Panel, settlement of the consideration to which any shareholder is entitled under the offer will be satisfied in accordance with the terms of the offer without regard to any other counterclaim to which the offeror may otherwise be entitled (Rule 24.12);
8. details of any arrangements in relation to certain dealings which exist between the offeror, or any person acting in concert with the offeror, and any other person, or a negative statement (Rule 24.13); and
9. a clear statement as to the procedure for shutting off any cash-underwritten alternative (Rule 24.14).

The complete and detailed list should be read from the Code itself, but there is one further and very important requirement which must be noted. According to Rule 24.7, the offer document must state the time allowed for acceptance of the offer and any alternative offer and must reflect appropriately the full terms relating to acceptance levels, time of announcements, rights of withdrawal, etc, which are contained in those parts of Rules 13.5(a), 13.6 (if applicable), 17 and 31–34 of the Code (see Ch.7). It must also reflect the terms of Notes 4–8 on Rule 10 relating to acceptances and purchases and confirmation of good title to shares. However, the amount of small print which would be required if all details were to be set out in full has been substantially reduced by the Code permitting a cross-reference to Notes 4–6 and Note 8 on Rule 10, since they deal with what are regarded as largely technical matters.

6.4.9   *Incorporation of information by reference: Rule 24.15*

In addition to the financial information required to be included or incorporated by reference in the offer document, Code documents may incorporate other information by reference to another source with the Panel's consent. If information is permitted to be incorporated by reference, then certain additional requirements need to be complied with under Rule 24.15 (including details of where the information is located) and recipients are entitled to request a hard copy of the relevant information.

6.5   Offeree circular contents: Rule 25

The offeree circular (which must be issued within 14 days after the issue of the offer document, if not combined with it or unless consented to by the Panel) is subject to various general requirements as set out in Rule 25.

6.5.1   *Offeree recommendation*

It must first contain the opinion of the board of the offeree on the offer and any alternative offers (together with the board's reasons for forming its opinion) and the substance of the advice given to it by its independent financial advisers (Rule 25.2). In a recommended offer, the opinion of the offeree board will be contained in the offer document itself. In a hostile offer, it will be contained in the "defence document" which will seek to refute the arguments and the commercial logic put forward by the offeror. The opinion of the offeree board must include its views on:

1. the effects of implementation of the offer on all the company's interests, including, specifically, employment; and
2. the offeror's strategic plans for the offeree and their likely repercussions on employment and the locations of the offeree's place of business as set out in the offer document pursuant to Rule 24.2.

If there is no clear opinion or there is a "divergence of views" among the offeree board, or between the board and its independent financial adviser, this must be made clear in the offeree circular and an explanation given, including the arguments for or against the acceptance or rejection of the offer (Note 2 on Rule 25.2). The views of any directors who are in a minority should also be included in the circular. The Panel will also require prior consultation on such opinions and related explanations. In addition, Note 1 on Rule 25.2 makes clear that the Code does not limit the factors that the board of the offeree is able to take into account in giving its opinion on the offer—in particular, that the offeree board is not bound to consider the offer price as the determining factor.

6.5.2 *Other specific content requirements*

Rule 25 also sets out specific content requirements for the first major offeree circular. To a large extent, this corresponds to the information requirements imposed on the offeror by Rule 24.

Under Rule 25.3, subject as set out below, the first major offeree circular advising shareholders on an offer must contain a description of any known "significant change" in the financial or trading position of the offeree since the end of the last financial period for which audited accounts, a preliminary statement of annual results, a half-yearly report or interim financial information has been published, or an appropriate negative statement.

Under Rule 24.3(e) of the Code, the offeror is generally required to include this information in its offer document in relation to an offeree. However, in a combined offer document (i.e. if the offer is recommended), this information is the responsibility of the offeree board and Rule 24.3(e) will not apply to such a statement. This gives the shareholders the benefit of knowing that such statements have been considered by those best placed to understand the offeree's affairs (i.e. the offeree's directors). In contrast, if the offeree circular follows the offer document, the information in the offeror document on any such changes need not be repeated as long as it is specifically referred to in the statement made by the offeree.

Other information that needs to be contained in the first major circular from the offeree includes:

1. interests and dealings in the offeror's and the offeree's shares and whether the offeree directors intend to accept or reject the offer in respect of their own beneficial holdings (and, if required by the Panel, which of any alternative offers they intend to elect for) (Rule 25.4);
2. information about directors' service contracts (including particulars of former contracts, if such contracts have been replaced or amended within six months of the date of the offeree circular) (Rule 25.5). This Rule is designed to ensure that any compensation payments to outgoing directors ("golden parachutes"), which are arranged at or shortly before the making of the offer, are fully disclosed to the public. Aggregation of the remuneration payable under service contracts is no longer permitted and full details of each director's remuneration package must be given;
3. any arrangement in relation to securities of the offeree, such as indemnities or options, must also be disclosed, or there should be an appropriate negative statement if there are none (Rule 25.6);
4. a summary of the principal contents of any material contract (not being a contract entered into in the ordinary course of business) entered into by the offeree or any

subsidiary in the two years before the commencement of the offer period (Rule 25.7(a));

5. details of any irrevocable commitment or letter of intent which the offeree or any person acting in concert with it has procured in relation to securities of the offeree (Rule 25.7(b));

6. any post-offer undertaking or post-offer intention statement made by the offeree in accordance with Rules 19.5 and 19.6 (Rule 25.7(c));

7. a list of the documents which the offeree has published on its website in accordance with Rules 26.1, 26.2 and 26.3 (Rule 25.7(d));

8. any profit forecast, or quantified financial benefits statement, and any related reports or confirmations, required by Rule 28 (Rule 25.7(e)); and

9. as mentioned in 6.4.6 above, details of any fees and expenses expected to be incurred by the offeree in connection with the offer (Rule 25.8).

6.5.3 *Opinions from employees and pension scheme trustees*

The offeree must also append to its document any opinion from its employee representatives and/or the trustees of its pension scheme(s) on the effect of the offer on employment and/or the offeree's pension scheme(s) respectively, provided that any such opinion is received "in good time before publication". It must also publish any employee opinion or pension scheme trustee opinion on a website (and announce via a Regulatory Information Service (RIS) that it has been so published) if it is not received prior to publication of the circular and provided that it is received within 14 days of the offer becoming or being declared wholly unconditional. Note 1 on Rule 25.9 also requires the offeree to pay for: (i) the costs of the publication of the employee opinion and of any pension scheme trustee opinion; and (ii) any costs reasonably incurred in obtaining advice on verification of the employee opinion.

Respondents to a Panel consultation on the 2006 changes to the Code in respect of employee representative opinions (which were required by the Directive) expressed concern that the effect of these Rules was to require the offeree to consult with its employees prior to the offer being announced. They claimed that this issue could be of particular concern in a recommended offer where both the announcement of a firm intention to make an offer and the combined offer document (containing information on the offeror and the offeree) could be published on the same day—this would not be possible if the offeree was required to obtain the opinion of employee representatives.

As a result, the Panel clarified that, in its opinion, both the Directive and the Code required information to be provided to employees but that consultation was not required and that there was no intention to change the practice of publishing a combined document in the case of a recommended offer. However, when the offeree makes a copy of an announcement or circular available to its employees or employee representatives at the beginning of an offer period, it must at the same time inform them of the right of employee representatives to have a separate opinion appended to the circular and of the offeree's obligation to pay for advice in connection with the verification of information in that opinion (see 6.11.4.2 below).

As mentioned above, in 2013 the above provisions relating to employee representatives were extended to any opinion of the trustees of an offeree's pension schemes, save in respect of the cost of verifying such an opinion (given that any such costs might be significant).

6.6 Other documents and announcements

6.6.1 Revised offers

Under Rule 32.1, if an offer is formally revised, a revised offer document must be drawn up in accordance with Rules 24 and 27. The same publication requirements apply to a revised offer document as for the original, including making the revised offer document readily available to employee representatives (or employees) and the trustees of the offeree's pension scheme(s), and informing them of the right to have a separate opinion on the revised offer appended to any offeree circular.

Similarly, under Rule 32.6, the board of the offeree must draw up a circular in accordance with Rules 25 and 27 containing its opinion on the revised offer. The same publication requirements apply to such a revised circular as for the original, including with regard to the opinion of employee representatives and the pension scheme trustees on the revised offer.

6.6.2 *General announcements and documents*

Irrespective of whether an offer is formally revised, after the initial offer and defence documents have been issued, particularly in hostile or competing offers there are likely to be a succession of documents issued by the offeror and offeree containing further arguments and information. These documents must comply with the provisions of Rule 27.2 and contain details of any changes in information previously published by the party in connection with the offer which are material in connection with that document and, if there have been no material changes, this fact must be stated. There must also be updated information on matters such as interests in shares and dealings, changes in the financial or trading position, offeror directors' emoluments, changes to offeree directors' service contracts, etc.

In addition, in relation to schemes of arrangement, certain key events must be announced and, in certain cases, then potentially posted to offeree shareholders (s.5 of Appendix 7).

Where a profit forecast, quantified financial benefits statement or asset valuation has been made, any subsequent document must also contain a statement by the directors that the forecast, quantified financial benefits statement or asset valuation remains valid for the purpose of the offer and, where applicable, that the financial advisers and accountants who reported on the forecast or qualified financial benefits statement have confirmed that their reports continue to apply, or the independent valuer who performed the asset valuation has confirmed that an updated valuation would not be materially different (see Rule 27.2(d)).

6.6.3 Continuous obligation to update material information

Prior to 2012, parties to an offer largely only had to update information previously published if they *chose* to issue a new document (subject to general Listing Rules and false market considerations). However, in 2012, the requirements to update previously published information were significantly amended so as to *require* parties to do so in certain circumstances.

In particular, a new Rule 27.1 was introduced which requires a party to an offer to disclose, after the date of the offer document or initial defence circular (as the case may be): (i) any material changes to information disclosed in any document or announcement previously published by it in connection with the offer; and (ii) any material new information which would have been required to be disclosed in any previous document or announcement published during the offer period had it been known at such time, in each case promptly by way of announcement—i.e. not merely when a subsequent document is published.

6.6.4 Equality of information to shareholders and persons with information rights: Rule 20.1

The Code generally requires information and opinions relating to an offer or a party to an offer to be made equally available to all offeree shareholders and persons with information rights as nearly as possible at the same time and in the same manner (Rule 20.1(a)). This Rule may require that any material new information or significant new opinion relating to an offer or a party to an offer that is inadvertently made public must be published in an announcement. The scope of Rule 20.1 was significantly expanded in 2016. For example, it now specifies certain persons to which the Rule applies if they receive such information, including holders of publicly-traded debt securities of an offeror or the offeree (Rule 20.1(b)). It also requires various documents given to certain persons to be published on a website regardless of whether they contain any material new information or significant new opinions (Rule 20.1(c)).

6.6.5   *Videos, social media and advertisements: Rules 20.3, 20.4 and 20.5*

As part of the amendments made in 2016, express rules were also introduced to govern the release of information regarding an offer via videos and social media.

A video published by or on behalf of an offeror or the offeree in relation to an offer or the financial performance of a party to an offer must be scripted and comprise only a director or senior executive and may only be published with the Panel's consent. The video must be published on a website but the fact of its publication need not be announced (Rule 20.3).

In addition, social media must not be used by an offeror or the offeree to publish information relating to an offer, other than for the publication of the full text of an announcement or document that has been published in accordance with the Code, a video which has been published with the prior consent of the Panel in accordance with Rule 20.3 or a notification of a link to a webpage on which such announcement, document or video has been published (Rule 20.4).

The provisions of the Code which apply to advertisements should also be noted. Rule 20.5 prohibits advertisements unless they fall within certain prescribed categories and (subject to limited exceptions) the Panel's consent is obtained. This Rule was introduced after a series of high-profile advertising campaigns which were generally not considered appropriate to the proper conduct of takeovers. Accordingly, advertisements relating to an offer are, in effect, limited to statements of fact (for example, reminders as to closing times, announcements which have to be made or advertisements of preliminary or interim results). Since 2016, advertisements no longer have to include a directors' responsibility statement.

6.6.6   Time limits on releasing material information

There is a limit to the time in which material information connected with offers can be released to shareholders. Rule 31.6 basically requires that, subject to limited exceptions, the acceptance condition must be satisfied by acceptances and purchases made by 13.00 on the 60th day after posting the offer document (commonly known as "Day 60"). Consequently, the last document from the offeror which can contain a revision of the offer must be issued on Day 46. This is because Rule 32, dealing with revised offers, requires any revised offer to be kept open for at least 14 days after posting to allow offeree shareholders sufficient time to reach a decision. This timing requirement applies in the absence of any competing offer, where an auction process will generally apply, or other exceptional circumstance (see Rule 32.5 and Panel Statements 2018/14, 2018/15 and 2018/16 concerning the competing offers for Sky PLC by Comcast Corporation and Twenty-First Century Fox Inc.).

In turn, in order to give the offeror seven days to consider the final material arguments of the offeree, the offeree is restricted by Rule 31.9 from issuing new material information after Day 39 (except with the consent of the Panel), though Day 39 may itself be suspended if, for example, anti-trust clearances have not been received by such time.

During the bid by The Great Universal Stores Plc (GUS) for Argos Plc in 1999, the Panel allowed Argos to release certain trading information after Day 39. GUS was allowed, as a consequence, to decide whether or not it wished, in the light of this information, to increase or extend its offer. GUS chose to do neither and its offer later succeeded. The Code has since been amended to deal with this issue expressly (see Rule 31.9 and Note 5 on Rule 32.2).

In addition, the Panel has amended the Code so as to make clear that, in schemes of arrangement, the latest day for revision should normally be 14 days prior to the shareholder meetings, absent Panel consent (which will normally only be given if the Panel receives certain confirmations from the offeree and its financial adviser to the effect, broadly speaking, that the revisions will not be detrimental to the likely success of the scheme) (s.7 of Appendix 7).

6.7 Schemes of arrangement

Takeovers are increasingly being implemented by way of schemes of arrangement. This was initially often done in order to avoid the half per cent stamp duty which arises on transfers of shares in a contractual takeover offer. However, even though this exemption is no longer applicable, schemes are still very common since they remove any risk of the offeror ending up owning less than 100% of the offeree securities if the offer succeeds (and so are generally preferred by offeror lenders) and the courts have shown themselves to be reasonably flexible in adapting to the sometimes rapidly evolving circumstances which may arise during a takeover.

In the case of a scheme, the circular which has to be sent to offeree shareholders is required to contain essentially the same Code information as an offer document in a recommended takeover. It also contains various sections necessary in order to implement the scheme itself—for example, the expected scheme timetable, an explanatory statement, notices of a general meeting and of a meeting of shareholders convened by the court, and the scheme of arrangement itself.

Takeovers implemented by way of a scheme of arrangement fall within the general scope of the Code and many of its Rules apply in exactly the same way in a scheme of arrangement as they do in a contractual takeover offer. However, some Rules are inevitably inapplicable to schemes given, for example, that there is no contractual "offer" or "acceptance" in a scheme of arrangement which is, in contrast, effected by way of a shareholder vote and court approval.

In light of this, the Panel has, over the years, applied the Code in relation to schemes of arrangement in a pragmatic way.

However, due in large part to the increasing number of schemes in recent years, a new Appendix 7 was included in the Code to deal with the differences between schemes of arrangement and contractual offers and to clarify which Rules should be disapplied when a scheme is used and to set out specific Code amendments. These include the following:

1. that a mandatory bid under Rule 9 should not be able to be undertaken by way of a scheme of arrangement without the Panel's prior consent. In deciding whether to give its consent, relevant factors will be the views of the offeree and its financial adviser and the likely timetable impact. In addition, if such a scheme lapses but an offer would not have done, the offeror will have to make a normal takeover offer immediately on such lapse and this must be stated in the scheme circular (s.2 of Appendix 7);

2. a requirement for holding statements to normally be clarified no later than 17.00 on the 7th day prior to the shareholder meetings but with Panel discretion to allow later clarifications prior to the court hearing to sanction the scheme (s.4 of Appendix 7 and related Notes) (see 6.3.4 above);

3. a requirement that announcements should be made as soon as practicable (and in some cases by no later than 08.00 on the following business day) following key events in a scheme (for example the shareholder and court meetings and the effective date (s.5 of Appendix 7));

4. disapplying the provisions of Rule 31 ("timing of the offer") but including new provisions relating to the timing of, and revisions to, a scheme (ss.6 and 7 of Appendix 7);

5. a requirement to consult the Panel if an offeror is considering announcing a scheme without beforehand obtaining the support of the offeree board (s.13 of Appendix 7); and

6. a requirement that, where securities are offered as consideration, the relevant admission to listing condition must be capable of being satisfied only when all steps required for the admission to listing have been completed other than the relevant regulatory announcement of admission to listing (s.15 of Appendix 7).

As part of their overall approach of protecting offerees, the 2011 Amendments prohibited many provisions in implementation agreements which had previously been generally used in schemes of arrangement and which had previously imposed various obligations on the offeree as to the timetable for it to seek to implement a scheme (see 6.8.2 below). Instead, the 2011 Amendments include specific requirements in Appendix 7 to deal with timing obligations, conditions and other rights or restrictions which would previously have been included in an implementation agreement.

For instance, under s.3 of Appendix 7, the offeree must: (i) ensure that the scheme circular is sent to shareholders (and persons with information rights) within 28 days of the announcement of the firm intention to launch the scheme (provided that the scheme is recommended); (ii) include in the scheme circular the expected timetable for the scheme (including certain key dates); and (iii) implement the scheme in accordance with the published timetable (for so long as the scheme remains recommended and subject to any proposed or actual adjournment of the shareholder meetings or court sanction hearing or the invocation of any condition to the scheme as permitted by the Code (see below)). On publication of the scheme circular, the offeree must also announce such publication and include the expected timetable in that announcement.

In addition, the parties to the offer are now permitted to include in the conditions to the scheme specific deadlines by when the shareholder meetings and court sanction hearing must be held (provided that the deadlines are more than 21 days after the relevant dates in the published timetable) and a long-stop date by which the scheme must become effective. Amongst other requirements, any such conditions must be given prominent reference in the offeror's firm intention announcement. While the offeror can agree an extended deadline or long-stop date with the offeree, if the relevant deadline is not met the offeror can walk away. In addition, if any condition is not capable of being satisfied by the relevant date, the offeror must make an announcement by no later than

08.00 on the business day following such date, stating whether the offeror has invoked or waived the condition or agreed a new deadline or long-stop date with the offeree.

Finally, following the 2011 Amendments, the Panel has also made clear that it will permit an offeror to switch from a scheme of arrangement to a contractual offer (with an acceptance condition of up to 90%) if: (i) the board of the offeree withdraws its recommendation of the scheme or proposes an adjournment of a shareholder meeting or the court sanction hearing or if any such meeting or hearing is adjourned; or (ii) if the Panel considers that the offeree has not implemented the scheme in accordance with the published timetable (see Note 2 on s.8 of Appendix 7).

6.8 Specific issues

6.8.1 Profit forecasts, quantified financial benefits statements and asset valuations (Rules 28 and 29)

It is not uncommon, particularly in contested offers, for the offeror or offeree to make a profit forecast in support of their respective positions, although this may not always be made in the first document from either side. Indeed, this may be unavoidable if, whether deliberately or not, a profit forecast has been made in some previous public statement (although this is now required in fewer situations following certain Rule changes). Similarly, statements quantifying financial benefits expected to accrue if the offer is successful, or expected cost savings if it is unsuccessful, (known as "quantified financial benefits statements") are also fairly common and the Panel has recently extended these statements to cover situations where an offeree announces that it has agreed terms on which it intends to sell all or substantially all of its assets (excluding cash and cash equivalents) and that it intends to return to shareholders all or substantially all of its cash balances (including the proceeds of any asset sale) in competition with an offer or possible offer. Asset valuations, which occur less

frequently, tend to be made in the case of offerees with a large and potentially undervalued asset base (for example property or mining companies).

The Code lays considerable emphasis on the standards of care which are required for these types of statements and imposes material additional safeguards in relation to them.

Rules introduced in 2013 made significant amendments to the requirements relating to profit forecasts and quantified financial benefits statements and Rules introduced in 2019 made significant amendments to the requirements relating to asset valuations. These amendments, and a summary of the more detailed Rules concerning profit forecasts, quantified financial benefits statements and asset valuations, are considered in more detail in Ch.8.

6.8.2   Offer-related arrangements: Rule 21.2

6.8.2.1   General prohibition on these arrangements

In recommended offers, it had become common for offerors to seek the benefit of a number of deal protection measures from the offeree, such as inducement fees. In its consultation on the 2011 Amendments, the Panel expressed the view that market practice had treated deal protection measures as standard packages, which would rarely provide much scope for negotiation or resistance by the offeree and which potentially made it more difficult for a competing offeror to enter the fray. Accordingly, in a drive to strengthen the position of the offeree, the 2011 Amendments introduced a general prohibition of inducement fees and other deal protection measures other than in certain limited cases.

Under Rule 21.2(a), except with the consent of the Panel, no offeree or any person acting in concert with it may enter into an "offer-related arrangement" with the offeror or any person acting in concert with it during an offer period or when an offer is reasonably in contemplation. This prohibition is widely drafted and includes any "agreement, arrangement or commit-ment in connection with an offer", which includes any inducement fee (or comparable arrangement) and extends to any other offer-related arrangement such as any exclusivity arrangements, matching rights, restrictive due diligence under-takings or where the offeree provides any ancillary benefits or undertakings to the offeror in support of the offer.

The restrictions are one-way in that, whilst they restrict the arrangements that can be entered into by the offeree, they do not prevent the provision of undertakings by the offeror (which can still, therefore, provide reverse break fees or agree to a standstill). Note, however, that the prohibition extends to the offeror (as well as the offeree) in the context of a reverse takeover since, in such a transaction, it may be arguable as to which party should be treated as the offeree (see Rule 21.2(b)(v)).

6.8.2.2   *Permitted offer-related arrangements*

Notwithstanding the above, implementation agreements are still frequently entered into in connection with offers, often to deal with regulatory filings and employee incentive arrange-ments.

Under Rule 21.2(b), the following offer-related arrangements are specifically permitted to be entered into: confidentiality undertakings; commitments to provide information or assis-tance for regulatory purposes or not to solicit employees, customers or suppliers; irrevocable commitments and letters of intent (as to which see below); agreements, arrangements or commitments which impose obligations only on offerors and their concert parties; and agreements relating to existing employee incentive arrangements. While not expressly permit-ted under Rule 21.2, the Panel has also said that the entry into management incentivisation arrangements between offeree management and an offeror continues to be permitted.

In 2013, this list of permitted offer-related arrangements was extended to include any agreement between the offeror and the trustees of any of the offeree's pension schemes—but only in relation to the future funding of the pension scheme. Any such agreement consequently needs to be summarised in the announcement of a firm intention to make an offer and in the offer document. However, unlike other offer-related arrangements (which all need to be published on a website), it will only need to be "published" on a website if it is material (Note 6 on Rule 26).

The way in which the Panel interprets these and other matters sometimes included in implementation agreements is set out in Practice Statement No.29. In particular, Practice Statement No.29 deals with the extent to which irrevocable commitments and letters of intent are permitted offer-related arrangements in the case of persons who are both shareholders and directors of the offeree. It states that shareholder directors are permitted to enter into irrevocable commitments or letters of intent in relation to the shares held or controlled by such individuals. However, they are not permitted to enter into other types of offer-related arrangements and the content of any irrevocable commitment or letter of intent is not permitted to extend beyond the scope of the decision to accept an offer or voting in favour of a scheme of arrangement. It also gives examples of provisions that the Panel Executive regards as being either permitted or prohibited in such commitments or letters.

In addition to these specific exceptions, Notes 1 and 2 on Rule 21.2 set out the following two situations when offer-related arrangements will still be permitted—namely in order to cater for offerees seeking a white knight and for formal sale processes:

1.   under Note 1, if a hostile offer has already been made and not subsequently withdrawn or recommended, the Panel will normally consent to the offeree entering into an inducement fee arrangement with any competing offeror—but only when any such white knight announces its firm intention to make a competing offer; and
2.   under Note 2, if the offeree initiates a formal sale process, the Panel will normally consent to the offeree entering into

an inducement fee at the conclusion of the process with one offeror who has participated in that process when such an offeror announces its firm intention to make an offer. (Note 2 also states that, in exceptional circumstances, the Panel may also consent to the offeree entering into other offer-related arrangements with that offeror.)

In each case: (i) the aggregate value of the inducement fee, or fees, that may be payable must be capped at 1% of the value of the offeree (calculated by reference to the price of the competing offer or, if there are two or more competing offerors, the first competing offer); and (ii) any fee must be payable only after an offer becomes or is declared wholly unconditional.

Practice Statement No.29 sets out, inter alia, various parameters for determining the maximum amount permitted for an inducement fee, in the few cases where an inducement fee is now possible. It states that the 1% limit may be calculated on the basis of the fully diluted equity share capital of the offeree and, where necessary, should take into account irrecoverable VAT payable on the fee. For the purposes of determining the offeree's fully diluted equity share capital, only options and warrants that are "in the money" may be included in the calculation and such instruments must be valued on a "see through" basis (being their value by reference to the value of the offer for the shares to which they relate, net of any exercise price). In a securities exchange offer, the value of the offeree will be fixed by reference to the value of the offer as stated in the Rule 2.7 firm offer announcement.

Inducement fees are from time to time entered into during the course of offers between offerees and third parties, for example as part of the disposal or acquisition of an asset or business by the offeree. These arrangements fell under close review by the Panel after SVG was allowed to sell nearly all of its business to HarbourVest in 2016. The review was triggered because the sale occurred after HarbourVest had made an offer for SVG which could not be increased and the sale of the SVG business to HarbourVest implied a higher price for SVG than the previous offer by HarbourVest.

The ability of an offeror to agree to buy the offeree's business at a higher value than a previous final offer was subsequently reversed by the Panel as part of its review. However, as part of the review, the Rules in relation to any inducement fee associated with such a sale were also clarified.

Such fees are, prima facie, caught by Rule 21.1(a)(v), under which an offeree is prohibited from entering into a contract otherwise than in the ordinary course of business during the course of an offer. In addition, the general exemptions available from this prohibition (i.e. the offeree obtaining prior share-holder approval or the contract being conditional on the offer lapsing or being withdrawn) are often be unlikely to be relevant in practice to such fees. Accordingly, a new Note 8 on Rule 21.1 was introduced, reflecting prior Panel Executive practice, stating that the Panel will normally consent to the offeree entering into an inducement fee arrangement with a counterparty to such a transaction, provided that:

(i) the aggregate value of the inducement fee or fees that may be payable by the offeree in relation to the same asset(s) is no more than 1% of the value of the transaction (or, if there are two or more transactions in respect of the same asset(s), the transaction with the highest value); and

(ii) the aggregate value of the inducement fee or fees that may be payable by the offeree in respect of all transactions to which Rule 21.1 applies is no more than 1% of the value of the offeree calculated by reference to the price of the offeror's offer (or, if there are two or more offerors, the first offer) at the time of the Rule 2.7 announcement.

6.8.2.3   *General provisions concerning offer-related arrangements*

The Panel should be consulted at the earliest opportunity if there is any doubt as to whether an agreement, arrangement or commitment is caught by the general prohibition or if the Panel's consent to an inducement fee, or dispensation from Rule 21.2, is sought.

As mentioned above, details of any permitted offer-related arrangement must be fully disclosed in the Rule 2.7 announcement of a firm intention to make an offer and in the offer document and (save for non-material agreements with pension scheme trustees) any relevant documentation or information must be put on display in accordance with Rule 26.2 (i.e. published on a website promptly following publication and in any event by no later than noon on the business day following the firm intention announcement until the end of the offer period) (see 6.11.5 below).

6.9 Offers to holders of convertible securities and options: Rule 15

Rule 15 requires that, when an offer is made for voting equity share capital or for other transferable securities carrying voting rights and the offeree has convertible securities outstanding, the offeror must make an appropriate offer or proposal to the holders of those securities to ensure that their interests are safeguarded. "Appropriate" is often fixed by reference to the "see through" price of the underlying securities but, in appropriate circumstances, may be more.

Whenever practicable, the offer or proposal should be sent out at the same time as the main offer but, if this cannot be done, the Panel should be consulted and it should be sent out as soon as practicable thereafter. It should contain the advice of a competent independent financial adviser and the offeree board's views on the offer or proposal.

Many offerees will have share option schemes outstanding and the provisions of Rule 15 will apply to those schemes. In most cases it will not be practicable to send out proposals to option holders until after the offer document has been published; indeed, in many cases, proposals will only be put to option holders after the offer has gone unconditional. Proposals on option schemes may take a number of forms, such as providing for cash payments to cancel options or rollover into an option scheme of the offeror or simply allowing option holders to exercise their options and accept the offer as shareholders. More detail is contained in Practice Statement No.24 which contains various examples of how the Panel Executive applies Rule 15 in practice.

Regardless of when an appropriate offer or proposal is made, all relevant documents issued to shareholders of the offeree should, if practicable, be issued simultaneously to holders of convertible securities and options (Note 1 on Rule 15).

6.10 Offeror documents required by the Listing Rules

In some cases, information will have to be given to the shareholders of a listed offeror. An announcement will have to be made if the takeover offer is a Class 2 transaction, which will generally be the case in a transaction in which the value of any factors such as the gross assets being acquired or the profits before tax of the offeree or the aggregate value of the consideration being given exceeds 5% (but is less than 25%) of the gross assets, profits before tax, or market value of the ordinary shares (as the case may be) of the offeror (as determined by the tests set out in Ch.10 of the Listing Rules).

If the tests in Ch.10 show that the value or amount of any of the factors applicable to the offeree is 25% or more of the appropriate measure for the offeror, the proposed takeover will qualify as a Class 1 transaction and the shareholders of the offeror will usually have to approve the takeover at a general meeting. In this case, a circular will be sent to them containing information about the proposed transaction (the detailed requirements are set out in Ch.13 of the Listing Rules) as well as any necessary resolutions to approve the acquisition, especially in share exchange offers. These may include, for example, resolutions to increase the directors' authority to allot shares.

A listed offeror may also have to prepare and publish a prospectus (or a document containing information which is regarded by the FCA as being equivalent to that of a prospectus—see further below) if it is offering its own securities, either as consideration or to its own shareholders to provide funds for a cash offer.

The information to be contained in the prospectus (or equivalent document) is set out in the Prospectus Rules. The prospectus should be incorporated in or sent out with the offer document. If a prospectus becomes necessary as a result of a revision to an offer, it should be sent out with the revised offer document, but it may be permitted to be sent out later. It should in any event be sent out before an offer goes unconditional in order to avoid having to adjust the information to take account of the offeree having become a member of the offeror's group.

The Prospectus Rules provide that there is no requirement for a prospectus to be published in relation to takeovers and mergers involving a securities exchange offer if an "equivalent document" is produced. However, the FCA applies a full vetting process to these documents to determine "equivalence" so the scope for circumventing the disclosure requirements of the Prospectus Rules is limited. One of the advantages of preparing an equivalent document is that there is no requirement to produce a supplementary prospectus with the effect that withdrawal rights under s.87Q(4) of the Financial Services and Markets Act 2000 (FSMA 2000) do not apply. On the other hand, the main advantage of preparing a prospectus is that "passport rights" are currently available enabling the document to be sent to the offeree's shareholders throughout the EU (subject to any translation requirements), although such "passport rights" may well fall away post Brexit, particularly in the event of a no-deal Brexit.

6.11   General publication requirements

6.11.1   *Publication of documents: Rule 30.2*

As a result of the increasing use of websites and electronic forms of communication between companies and their shareholders, the Code was amended in 2009 in order to relax the provisions dealing with the publication and circulation of takeover documents. A summary of these provisions (as subsequently further amended) is set out below.

Under Rule 30.2, Code documents must be published in one of the following three ways:

1.   in traditional hard copy form;
2.   by communication in electronic form (for example email); or
3.   by publication on a website, provided that shareholders are notified of such website publication in accordance with (1) or (2) above (see 6.11.2 below).

These publication requirements cover all documents that are required to be issued under the Code, except that forms of acceptance, withdrawal forms and proxy forms still need to be sent out in hard copy form (and must not be published in newspapers).

6.11.2   *Website notifications*

If a party publishes Code documents on its website, rather than publishing them electronically or in hard copy, it is also required to send a website notification to alert recipients to the website publication of such Code documents. The notification must be sent electronically or by hard copy no later than the date on which the relevant document is published on the website.

Website notifications are subject to strict content requirements (see the Note on the definition of a "website notification" in the Code). In summary, they are required, inter alia, to:

1. give notice of the publication of a document on a website and identify the website;
2. be prepared to the highest standards of accuracy and contain a directors' responsibility statement;
3. contain a summary of the provisions of Rule 8;
4. only include non-controversial information about an offer or a party to an offer (and not, for example, include a recommendation);
5. only include certain other limited information in the same envelope as the notification;
6. include a statement about the recipient's entitlement to receive information in hard copy and details of how to do so; and
7. include a statement that the notification is not a substitute for, or a summary of, the relevant information.

6.11.3 *Ability to choose method of publishing: Rule 30.3*

Save for forms of acceptance, withdrawal forms, proxy forms and any other form connected with an offer, each of which must be sent by hard copy, parties to an offer are generally able to choose which method of publishing a document they use, subject to previous elections by offeree shareholders.

Accordingly, if an offeree shareholder (or person with information rights) has elected to receive documents generally from the offeree in electronic form, then Code documents can be sent to him or her electronically without the need for further consent. To bolster this requirement, the offeree is required to provide the offeror with offeree shareholders' email addresses upon request following the announcement of a firm intention to make an offer.

Conversely, however, a fresh consent is required if a person has limited its e-communications election to specific documents, such as notices of meetings. Similarly, previous general elections by offeree shareholders to receive documents in hard copy form prior to any offer are binding on parties to an offer during an offer.

Any person to whom a Code document is sent either electronically or by website publication is also entitled to request to receive a hard copy of that document or any future Code documents sent to him or her in connection with that offer (Rule 30.3). This right must be made clear in any electronic communication or website publication, together with details of how a hard copy may be obtained. A person who requests a hard copy should receive it by no later than two business days following receipt of that request.

If a person sends a request for a hard copy to an offeror, the offeror must notify the offeree of such request, and if sent to the offeree (including by an offeror), the offeree must notify the other parties, without that person having to make separate requests of those other parties.

6.11.4 Distribution of announcements and documents

The Code contains various provisions designed to ensure that announcements and documents are distributed to shareholders and other parties which may be interested in their contents and the outcome of an offer or possible offer.

6.11.4.1 General Rules on distribution

Any announcement required to be published under the Code must be published via an RIS and, except with the consent of the Panel, if an announcement is published when the relevant RIS is not open for business, it must be distributed to not less than two newswire services operating in the UK and submitted for publication as soon as the relevant RIS re-opens. The Panel may also require such an announcement, or a document including its contents, to be sent to offeree shareholders, persons with information rights, offeree employee representatives and trustees of offeree pension schemes (Rule 30.1).

The offer document must be sent in hard copy and electronic form: (i) to the Panel prior to publication; and (ii) to the advisers to all other parties at the time of publication (Rule 30.5(a)). Copies of all other documents, announcements and information published in connection with an offer by or on behalf of the offeror or the offeree must be sent in electronic and hard copy form to the Panel and the advisers to all other parties at the time of publication and must not be released to the media under an embargo (Rule 30.5(b)).

In addition, if a party publishes a document, an announcement or any other information outside normal business hours, that party must inform the advisers to all other parties of its publication immediately (Rule 30.5(c)).

6.11.4.2 Distribution of early stage announcements

Possible offer announcements starting an offer period and announcements of a firm intention to make an offer (or a circular summarising its terms) must be sent promptly by the offeree to its shareholders, persons with information rights and to the Panel (Rule 2.11). They must also be made promptly and "readily available" by the offeree to its employee representatives or, where there are no such representatives, its employees and to the trustees of the offeree's pension scheme(s) (Rule 2.11(a)(ii)). For these purposes, and for the purposes generally of the Code, "pension schemes" must include a defined benefit element for the relevant Rules to apply.

These documents will often be accompanied by the offeree board's preliminary views, for example advising shareholders to take no action pending further consideration by the board, or outright rejection.

When an offeree makes an announcement or circular available to its employee representatives (or employees) and to the trustees of its pension scheme(s) pursuant to Rule 2.11, it must at the same time inform them of the right of employee representatives and pension scheme trustees to have separate opinions appended to the offeree board circular pursuant to Rule 25.9. In addition, the offeree must inform its employee representatives (or employees) of the offeree's responsibility to pay the costs reasonably incurred in obtaining advice required for the verification of the information contained in their opinion (Rule 2.11(d)).

Both the offeror and the offeree must explain the implications of the relevant announcement and the offeree must make clear that certain information, relating to the receipt of communications from the offeree, provided by offeree shareholders, persons with information rights and other relevant persons may be provided to an offeror during the offer period and any circular published should include a telephone number so that such shareholders and persons may contact the offeree regarding administrative matters (Rule 2.11(c)).

Note 1 on Rule 2.11 makes clear that, where a circular summarising the terms of the offer is sent to shareholders, persons with information rights, employee representatives (or employees) and/or pension scheme trustees, the full text of the announcement must be made "readily and promptly available" to them, for example by posting it on the offeror's or offeree's respective websites. Any circular summarising the Rule 2.7 announcement must also include details of the website on which a copy of the announcement is published in accordance with Rule 26.1 (see 6.11.5).

6.11.4.3   *Distribution of the offer document*

Under Rule 24.1(a), except with the consent of the Panel, the offeror must send the offer document to shareholders of the offeree and persons with information rights in accordance with Rule 30.2 within 28 days of the announcement of a firm intention to make the offer. At the same time as the offer document is published, both the offeror and the offeree must make the offer document "readily available" to their employee representatives or, where there are no employee representatives, to the employees themselves, and the offeror must make the offer document "readily available" to the trustees of the offeree's pension scheme(s). It is likely that website publication will be sufficient to discharge this obligation. Under Rule 24.1(b), promptly following the offer document being sent to shareholders, the offeror must also publish it on a website and announce that the offer document has been so published (see 6.11.5 below).

6.11.4.4   Distribution of the offeree circular

Except with the consent of the Panel, if it is not combined with the offer document, the board of the offeree must send a circular to its shareholders (and persons with information rights) in accordance with Rule 30.2 within 14 days of the despatch of the offer document (Rule 25.1(a)). Similarly to the case of offer documents, at the same time as the circular is published, the offeree must make the offeree circular "readily available" to its employee representatives or, where there are no employee representatives, to the employees themselves and also to the trustees of its pension scheme(s). Again, website publication is likely to be sufficient.

Finally, the offeree must also publish the offeree circular on a website, and announce that the offeree circular has been so published, promptly following its publication (Rule 25.1(b)).

6.11.5   Information must be published on a website

A copy of most information published in relation to an offer by a party to an offer or a possible offer is required to be made available on a website (and any such document must provide details of the relevant website) on an ongoing basis promptly following the publication of the relevant document, announcement or information and, in any event, by no later than noon on the following business day, even if that party does not intend to publish documents in electronic form or by means of website publication (Rule 26.1). These documents include:

1.   Code documents and other information sent to offeree shareholders, persons with information rights and other relevant persons;
2.   any RIS announcements made by that party during the offer (whether related to the offer or not). However, this does not apply to: (i) transaction disclosures made by

directors and similar persons; (ii) sales/acquisitions of major shareholdings; (iii) disclosures of increases or decreases in total voting rights and share capital; and (iv) announcements by offerees at the start of an offer period of the offeree's issued share capital (as required by Rule 2.9); and

3. any document or information required to be published on a website under Rule 20.1 or any other provision of the Code (other than Rules 26.2 or 26.3).

Conversely, however, companies are not required to publish the documents produced by another party to an offer, though they may well choose to do so in practice in the context of a recommended offer.

If a party does not have its own website (for example a bid vehicle in a P2P), the Panel may allow it to use a website belonging to a third party. The website must be maintained for the duration of the offer period as well as during any competition reference period related to the offer and all Code documents must include details of the website on which a copy is published.

In addition, certain specific documents are required to be published on a website promptly following the publication of the announcement of a firm intention to make an offer (or, if later, following the date of the relevant document) and, in any event, by no later than noon on the following business day (Rule 26.2).

This requirement applies to any irrevocable commitment or letter of intent, any documents relating to the financing of the offer (save potentially for market flex arrangements), any indemnities and any offer-related arrangement permitted under Rule 21.2 on inducement fees (save for any such arrangements with pension scheme trustees which are not material (Note 6 on Rule 26: see 6.8.2 below)) and any agreements or arrangements which relate to the circumstances in which the offeror may or may not invoke or seek to invoke a pre-condition or condition to its offer (or, if not reduced to writing, a memorandum of all the terms of such agreements or arrangements).

Rule 26.3 then lists a wider number of documents that must be published on a website following the publication of the offer document and any offeree board circular (or, if later, the date of the relevant document).

All such documents must continue to be available on the website until the end of the offer (including any related competition reference period).

Finally, Note 5 on Rule 26 makes clear that, if any relevant document is amended, varied or replaced during the period in which it is required to be published, the amended, varied or replaced document must be put on the relevant website and, except as provided in Note 8 on Rule 20.1, an announcement made explaining that this has been done.

6.11.6 *Publishing documents to persons with "information rights"*

Under ss.145 and 146 of the Companies Act 2006, shareholders may notify companies or other persons that they wish to receive information from the relevant company (for example a nominee shareholder might notify the details of the beneficial owner of the relevant shares). Persons granted such information rights will be entitled to receive Code documents at the same time and in the same manner as they are sent to offeree shareholders.

Forms of acceptance relating to an offer, however, do not need to be sent to persons with information rights on the basis that such persons are not able to transfer or dispose of the whole or any part of a shareholder's interest in shares.

6.11.7 Circulation of documents to overseas shareholders: Rule 30.4

Rule 30.4 provides that the requirement to make information and documents available to shareholders, persons with information rights and employees or their representatives applies wherever those shareholders or employees are located, unless there is "sufficient objective justification" for the requirement not applying.

The Note on Rule 30.4 provides a derogation setting out the circumstances in which there would be "sufficient objective justification" for not applying the Rule. Dispensations will not normally be granted in relation to recipients who are located within the EEA (or, following Brexit, within the UK, the Channel Islands or the Isle of Man). However, in jurisdictions outside those specified above, circumstances for dispensations include where the laws there may result in a significant risk of civil, regulatory or criminal exposure for the offeror or offeree if the information or document is sent into that jurisdiction without amendment and either:

1. less than 3% of the shares of the offeree are held by registered shareholders located there; or
2. circumstances are such that it would be proportionate for the Panel to grant a dispensation (having regard to factors such as the cost involved, number of shares involved and any delay to the timetable).

The introduction of this Rule in 2006 led to an updating of past advice about the risks of posting documents into certain jurisdictions and the result, in practice, has been that offer documentation is now often posted to some jurisdictions where it had not been in the past.

Overseas shareholders are also entitled to enjoy the same rights of electronic access to offer-related documents unless there is a sufficient objective justification for not doing so on the current bases set out in Rule 30.4 (see Note 4 on Rule 26).

6.12 Liability for inaccurate or misleading statements in offer documentation

The inclusion of an inaccurate or misleading statement in offer documentation (including announcements) may give rise to liability in various ways, including in particular those set out below.

6.12.1 Complaints to the Takeover Panel

The most immediate remedy, used particularly in hostile or competing bids, is for parties to bids (or occasionally share-holders) to complain to the Panel about the accuracy of statements made by others involved in a particular bid with a view to seeking a public retraction or clarification. In hostile or competing bids, such complaints can occur on an almost daily basis.

6.12.2 Liability in tort

The public assumption of responsibility in the directors' responsibility statement under Rule 19.2 may result in such directors taking on a potential personal liability in tort to persons who act in reliance on statements contained in a document under the principle established in *Hedley Byrne & Co Ltd v Heller & Partners Ltd* [1964] A.C. 465; [1963] 3 W.L.R. 101 HL. In effect, this states that, if a mis-statement has been made negligently to a person who is sufficiently proximate in circumstances where it is foreseeable that such person may suffer economic loss, the person making the statement will be liable in damages to a person who suffered loss by relying on the statement.

In many cases, it would be reasonable to assume that a shareholder to whom a document or advertisement is addressed may be able to show reliance on the information presented to him or her in considering what action he or she should take with regard to a takeover. The offeror or offeree making the statement may also share similar liability.

In addition, liability may arise for defamation if untrue or misleading statements are made.

6.12.3 *Duty to exercise reasonable care, skill and diligence under the Companies Act 2006*

Similarly to liability in tort, directors may now incur liability under s.174 of the Companies Act 2006 for inaccurate or misleading statements if they fail to exercise reasonable care, skill and diligence.

6.12.4 *Criminal liability for non-compliant documents under the Companies Act 2006*

Since the introduction of s.953 of the Companies Act 2006, all parties involved in a takeover offer need to take into account the criminal offence for non-compliance with the contents requirements for offeror and offeree documents set out in Rules 24–27 of the Code. The offence is punishable by a fine. It catches not only wilful non-compliance, but also non-compliance due to recklessness and failure to take "all reasonable steps" to ensure compliance.

With regard to the offer document, the offence is committed by "the person making the bid" and also by any of such person's directors, officers or members who caused the document to be published. It seems logical that directors, as persons responsible for the offer document under Rule 19, should be caught by this new offence but the term "officer" extends to both the company secretary and a "manager" (a term of somewhat imprecise scope in an English context).

Directors and officers of the offeree are also at risk of prosecution for the new offence, so far as offeree documents are concerned. "Members" (i.e. shareholders) of the offeror are also at risk where they cause the offer document to be published—and the scope of the offence is such that directors and officers of that member, if it is a body corporate, may also be criminally liable. This is of particular concern in the case of "take private" bids where a new bid vehicle is traditionally used, and in the case of takeover offers by wholly-owned subsidiaries.

Historically, it had been common practice for the offeror's financial adviser to make the offer to offeree shareholders on the offeror's behalf. Whilst it was arguable that it was the offeror and not the financial adviser (as the offeror's agent) who should be regarded as "the person making the bid" in these circumstances, the legislation's lack of clarity in this regard encouraged a cautious approach from financial advisers, with the result that offers are now almost always made directly by the offeror itself.

6.12.5 *Liability under Financial Services Act 2012 (and the EU Market Abuse Regulation)*

Parties must also bear in mind the provisions of s.89 of the Financial Services Act 2012 which makes it an offence knowingly or recklessly to make a statement which is false or misleading in a material respect or dishonestly to conceal any material facts, if the statement or concealment is made with the intention of inducing another person to enter or offer to enter into, or to refrain from entering or offering to enter into, an investment agreement or to exercise, or refrain from exercising, any rights conferred by an investment. Thus, if misleading statements are made or material facts are concealed by either side in a takeover bid which induce a shareholder to accept or reject an offer or to vote a particular way on a resolution and if the statement is made deliberately or recklessly or if the concealment is made dishonestly, criminal sanctions may follow.

Similarly, liability may arise for market abuse.

6.12.6 *Avoiding liability in practice*

The potential liabilities described above mean that great lengths are taken in order to seek to ensure the accuracy of offer documentation. In particular, the directors and their advisers usually undertake a full and detailed verification exercise to check all of the facts, and the bases and assumptions for any statements of opinion or belief, contained in such documentation.

6.13   FSMA 2000: financial promotion

Offer documents will be, but defence documents will often not be, financial promotions pursuant to s.21 of the FSMA 2000—that is, communications of "an invitation or inducement to engage in investment activity". These documents can only be communicated by, or with the approval of, an authorised person unless they fall within the exemptions contained in the FSMA (Financial Promotion) Order 2005 (the Order).

Article 62 of the Order exempts from s.21 of the FSMA 2000 any communication in connection with the sale of a body corporate. Offer documents appear, on their face, to fall within this exemption and this interpretation seems to have been approved by the FCA (although the exemption was envisaged to deal with more limited transactions). However, care needs to be taken before proceeding in reliance on this exemption. If this exemption is not available, offer documents do not fall within any of the exemptions contained in the Order and would, therefore, need to be communicated and/or approved by an authorised person.

The making and/or approval by authorised persons of financial promotions is governed by the FCA's Conduct of Business Rules. It contains various provisions limiting its application in respect of takeovers.

Defence documents will not, in many circumstances, fall within the definition of financial promotion (by virtue of their encouraging the offeree shareholders not to accept the offer) but, even if they do, if sent only to shareholders of the offeree, they will often be exempt by virtue of art.43 of the Order.

6.14 Companies Act 2006

6.14.1 Payments to directors for loss of office

Section 314 of the Companies Act 1985, which previously required disclosure in relation to compensation for loss of office in the offer document, was repealed by the Companies Act 2006 with effect from 1 October 2007. Sections 215 and 219 of the Companies Act 2006, which deal with payments for loss of office, do not require such disclosure. However, details of agreements between the offeree and directors or employees in relation to compensation for loss of office/employment that occurs because of a takeover bid are now required to be disclosed in the directors' report in the relevant financial year (see Ch.4 Pt 28 of the Companies Act 2006).

6.14.2 Squeeze out and sell out

Sections 974 to 982 of the Companies Act 2006 provide a procedure whereby a person who has made a takeover offer can compulsorily acquire the shares held by non-accepting shareholders. However, it can only do so if inter alia it has received acceptances in respect of: (i) 90% in value of the relevant shares; and (ii) 90% of the voting rights of those shares (if they are voting shares). Assuming the relevant conditions are met, the documents sent to offeree shareholders to effect this will generally be prescribed forms of notice under s.979 of the Companies Act 2006.

Similarly, ss.983 to 985 of the Companies Act 2006 also provide a procedure whereby offeree shareholders who have not accepted an offer can "sell out"—i.e. force the offeror to buy them out if the offeror comes to hold more than 90% in value of the shares in the offeree (or any class of such shares) as well as 90% of the voting rights in the offeree.

Chapter 7

Conduct During the Offer; Timing and Revision; and Restrictions Following Offers

Lee Coney
Partner
Clifford Chance LLP

Rui Huo
Senior Associate
Clifford Chance LLP

7.1 Introduction

The Code is designed principally to ensure that shareholders are treated fairly and are not denied the opportunity to decide on the merits of a takeover, and that shareholders of the same class in the offeree company are afforded equivalent treatment. The Code is also designed to ensure that takeovers are conducted within an orderly framework, which helps to promote the integrity of the financial markets. The three areas of the Code which are the subject of this Chapter play an important role in achieving these goals and involve the balancing of the, often conflicting, interests of the offeror, offeree company shareholders, the offeree company itself and potential competing offerors.

The Panel has a statutory footing and a range of sanctions and powers to regulate the conduct of offers including the power to require disclosure to it of documents and information, the ability to require compensation to be paid to target shareholders and the power to seek enforcement orders from the courts.

The Panel operates largely on a consensual basis relying, principally, on its time-honoured sanctions of private and public censure.

The High Court decision in June 2008 in relation to the competitive bids for Expro International Group reaffirmed the reluctance on the part of the courts to take a more active role in determining the outcome of offers which are subject to the Code. The Court, in particular, emphasised that there should be a common approach to the conduct and regulation of bids, whether structured as a contractual offer or a court-approved scheme of arrangement. That said, the Panel initiated its first ever enforcement proceedings in the Court of Session in April 2017, seeking an order under s.955 of the Companies Act 2006 (CA 2006) to require David King to comply with rulings of the Panel Executive and Hearings Committee in relation to his shareholding in, and Rule 9 obligations in relation to, Rangers International Football Club. In December 2017, the Court of Session, in exercising its discretion under s.955, granted the order sought by the Panel. The Court of Session subsequently refused an appeal against the order and contempt proceedings were commenced against Mr King for his failure to publish an offer document within 28 days of the announcement of the mandatory offer. The Panel sought the imposition on Mr King of "such penalty, whether by fine, imprisonment or otherwise as to the court shall seem appropriate in respect of that contempt". Mr King challenged the contempt of court proceedings but his challenge was rejected. Subsequently, Mr King provided an undertaking to the court to take the necessary steps to post the mandatory offer document by no later than 5.30pm on 25 January 2019 (and complied with the undertaking).

Whilst the courts may be reluctant to intervene in determining issues which are subject to the jurisdiction of the Panel, the FCA is responsible for taking enforcement action in all cases of market abuse. Although compliance with the Code will not always ensure immunity from allegations of market abuse, behaviour conforming to certain specific Rules of the Code and/or the Market Abuse Regulation (2014/596/EU) is unlikely to constitute market abuse.

Legislative changes in connection with the UK's withdrawal from the EU impact the statutory regime underpinning the Code. The Takeovers Directive, which: (i) established the legal framework through which company takeovers are regulated in the EEA; and (ii) was implemented into domestic law in the form of Pt 28 of the CA 2006, will cease to apply once the UK is no longer a member of the EU.

The Takeovers (Amendment) (EU Exit) Regulations 2019 (2019 Regulations): (i) amend Pt 28 of the CA 2006 (to, among other things, remove references to the Directive, Directive definitions and provisions specifically for EEA member states); and (ii) transpose into a new Sch.1C to the CA 2006, certain articles of the Directive (modified as necessary for UK legislation). The amendments will come into effect on exit day (within the meaning of s.20 of the European Union (Withdrawal) Act 2018 (WA 2018)).

In 2018, the Code Committee consulted on proposed amendments to the Code as a result of the UK's withdrawal from the EU and subsequently published RS 2018/2 setting out the amendments to the Code. The amendments will come into effect on exit day (within the meaning of s.20 of the WA 2018). References in this Chapter to exit day are references to exit day within the meaning of s.20 of the WA 2018. A detailed review of the conduct of schemes of arrangement and the related court process in takeover situations is beyond the scope of this Chapter but it should be noted that a separate Schemes Appendix (Appendix 7 to the Code) addresses the application of the Code to schemes. The most significant area of divergence between schemes and contractual offers in relation to conduct during an offer, however, concerns the timetable for implementing the transaction. The scheme timetable is more flexible and is, to a very large extent, determined by the court process. Many of the general themes of this Chapter will, however, apply equally to contractual offers and to schemes.

7.2 Conduct during the offer

The first area covered in this Chapter, "Conduct during the offer" (Rules 19–22, Rule 27 and Rule 30), is principally concerned with the Rules governing the release of information during the course of a takeover and the Rules which control the taking of frustrating action by the board of an offeree company faced with a hostile takeover bid.

The cornerstone is Rule 19 (which is also addressed in Ch.6). This Rule deals with both responsibility for information released during the course of an offer and the manner of its release.

The Panel has made it clear that a breach of the Rules relating to the release of information during a bid will be treated as "a grave matter". There was in the past a perception that if the bid parties or financial advisers wanted to leak something then the public relations advisers could be left to talk freely to the press. As is made clear in the Introduction to the Code, however, the Panel regards the Code as applying not only to financial advisers and their clients but also to any other advisers to or representatives of any entity to which the Code applies. In 1997, the Panel was heavily critical of Triplex Lloyd and its PR advisers, Citigate, over the leak by Citigate of confidential information obtained by Triplex Lloyd under Rule 21.3 (equality of information to competing offerors, then Rule 20.2) in the course of the competing bids for William Cook.

7.2.1 Rule 19.1

Rule 19.1 sets out the standard of care which must be adopted not only in the preparation of formal offer documents, announcements or other information, but also in the making of statements to the media. Each document, announcement, other information published or statement must be produced to the highest standards of care and accuracy, the language used must clearly and concisely reflect the position being described and the information given must be adequately and fairly presented.

The Notes on Rule 19.1 deal with the following areas which are of particular concern to the Panel based on its past experience of dealing with over-imaginative offer participants:

1. the Panel regards financial advisers as being responsible to the Panel for guiding their clients and any relevant public relations advisers with regard to any information published during an offer (including information published using social media);
2. the source for any fact which is material to an argument must be clearly stated, including sufficient detail to enable the significance of the fact to be assessed;
3. quotations (e.g. from a newspaper) must not be used by a party to the offer out of context, details of the origin must be included and must be capable of being substantiated; and
4. diagrams should not be distorted and, when relevant, should be to scale.

A high-profile example of the high standards required in this regard was the Panel's public criticism of Kraft Foods in 2010 in relation to its statement of belief concerning its plans for Cadbury's Somerdale facility. The Panel reiterated that where a party makes a statement of belief, that party must both honestly and genuinely hold that belief (a subjective test) and have a reasonable basis for holding that belief (an objective test). Whilst the Panel accepted that Kraft honestly and genuinely believed that it would be able to keep open Cadbury's Somerdale facility, such belief was not one which Kraft had a reasonable basis for holding. Such intention statements are now covered by specific rules (post-offer undertakings and post-offer intention statements, described in 7.2.4.5 below).

7.2.2 Responsibility for information

Rule 19.2 provides that subject to certain limited exceptions, each document published in connection with an offer must state that the directors of the offeror and/or, where appropriate, the offeree company, accept responsibility for the information contained in it. This involves the inclusion of a statement that, to the best of the relevant directors' knowledge and belief (having taken all reasonable care to ensure that such is the case), the information contained in the document is in accordance with the facts and, where appropriate, that it does not omit anything likely to affect the import of such information. The implications of such an express acceptance of responsibility have been discussed in Ch.6.

7.2.3 Unacceptable statements

Rule 19.3 prohibits the issue of statements which, while not factually inaccurate, may mislead shareholders and the market or may create uncertainty. In particular, an offeror should not make a statement to the effect that it may improve its offer or make a change to the structure, conditionality or non-financial terms of its offer without committing itself to doing so and specifying the improvements or changes to its terms.

In 2007, Standard Life was required by the Panel to confirm publicly that there was no certainty it would ultimately restructure its offer for Resolution Plc following an earlier announcement in which it indicated that it was exploring a number of options for restructuring the offer, including the possibility of switching from a scheme to a conventional takeover offer.

Practice Statement No.19 emphasises that, particularly in the context of a competitive or hostile bid, any suggestion of the possibility of an improvement to an offer or change to the structure, conditionality or non-financial terms of an offer (including, for example, a switch from a scheme of arrangement to a contractual offer, or vice versa) will be particularly sensitive as it may lead to a false market being created in the shares of the offeree company. Therefore, while an offeror may publicise its initial reaction to a particular development and may state, for example, that it is "considering its options", an offeror should not use any language which implies that it might improve or change the terms, structure or conditionality of its offer as such statements must be made in unambiguous terms.

This Rule was applied in 2010 in relation to URS Corporation's offer for Scott Wilson Group, when URS was publicly rebuked by the Panel for stating that it was considering increasing its offer without committing itself to doing so following a competing offer announced by CH2M HILL.

The Note on Rule 19.3 also highlights that neither the offeror nor the offeree may make statements about the level of support from shareholders or other persons (for example, holders of derivatives such as contracts for differences or persons with de facto control over the shares in question) unless their up-to-date intentions have been clearly stated to the offeror or offeree (as appropriate) or their respective advisers. The Panel will require any such statements to be verified to its satisfaction. This means that a relatively simple statement about the level of shareholder support for (or opposition to) a bid can involve considerable discussion with the Panel concerning precisely what evidence is required. The evidence will normally take the form of a written confirmation from the person concerned and such confirmation is treated as a letter of intent.

One example of this Rule being enforced by the Panel occurred in relation to AbbVie's possible offer for Shire in 2014. AbbVie was required to retract comments by its CEO that he believed major Shire investors were "generally supportive of" AbbVie's £30.14 billion possible offer. In the retraction announcement AbbVie stated that it had "not received any written commitments of support and accordingly retracts the statements". Another example of this Rule was in relation to Deltic Group's merger proposal for Revolution Bars in 2017. Deltic included a statement in its announcement that it had received positive feedback from a significant number of shareholders of Revolution Bars in respect of its merger proposal. It was required to withdraw its statement by issuing an announcement on the following day clarifying that the feedback had been oral and no shareholder had formally confirmed its preference for Deltic's merger proposal over the offer for Revolution Bars by Stonegate (a competing bidder). The swift actions taken by the Panel in forcing a retraction highlight how closely the Panel monitors statements made by the parties to a bid.

The inclusion of an express responsibility statement by the directors, the requirement for documentation to be prepared to the highest standards of accuracy and the provisions of Rule 19.3 plus the risk of civil or criminal liability for knowingly or recklessly making misleading statements have combined to make it essential to conduct a proper verification exercise. This normally involves the preparation of detailed verification notes. It is generally regarded as insufficient simply to refer to the directors' responsibilities in the board minutes which approve the relevant document. Non-compliance with certain of the content requirements for offer and defence documentation is a criminal offence, referred to as the "bid documentation offence". Whilst scheme documents must include equivalent information to that found in offer documents and must be prepared to the same standard of accuracy, the bid documentation offence does not apply to bids implemented by way of a scheme of arrangement. The Rules covering content requirements for the purposes of the bid documentation offence are set out in Appendix 6 to the Code and principally relate to Rules 24 and 25 of the Code. The offence can be committed by the person making the bid and any director, officer or member of the bidder who caused the offer document to be published, and in the case of the defence document, any director or officer of the company for which the bid is made (s.953 of the CA 2006).

From the perspective of the offeror and its directors and the offeree and its directors, comfort can be taken from the fact that criminal liability will only arise where the person knew that the offer or defence document did not comply, or was reckless as to its compliance, with the relevant disclosure obligations and failed to take reasonable steps to ensure compliance. In addition, a criminal standard of proof would apply. A properly conducted verification exercise should be effective to mitigate this risk. At the time of writing, no prosecutions have been brought in respect of the bid documentation offence.

7.2.4 Release of information

The following are some of the different ways in which information can be released during an offer.

7.2.4.1 Advertisements

Takeover advertisements are relatively rare, largely as a result of the Panel introducing Rules controlling their use following some of the more heated battles in the mid-1980s.

Rule 20.5 provides that the publication of advertisements during the course of an offer by or on behalf of an offeror or offeree company is prohibited unless the advertisement falls within one of the specific exempt categories listed in the Rule or is being made with the consent of the Panel. Advertisements include not only press advertisements but also advertisements in other media such as television, radio, video, audio tape, and poster.

Three of the key exemptions are:

1. product advertisements published by the offeror or offeree company in the ordinary course of its business which do not relate to the offer (these do not have to receive prior clearance from the Panel although where there could be any doubt the Panel must be consulted);
2. corporate image advertisements published by the offeror or offeree company in the ordinary course of its business which do not relate to the offer or the financial performance of a party to the offer, but these must be cleared by the Panel in advance unless/until there is an announcement of a recommended and non-competitive firm offer.

This is presumably because there is a fine line between genuine corporate image advertisements and those which, although they do not refer to the existence of an offer, are nevertheless geared to affect the market's perception of an offer; and

3.   advertisements which contain only factual information in relation to an offer (for example, reminders as to closing dates or times or the value of an offer) and not any argument or opinion in relation to an offer. These advertisements must be cleared by the Panel in advance. During Banco Santander's offer for Abbey in 2004, advertisements were placed in national newspapers to remind Abbey's 1.8 million retail shareholders of approaching deadlines and of the existence of a shareholder telephone helpline.

Where Panel consent to the publication of an advertisement is sought, the Panel should be given at least one business day to clear the advertisement and the proofs submitted to them must have been reviewed by the financial adviser (Note on Rule 20.5). The Panel will not verify the accuracy of statements submitted for clearance but may comment on proposed wording.

7.2.4.2   *Telephone campaigns*

Telephone campaigns designed to sway wavering shareholders or other persons interested in shares are not all that common and the Rules relating to them are complex. The key requirement is contained in Rule 20.6 which provides that, except with the consent of the Panel, telephone campaigns may only be conducted by staff of the financial adviser who have a thorough understanding of the requirements of, and their responsibilities under, the Code. Where this is impractical (for example because of the large number of shareholders concerned), other persons can be employed with the consent of the Panel but only in accordance with the strict procedures laid down in the Code, including supervision by the financial advisers. The Panel must approve the written script for any such campaign and its principal concern will be to ensure that

only previously published information which remains accurate, and is not misleading at the time it is quoted, may be
used.

7.2.4.3   *Interviews and debates*

As regards television and radio interviews, the Rules which
apply here probably explain why most interviews of parties
involved in takeover bids are particularly dull (except where
the chairman or finance director has not been properly
briefed!). Parties should in general avoid the release of any
new material and any public confrontation between representatives of the offeror and offeree company, or between
competing offerors. In the Panel's own words, the parties
should also avoid "anything … which leads to any kind of
gladiatorial combat". Rule 19.4 which applies here does not say
much for the level of confidence in the integrity of our media:

> "Parties to an offer should, if interviewed on radio or
> television or any other media, seek to ensure that the
> sequence of the interview is not broken by the insertion of
> comments or observations by others not made in the
> course of the interview."

In other words, it is important for the parties to lay down the
ground rules before agreeing to be interviewed so as to avoid a
misleading message being broadcast.

7.2.4.4   *Videos and social media*

In 2016, RS 2016/1 introduced a new Rule 20.3 in relation to
videos and a new Rule 20.4 in relation to social media—these
methods of communication were previously not covered by the
Code. The Code severely limits the contents of videos and
publications via social media, in keeping with its approach to
interviews and debates (RS 2017/1 subsequently lessened
some of the requirements introduced by RS 2016/1 as they
caused practical difficulties for companies seeking to comply
with them and for the Panel to police them). Under Rule 20.3,
videos which include any information or opinions relating to

an offer or the financial performance of a party to an offer must comprise only a director or senior executive reading from a script or participating in a scripted interview and the Panel must consent to their publication. In addition, approved videos must be published on a website. Under Rule 20.4, social media must not be used by or on behalf on an offeror or offeree company to publish any offer-related information other than: (i) the full text of offer-related announcements or documents, or offer-related videos, in each case which have already been published in accordance with the Code; or (ii) notifications of website links on which such announcements, documents or videos have already been published in accordance with the Code. The Panel should be consulted if an offer is to be announced at a presentation which is to be broadcast by webcast, such as a results presentation.

7.2.4.5 *Post-offer undertakings and post-offer intention statements*

In January 2015, RS 2014/2 amended the Code to introduce a new framework for the regulation of statements made by bid parties relating to any particular course of action they commit or intend to take, or not take, after the end of the offer period—this framework is now found in Rules 19.5 (post-offer undertakings) and 19.6 (post-offer intention statements). The introduction of these Rules was triggered by the Pfizer/ AstraZeneca possible offer in connection with which Pfizer made a number of five-year commitments relating to Astra-Zeneca's R&D capabilities. The Code Committee of the Panel noted (in PCP 2014/2) that Pfizer's statements were unusual in that a bidder would normally express such statements as statements of intention rather than as commitments and the commitments were long-term (as compared to the 12-month period applicable to statements of intention as set out in the then existing Note 3 on Rule 19.1 of the Code).

Post-offer undertakings are covered by Rule 19.5. They are statements made by a bid party in any document, announcement or other information published by it in relation to the offer relating to any particular course of action that the party commits to take, or not take, after the end of the offer period and which is described by that party as a post-offer undertaking. The consent of the Panel is required for any such post-offer undertakings.

A post-offer undertaking must: (i) state that it is a post-offer undertaking; (ii) specify the period of time for which the undertaking is made or the date by which the course of action committed to will be completed (the Panel has indicated that it would generally expect post-offer undertakings to be made for a period of no more than five years, however the Code does not contain any express restriction on the time period for which post-offer undertakings may be made. If an undertaking is proposed to be made for an extended period, the Panel would wish to seek appropriate assurances from the party and its advisers as to its lawfulness); and (iii) prominently state any qualifications or conditions to which the undertaking is subject. The bid party concerned will normally be bound by the terms of the undertaking for the period specified in the undertaking (unless an express and specific qualification or condition set out in the undertaking applies and the Panel consents to that party relying on such qualification or condition).

The bid party giving the undertaking must also submit written reports to the Panel after the end of the offer period at such intervals and in such form as the Panel may require. Amendments to the Code (introduced by RS 2017/2) in January 2018 clarify that such interval periods should not be longer than 12 months. These periodic reports must: (i) indicate whether any course of action committed to be taken has been completed within the specified time-period, or if not, the progress made to date, the steps being taken and the expected time of completion; and (ii) confirm that any course of action the party had committed not to take has not been taken; (iii) be published in accordance with the Code in whole or in part (as required by the Panel).

As part of the Panel's powers to monitor compliance with, and enforce, post-offer undertakings, it has the ability to require a bid party that has made a post-offer undertaking to appoint an independent supervisor to: (i) monitor compliance; and (ii) submit written reports to the Panel at such intervals and in such form as the Panel may require in relation to compliance with the undertaking.

The first ever post-offer undertakings were entered into by SoftBank Group Corp. in July 2016 in relation to its offer for ARM Holdings. Against a background of political upheaval (including the unexpected result of the UK's referendum on membership of the EU in June 2016 and Theresa May's willingness to introduce new powers for the Government to intervene in UK public M&A deals, with the ability of "stepping in to defend a sector"[1]), concerns about the risks of losing an important UK technology company, UK technical capability and UK jobs, the Japanese bidder agreed, in relation to a five year period, to maintain ARM's corporate head-quarters in Cambridge and to increase or maintain ARM's UK, non-UK and technical employees. Additional detail and historical data were provided in the scheme document to assist with interpretation of these undertakings. An accountancy firm was appointed as an independent supervisor. SoftBank has periodically published excerpts of reports it has submitted to the Panel in relation to its post-offer undertakings.

The second post-offer undertakings were given by Melrose in March 2018 in relation to its hostile share and cash offer for GKN, pursuant to which Melrose agreed, for five years from completion of its offer, to maintain Melrose's headquarters and listing in the UK, to maintain a board comprising of a majority of UK residents and to retain GKN trade marks for GKN's Aerospace and Driveline businesses. In addition, Melrose also gave certain undertakings in relation to research and develop-ment expenditures of the GKN Group following completion of

---

[1] In her speech on 11 July 2016, launching her successful bid to become Prime Minister and setting out her vision for the UK, Theresa May made express reference to UK-bidder Pfizer's failed approach for AstraZeneca and the need for a "proper industrial strategy" which would enable the Government to intervene in transactions to protect important sectors. Subsequently, in 2018, the Enterprise Act 2002 was amended to enable regulatory intervention in relation to transactions involving targets operating in certain sectors, including certain technology sectors.

its offer. On 1 April 2019, Melrose published via RNS its 12-month report which it had submitted to the Panel.

The third post-offer undertakings were given by Comcast Corporation in May 2018 in relation to its offer for Sky. The post-offer undertakings related to maintaining Sky-branded news service and a minimum level of expenditure for Sky's news business, keeping Sky's UK headquarters in Osterley, the establishment of an editorial board of Sky (the Sky News Board), and the restriction on Comcast from acquiring any majority interest in any daily, Sunday or local UK newspaper (in most cases, for approximately five years after completion of its offer). In addition, Comcast also gave binding and enforceable commitments by way of a deed poll in favour of the Sky News Board in relation to certain actions already covered by its proposed post-offer undertakings, with such commitments continuing to apply for approximately 10 years after completion of its offer.

Post-offer undertakings could potentially be given by the bidco of a consortium (comprised of Apax Partners, Warburg Pincus International, Canada Pension Plan Investment Board and Ontario Teachers' Pension Plan Board) bid for Inmarsat, which operates in the telecommunications sector. On 18 April 2019, bidco announced that was is in discussions with the UK government regarding the potential for bidco to provide undertakings in connection with the acquisition, which may include post-offer undertakings under the Takeover Code and that bidco would make a further announcement with details in the event that it provides post-offer undertakings.

It would not be surprising to see more offerors using post-offer undertakings as a means to address public, political or regulatory concerns around the offeree company's business, employees and locations following the completion of the offer.

Post-offer intention statements are covered by Rule 19.6. They are statements made by a bid party in any document, announcement or other information published by it in relation to the offer relating to any particular course of action that the party intends to take, or not take, after the end of the offer period. Any post-offer intention statement made by a party to an offer must be: (i) an accurate statement of that party's intention at the time it is made; and (ii) made on reasonable grounds. Where a bid party makes a post-offer intention statement, it must consult the Panel if, during the 12 months from the end of the offer period or such other period specified in the statement, it decides to take a different course of action.

In addition, RS 2017/2, which amended the Code in January 2018, introduced a new requirement on a bid party who had given post-offer intention statements: such party must, at the end of the 12 months from the end of the offer period or such period specified in the statement, confirm in writing to the Panel whether it has complied with its stated intentions and publish such confirmation in accordance with the Code. To date, in the relatively rare instances where there has been a revision of a bidder's stated intentions, or non-compliance with stated intentions, bidders have attempted to provide clear explanations for the revision or non-compliance (as appropriate). One bidder, TT Electronics, revised its original stated intentions nine months after the end of the offer period for Stadium Group, stating that it intended to reduce the Stadium workforce headcount by no more than 4% rather than by no more than 3% as originally anticipated. TT Electronics subsequently announced it had complied with its revised intention statements. Another bidder, Newfield Resources, announced that it had complied with its post-offer intention statements except in relation to its intention to provide its shareholders within three months following completion of its offer for Stellar Diamonds with a facility under which holdings of less than A$500 could be aggregated and sold with proceeds returned to the participants, so that shareholders would not incur selling costs that would otherwise render a sale of their shares uneconomic. In its announcement, Newfield explained the reasons for the failure to comply (citing problems relating to the transition of the Stellar shareholder register from Stellar's registry to Newfield's share registry) and clarified that it still intended to establish such a facility but would do so once those transitional issues had been resolved.

Post-offer intention statements have been more widely used by bidders than post-offer undertakings.

For both post-offer undertakings and post-offer intention statements, if an alternative course of action is then taken, the bid party concerned must promptly make an announcement describing the course of action taken, or not taken, and explaining its rationale for the change (and, in the case of a post-offer undertaking, explaining how and why the relevant qualification or condition applies).

7.2.5 *Distribution and availability of documents and announcements*

Rule 30.5 imposes certain practical obligations in relation to the distribution of offer documents and announcements. Before the offer document is made public, a copy must be lodged with the Panel in hard copy and electronic form. Copies of all other documents, announcements and information published relating to a takeover must be lodged with both the Panel and also with the advisers to all other parties to the offer in both hard copy and electronic form. Where information has been incorporated into a document by reference, a copy of the relevant information should also be provided. Where the release of documents occurs outside normal business hours, the advisers to the other parties must be informed of the release immediately.

Rules 30.2–30.5 deal in some detail with the Code requirements for the distribution of documents both in hard copy and electronic form. The principle behind these Rules is that no party to an offer should be put at a disadvantage owing to a delay in receiving new information. A Code document will be treated as having been "sent" to a person if it is: (i) sent to the relevant person in hard copy form; (ii) sent to the relevant person in electronic form; or (iii) published on a website, provided that the relevant person is sent a notification in respect of its publication by no later than the date on which the Code document is published on the website. It remains market practice, however, for offer and scheme documents to be sent to offeree shareholders in hard copy form. Acceptance forms, withdrawal forms, proxy forms or any other forms relating to an offer must be published in hard copy form-only (in accordance with the Note on Rule 30.2, which also clarifies that such forms must not be published in newspapers).

In addition, in accordance with Rule 30.4, if a document, announcement or any information is required to be sent, published or made available to: (i) shareholders in the offeree company; (ii) persons with information rights; or (iii) employee representatives (or employees) of the offeror or the offeree company, it must be sent, published or made available (as the case may be) to all such persons, including those located outside the EEA (or from exit day, outside the UK, the Channel Islands and the Isle of Man), unless there is a sufficient objective justification for the party which publishes it not doing so on the basis described in the Note on this Rule (see below in 7.2.6). Certain information can be incorporated into the relevant documents by reference to another source of information (for example Annual Report and Accounts etc), provided that such information is sent to shareholders and other relevant persons if so requested.

Rule 26.1 requires that the offeror or offeree (as relevant) must publish on a website promptly following publication and in any event by no later than 12.00 noon on the following business day: (i) any document or information in relation to an offer sent to offeree shareholders, persons with information rights or other relevant persons in accordance with Rule 30.2; (ii) any announcement (subject to limited exceptions) published via a RIS (whether related to the offer or not); and (iii) any document or information required to be published on a website under any other provision of the Code (except Rules 26.2 (Documents to be published on a website following the announcement of a firm offer) or 26.3 (Documents to be published on a website following the making of an offer)).

The relevant website forms a single point of reference for all information published by a party in relation to an offer thereby affording easy access to such information by shareholders, potential investors and other interested persons. Access to the website can, however, be restricted via firewalls and disclaimers to address any potential securities laws issues (such as restricting access for shareholders in certain overseas jurisdictions).

7.2.6 Equality of information to shareholders

Rule 20.1(a) seeks to ensure that all shareholders (and persons with information rights) are kept properly informed by requiring that information and opinions relating to an offer or a party to an offer be made equally available to all offeree shareholders (and persons with information rights) as nearly as possible at the same time and in the same manner. Not only does this preserve equal treatment for shareholders but it helps to avoid the creation of a false market and reduces the potential for insider dealing.

Rule 20.1(b) (introduced in 2016 by RS 2016/1) requires the publication (except with the consent of the Panel and subject to certain limited exceptions in the Notes to Rule 20.1) via a RIS of any material new information or significant new opinion relating to an offer, or a party to an offer, which is: (i) published by or on behalf of an offeror or offeree company (other than a document sent to all offeree company shareholders and persons with information rights); or (ii) provided by or on behalf of an offeror or the offeree company to offeree or offeror shareholders (or other persons with interests in their securities), to any holder of publicly-traded debt securities of the offeror or offeree, or to any investment manager, investment adviser, investment analyst, or the media (whether in an interview, discussion, article, press release, letter or other document).

Rule 20.1(c) (also introduced in 2016 by RS 2016/1) requires publication (again, except with the consent of the Panel) on a website, accompanied by a RIS announcement noting the publication and providing a link to the website, of: (i) any presentation or other document relating to an offer (or a party to an offer) provided to, or used in a meeting (including a telephone call or meeting held electronically) with, any offeror/offeree shareholder (or other person interested in any relevant offeror/offeree securities), an investment manager, investment adviser, investment analyst or any holder of publicly-traded debt securities of the offeror/offeree, promptly following its provision or use; and (ii) any article, letter or other written communication relating to an offer or the financial performance of a party to an offer provided to the media, promptly following its publication by the media. This Rule 20.1(c) applies regardless of whether the relevant documents contain any material new information or significant new opinions.

Information, announcements and offer documentation must be made readily and promptly available to shareholders of the offeree company, persons with information rights, employee representatives (or employees) of the offeror or the offeree company and trustees of the offeree company's defined benefit pension schemes, including those who are located outside the EEA (or from exit day, outside the UK, the Channel Islands and the Isle of Man), unless there is sufficient objective justification for not doing so. Certain limited dispensations are available in respect of shareholders, persons with information rights and employee representatives (or employees) in non-EEA jurisdictions (or from exit day, outside the UK, the Channel Islands and the Isle of Man) (Note on Rule 30.4). Unless significant criminal, regulatory or civil exposure can be avoided by making minor amendments to the documents, a general dispensation will be available (without the need to consult the Panel) if less than 3% of the offeree company's shares are held by registered shareholders in a particular non-EEA jurisdiction (or, from exit day, a particular jurisdiction outside the UK, the Channel Islands and the Isle of Man). In other instances, the Panel may grant a specific dispensation where it would be appropriate to do so.

The same dispensations are generally available in relation to electronic communications, including the use of disclaimers on the gateway to a website or restrictions on access to websites from certain jurisdictions to restrict access to information where necessary, although no express reference to such mechanisms is made in the Code.

As a practical matter, the relevant overseas securities law implications need to be considered early in the bid process in order to determine whether there is a significant risk of criminal, regulatory or civil exposure in sending documentation into a particular jurisdiction.

As regards employees, employee representatives and trustees of the offeree company's defined benefit pension schemes (as opposed to shareholders), the Code does not require that a copy of the relevant information or document is sent to all employees/employee representatives or the defined benefit pension trustees; it must simply be made available to them. Accordingly, this obligation can be satisfied by placing the information on an appropriate part of the company's website. However, the Panel does have a right to require a copy of any announcement (or document which includes the contents of an announcement) to be sent to the offeree company's employee representatives (or employees) and defined benefit pension trustees (Rule 30.1(c)).

The Notes on Rule 20.1 contain certain exceptions to the equality of information principle. The most important of these Notes relates to the provision of information in confidence by an offeree company to a bona fide potential offeror or vice versa (Note 2). The reason for this exemption is to allow an offeree company to provide a prospective offeror with certain confidential information to enable it to decide whether to proceed with an offer; without this, the offeree company's shareholders might well be deprived of the benefit of an offer which would otherwise have been made for their shares (this is a theme that runs through the Code).

7.2.7 Meetings

Meetings are dealt with in Rule 20.2. Meetings include telephone calls (but not telephone campaigns) and meetings held by electronic means, such as video conferences. Although meetings with selected shareholders, analysts or brokers are not prohibited, the Rules reflect the fact that the overriding objective is to prevent material new information being disclosed selectively.

The offeror or offeree company (or either of their advisers) may, for example, hold meetings with selected shareholders of, or other persons interested in any relevant securities of the offeror or offeree company, or with investment managers, investment advisers or investment analysts, provided that:

1. no material new information or significant new opinion relating to the offer or a party to the offer is provided during the meeting; and
2. except with the consent of the Panel, an appropriate financial adviser or corporate broker to the party convening the meeting is present at the meeting. That representative must then confirm in writing to the Panel, not later than 12.00 noon on the business day following the date of the meeting, that no such material new information or significant new opinion was provided at the meeting. The Panel polices this requirement strictly.

If any material new information or a significant new opinion does emerge during a meeting, an announcement giving all relevant details must be made as soon as possible thereafter and, where appropriate, the Panel may, in addition, require a document to be sent to shareholders and the other persons listed in Note 3 on Rule 20.1.

If, however, the meeting is held before the offer period begins or before an announcement of a firm (or revised) offer is made, the Panel will allow the material new information and/or significant new opinions to be published in the announcement of the firm (or revised) offer (or the first substantive announcement by the board of the offeree company if the offer is not recommended) rather than requiring a separate document to be sent to shareholders, as long as the financial adviser or corporate broker attending the meeting confirms this in writing to the Panel (Note 1 on Rule 20.2). If the new information or opinion cannot be properly substantiated, this must be made clear and it must be formally withdrawn.

The question of what constitutes "material" new information has to be judged on a case-by-case basis. However, the Panel adopts a strict approach and the fact that information given during meetings is based upon information which has previously been made publicly available does not preclude it from being regarded as "new". For example, the provision of financial data or statistics which have been calculated from publicly available information may constitute new information, even where the data or statistics have been arrived at following a simple arithmetic process. It is therefore important to consider both the nature of the information which is given and the manner in which it is presented.

The Code Committee recognised in 2016 that there are significant costs and practicalities associated with the requirement for financial advisers/corporate brokers chaperoning meetings and it noted that the Executive had received an increasing number of requests for dispensations from the requirement, in particular where the offer is recommended and uncompetitive and the offer period is lengthy (e.g. due to official authorisations and regulatory clearances). RS 2016/1 therefore introduced a new Note 2 to Rule 20.2 which provides that the Panel will normally grant a dispensation (subject to prior consultation) from the Rule 20.2 requirement for financial adviser chaperoning following the announcement of a recommended firm offer which is not competitive, provided that the meeting attendees are appropriately briefed by the financial adviser and a senior representative of (or adviser to) the offeror/offeree attends the meeting and provides the usual confirmation to the Panel. Note 3 on Rule 20.2 was also introduced, allowing further dispensations for meetings attended by advisers only and not also by a representative of the offeror or offeree.

7.2.8 *Equality of information to competing offerors*

As noted above, one exception to the rule on equality of information to all shareholders is the provision of information in confidence by an offeree company to an offeror or potential offeror. Rule 21.3 provides that any such information must, however, be given on request equally and promptly to another offeror or bona fide potential offeror even if that other offeror is less welcome. This requirement will usually only apply when there has been a public announcement of the existence of the offeror or potential offeror to which information has been given. However, this obligation can also be triggered where one offeror or potential offeror is informed authoritatively (normally by the offeree company or its advisers) of the existence of another potential offeror even if there has been no public statement made to this effect. Equally it will be triggered if there is a public announcement of an approach or talks concerning a possible offer even if an exemption from naming is available such that the potential offeror involved is not identified in that announcement.

There is a practical limitation to this Rule as the Code provides that the less-welcome offeror must specify the questions to which it requires answers. It cannot simply make a general request to receive all information provided to its competitor. This tends to lead to extremely lengthy and detailed question-naires being sent to the offeree company's advisers by the offeror's advisers in an attempt to catch any and all information which might conceivably be of interest.

It is important, therefore, that the flow of information from an offeree company to its preferred offeror is carefully controlled not only to avoid the prospect of having to give valuable commercial information to an unwelcome offeror but also to ensure that there is an accurate record of what information has been provided to any particular potential offeror.

It has always been clear that Rule 21.3 applies not just to information which is provided in written form but also to information which is provided orally. However, Practice

Statement No.2 clarified that Rule 21.3 also extends to site visits and meetings with the management of the offeree company. As a result, if one offeror (or potential offeror) has been granted access to conduct a site visit or to talk to management then equal access must be granted to any other offeror (or potential offeror) that requests it. Offeree companies will therefore need to give particular thought to whether to allow an offeror, such as a potential white knight, to talk to management in light of the prospect of having to allow a hostile bidder similar access.

Rule 21.3 (then Rule 20.2) was in issue in the battle for Midland Bank in 1992. HSBC Holdings (a Hong Kong and Shanghai Bank subsidiary) announced a recommended offer for Midland and some weeks later Lloyds Bank announced that it was considering making an offer for Midland. One pre-condition of Lloyds making an offer was that it received all the information which HSBC had received from Midland and such information being satisfactory to it. Midland was concerned that passing confidential commercially sensitive information to a competitor could ultimately cause damage to its shareholders. The Panel had to decide whether it should modify or relax the then Rule 20.2 since it was not disputed that Lloyds was other than a "bona fide potential offeror" for the purposes of the Rule. In the circumstances the Panel decided not to modify or relax the Rule and Midland was obliged to hand over to Lloyds the information which had previously been passed to HSBC. In the Panel's view the likelihood of damage being done to Midland shareholders was greater if the relevant information was withheld than if it were given to Lloyds.

RS 2017/1 introduced a new Note 6 on Rule 21.3 that extended the application of Rule 21.3 to information given to substantial asset purchasers. If the offeree company commences discussions with one or more persons in relation to the sale of all or substantially all of its assets (excluding cash and cash equivalents) during an offer or following the date on which the board of the offeree company has reason to believe that a bona fide offer might be imminent, information given by the offeree company to the potential asset purchaser(s) must, on request, be given to an offeror or bona fide potential offeror. As for competing offerors, this requirement will usually only apply when there has been a public announcement of the discussions between the offeree company and the potential asset purchaser(s) or, if there has been no public announcement, when the offeror or bona fide potential offeror requesting information has been informed authoritatively that the offeree company and the potential asset purchaser(s) are having such discussions.

If a company was in discussions with potential purchaser(s) regarding the sale of all or substantially all of its assets prior to an offer being made or the date on which the board had reason to believe that a bona fide offer might be imminent, Rule 21.3 will not apply in relation to any information given to the potential asset purchaser(s) (including information given after the offer was made or the date that the board had reason to believe that a bona fide offer might be imminent) and accordingly there is no requirement for such information to be given to an offeror or bona fide potential offeror.

The only restrictions which may be placed on information which is provided under Rule 21.3 (as set out in Note 2 on that Rule) relate to:

1. maintaining the confidentiality of the information passed;
2. preventing the use of the information to solicit customers or employees; and/or
3. restricting the use of the information solely in connection with an offer or potential offer.

Any conditions imposed in this way should be no more onerous than those imposed on any other offeror or potential offeror or substantial asset purchaser to whom information is provided.

More recently, against a background of increasing regulatory focus, clean team agreements (or confidentiality and joint defence agreements) have been entered into to address concerns around sharing confidential commercially sensitive information and Rule 21.3. The Panel published Practice Statement No.30 in 2015 relating to Rule 21.3 confirming its approach to clean team arrangements in UK public deals. The Executive noted that an offeree may consider it necessary to provide a limited amount of commercially sensitive information to a "clean team" (composed of lawyers or economists advising the offeror on an "outside counsel" basis) in order to consider the need for and, if necessary, obtain antitrust or other regulatory clearances but the offeree may not wish to provide this information directly to the offeror or to any competing offeror. The Practice Statement states that the Panel will normally agree that the requirements of Rule 21.3 will be satisfied if the restricted information which is provided to the clean team of the first offeror is also provided on request to the clean team of the competing offeror. The consent of the Panel must be obtained in advance before any clean team arrangements are made with any offeror and the Practice Statement sets out the factors that the Panel will take into consideration when considering whether to grant this consent as well as the details that must be provided to the Panel and the procedures that must be followed. Such clean team arrangements were used recently for example on John Wood Group's offer for Amec Foster Wheeler, Standard Life's offer for Aberdeen Asset Management, and Tesco's merger with Booker Group.

There are specific provisions of the Code (see Note 3 on Rule 21.3 and Rule 21.4) which deal with equality of information where the offer is a management buyout (MBO). An MBO competing offeror or potential offeror must, on request, promptly be provided with all the information generated by the offeree company (including the management of the offeree company acting in their capacity as such) which is passed to the offeror's/potential offeror's external providers or potential providers of equity or debt finance. The Panel expects the directors of the offeree company who are involved in making the MBO offer to cooperate with the independent directors of the offeree company and its advisers in assembling such information. The independent directors of the offeree company or its advisers must, on request, be provided with the all the information which the offeror/potential offeror has provided to external providers or potential providers of equity or debt finance for the buy-out.

7.2.9 Restrictions on frustrating action: Rule 21

The vast majority of takeovers in the UK are recommended at the time of launch. However, there have been several high-profile hostile offers in recent years, including the offer for Eurasian Natural Resources Corporation by its founders, Essar Global Fund Ltd's offer for Essar Energy, HarbourVest Partners' offer for SVG Capital, TVH Group's offer for Lavendon Group, Melrose's offer for GKN and Non-Standard Financial plc's (NSF) offer for Provident Financial plc (Provident). As a consequence, the provisions of the Code which restrict the ability of the offeree company to take action which might frustrate an offer must be considered carefully in practice.

7.2.9.1 Shareholder approval

The restrictions on frustrating action are contained in Rule 21 of the Code and are reinforced by General Principle 3. Rule 21.1 prohibits the offeree board from taking any action which may result in any offer or bona fide possible offer being frustrated unless the board has obtained shareholder approval. This applies during the course of an offer, or even before the date of the offer if the board of the offeree company has reason to believe that a bona fide offer might be imminent. If the proposed action is in pursuance of a contract entered into earlier or another pre-existing obligation or decision of the offeree company's board, the Panel must be consulted and its consent to proceed without a shareholders' meeting obtained. It should, however, be noted that the board of a company is, subject to directors' fiduciary duties, free to put in place defence planning initiatives (for example poison pills) at any time when an offer is not in contemplation (although these are very rarely employed in the UK).

Rule 21.1 specifically prevents any decision by the offeree company directors (without shareholder approval) to:

1. issue any further shares or transfer/sell any treasury shares or redeem or purchase any shares in the offeree company;
2. issue or grant any options over any unissued shares in the offeree company;
3. create or issue any convertible securities (for example convertible loan stock) or securities carrying the right to subscribe for company shares (for example warrants);
4. make any disposal or acquisition of assets of a "material amount" (the Panel will normally consider relative values of 10% or more as being of a material amount, although relative values lower than 10% may be considered material if the asset is of particular significance. Note also that the 10% becomes 15% in the event that the disposal or acquisition takes place during a Phase 2 reference to the Competition and Markets Authority or where the European Commission has initiated Phase 2 proceedings); or
5. enter into any contracts other than in the ordinary course of business.

Generally, it should be appreciated that this is a non-exhaustive list of prohibited acts. As a result, it is important that the Panel is consulted in advance if there is any doubt as to whether any proposed actions would fall foul of General Principle 3 or Rule 21.1.

General Principle 3 and Rule 21 are based on the premise that it is for the shareholders of the offeree company (not its directors or management) to determine the outcome of the offer. It is open to the offeree company directors to publish profit forecasts and other indications of the expected future performance of the offeree company's business and to lobby competition authorities to investigate the bid. Equally, the offeree board can put proposals to shareholders which would have the effect of defeating the bid, so long as those proposals can only be implemented with the consent of shareholders. As part of its defence against the unwelcome bid from NASDAQ in 2007, the London Stock Exchange announced that it would return an additional £250 million to investors via a share buy-back programme. The vote on a proposal which might potentially frustrate an offer is, of course, open to all shareholders and therefore if the potential offeror has managed to establish a significant shareholding in the offeree company, it would be free to vote against the proposed course of action.

Where shareholder approval is to be sought in general meeting for a proposed action, the board of the offeree company must obtain competent independent advice as to whether the financial terms of the proposed action are fair and reasonable, the Panel must be consulted regarding the date of the general meeting, and the board of the offeree company must send a circular to shareholders containing the details set out in Note 1 to Rule 21.1 as soon as practicable after the announcement of the proposed action.

The Panel will normally grant dispensation from the requirement for shareholder approval if: (i) the taking of the proposed action is conditional on the offer being withdrawn or lapsing (provided the offeree company announces the details of the proposed action in accordance with Note 1 on Rule 21.1); (ii) the offeror consents to the proposed action; (iii) offeree shareholders holding more than 50% of the voting rights of the offeree company state in writing that they approve the proposed action and would vote in favour of any resolution to that effect proposed at a general meeting; (iv) the proposed action is in pursuance of a contract entered into before the beginning of the period that Rule 21.1 started to apply (as set out above) or another pre-existing obligation; or (v) a decision to take the proposed action had been taken before the beginning of the period that Rule 21.1 started to apply (as set out above) which either has been partly or fully implemented before the beginning of that period or is in the ordinary course of business.

In deciding how best to defend the company against an unwelcome bid, the directors of the offeree company must, of course, have regard to their general duties as directors and in the exercise of their powers be satisfied, after taking advice, that such powers are being exercised for a proper purpose and that they are acting in accordance with their duties.

It may be tempting for the board of directors of an offeree company to consider extending service contracts or amending them to increase directors' remuneration as a protective reaction to a bid. The Panel will regard this as entering into a contract other than in the ordinary course of business and therefore as outlawed if the new or amended contract or terms constitute "an abnormal increase" in the directors' emoluments or a "significant improvement" in the directors' terms of service (Note 5 on Rule 21.1).

The offeree company may well have an existing executive share option scheme and the question may arise of granting further options to executives over shares in the offeree company. As already mentioned, the grant of options over unissued shares in the offeree company is prohibited unless approved by shareholders in general meeting. However, the Panel will normally permit the grant of options under an existing established share option scheme where the timing and level of the grants are in accordance with the company's normal practice (for example as regards timing, during a "window" period after the announcement of year-end or interim results). The Panel will also normally permit the issue of shares on the exercise of employee share options in accordance with their normal terms (Note 6 on Rule 21.1). However, a company will also need to ensure that it complies with any other obligations to which it is subject, such as art.19 of the Market Abuse Regulation (2014/596/EU) relating to transactions by persons discharging managerial responsibilities.

Other things to watch out for include the payment of interim dividends otherwise than in the normal course or the making of changes to the pension scheme arrangements; in such circumstances the Panel should always be consulted in advance (see Notes 3 and 7 on Rule 21.1).

Further, it is important for an offeree board to bear in mind the aggregation principle. Separate matters may be aggregated and treated as covered by Rule 21.1 notwithstanding that individually they might not be regarded as sufficiently material (see paragraph (d) of Note 2 on Rule 21.2).

In the case of a scheme, the offeree board should consult the Panel prior to taking any action which could lead to a scheme lapsing (where the offeror has not been given an opportunity to switch the structure of the transaction to a contractual takeover offer), in order to determine whether such action might constitute frustrating action.

RS 2017/1 introduced an additional type of permitted break fee payable by the offeree to a counterparty (or counterparties) to transaction(s) to which Rule 21.1 applies. This is explained further in 7.2.9.2 below.

7.2.9.2 Deal protection measures

Except in very limited circumstances, Rule 21.2 prohibits an offeree company and its concert parties from entering into any offer-related arrangement with either the offeror or any of its concert parties. The prohibition covers an inducement fee (often called a "break fee") arrangement, or any other deal protection measures, such as an undertaking from the offeree board to take certain actions to implement an offer (or refrain from taking action which might facilitate a competing bid) or "matching rights" provisions in the event of a competing offer. The prohibition applies both during an offer period and when an offer is reasonably in contemplation.

Derogation from this prohibition is only permitted in very limited circumstances. The prohibition does not apply where an offeree board has initiated a formal sale process to identify a buyer (at any time up to a Rule 2.7 firm intention announcement), although any break fee entered into must not exceed 1% of the offer value/market capitalisation of the offeree company, may only be agreed with a single preferred participant in the formal sale process, and may only be payable after a third-party offer becomes or is declared wholly unconditional. In exceptional circumstances, the Panel may also be prepared to consent to the offeree company entering into other offer-related arrangements with the preferred offeror.

An additional white knight exception is also available in circumstances where a non-recommended offer has been announced and the offeree company wishes to obtain a competing offer from a more welcome bidder. This exception applies solely to break fees (not other offer-related arrangements); however, a white knight break fee can be agreed with more than one party provided that the maximum aggregate payment under any such break fee arrangements is 1% of the value of the offeree company. Any such break fee agreements can only be entered into following the announcement of a firm intention to make a non-recommended offer by an initial offeror, and the fee must only become payable once a third party's offer becomes or is declared wholly unconditional. The first ever white knight break fee was entered into in 2016 on Loxam SAS's offer for Lavendon Group where Loxam was a competing offeror to TVH Group's hostile offer for the target.

The Panel Executive has the discretion to grant a dispensation from the prohibition on inducement fees and deal protection measures (including work fees) to a company in serious financial distress. This discretion arises under the Panel's general rights of derogation set out in the Introduction to the Code.

RS 2017/1 introduced an additional type of permitted break fee payable by the offeree to a counterparty (or counterparties) to transaction(s) to which Rule 21.1 (frustrating action) applies, provided that: (a) the aggregate value of the inducement fee(s) that may be payable by the offeree company in relation to the same asset(s) is no more than 1% of the value of the transaction (or, if there are two or more transactions in respect of the same asset(s), the transaction with the highest value); and (b) the aggregate value of the inducement fee(s) that may be payable by the offeree company in respect of all transactions to which Rule 21.1 applies is no more than 1% of the value of the offeree company calculated by reference to the price of the offeror's offer (or, if there are two or more offerors, the first offer) at the time of the firm offer announcement made under Rule 2.7.

The prohibition on deal protection measures does not apply to arrangements between an offeror and an offeree company entered into in the ordinary course of business (although the Panel should be consulted in such circumstances), nor does it apply to any offer-related agreement which relates to an existing employee incentive arrangement. An offeror is not prevented from seeking irrevocable undertakings or letters of intent, confidentiality undertakings, commitments not to solicit the offeror's employees, customers or suppliers, undertakings from the offeree company to provide information or assistance for the purposes of obtaining any official authorisation or regulatory clearance, or commitments imposing obligations on the offeror (except in the context of a reverse takeover). These exceptions are listed in Rule 21.2(b)(i)–(vii) and Practice Statement No.29 gives guidance on the Panel's interpretation and application of these exceptions.

Cooperation agreements (or bid conduct agreements) have become a regular feature of takeovers since the introduction of Rule 21.2 and contain obligations on both the offeree and offeror. The offeree's obligations are limited to those listed in Rule 21.2(b)(i)–(vii). Practice Statement No.29 lists provisions that the Panel views as not falling within these exceptions (and therefore not permitted in a co-operation agreement), such as obligations on the offeree to assist with the offer documentation or integration planning, conduct of business undertakings or information warranties from the offeree and restrictions on offeree dividends. A co-operation agreement will therefore typically contain commitments from the offeree to provide information and assistance for the purpose of obtaining official authorisation or regulatory clearance and in relation to existing employee incentive schemes. There are no restrictions on the obligations that can be imposed on an offeror in a cooperation agreement. Typically, the offeror will give undertakings in relation to official authorisations and regulatory clearances, assistance with the implementation of the offer (including if the structure of the offer changes from a scheme to an offer or vice versa), recommending the offer to its shareholders, maintaining D&O insurance for the outgoing offeree directors and, in some cases, a reverse break fee. The Panel expects cooperation agreements to contain a standard clause acknowledging that if the Panel determines that any provision in the agreement is not permitted by Rule 21.2 that provision will have no effect.

Reverse break fees (paid by the offeror to the offeree) have become a popular form of deal protection, particularly on large deals where there is significant risk of the deal not receiving antitrust or regulatory clearance or shareholder approval. A reverse break fee is intended to compensate the offeree for any loss incurred preparing and negotiating the offer. Significant reverse break fees have been agreed on a number of deals in recent years including Anheuser-Busch InBev SA/NV's offer for SABMiller, Ball Corporation's offer for Rexam, Royal Dutch Shell's offer for BG Group, 21st Century Fox's offer for Sky and AbbeVie's offer for Shire. AbbeVie then paid a reverse break fee of approximately US$1.635 billion to Shire when AbbeVie's board withdrew support for the transaction in 2014.

The boards of UK companies also need to have regard to the Listing Rules, the prohibitions on providing financial assistance and their own directors' duties when considering whether to agree to enter into a cooperation agreement and a reverse break fee and, if so, the terms of that agreement and the amount of any such fee.

Irrevocable commitments and letters of intent are included within the exceptions allowed by Rule 21.2 and continue to be widely used as a form of deal protection. There has been a notable increase in the use of matching rights and exclusivity provisions in irrevocable undertakings since 2011. Care must be taken when drafting such provisions in irrevocable undertakings given by offeree company concert parties. For example, directors and 20% plus shareholders (unless the presumption of concertedness is capable of being rebutted) are presumed to be concert parties of the offeree company and will also be caught by the prohibition in Rule 21.2. In Practice Statement No.29, the Panel makes clear that offeree director shareholders are permitted to enter into irrevocable commitments in relation to their shares, however, they are not allowed to enter into other types of offer-related arrangement, for example, a deal protection undertaking in favour of the offeror (or its concert parties). Undertakings aimed solely at giving effect to the irrevocable are, however, permitted, for example, an undertaking not to dispose of the shares or withdraw acceptance of the offer; an undertaking to elect for a particular form of bid consideration; and representations as to title to the relevant shares.

In connection with General Sales and Leasing's bid for Xenetic Biosciences, the offeree directors' irrevocable undertakings contained a non-solicit undertaking contrary to Rule 21.2 and Practice Statement No.27 (subsequently withdrawn and replaced by Practice Statement No.29). The Panel required the directors to enter into new irrevocable undertakings without the offending undertaking.

7.2.10 Prohibition on share dealings by offeree company advisers

During the offer period, no financial adviser or corporate broker (or any persons in the same group/under the same control) to an offeree company (or any member of its group) is permitted to deal (or procure, facilitate, or encourage a person to refrain from, dealing) in offeree company shares without the consent of the Panel (see Rule 4.4). This reflects the view of the Panel that it is for the offeree shareholders and not its financial advisers or other connected persons to determine the outcome of a bid. There is, however, a carve-out for the activities of exempt principal traders and exempt fund managers connected with the relevant financial adviser or broker.

The Code also contains restrictions on securities borrowing and lending transactions without the Panel's consent by offerors, the offeree company and certain other persons acting in concert with them (Rule 4.6).

7.3 Timing and revision

The second main area covered in this Chapter, "Timing and Revision" (Rules 24.1 and 25.1 and Rules 31–35), is very much the "nuts and bolts" of takeover practice in that it covers the detailed and somewhat technical Rules governing the timing of the various steps in a takeover bid, the Rules relating to the introduction of different forms of bid consideration and those relating to increased offers.

The two most important basic principles underlying the Rules relating to the timing and revision of offers are as follows:

1.   the duration of a bid should be limited. This is in recognition of the disruption caused by a hostile bid to the offeree company and its board in taking their attention away from the day-to-day management of the offeree group's business; and
2.   the shareholders of the offeree company should, however, have sufficient time to be able to consider any offer for their shares and any competing offer for their shares on their merits.

As a result, certain events have to happen by certain times, whilst other events cannot happen before certain periods of time have elapsed.

7.3.1   Offer timetable

This section focuses on the Code timetable for a contractual offer (although commentary is provided on how the timetable differs on a takeover structured as a scheme of arrangement). Schemes are conducted by reference to a largely court-driven timetable and, in the absence of a competitive bid, there are no maximum time periods set out in the Code for the holding of shareholder meetings and/or the fulfilment of other conditions to a recommended scheme. As a result, a scheme can provide a greater degree of flexibility in the timetable than is the case with a contractual offer. The rules on the application of the Code to schemes are largely contained in the Schemes Appendix.

In the case of a scheme, the timetable will need to be published in the scheme circular and then adhered to by the offeree company. If the board of the offeree company withdraws its recommendation, announces its decision to propose an adjournment of a shareholder meeting or the court sanction meeting, any shareholder meeting or the court sanction meeting is adjourned, or the Panel considers that the offeree company has not implemented the scheme in accordance with the published timetable, the offeror will normally be permitted to switch to a contractual offer with up to a 90% acceptance condition. An offeror may protect itself by including timetable-related conditions in its offer (for example, a condition that the shareholder meetings and/or the court sanction hearing must be held on or by a specific date). The inclusion of such a condition allows an offeror to lapse the scheme in the event of it being breached, without reference to the materiality thresholds set out in Rule 13.5. However, the Panel expects that any such dates stipulated in a formal condition should be more than 21 days after the date set for the relevant event in the expected scheme timetable in order to allow the offeree board flexibility to adjourn the shareholder meeting or court hearing for a short period without the offeror being immediately able to invoke a condition.

The key times or dates in a contractual offer timetable are as follows.

7.3.1.1 Posting date (Day 0)

The offer document should normally be sent to offeree company shareholders (and persons with information rights) within 28 days of the announcement of a firm intention to make an offer (Rule 24.1(a)). References to days are generally to calendar days-weekends and public holidays are treated like any other day. The Panel will not usually grant an extension of time for publishing it unless the offeree company consents.

RS 2017/2 introduced a new provision in Rule 24.1(a) that the offeror may only publish the offer document within 14 days following its firm intention announcement with the consent of the board of the offeree company. The purpose of this new requirement is to ensure that the offeree company has at least 28 days from the offeror's firm intention announcement to prepare its defence document in a hostile situation (see 7.3.1.2 below). On a recommended offer, the offer document will be a combined document of the offeror and the offeree, hence the parties would mutually agree a date for its publication (see 7.3.1.2 below).

Rule 24 is similarly applied to the publication of a scheme circular, requiring the circular to be sent to target shareholders within 28 days of the announcement of a firm intention to make a bid. In practice, however, the Panel will normally grant an extension to the publication date if that is supported by the target board as it may not always be possible to publish a scheme circular within 28 days of announcement.

Rule 24.1(b) requires the offeror to make the offer document readily available to the trustees of the offeree company's defined benefits pension scheme(s). At the same time both the offeror and the offeree company are required to make the document available to their employee representatives or, where there are no such representatives, to the employees themselves. These requirements apply equally on a scheme.

Rule 24.1(c) requires the offer document to be published on a website and such publication announced via a RIS.

The Code provides for the opinion of employee representatives on the effects of the offer on employment and/or the opinion of the trustees of the offeree company's pension scheme(s) on the effects of the offer on the pension scheme(s) to be appended to the recommended offer document (or the offeree defence document in the case of a hostile offer—see 7.3.1.2 below), if it is received in good time (Rule 25.9). If any such opinion is not provided to the offeree company in time, then the offeree company is required to publish the opinion on its website and to announce that this has been done via a RIS (for example an RNS announcement), provided that the opinion is received no later than 14 days after the date on which the offer becomes or is declared wholly unconditional. It should be noted that the offeree company is required to pay for the reasonable costs incurred by the employee representatives in obtaining advice in preparing their opinion on the effects of the offer on employment (Note 1(a) on Rule 25.9).

7.3.1.2 Day 14 (counting forwards from the posting date and excluding the posting date)

This is (normally) the last day for the offeree board to advise shareholders (and persons with information rights) of its views on the offer. Rule 25.1(a) provides that the board of the offeree company must, within 14 days of the publication of the offer document, send a circular to its shareholders (and persons with information rights). Rule 25.1(b) requires that at the same time as the circular is published, the offeree company must make it readily available to the trustees of its defined benefit pension scheme(s) and its employee representatives (or, where there are no such representatives, the employees themselves). The circular must set out the opinion of the board on the offer and the board's reasons for forming its opinion in accordance with Rule 25.2. As with the publication of an offer document, the circular must be made available on a website in accordance with Rule 26.1 and such publication announced via a RIS. As mentioned above, the offeree board is required to append to the circular any opinion from the trustees of its pension scheme(s) on the effects of the offer on the pension scheme(s) and/or the representatives of its employees on the effects of the offer on employment, provided any such opinion is received in good time before publication of the circular (Rule 25.9). If any such opinion is not received in good time, then the offeree company is required to publish the opinion on a website and to announce that this has been done via a RIS—see 7.3.1.1 above.

On a recommended offer, the offeree board circular would normally be incorporated within the offer document. Similarly, under a scheme of arrangement, the information required to be contained in an offer document and the information required to be contained in the offeree board circular is included in a single document, the scheme circular. Therefore, the reference to the offeree board's circular being published and made readily available after publication of the bid document is not applicable to a recommended contractual offer or a scheme.

7.3.1.3 *Day 21*

An offer must initially be open for at least 21 days following the date on which the offer document is published (Rule 31.1). Therefore, the first closing date of an offer will normally be 21 days from the date of publication of the offer document, although it can be later than Day 21. This does not, however, prevent the offer from becoming unconditional at an earlier date or, alternatively, the first closing date being set for a date which is more than 21 days after publication (for example, to avoid public holidays etc).

Since a scheme of arrangement does not remain "open for acceptance" in the way that a contractual offer does, Rule 31.1 is disapplied in relation to schemes. However, in order to be consistent with the position under a contractual offer, Section 3 of the Schemes Appendix provides that shareholder meetings must normally be convened for a date which is at least 21 days after the date of the scheme circular, except with the consent of the Panel.

7.3.1.4 *Day 35*

This is the first day on which an offer may close (i.e. no longer be open for acceptance), assuming it has been declared unconditional as to acceptances on the first closing date (assuming that is Day 21). This is because Rule 31.4 provides that after an offer has become or is declared unconditional as to acceptances, the offer must remain open for acceptance for not less than 14 days after the date on which it would otherwise have expired.

This Rule allows a shareholder who has been unable to make up his or her mind, or who perhaps wanted to see whether control would pass without his or her support, a period of 14 days beyond the date when the offer would otherwise have expired to accept the offer. When, however, an offer is unconditional as to acceptances from the outset, it is not necessary to keep the offer open for a further 14 days, provided the position has been set out clearly and prominently in the offer document.

Since a scheme of arrangement is immediately binding on all shareholders once it has become effective, the concept of an offer remaining "open" after control has passed is not relevant and Rule 31.4 is therefore not applicable.

If the offer became wholly unconditional on Day 21, then Day 35 will also be the last date for payment of the consideration under the offer to shareholders who accepted the offer. The reason for this is that Rule 31.8 requires the consideration to be sent to accepting shareholders within 14 days of the later of:

1. the first closing date of the offer (normally "Day 21");
2. the date on which the offer became or was declared wholly unconditional; and
3. the date of receipt of a valid acceptance complete in all respects.

As a result, where an offer becomes or is declared unconditional as to acceptances on Day 60 but does not become unconditional in all respects (i.e. all other conditions satisfied or waived) until Day 81, the consideration will not have to be sent until Day 95.

A scheme of arrangement has no "first closing date", is not "accepted" by target shareholders and becomes effective once the relevant court order has been duly filed, or if required by the court registered, at Companies House rather than on becoming or being declared "wholly unconditional". As a result, s.10 of the Schemes Appendix provides that the consideration under a scheme must be sent to offeree company shareholders within 14 days of the scheme becoming effective, except with the consent of the Panel.

7.3.1.5   Day 39

Except where the Panel has otherwise consented (having been consulted "in good time"), this is the last day of the offer period for the offeree board to announce "any material new information" (Rule 31.9). This Rule covers announcements relating to trading results, profit or dividend forecasts, asset valuations, quantified financial benefits statements, proposals for dividend payments and material acquisitions or disposals. This is a non-exhaustive list and these matters are referred to in the Rule as illustrative examples of the types of new information which could be considered material.

Rule 31.9 provides that, where a matter which might result in a Rule 31.9 announcement being made after Day 39 is known to the offeree company, every effort should be made to bring forward the date of the announcement. If it is not practicable to make the announcement before Day 39 or the matter arises after Day 39, the Panel will normally give its consent to a later announcement and will normally be prepared to extend the offer period and, in particular, move Day 46 (the last day for posting a revision of the offer); Day 53 (the date by which any potential competing offeror is required to confirm its position) and/or Day 60 (the final date for declaring the offer uncondi-tional as to acceptances), as appropriate, to a later date.

This happened in 2003, in the context of the competing bids for Oxford Glycosciences by Celltech Group and Cambridge Antibody Technology. The Panel Executive extended Day 39 for up to 20 days to allow Oxford Glycosciences to announce its trading results. The offer timetable was subsequently reset, with Day 46 deemed to fall seven days after the announcement of the trading results. The Panel also granted an extension under this Rule in relation to Kraft Foods' bid for Cadbury in 2009, so as to enable Cadbury to release its annual trading results up to three days after the original Day 39 deadline, although the offer timetable was not reset in any other respect.

In cases where an offer is subject to a competition condition and the Competition and Markets Authority or the European Commission (as the case may be) has not yet announced whether or not a Phase 2 investigation will be initiated, the Panel will normally extend Day 39 to the second day following the announcement of the relevant decision with consequent changes to Day 46, Day 53 and Day 60 (see Note 5 on Rule 31.6). Such an extension was granted in relation to Reckitt Benckiser's bid for SSL International in 2010, Greencore's offer for Uniq in 2011, Motorola Solutions bid for Psion in 2012, IP Group plc's offer for Touchstone Innovations plc in 2017 and NSF's hostile offer for Provident in 2019, and the offer timetables were reset accordingly. Note that an offeror or an offeree can request an extension of Day 39.

During the hostile bid by Saint-Gobain for BPB in 2005, Saint-Gobain sought an extension of Day 39 in circumstances where it had been delayed in making the requisite competition filing with the European Commission with the inevitable consequence that the relevant decision would be delayed beyond Day 39. Although the Panel was prepared to grant the timetable extension in these unprecedented circumstances, Saint-Gobain was required to undertake that neither it nor any of its concert parties would acquire any interest in or rights over any BPB shares (other than in very limited circumstances) until such time as the European Commission published its decision as to whether or not to initiate a second stage investigation.

The Day 39 Rule (Rule 31.9) is disapplied in relation to schemes of arrangement. Generally, schemes are implemented by agreement between the target and the bidder, therefore no specific deadline for the announcement of material new information by the target is imposed by the Code.

7.3.1.6   Day 42

This is the last date for fulfilment of all other conditions of the bid, assuming the offer became or was declared unconditional as to acceptances on the first closing date and the first closing date was Day 21.

Rule 31.7 provides that, except with the consent of the Panel, all conditions must be fulfilled or the offer must lapse within 21 days of the first closing date or the date the offer becomes or is declared unconditional as to acceptances, whichever is the later. The Panel will normally only grant consent for an extension if the outstanding conditions involve a material official authorisation or regulatory clearance relating to the offer, and it has not been possible to obtain an extension under Rule 31.6 (see 7.3.1.5 above). Thus, if an offer is not declared unconditional as to acceptances until Day 60 (which is common where there are competing offers), all other conditions must normally be satisfied by Day 81 (i.e. Day 60 plus 21). (Timetable extensions are discussed in 7.3.2 below.)

The rationale behind Rules 31.6 and 31.7 is that the offeree company should not be hindered in its affairs for longer than is reasonable. On a scheme of arrangement, it is generally the target company that controls the timetable and therefore the Schemes Appendix disapplies both these Rules in relation to schemes.

Day 42 is perhaps best known because of Rule 34 which provides that the offer must confer upon an accepting shareholder a right to withdraw his or her acceptance from the date which is 21 days after the first closing date of the initial offer (which, as indicated above, is normally Day 21) if the offer has not by such date become or been declared unconditional as to acceptances. This is of considerable importance in a competitive bid situation since this enables an accepting shareholder to change his or her mind at the last minute; it is not possible for an offeror to provide in the offer document that acceptances of the offer should be irrevocable (i.e. not capable of being withdrawn) after Day 42. Equally, it is important that an offeror clearly sets out this withdrawal right in its offer document. Confusion over the timing of withdrawal rights in the Thistle/BIL bid in 2003 resulted in BIL having to allow Thistle shareholders withdrawal rights from an earlier date than the Code would otherwise have strictly required.

Competing offerors and offeree companies in hostile bids commonly try to take advantage of the existence of withdrawal rights by sending withdrawal forms to offeree shareholders pointing out that they have the right to withdraw any acceptance of the relevant offer. (This does not, however, prevent the offer from being declared unconditional at an earlier date.)

The right of withdrawal conferred by Rule 34 may, however, be varied by individual agreement and an offeror will normally attempt to extract a waiver of this right from those offeree shareholders who agree to give irrevocable undertakings to accept the offer.

A right of withdrawal can also be imposed by the Panel as an alternative to allowing an offeree company to invoke, or cause or permit an offeror to invoke, a so-called "offeree protection condition" (see Rule 34.2 and Note 2 on Rule 13.6).

See also 7.4 below, for a discussion of the unusual circumstances in which a right of withdrawal was made available in the context of Guoco's mandatory bid for Rank in the summer of 2011.

In addition to withdrawal rights under the Code, accepting offeree company shareholders may, in certain circumstances, benefit from the protection offered by a statutory right of withdrawal when a securities exchange bidder publishes a supplementary prospectus. Section 87Q(4) of the Financial Services and Markets Act 2000 (FSMA 2000) provides that offeree company shareholders who have, at the time a supplementary prospectus is published, accepted the offer, will have the statutory right to withdraw their acceptances within two working days of publication of the supplementary prospectus.

In the hostile offer for Provident by NSF, NSF published (on 28 May 2019) a supplementary prospectus which gave rise to withdrawal rights under s.87Q(4) of the FSMA 2000 (the offer had been declared unconditional as to acceptances on 15 May 2019). However, on 28 May 2019, NSF announced that it had agreed with the Panel an extended period of time (until 5 June 2019, which is also the last date on which the offer may become or be declared wholly unconditional) during which Provident shareholders would be able to withdraw their acceptances, in light of the specific circumstances surrounding the deal.[2] NSF's hostile offer lapsed pursuant to Rule 31.7 on 5 June 2019 due to non-satisfaction of the regulatory condition.

The Schemes Appendix disapplies Rule 34 in the case of a scheme of arrangement because shareholders generally retain the right to control and/or dispose of their shares in the target company until the scheme becomes effective and there is therefore no need for a right of withdrawal. However, s.9(b) of the Schemes Appendix provides that a shareholder who has elected to receive a particular form of consideration in respect of any of his or her shares should be entitled to withdraw his or her election up to one week prior to the court sanction hearing.

7.3.1.7 Day 46

This is the last day for publishing a revision of the offer since an offer must be kept open for at least 14 days from the date of publishing the revised offer document to shareholders (Rule 32.1(c)) (thus giving them time to consider the revised offer on its merits) and the last day on which the offer is able to become unconditional as to acceptances is Day 60.

---

[2] The specific circumstances included the likelihood that following completion of the offer two of NSF's shareholders (Woodford and Invesco) would each become interested in NSF shares carrying 30% or more of its total voting rights in circumstances where there would be no requirement for a general offer under Rule 9 (as NSF's independent shareholders had agreed to a Rule 9 whitewash).

Rule 32.1(c) is disapplied in the case of a scheme and s.7 of the Schemes Appendix states that any revision to a scheme should normally be made no later than the date which is 14 days prior to the date of the shareholder meetings, with revisions after that date requiring the Panel's consent. In practice, this means that there is a much shorter period in which to revise the terms of a bid which is being implemented by way of a scheme.

At the same time as publishing the revised offer, the offeror must make the revised offer document readily available to the trustees of the offeree company's pension scheme(s) and both the offeror and the offeree company must make the revised document readily available to their employee representatives (or, where there are no such representatives, to the employees themselves). The offeree company must inform the trustees of its pension scheme(s) and its employee representatives (or employees) of their right under Rule 32.6 to have a separate opinion on the revised offer appended to any response published by the offeree company in relation to the revised offer.

Day 46 will also normally be the last day for the offeror to make an announcement as to trading results, profits, dividends etc. where the offer involves an element of share exchange (i.e. the offeror is offering its shares). This is because such an announcement may have the effect of increasing the value of the offeror's shares and thus amount to a revision of its bid.

The Code contains specific Rules which address what happens if there are still two (or more) competing bidders at Day 46 (see 7.3.1.13 below).

7.3.1.8 Day 53

Under Rule 2.6, a potential second/competing offeror, who has been the subject of a "possible offer" announcement, must clarify its position by 17.00 on the 53rd day after the publication of the first offeror's offer document.

Similarly, on a scheme of arrangement where the first offeror's offer is to be implemented by way of a scheme of arrangement, the deadline by which the second/competing offeror would normally be required to clarify its position is 17.00 on the seventh day prior to the date of the shareholder meetings. The Panel may in appropriate cases permit the second/competing offeror to clarify its position after the date of the shareholder meetings but before the date of the court sanction hearing in relation to the scheme.

The second/competing offeror must clarify its position by either: (i) announcing a firm intention to make an offer (under Rule 2.7); or (ii) confirming to the offeree company that it does not intend to make an offer and the offeree must announce this and it will be considered to be a no intention to bid statement (under Rule 2.8).

7.3.1.9 *Day 60*

As indicated above, this is the final day for an offer to become or be declared unconditional as to acceptances (Rule 31.6). In other words, if the offeror has not achieved the minimum level of acceptances on which its bid is conditional by Day 60, its offer will lapse.

Day 60 can be extended with the consent of the Panel but Rule 31.6 makes it clear that the Panel will normally only consent to such an extension if:

1. a competing firm offer has been announced;
2. the board of the offeree company consents to an extension;
3. there is a significant delay in the decision on whether there is to be a Phase 2 CMA reference or initiation of Phase 2 European Commission proceedings (as already mentioned in 7.3.1.5 above);
4. there is an announcement of the offeree company's results after Day 39 (as already mentioned in 7.3.1.5 above);
5. the offeror's receiving agent requests an extension for the purpose of issuing to the offeror or its financial advisers a certificate stating the number of acceptances and shares

otherwise acquired, such certificate being required before an offer may be declared unconditional as to acceptances (Note 7 on Rule 10); or

6. withdrawal rights are introduced by the Panel under Rule 13.6 as a result of an "offeree protection condition" being triggered.

Note 1 on Rule 31.6 clarifies that where the Panel consents to an extension in accordance with points (1)–(4) listed above, it will normally also grant an extension to or, if appropriate, re-set Day 39, Day 46 and Day 53.

The date of the shareholder meetings in a scheme of arrangement is considered to be analogous to Day 60 of a contractual offer (on the basis of this being the time by which investment decisions need to be made by offeree shareholders). Accordingly, as mentioned previously, Rule 31.6 is disapplied in relation to schemes.

An example of an extension of Day 60 occurred during the Ferrovial Consortium bid for BAA in 2006. With the support of the BAA board, the Panel granted a seven day "stay of execution" to the usual requirement under Rule 32.1 that no revised offer may be posted to offeree shareholders after Day 46 of the offer timetable, with a consequent extension of Day 60. The Panel agreed that the deadlines could be extended on the basis that a rival potential bidder in the form of a consortium led by Goldman Sachs had yet to declare its hand formally, and shareholders in BAA should be afforded the possibility of receiving a higher offer from the Ferrovial Consortium in the event of a rival bid emerging which was, indeed, what happened.

In 2007, with the consent of the board of EMI, the Panel granted Terra Firma an extension of Day 60 to allow it more time to satisfy the 90% acceptance threshold required for its offer for EMI to become unconditional. There was speculation that, at the time of the "original" Day 60 deadline, Terra Firma had not received all of the necessary supporting documentation to be able to count all of the acceptances it had received towards the 90% threshold and that, due to the upheaval at the time in the debt markets, its lending banks were unwilling to allow it to waive down the 90% threshold.

On 11 March 2019, the Panel granted (after day 46) an extension of Day 60 in relation to Visa International Service Association's offer for Earthport plc as the CMA had not (as at that date) made a decision as to whether there would be a Phase 2 CMA reference. The Panel consented to the extension of Day 60 of the offer timetable until the date falling 14 days after the date on which Visa announced that the condition relating to there not being a Phase 2 CMA reference being made was satisfied or waived. On 8 May 2019, Visa announced that the CMA had notified it that the offer for Earthport did not qualify for Phase 2 investigation and that the offer had become unconditional in all respects.

In circumstances where a competing firm offer has been announced, both offerors will normally be bound by the timetable established by the publication of the competing offer document. In addition, the Panel will extend Day 60 in accordance with any auction procedure established by the Panel in accordance with Rule 32.5. As a result, the normal bid timetable can be extended considerably in the event of competing bids (especially where complex competition issues are involved) and become somewhat of a marathon. This explains why bid battles can go on for some months in spite of the normal 60-day rule.

Where competing firm offers have been made, it is worth noting that the Panel will not normally give its consent to an extension of Day 60 under Rule 31.6(a)(ii) (where the board of the offeree company consents to the extension) unless the Panel's consent is sought before Day 46 (being, in this case, the 46th day following the publication of the competing offer document).

Note 4 on Rule 31.6 deals with extensions of Day 60 after Day 46. This note states that the Panel will normally grant an extension to Day 60 (with a corresponding extension to, or re-setting of, Day 46) of an offeror's timetable where the board of the offeree company consents to such an extension. Therefore, provided that such consent is obtained, and subject to no unreserved "no extension" statement (see Rule 31.5) or "no increase" statement (see Rule 32.2) having been made, the offeror will normally be able to revise its offer, notwithstanding that the original Day 46 has passed.

Where an offeror has made an offer and it has been announced that a potential offeror might make a competing offer (see Rule 2.6(d) and (e)), the Panel will normally, at the request of the first offeror and with the consent of the board of the offeree company, consent to an extension of Day 60 (with a corresponding extension to, or re-setting of, Day 46) as described above. In such cases, the Panel will normally also require a corresponding extension to, or re-setting of, Day 53, being the date by which the potential competing offeror is required to confirm its position in accordance with Rule 2.6(d) or (e) (as applicable).

7.3.1.10 Day 81

As referred to in 7.3.1.6 above, this will be the last day for fulfilment of all other conditions if the offer is declared unconditional as to acceptances on Day 60. This is another example (Day 42 was the first) of the application of Rule 31.7 (i.e. that all conditions must be fulfilled or the offer must lapse no later than 21 days after the date the offer becomes or is declared unconditional as to acceptances). A recent example of an offer lapsing on day 81 pursuant to Rule 31.7 was the hostile offer for Provident by NSF, discussed in 7.3.1.6 above.

As mentioned previously, Rule 31.7 is disapplied in relation to schemes of arrangement.

7.3.1.11 Day 95

As already mentioned in 7.3.1.4 above, the consideration must be sent to accepting shareholders no later than 14 days after the offer becomes or is declared wholly unconditional (Rule 31.8).

Therefore, this is the latest theoretical date for such settlement (assuming that the offer is declared unconditional as to acceptances on Day 60 and that Day 60 is not extended).

As mentioned above, Rule 31.8 is disapplied in the case of a scheme of arrangement; in its place, Section 10 of the Schemes Appendix imposes a 14-day time limit for the settlement of consideration after the scheme has become effective.

7.3.1.12 *Trigger date for compulsory acquisition of the minority*

In order for an offeror to implement the compulsory acquisition of minority shareholders pursuant to the CA 2006 (squeeze out), an offeror must satisfy a dual test: it needs to have acquired or unconditionally contracted to acquire both 90% of the shares to which the offer relates and 90% of the voting rights in the company to which the offer relates.

The squeeze-out rights must then be exercised within the period of: (i) three months from the end of the time allowed for acceptance of the offer where the offeree company is a listed issuer; and (ii) six months from posting the offer document in relation to all other offeree companies (for example AIM companies and non-traded companies). This potentially provides an offeror bidding for a listed offeree company with an indefinite period of time in which to implement the squeeze-out as offers are often left open for acceptance once control has passed. In practice, however, an offeror will normally want to acquire any remaining minority as quickly as possible and the terms of any bank financing for the offer are likely to impose obligations on the offeror to implement the squeeze-out as soon as practicable.

Similarly, a minority holder has the right to require a bidder to buy his or her shares at the offer price if the bidder has obtained 90% of the issued shares and the voting rights in the company.

Squeeze-out and sell-out provisions are not relevant in the context of a scheme of arrangement. Once a scheme has become effective, all of the target shareholders are bound by it regardless of whether or not they voted in favour of the scheme.

7.3.1.13   Competing bids on Day 46

The rules dealing with the relatively rare situation where there are two outstanding offers, neither of which is a "final" offer, for an offeree company on Day 46 (the last day for posting a revised offer) have undergone a number of modifications since they were first introduced.

The process is now governed by Rule 32.5 and Appendix 8. Rule 32.5 provides that if a competitive situation continues to exist in the later stages of the offer period, the Panel will normally require revised offers to be announced in accordance with an open auction procedure, the terms of which will be determined and announced by the Panel. That procedure will normally follow the auction procedure set out in Appendix 8. However, the Panel will consider applying any alternative procedure which is agreed between competing offerors and the board of the offeree company.

The auction procedure set out in Appendix 8 involves a maximum of five rounds of bidding, taking place over the five business days immediately following Day 46. Previously, the Code did not provide for a specified number of bidding rounds but the Panel was able to impose a final time limit, or "guillotine", for announcing revisions to competing offers. Other features of the default auction procedure in Appendix 8 include:

1.   either or both competing offerors are permitted to announce a revised offer in the first round of the auction, but in the second, third and fourth rounds, a competing offeror is permitted to announce a revised offer only if the other competing offeror has announced a revised offer in the previous round. This is intended to avoid the auction process being undermined by a competing offeror making only minor revisions to its offer in each round that are not

made in response to a revision by the other competing offeror. If, on any day of the auction, the relevant competing offeror, or offerors, permitted to announce a revised offer on that day do not do so, the auction ends;

2. if the auction has not ended by the fifth business day, both competing offerors are permitted to announce a revised offer in the fifth and final round. In the fifth and final round only, a competing offeror is entitled to submit its revised proposal to the Panel subject to the condition that the offer will only be required to be announced if the other competing offeror also submits a revised proposal to the Panel. This is intended to avoid a competing offeror from effectively bidding against itself by announcing a revised offer when the other competing offeror does not announce a revised offer;

3. there is no requirement for revised offers to incorporate minimum incremental increases to previous offers;

4. a prohibition on formula offers (the Code Committee noted that it is open to the parties to an offer to permit formula offers in any alternative auction procedure which they are able to agree);

5. there is no prohibition on the introduction of new forms of consideration during the auction;

6. a prohibition on the parties to the offer and persons acting in concert with them from dealing in the relevant securities of the offeree company, and from procuring or amending irrevocable commitments and letters of intent, during the auction procedure;

7. a prohibition on a competing offeror and any person acting in concert with it from acquiring any interest in target shares between the end of the auction procedure and the end of the offer period if it would then be required to revise its offer; and

8. a prohibition on announcements by the competing offerors and the offeree company (or their concert parties) that affect the orderly operation of the auction procedure.

An "open" auction process (although not in the form of Appendix 8) approach has been either utilised or proposed during takeover bids for Debenhams, QXL Ricardo, Canary Wharf and Cove Energy.

An alternative auction process considered by the Code Committee in 2014 (in PCP 2014/1) was an "accelerated" auction procedure such as was first utilised during the takeover battles for Corus and for Imprint.

On 20 October 2006 Tata Steel and Corus announced a recommended bid to be implemented by a scheme of arrangement. On 17 November, Companhia Siderugica Nacional (CSN) approached Corus with a higher competing bid which culminated in a pre-conditional Rule 2.7 announcement on 11 December. The CSN offer was also to be implemented by way of a scheme of arrangement but due to concerns over whether a target company could legitimately run parallel, competing schemes, the CSN scheme was conditional upon the Tata scheme lapsing or being withdrawn. Corus shareholders were to vote on the Tata scheme on 20 December 2006. To ensure equality of information, the Panel required CSN to post an information document (containing most of the information which would have been included in a scheme document) to Corus shareholders.

In accordance with the "accelerated" auction procedure the Panel set an end date of 30 January 2007 (which would have equated to approximately Day 46 of a reset timetable if CSN had posted its scheme document shortly after announcing its bid) for the parties to announce their final offers. Although the usual position when a second bidder intervenes is for the first bidder's timetable to be reset according to when the second bidder posts its offer or scheme document (Note 4 on Rule 31.6), this could not happen in relation to CSN's bid as it was a pre-condition of CSN's bid that it would only post its scheme document if the Tata scheme failed.

On 30 January 2007 neither Tata nor CSN declared its offer as final and therefore the Panel proceeded with the "accelerated" auction process. This differed from previous "open" auction procedures where the parties had to announce their bids over a number of days as it was agreed that there would be a maximum of nine rounds of bidding to take place between 16.30 on 30 January and 02.30 on 31 January 2007. This timing ensured that most of the auction would take place when the three stock markets on which the parties' shares were traded (London, New York and Mumbai) were closed in order to minimise market speculation during the bidding process. Bids were made in private to the Panel and communicated by the Panel to the bidders.

For the first eight rounds, the parties had to make fixed price bids, but for the ninth and final round they could make a formula bid stating a specified amount in cash that they would pay more than the other bidder's highest offer, subject to a specified maximum amount.

The auction was completed after Tata submitted a winning bid of 608 pence per share (significantly above the 500 pence per share that Tata was offering prior to the start of the auction process) which valued Corus at £6.7 billion. Corus posted a revised scheme document to its shareholders on 12 February 2007 and reconvened the adjourned court and shareholder meetings which then duly approved the Tata scheme.

This procedure was also adopted in February 2008 in relation to the competing bids from Hydrogen Group (by way of scheme) and OPD Group (by way of offer) for Imprint. On 7 November 2007, OPD announced a recommended bid for Imprint to be implemented by way of a traditional cash offer; on 20 December, Hydrogen announced a recommended offer for Imprint to be implemented by way of a scheme, and the shareholder meetings to approve the scheme were scheduled for 27 February 2007. In accordance with the "accelerated" auction procedure the Panel set an end date of 4 February 2008 for the parties to announce their final offers. On 8 February neither party had declared its offer final and therefore the Panel proceeded with the "accelerated" auction process whereby the three rounds of the auction took place on 11, 12, and 13 of February with each party announcing its revised bid for each round by means of an announcement released via a RIS after the close of trading on the London Stock Exchange on the relevant day.

Following the auction procedure, both Hydrogen and OPD Group reissued scheme and offer documentation respectively, leaving it to the Imprint shareholders to resolve the impasse.

However, on 26 February 2008, a further new offeror, Premier, emerged and the Panel again determined that a competitive situation had arisen for the purposes of Rule 32.5 and held a further auction process in which all three offerors were entitled to participate. However, as none of the offerors submitted an increased offer, the Imprint board continued to recommend Premier's offer, which was ultimately successfully implemented by way of a scheme.

Also considered by the Panel in 2014 (in PCP 2014/1) was an out of hours sealed bid process such as was used in June 2008 in relation to the competing bids from ITW and Manitowoc for Enodis. The procedure established by the Panel for this auction consisted of a single round, which took place after markets closed. Any increased bid by either bidder was required to be at a fixed price in cash being not less than five pence higher than the price of the highest cash offer announced by either bidder prior to the commencement of the auction procedure. Any increased bid made by ITW could only be at an odd-numbered price, and any increased bid by Manitowoc could only be at an even-numbered price. As with the Imprint auction, formula bids were not allowed. Each offeror was, however, permitted to stipulate to the Panel that its bid was conditional on the other offeror also lodging an increased bid. Following the conclusion of the auction procedure, Enodis agreed to recommend Manitowoc's offer and, once the offer documentation was posted, ITW was required to withdraw its offer.

During the competitive bid for Cove Energy in 2012 which followed a formal sale process, Shell and PTTEP were unable to agree a resolution process to determine the "winning" bid, so the Panel ruled that an open auction should be conducted. The rules of the auction permitted each bidder to announce to the market one revised bid per day, such bid being revised by a fixed amount in whole pence (i.e. no minimum increment bids or by reference to a formula). The Panel had discretion to impose a final "guillotine" on the time-period for announcing revised offers; in this event, the cash consideration payable under any revised offer announced by Shell needed to be at an odd-numbered price and that announced by PTTEP needed to be at an even-numbered price. A few hours before the auction was due to start, Shell announced that it would not be increasing its offer nor would it be participating in the process.

An auction procedure was also adopted in September 2018 on the competing bids by Fox and Comcast for Sky.

On 20 September 2018, the Panel announced that following talks with the parties concerned, a three-round auction process would commence ending on the evening of Saturday, 22 September 2018. In line with the previous practice of the Panel, formula bids were not permitted and there was no requirement for an increased bid to be higher by any minimum increment than the other bidder's bid. The Panel announced the results of the auction after the conclusion of the procedure and required the bidders to publish their respective revised offer documents on or before 27 September 2018, with 11 October 2018 being the last date on which either bidder's offer could become or have been declared unconditional as to acceptances. The auction completed, with Comcast making the winning bid (£17.28 per Sky ordinary shares compared to Fox's offer of £15.67 per Sky ordinary share). Comcast duly proceeded to complete the acquisition of Sky in October 2018.

The Code does not prescribe what timetable should apply where a scheme is proposed in competition with an existing contractual offer, or with an existing scheme, and instead this is left to the Panel to determine in the light of all the prevailing circumstances. Note 2 on Rule 32.5 requires the parties to consult with the Panel as to the applicable timetable following which the Panel will determine the date or dates on which final revisions to competing offers must be announced and on which any auction procedures will commence. It is likely that the Panel will take a stance in relation to so-called "parallel" schemes (i.e. two competing schemes), similar to its approach in relation to the situation where a scheme is proposed in competition with an existing contractual offer. In such a case, the Panel will determine the precise dates on which final revisions to the competing offers should be announced and on which the auction procedure should commence. The Corus situation provides a useful precedent in this regard as does the Costain Group and Kier Group offers, both by way of scheme, for May Gurney in 2013.

7.3.2 Timetable extensions

As already mentioned, regulatory issues can impact on the offer timetable. Whilst the Panel attaches considerable importance to the strict offer timetable, it is prepared to be flexible in accommodating delays or extensions which arise from regulatory issues (particularly, in the case of recommended offers).

So what are the available options if the required regulatory clearances are unlikely to be obtained within the normal offer timetable?

There are, principally, three options:

1. make the offer subject to a pre-condition that regulatory approval is obtained—this approach has recently been very popular and was adopted, for example, on Fox's, offer for Sky, Comcast's competing offer for Sky, Tesco's merger with Booker Group, Equinix's offer for Telecity Group, Anheuser-Busch InBev's offer for SABMiller, Ball Corporation's offer for Rexam and Royal Dutch Shell's offer for BG Group. The Panel must be consulted in advance if such a pre-conditional bid is to be announced;
2. seek consent from the Panel to an extension to Day 60 in accordance with Rule 31.6 (the requirement that the acceptance condition must be satisfied by midnight on

Day 60). This has the effect of also extending what would otherwise be the last date for satisfying or waiving all other offer conditions (as Rule 31.7 provides that all conditions must be fulfilled or the offer must lapse by no later than the date the offer becomes or is declared unconditional as to acceptances); or

3. seek an extension of Rule 31.7 (the requirement that all other conditions must be satisfied within 21 days of the first closing date or the date the offer becomes or is declared unconditional as to acceptances, whichever is the later), in order to be able to close off withdrawal rights by declaring the offer unconditional as to acceptances whilst allowing more time to satisfy the other conditions.

Following the announcement of a firm intention to make an offer, the offeror must use reasonable endeavours to ensure the satisfaction of any conditions or pre-conditions to which the offer is subject.

Pre-conditional offers have become increasingly popular particularly due to the complex antitrust issues on large deals where it is often not possible to obtain the required regulatory clearances within the Code timetable. If an offeror announces a scheme as pre-conditional it can defer publication of the formal offer documentation and offeree shareholder approval until the required regulatory clearances have been received, allowing more visibility over the transaction and any antitrust remedies that may subsequently be required. The Panel should be consulted in relation to any pre-conditions to which the offer is to be subject and if the relevant pre-condition has not been satisfied or waived within the period agreed with the Panel, the offeror will be required to withdraw its proposed offer.

An example of an extension of Rule 31.7 (Day 81) arose on the Federal Mogul/T&N bid. The bid was announced on 16 October 1997 (with the offer document published on 13 November 1997) and was declared unconditional as to acceptances in early January 1998 before withdrawal rights arose. The Panel granted an extension under Rule 31.7 in order to allow more time in which to obtain the necessary regulatory clearances and the offer only became unconditional in all respects in early March 1998 (before the extended deadline). During this period the T&N shareholders who had accepted the offer could not receive their consideration and were not free to withdraw acceptances and sell their shares in the market. There was press criticism of the Panel and the parties to the bid and questions were raised as to whether Federal Mogul should have been required to pay interest to those accepting shareholders or, alternatively, the Panel should have reintroduced withdrawal rights.

The Panel is now reluctant to accede to requests to extend Rule 31.7 and instead prefers to grant extensions to Rule 31.6 to avoid shareholders being locked in or agree to a pre-conditional offer. Granting an extension under Rule 31.6 means that the offeror has an extended timetable in which to complete the offer but cannot declare its offer unconditional as to acceptances (thereby ending withdrawal rights) until it is satisfied that all other conditions to the offer can be fulfilled (or waived) within the next 21 days. Where it is considered more likely than not that competition issues will arise, the Panel prefers the parties to use the full 28 days following the Rule 2.7 announcement to post the offer document (or potentially a longer period, with an extension), rather than announcing and posting in quick succession and then requesting an extension in the latter stages of the bid timetable. Where it only becomes apparent later in the timetable that there will be a delay in obtaining competition clearances, the Panel is more likely to be receptive to a request to grant an extension to Day 60 (albeit still somewhat reluctant unless the target is supportive of this course of action).

In order to ensure that shareholders and other market participants are kept properly informed of the progress of a scheme, Section 6 of the Schemes Appendix provides that certain changes to the expected scheme timetable (for example, any adjournment of a shareholder meeting or court sanction hearing, or any decision by the target board to propose such an adjournment) should be announced promptly by the target. In addition, it is worth noting that the Code Committee's response statement RS 2007/1 indicates that the Panel may hold a bidder or the target to any statements which they may make in relation to not extending the scheme timetable, including any "no adjournment statements" if it believes that shareholders or others may have relied on such statements.

7.4   Extensions of the offer

In what circumstances will an extension of the offer be important?

1. If an offeror has failed to achieve a sufficient level of control by a specified closing date, it may well wish to extend its offer to give itself more time to persuade shareholders by its arguments to accept it. As mentioned above, an offer may not be extended beyond Day 60 unless the offer has become or been declared unconditional as to acceptances by that date. Subject to this, if an offeror wishes to extend its offer, it has two options: it can either announce an extension specifying the next closing date or, if the offer is unconditional as to acceptances, it may state that the offer will remain open until further notice (Rule 31.2).
2. Once an offeror has gained control it will normally leave its offer open in order to allow dissentients to accept and to allow it to gather in further acceptances to the extent necessary to be able to utilise the compulsory acquisition provisions under the CA 2006 to "squeeze out" the outstanding minority (see 7.3.1.12 above).

An offeror is not, however, obliged to extend its offer (Rule 31.3). If, for example, its acceptance condition has not been satisfied by a specified closing date then, as was the case in Vinci's bid for TBI following the 9/11 attacks in 2001, Macquarie Bank's bid for the London Stock Exchange in 2007 and KiFin's offer for Minerva in 2009, the offeror is free to lapse its offer and walk away without consequence under the Code.

Whilst an offeror is free to decide whether or not to extend its offer beyond a specified closing date where the acceptance condition has not been satisfied as at that date, it can contract out of that right. In 2008, Barings Private Equity Asia agreed with the offeree company, Nord Anglia, that it would only be able to invoke the acceptance condition to lapse the offer if, at the relevant closing date, the level of acceptances was below 75%, and that it would give Nord Anglia seven days advance notice of its intention to invoke such condition. This meant that if Barings were to have given notice of its intention to lapse the offer, the offeree company would have had an opportunity to seek to obtain sufficient acceptances during this notice period to prevent the offer from actually lapsing. In 2010, on the Apollo/CVC consortium bid for Brit Insurance, Achilles (the consortium bidco) agreed not to cause the offer to lapse before Day 60 by reference to any non-fulfilment of the acceptance condition except in certain specified circumstances (the announcement of a competing offer, certain breaches by Brit Insurance of its covenants in the implementation agreement or a change in the independent directors' recommendation). In 2010, in the takeover of Wellstream by GE, GE agreed to keep its offer open beyond the initial closing date regardless of the level of acceptances it received. These sorts of provision are relatively unusual but do provide considerable benefits for the offeree company and its shareholders, as they reduce the flexibility of the offeror to lapse its offer.

Rule 31.5 (and the Notes on that Rule) deal in some detail with what are known as "no extension statements". The basic idea is that shareholders should not be misled into thinking that they must accept an offer by a certain date only to find later that the offeror has granted a further extension. Accordingly, if an offeror (or its directors, officials or advisers) makes a no extension statement (that is not withdrawn immediately if incorrect) the offeror will not be allowed subsequently to extend its offer beyond the stated date except: (i) where the right to do so in certain circumstances is specifically reserved at the time the no extension statement is made and those circumstances subsequently arise; or (ii) in wholly exceptional circumstances. If the offeror wishes to include a reservation to a no extension statement the Panel must be consulted. Note 1 on Rule 31.5 provides that any such reservation must not depend solely on subjective judgments by the offeror or its directors or the fulfilment of which is in their hands (which is the same test which governs the acceptability of conditions and pre-conditions to an offer under Rule 13.1). The first document published, in connection with an offer in which the no extension statement is mentioned, must contain prominent reference to any reservation to set it aside and must include precise details of both the statement and the reservation.

Note 3 on Rule 31.5 provides that if the offeror has made a reservation relating to competitive situations with its no extension statement and a competitive situation subsequently arises, and the offeror wishes to set aside its no extension statement, it must make an announcement to that effect as soon as possible and in any event within four business days of the firm intention announcement of the competing bidder, and in addition, give shareholders who accepted the offer after the no extension statement withdrawal rights for a period of eight days following the offeror's announcement.

In addition, Note 4 on Rule 31.5 provides that an offeror may reserve the right to set aside a no extension statement in the light of material new information announced by the offeree company after Day 39 of the offer timetable, only if the no extension statement is made after that day. If such an announcement is subsequently made by the offeree company and the offeror wishes to set aside its no extension statement, the offeror must make an announcement to that effect as soon as possible, and in any event within four business days after the offeree company's announcement, with shareholders being informed in writing of this extension at the earliest opportunity.

A somewhat unusual situation arose in June 2011 when, after Guoco's hostile mandatory bid for Rank had become wholly unconditional. Guoco was permitted, with the consent of the Panel, to extend its offer until 15 July 2011 notwithstanding a previous statement that its offer would close on 1 July. Guoco agreed that if, by 15 July 2011, it had received acceptances which, when combined with the Rank shares already owned by the Guoco group, represented more than 75% of Rank's share capital, then the offer would remain open for acceptance for a further seven days until 22 July 2011. This arrangement was designed to allow Rank shareholders the opportunity to wait and see whether Guoco achieved the 75% threshold before deciding whether to accept the offer. In addition, Rank shareholders who had already accepted the offer were permitted to withdraw their acceptances. Guoco agreed that if it failed to reach the 75% threshold by 15 July 2011, then the offer would close at that time and would not be extended further.

The driver behind these arrangements was to minimise the risk of minority shareholders being "left behind" in Rank given the possibility of the company being delisted in the event that Guoco acquired 75% or more of Rank's shares. Guoco had consistently stated that it intended to retain Rank's London Stock Exchange listing regardless of the level of support for its offer but if it had ended up acquiring over 75% of Rank's shares then either the London Stock Exchange could have terminated the listing (as the free float would have fallen below 25%) or Guoco would have been in a position at any point in the future to proceed to delist Rank. De-listing would have had a significant adverse impact on the value of any shares held by minority shareholders. These arrangements were therefore intended to ensure Guoco remained below the 75% threshold and, failing that, to give Rank shareholders an opportunity to accept the offer if the 75% threshold was reached. As it turned out, Guoco ended up with 74.5% and Rank remained as a listed company.

7.5 Revisions and increases

The timing requirements relating to revisions are referred to above, for example no revision after Day 46 (see 7.3.1.7 above). Revisions will be obligatory in certain circumstances such as an acquisition by the offeror (or any person acting in concert with it) of any interest in shares in the offeree company above the offer price (Rule 6.2) or in the event of an obligation to introduce a cash offer under Rule 11.1. Rule 32.3 provides that if an offer is revised, all shareholders who accepted the original offer must be entitled to the revised consideration.

As regards increased offers (as distinct simply from offers which are revised, although it is rare for a revision not to represent an increase), Rule 32.2 contains substantially equivalent restrictions on no increase statements as those outlined in relation to no extension statements and dealt with in Rule 31.5 (see 7.4 above). Under Note 6 on Rule 32.2, where an offeror has made a no increase statement under Rule 32.2, and the offeree company subsequently pays a dividend (or other distribution), the offeror will normally be required to reduce the offer consideration by an amount equal to that dividend (or other distribution) so that the overall value receivable by the offeree company shareholders remains the same, unless the offeror has stated that the offeree company shareholders would be entitled to receive and retain all or part of the specified dividend (or other distribution) in addition to the offer consideration. As a general rule, if an offeror wishes to protect against value leakage from the offeree caused by the payment of a dividend, it must do so by reserving the right to reduce the bid consideration if a dividend is paid, rather than trying to restrict the board of the offeree from paying dividends (as the Panel may treat any such agreement as being prohibited pursuant to Rule 21.2). However, on Tesco/Booker and Kennedy-Wilson Holdings/Kennedy Wilson Europe Real Estate, both in 2017, the offeree shareholders were entitled to receive a closing dividend in order to compensate them for the dividends that they would have expected to receive in the time between the last ordinary course dividend and the scheme of arrangement becoming effective.

The reasons for these restrictions were explained in the 1999 Panel ruling in the context of the competing bids for CALA Plc. An MBO vehicle, Dotterel Ltd, and Miller 1999 Plc had each announced bids for CALA. Miller announced the revised offer of 200 pence per CALA share and stated that this increased offer was final and would not be increased further except that

Miller reserved the right to increase its offer up to a maximum of 210 pence per share in the event of a bid being made for CALA at a higher value than its increased offer of 200 pence in cash.

Dotterel indicated its intention to announce a matching offer of 200 pence per share—basically relying on the shares held by management and the support of institutional shareholders for existing management to win the day. Miller sought consent from the Panel to increase its offer if a matching offer was made. The Panel ruled that as Miller had not reserved the specific right to increase its offer in the event of a matching (as opposed to higher) bid, then Miller was prohibited from doing so.

The Panel ruling went on to explain that:

> "This Rule seeks to set a balance between the potential disadvantages to shareholders from this consequence and the undesirable consequences for shareholders and the markets if they cannot rely on the accuracy of statements made by an offeror. As a matter of policy, and in the absence of 'wholly exceptional circumstances', it is more important that the principle of certainty and orderly conduct should be upheld rather than to risk compromising this principle to accommodate the apparent disadvantages which may result from the application of the Rule in a particular case."

This ruling was, however, the subject of a certain amount of press criticism on the basis that this apparently inflexible application of Rule 32.2 potentially deprived the CALA shareholders of a further higher bid from Miller.

Care should also be taken to ensure that statements made by the offeror company, or its controlling shareholder, cannot be construed under Rule 32.2 as a no increase statement. It is relatively easy to be inadvertently tripped up by this Rule. In 2002 Hugh Osmond, a controlling shareholder in Twigway which had made an indicative offer of 320–350 pence per share for the Pizza Express restaurant group, was quoted in the press as saying that the offeror company would "not reconsider the price under any circumstances unless there's some bloody good reason, and right now I can't think of one". The Panel immediately required a statement from Twigway clarifying that Mr Osmond's comments did not represent a no increase statement under Rule 32.2.

Whilst on the subject of increased offers, it is worth noting that Rule 32.4 recognises that the offeror may need to introduce new conditions into its bid in the event of a revision or an increase. For example, if it introduces a securities element to the consideration it will need a condition that the new securities be admitted to listing and/or trading. Panel consent is, however, required for inclusion of any such condition. This will only be permitted to the extent necessary to implement the revised offer.

If an offer includes both a cash and a securities element to the consideration, Panel consent will be required on a subsequent revision of the offer if the offeror wishes to remove, or reduce the amount of, one element of the consideration in substitution for an increase in a different element. The Panel is unlikely to give its consent unless the offeree company agrees to such revision.

As mentioned above, the Schemes Appendix addresses various issues in relation to the revision of a scheme. In particular, Section 7 provides that a revision to a scheme should normally be made no later than the date which is 14 days prior to the date of the shareholder meetings (or any later date to which such meetings are adjourned), with revisions after that date requiring the Panel's consent. Section 7 also provides that the Panel's consent must be sought to any revision of a scheme following the shareholder meetings but before the court sanction hearing. Details of the confirmations that are likely to be required from the target board and its Rule 3 adviser in such circumstances are set out in the Code Committee's response statement RS 2007/1 (but have not been reflected in the Code in order to preserve the Panel's flexibility in such circumstances).

Section 8 of the Schemes Appendix provides that the offeror may only switch from contractual takeover offer to a scheme (or vice versa) with the consent of the Panel, although it is not required to reserve the right to do so. The circumstances in which the Panel would withhold its consent are likely to be limited.

7.6 Alternative offers

Generally, the provisions of Rules 31 and 32 outlined above apply equally to alternative offers (including cash alternative offers as specified in Rule 33.1). Difficult questions arise, however, with regard to alternative offers, in particular in relation to closing or shutting them off.

Note 1 on Rule 33.1 deals with "elections" or "mix and match" offers where shareholders may elect to vary the proportion in which they are to receive different forms of consideration subject to other shareholders making contrary elections (because there are limits on the different forms of consideration available). Note 1 makes it clear that these are not regarded as alternative offers and the availability to "mix and match" may be closed without notice on any closing date provided this has been clearly stated in the offer document.

Note 2 on Rule 33.1 deals with shutting off alternative offers (other than cash underwritten alternatives, which are dealt with by Rule 33.2 and discussed below). The general rule is that once an offer has become or is declared unconditional as to acceptances, all alternative offers (in the same way as the principal offer itself) must remain open for a minimum of 14 days in accordance with Rule 31.4. Thus, waverers must also be given the benefit of jumping on the bandwagon with regard to alternative offers.

Also, as with the principal offer under Rule 31.3, if on a closing date an offer is not unconditional as to acceptances, an alternative offer (except a cash alternative provided to satisfy the requirements of Rule 9, i.e. on a mandatory bid) may be closed without prior notice (i.e. there is no obligation to extend it). However, if on the first closing date on which an offer is capable of being declared unconditional as to acceptances, the offer is not so declared and is extended, all alternative offers must, except as permitted by Rule 33.2, remain open for 14 days thereafter but may then be closed without prior notice.

Rule 33.2 deals with shutting off cash underwritten alternatives. Cash underwritten alternatives involve large underwriting fees and offerors are naturally keen to stop commitment commissions running as soon as control of the offeree company has been won. The effect of this Rule is to allow an offeror to shut off a cash alternative earlier than other forms of consideration provided:

1.   the value of the cash underwritten alternative (which must be provided by third parties) is, at the time of announcement, more than half the maximum value of the offer; and
2.   it has sent a notification to offeree company shareholders (and persons with information rights) that it reserves the right to close the cash alternative on a stated date, being not less than 14 days after the date on which the notification is published, or to extend it on that stated date.

Notice under Rule 33.2 may not be given between the time when a competing offer has been announced and the end of the resulting competitive situation.

Rule 33.2 will not apply to a cash alternative which is provided to satisfy the requirements of Rule 9. In other words, an offeror required to make a cash bid under Rule 9 will not be able to shut it off on the date its offer becomes or is declared unconditional as to acceptances but must keep it open for a further minimum period of 14 days.

Rule 33.3 deals with the reintroduction of alternative forms of consideration. Generally, unless a firm statement has been made that an alternative offer will not be extended or reintroduced, it may be reintroduced at a later date, even if it has lapsed or closed for acceptance in the interim. Reintroduction is treated as a revision of the offer and is therefore subject to the requirements of, and only permitted as provided in, Rule 32 (i.e. it must be open for 14 days and cannot be effected later than Day 46).

In the context of schemes, Section 9 of the Schemes Appendix provides that an election for alternative consideration under a scheme should be capable of being made at least until the date of the shareholder meetings and target shareholders who elect for alternative consideration in a scheme should have a right to withdraw such an election. The right of withdrawal must be exercisable at least until one week prior to the court sanction hearing.

7.7 Restrictions following offers and possible offers

The final area covered by this Chapter deals principally with Rule 35.1 of the Code which contains the Rule restricting a new offer from being launched within 12 months of the lapsing or withdrawal of a previous offer.

7.7.1 Circumstances when an offer must lapse

An offer must lapse in accordance with:

1. Rule 31.6 if an offeror does not obtain sufficient acceptances to be able to declare its offer unconditional as to acceptances by Day 60 (examples of this have included the NASDAQ/LSE bid; OPD's bid for Hydrogen; and TPG Capital/GlobeOp Financial Services);
2. Rule 12.1 if the offer becomes subject to a Phase 2 review by the UK's Competition and Markets Authority or by the European Commission before the later of: (i) the first

closing date; and (ii) the date on which the offer becomes or is declared unconditional as to acceptances (examples of this are the lapse of the original bid announced by William Morrison Supermarkets for Safeway; the HMV bid for Ottakers; and AG Barr's all-share merger with Britvic); or

3.   Rule 31.7 if, having declared the offer unconditional as to acceptances, the other conditions to the offer are not satisfied within 21 days (unless extended with the Panel's consent) (one example of this is NSF's lapsed bid for Provident).

In 2008, BHP Billiton's offer for Rio Tinto lapsed when it became clear that competition clearance, which was a pre-condition for the offer, would not be given without requiring significant divestments, which BHP was not prepared to make.

When an offer lapses any tendered acceptances also lapse. The offeror is therefore left with only the shares it has acquired through purchases. Its stake will usually be less than 30% of the offeree company. However, if as a result of acquisitions, it was forced to make a Rule 9 offer which failed, an offeror could be left with a stake of 30% or more.

Since the Schemes Appendix disapplies timing restrictions in relation to schemes, there is no pre-determined time limit by which a scheme must become effective or lapse. However, Rule 12.1 of the Code provides that: (a) where an offer comes within the statutory provisions for a possible Phase 2 CMA reference; and (b) where an offer would give rise to a concentration with an EU dimension for EU competition law purposes, the offer must contain a term that the offer will lapse and the scheme will not become effective if it is the subject of a Phase 2 reference to the Competition and Markets Authority or if Phase 2 European Commission proceedings are initiated before the shareholder meetings have taken place. However, if the competition reference occurs after the date of the shareholder meetings, the Code will not require the scheme to lapse as a result although it may give rise to the right for an offeror to invoke a condition to seek to lapse the offer. Such a right arose on the London Stock Exchange and Deutsche Börse merger in 2017 where the European Commission decided to prohibit the merger and therefore the relevant condition was invoked and the scheme of arrangement lapsed.

7.7.2 Dealing in offeree company shares

Once the offer has lapsed, the offeror is no longer subject to the Code restriction on disposing of offeree company shares (Rule 4.2) and can therefore sell down any shareholding it has acquired in the offeree company (subject to insider dealing restrictions, if any). If it decides to retain all or some of its holding then the degree of influence it can exert over the offeree company will depend on the size of its stake.

There is generally no restriction on an offeror making market purchases after its offer has lapsed save for the restrictions set out in this paragraph and 7.7.3 below. Where there have been competing offers, neither a lapsed offeror (nor any of its concert parties) may acquire any interest in shares in the offeree company on more favourable terms than those made available under its lapsed offer until such time as each of the competing offers has either lapsed or been declared unconditional in all respects (Rule 35.4). This is intended to prevent an offeror which has lapsed its offer from making market purchases with a view to frustrating a competing offer which is still continuing. It does not, however, prevent an unsuccessful offeror from acquiring an interest in offeree company shares once the "successful" offer has become wholly unconditional, which could potentially still frustrate the ability of the successful offeror to obtain 100% control of the offeree company.

7.7.3 Rule 35: delay of 12 months

Whatever the size of the offeror's stake in the offeree company, its continued presence on the shareholder register is likely to be a source of both concern and possible irritation to the offeree company. The offeree company will not know what the offeror's intentions are.

The Code provides some protection against the "siege" being renewed immediately. Rule 35.1 provides that except with the consent of the Panel, in the 12 months following an offer lapsing, neither the offeror nor its concert parties can: (i) announce an offer or possible offer for the offeree company; (ii) acquire any interest in shares of the offeree company if this would give rise to an obligation to make a mandatory bid under Rule 9; (iii) acquire any interest in, or procure an irrevocable commitment in respect of, shares in the offeree company if the shares in which such person, together with persons acting in concert with him, would be interested and the shares in respect of which he, or they, had acquired irrevocable commitments would in aggregate carry 30% or more of the voting rights of the offeree company; (iv) make any statement which raises or confirms the possibility that an offer might be made for the offeree company; (v) take any steps in connection with a possible offer for the offeree company where knowledge of the possible offer might be extended outside those people within the offeror and its immediate advisers who need to know about it; or (vi) purchase, agree to purchase, or make any statement which raises or confirms the possibility that it is interested in purchasing assets which are significant in relation to the offeree company. However, (iv) and (v) above will not normally apply to the extent that the offer lapsed as a result of the offeror failing to obtain a material official authorisation or regulatory clearance relating to the offer within the usual Code timetable, and the offeror is continuing to seek the relevant approval with a view subsequently to making a new offer with the consent of the Panel.

The restrictions do not, however, prevent a lapsed offeror from acquiring further shares in the offeree company (save in the circumstances described in 7.7.2 above). However, an important restriction is that if the offeror has less than 30%, it cannot acquire shares or rights over shares taking it to 30% or more. Equally, if the unsuccessful offeror has between 30% and 50%, it cannot acquire any more shares during that 12-month period.

Note 1 on Rules 35.1 and 35.2 provides that the Panel will normally only give its consent if: (i) the board of the offeree company so agrees (such consent will not normally be given within three months of the lapsing of an earlier offer in circumstances where the offeror was prevented from revising or extending its previous offer as a result of a no increase statement or a no extension statement); (ii) the action follows the announcement by a third party of a firm intention to make an offer for the offeree company; (iii) the action follows the announcement by the offeree company of a "whitewash" proposal or a reverse takeover; or (iv) the Panel determines that there has been a material change of circumstances.

The Panel may also grant consent for a new offer to be made in circumstances where it is likely to prove, or has proved, impossible to obtain material regulatory clearances relating to the offer within the Code timetable. Accordingly, Morrison's was able to announce a renewed recommended offer for Safeway in December 2003 following the completion of the detailed review of the supermarket industry undertaken by the UK's competition authority as a result of Morrison's initial offer for Safeway in January 2003.

The Panel's general approach to Rule 35.1 was explained in its statement of 17 March 1995 relating to the appeal by Trafalgar House against a Panel Executive decision that Trafalgar House should not be permitted to make an immediate new offer for Northern Electric:

> "Rule 35.1 is designed to create a reasonable balance between giving shareholders an opportunity to consider offers for their shares and enabling the business of the company in which they have invested to be carried on without continuous uncertainty and dislocation. Inevitably the effect of this Rule may be to prevent for a period of time a new offer by a failed offeror, at whatever price, being made to shareholders in the offeree company."

On that occasion the Panel made it clear that Rule 35 is regarded as one of the more important Rules of the Code and that only on rare occasions would it be prepared to grant a dispensation. Trafalgar House allowed its offer to lapse on Day

60 (with acceptances of 76.5%) three days after a pricing review of all electricity companies which led to a substantial fall in the market value of shares in electricity companies generally. The Panel ruled that those circumstances did not warrant the granting of a dispensation to enable Trafalgar House immediately to make a new offer at a lower price to take account of the pricing review without having first obtained the consent of the board of Northern Electric.

Rule 35.2 makes it clear that Rule 35.1 also applies following partial offers which could result in the offeror (and its concert parties) being interested in shares carrying between 30% and 50% of the voting rights of the offeree company whether or not that offer has become or been declared wholly unconditional. This is to cover the possibility of successive partial offers. When such an offer has become or been declared wholly unconditional, the 12-month period runs from that date. In addition, Rule 35.1 applies following a partial offer for more than 50% of the voting rights of the offeree company which has not become or been declared wholly unconditional (see Rule 35.2(b)).

Once the 12 months have elapsed, an offeror is free to acquire further shares or make another offer. Rule 9 does, however, continue to apply and the offeror will be forced to make an offer if it (together with its concert parties) takes its stake from below 30% to 30% or more, or if it acquires any interest in further shares in the company where it already has between 30% and 50%.

7.7.4 Rule 35.3: six-month delay before offering better terms to any remaining minority

If an offer is declared unconditional in all respects but a minority remains outstanding, then a six-month delay is likely to be required by the Panel before the offeror or any person acting in concert with him or her can make a second offer, or acquire any interest in shares, on more favourable terms than those which were available under the previous offer (Rule 35.3). Again, this is to ensure fair treatment for offeree shareholders and to seek to establish a level playing field as between competing offerors or potential offerors.

Chapter 8

Profit Forecasts, Quantified Financial Benefits Statements and Asset Valuations

Ursula Newton
Partner
PricewaterhouseCoopers LLP

8.1   Introduction

Rule 28 of the Code states that if during an offer period, or in an announcement which commences an offer period, a profit forecast or a quantified financial benefit statement is made reporting will be required from the reporting accountant and the financial adviser. The Rules also give guidance to directors as to the expected level of confidence required prior to making any such forecasts or statements in an offer period. This Chapter also considers Rule 29 regarding asset valuations.

All of the Code Rules exist for a reason and Rules 28 and 29 are no exception. The Code Rules concerning profit forecasts, quantified financial benefits statements and asset valuations are in place principally to protect shareholders in the offeree company against all offers, not just hostile ones. Prior to the Code's introduction in the late 1960s, there were a number of scandals where takeovers were effected in circumstances where profit forecasts had been made which subsequently proved to have been exceedingly optimistic. More recently we have also seen a rise in the number of quantified financial benefits statements being made. The Rules have been developed over time as precedents have been established, particularly in how deals are presented in announcements and through the media by the directors of both the bidder and target.

Rule 28 does not apply to forecasts or statements made by an offeror offering solely cash, given the Rules are designed to ensure that shareholders are protected from being misled by inaccurate forecasts or statements, whether too high or too low.

It should be noted upfront that there are various complexities regarding what would and wouldn't be considered as a profit forecast under the Code or which may receive a reporting exemption. There is a strong recommendation within the Code, in the majority of cases for the advisers to consult with the Panel as early as possible, in order to provide the necessary time, prior to any announcements, for appropriate diligence to be performed regarding any reporting required.

8.2   Profit forecasts

8.2.1   *When reporting is required*

In common with the Financial Conduct Authority Listing Rules (FCA Listing Rules) and the Prospectus Directive, there is no requirement under the Code for a company to issue a profit forecast.

If a forecast is issued for the first time during an offer period (or in an announcement which commences an offer period), or an existing forecast is revised, this will need to be reported on by the company's reporting accountants and the financial adviser. Where a forecast made in an offer period is repeated in a subsequent document and still within the offer period, the document must include a statement that the profit forecast remains valid and that the reporting accountant and financial adviser have confirmed that their reports continue to apply.

If there is already a profit forecast on the public record before a bid is made, this will normally have to be repeated or, a revised forecast may be substituted. Where the directors reaffirm a forecast that was made prior to an offer period commencing separate reporting by reporting accountants and the financial adviser is not required. Instead a statement is made by the directors reaffirming the profit forecast in any subsequent document published in the offer period. In the event that the Board does not wish to repeat the previously published statement the Code allows that it can either include in the announcement or document a statement that the previous forecast is no longer valid and provide an explanation as to why this is the case, or can amend the previous statement to produce a new forecast.

It is therefore key at the outset for the advisers to check whether or not their client has a forecast on the record. Particular areas to note relate to trading statements and cross-border transactions from territories where it is common practice to provide earnings guidance in communications with the markets.

There are no rules concerning the format in which the profit forecast must be made. Indeed the forecast need not even mention a number. A statement that profits will be higher than last year or that the result will be breakeven, are both fully acceptable ways of making a forecast.

Whilst the directors and their advisers would often feel that giving a range of profits might be the most realistic approach, in practice a single figure is usually given, qualified by the words "not less than", "of the order of", or "approximately". These phrases have tended to be interpreted in subtly differing ways, with "not less than" meaning that one might actually expect to exceed the stated number by a small amount, perhaps a few percentage points. "Of the order of" might imply that one would expect the result to be a few percentage points either side of the stated figure. However, this form of disclosure is a lot less attractive than "not less than" as it implies much less certainty in the minds of the directors about the robustness of their forecast.

It is worth noting that the more precise or comprehensive the forecast, the greater the amount of work required by the company and its advisers. The directors may find that they have to balance their preference for more detailed information, for example profit by division or country, against the downside risk of any published element of the forecast not being achieved. In such circumstances, it would be expected that each published element of the forecast would require the same degree of rigorous analysis (and prudence) as that which would be applied to a total number.

If there is anything out of the ordinary which means it is not possible simply to tax-effect the pre-tax figure to arrive at earnings, the abnormal items, such as unusual tax charges, must also be given.

It is very easy to get a forecast wrong and thus a forecast should be prepared with scrupulous care and objectivity by the directors, who have sole responsibility for it.

8.2.2 Definition of a profit forecast

The Code's definition of a profit forecast is consistent with the definition in the FCA's Prospectus Rules. The principle being that a profit forecast arises from the issue of any published expectation of financial results for the last financial period (if it has not yet been audited), the current period or for a future period. Where the period has already finished, the term employed is a profit estimate, but essentially all the same rules apply whether it is a profit estimate or a profit forecast.

This principle may appear straightforward but a company and its advisers have to take great care to ensure that the company does not inadvertently make a profit forecast. This was demonstrated in the bid by Kvaerner for AMEC several years ago, when a director of Financial Dynamics, the public relations adviser to AMEC, gave:

"an impression of a level of AMEC's future profits that was not being made public, and had not been prepared and reported on in accordance with the Code."

AMEC subsequently had to disassociate itself from the information, and Financial Dynamics was criticised by the Panel for failing to take sufficient care in its discussions with analysts which resulted in what were described as "serious breaches of the Code". Similarly, during the TI Group bid for Dowty Group, Dowty's public relations adviser was criticised by the Panel for making a profit forecast which failed to meet the standards required by the Code and for giving out material new information in conversations with certain journalists and investment analysts which was not correct.

Any public statement that can be construed as putting a floor or ceiling on anticipated results would be regarded as a profit forecast, as would a statement of any data from which a calculation of future profits may be made, although as noted later in this chapter the Panel may grant a dispensation in the case that just a ceiling to the level of profits is given. The Code makes it clear that it is not necessary for the statement to mention a particular figure or even the word profit.

For example, a chairman might respond to questions at an AGM regarding the current year performance by commenting that the current year's results will be better than the previous year's. Such a statement would be regarded as a forecast. In the 2015 takeover of Telecity by Equinox, Telecity were required to report under the Code as they had given guidance on revenue and EBITDA margin, which was deemed enough information to calculate an earnings figure. Therefore the Panel required the statement to be reported on as a profit forecast in the offer documents. Another recent example would be the 2018 takeover of Hogg Robinson Group Plc by Global Business Travel Holdings Ltd (the business travel arm of American Express). Hogg Robinson Plc had previously provided some guidance on a three-year revenue CAGR (compound annual growth rate) and an underlying operating profit margin. As such the Panel deemed that this statement gave a measure of earnings and was to be treated as a profit forecast.

The Code also requires that where a forecast does not relate to the current financial year, the document or announcement must include a corresponding profit forecast for the current and each intervening financial year(s). The reporting requirements concerning profit forecasts will then apply to each statement for a financial year ending 15 months or less from the date on which the forecast is first published.

An example of this occurred in the 2015/16 acquisition of Rexam by Ball Corporation. Under the US rules Ball had to include prospective financial information (PFI) within the proxy statement issued to its shareholders. Although several years of information was presented, only the first financial period required reporting due to the 15-month rule. An important planning point to also note from this example is that given the PFI in the proxy statement was a specific estimate (therefore very hard to substantiate and to report on) and given it related to information that would no longer be considered current, Ball management decided to update this forecast using current information at the same time as publishing the proxy statement and therefore the required reporting was made on the updated forecast.

There have also been examples of cash profit measures such as adjusted funds from operations, in sectors such as property, being treated as profit forecasts which were subsequently required to be reported on under the Code.

In addition the Code extends the reporting requirements to cover references to a forecast published by third parties. Thus, if a company refers to or quotes a profit forecast relating to it that has been published by a third party, for example an investment analyst, it will be treated as having endorsed and published that profit forecast itself for the purpose of the Code. The requirements concerning profit forecasts will therefore then apply to this statement.

The Code does provide an exemption where a company merely continues to provide details on its website of all published analyst forecasts, but as with many of the Rules, companies and their advisers are recommended to consult with the Panel in advance of making any statements in order to ensure that they have an agreed understanding of the requirements.

The Rules are also clear that the reporting requirement applies to a forecast which relates to any part of a company's business in the same way as to a forecast which relates to the whole of a company's business. However, in circumstances where a forecast is published for both the whole and a part of a company's business it is not the Panel's intention to require separate reports in respect of each forecast and a report on the forecast for the whole of the business would be sufficient.

8.2.3   Exemptions

There are certain exemptions to the requirement for a profit forecast to be reported on. These exemptions are set out in the Rules, which also make it clear, as previously stated, that advisers should consult with the Panel over the application of these exemptions:

1. Where a profit forecast has been published prior to any approach, and concerns a period less than 15 months from the date on which the forecast was made, there is no specific requirement for reporting.
    In such circumstances, within the first document published in connection with any possible offer, the directors of the company making the forecast must either:
    (a) repeat the existing forecast and confirm in the offer document or offeree board circular that the forecast remains valid and has been properly compiled and that the basis of accounting used is consistent with the company's accounting policies and includes the assumptions on which the forecast is based;
    (b) include a statement that the forecast is no longer valid, with an explanation of why that is the case; or

(c) publish a new forecast, with appropriate reporting thereon.

2. There is a general exemption to reporting requirements for any profit forecast where the forecast concerns a period greater than 15 months from the publishing date, but such forecasts must be repeated and confirmed as previously described.

3. The Code also contains a concept of "Ordinary course profit forecasts" in contrast to "One off profit forecasts" as described above. These are defined in the Rules as a profit forecast published by either the target or bidder in accordance with its established practice and as part of the ordinary course of its communications with its shareholders and the market. There are no set criteria in the Rules as to how long it takes for a practice to become "ordinary course". The Code specifically requires advisers to consult the Panel if they consider that a profit forecast should be treated as ordinary course, since the Panel has retained the right to require such forecasts to be reported on.

The Rules provide the following exemptions from the requirement for "ordinary course profit forecasts" to be reported on:

(a) where an "ordinary course profit forecast" was made prior to an approach regarding a possible offer (consistent with "one off profit forecasts" and treatment noted previously);

(b) where the "ordinary course profit forecast" is for a period ending more than 15 months after the date on which the forecast is made (consistent with "one off profit forecasts" and treatment noted previously); and

(c) where an "ordinary course profit forecast" is issued during an offer period and the other party to the offer agrees to the exemption.

In the latter case, when the other party to the offer does agree to the exemption, the directors of the company making the forecast would again be required to confirm in the offer document or offeree board circular that the forecast remains valid and has been properly compiled and that the basis of accounting used is consistent with the company's accounting policies and includes the assumptions on which the forecast is based.

The "ordinary course profit forecast" exemption has been particularly relevant in recent years, due to a number of takeovers by US companies of UK companies. In the US it is very much the norm that companies provide earnings guidance to the market. However, whilst one would initially expect that the regular provision of such forward guidance would be within the ordinary course exemption it should be remembered that approval is required from all parties in order for this exemption to apply and such approval might not be obtained, particularly in a hostile bid.

It is also worth noting, that if an "ordinary course profit forecast" is revised or amended during the course of the offer period then this would be regarded by the Panel as a new forecast which would need to be reported on by the reporting accountants and financial advisers.

4.   There is also an exemption in relation to unaudited preliminary statements of annual results published during the offer period such that these are outside the scope of Rule 28. Preliminary results, as long as they are prepared to the standard required by the FCA Listing Rules, will never have to be repeated and reported on because it is assumed that the results will subsequently be audited. Similarly half-yearly financial reports, or "interims", which comply with the relevant provisions of the FCA Listing Rules, the AIM Rules for Companies or the ISDX Growth Market Rules for Issuers also do not need to be repeated or reported on.

Rule 28 also excludes any other interim information which has been published by virtue of a regulatory requirement and has been prepared in accordance with International Accounting Standard 34 (or an equivalent accounting standard). It is worth noting however that this would generally mean that interim management statements would be caught by the Code and would be required to be reported on since they would not normally comply with International Accounting Standard 34.

Such a situation arose during the 2014 TUI AG merger with TUI Travel Plc; when TUI Travel Plc published its third quarter interim management statement during the offer period it included financial information not prepared in accordance with International Accounting Standard 34 and this therefore required reporting under the Rules by the reporting accountants and the financial adviser.

5. The Rules also provide the following additional exemptions from the requirement for a profit forecast to be reported on:

    (a) where a profit forecast states only a maximum figure for the likely level of profits for a particular period (a profit ceiling); and

    (b) in the case of an offeror, where the consideration securities will not represent a material proportion of its enlarged share capital or, alternatively, a material proportison of the value of the offer.

    Each of these two exemptions is only available with the specific approval of the Panel.

It is also worth noting that the exemptions set out above do not apply where the offer is a management buy-out or an offer being made by a controlling shareholder. An example of the latter is when TUI AG, the controlling shareholder, completed the takeover of the minority interest of TUI Travel Plc in 2014. In this instance both companies regularly made "ordinary course" profit forecasts as part of their regular financial reporting to the market. However, the statements that were made by TUI Travel Plc during the offer period where caught by the Rules and required public reporting by the reporting accountant and the financial adviser.

8.2.4 The forecast: Code requirements

In making a profit forecast the directors must ensure that it is:

- understandable: it must not be presented in such a way that it is so complex that it cannot be readily understood;
- reliable: it must be supported by thorough analysis and represent factual strategies, plans and risk analysis; and

- comparable: it should be capable of comparison with information included in the historical financial information.

The principal assumptions on which the forecast is based must be stated and these should provide useful information as to the forecast's reasonableness and reliability. In the case of a profit estimate there will be no such assumptions disclosed as the period being reported on will have already finished with the only uncertainties being around year-end management and audit adjustments. If the forecast is required to be reviewed and reported on by the reporting accountants and the financial advisers, these reports need to be included in the offer or defence document and also in any announcement of the transaction, if that is made earlier.

An example of a profit estimate made during an offer period is in relation to the Hammerson Plc offer to acquire intu properties plc during 2017 and 2018 and the leaked proposal by Klépierre S.A. to acquire Hammerson Plc.

During this period Hammerson Plc released a Q1 business update which included trading results in the form of EPRA NAV per share (European Public Real Estate Net Asset Value) disclosure. Under the Code the business update statement regarding the estimated EPRA NAV per share for the quarter was regarded as a profit estimate, being a period which had already finished but had not been reported on. As such, under Rule 28.1(a) of the Code, the Panel required that the estimate was reported on by both the Reporting Accountant and the Financial Advisers to Hammerson Plc.

Once a forecast has been made, its continuing validity must usually be confirmed in each subsequent document that is issued, so as to make sure that any significant changes are notified to shareholders.

The degree of risk of getting a forecast wrong increases with the length of time that is forecast ahead. For this reason, it is relatively unusual for a forecast to extend beyond the current financial year, particularly if the current year is not well advanced. As previously noted, the Panel will normally grant dispensation over the requirement for reporting from reporting accountants and financial advisers where the period of the profit forecast ends more than 15 months after the date it was first published. The directors are however still required to confirm that the forecast has been properly compiled.

Whether a forecast can actually be reported on at all can depend upon the nature of the business. It is much easier to forecast the results of a business such as an aircraft manufacturer (with its long order books) than it is for a high street retailer where a week of seasonal trading can result in a significant range of possible financial results. Equally, in the financial services industry, the results of a life assurance company are so highly dependent upon its annual actuarial valuation (carried out at the end of each financial year) that any forecast issued prior to that exercise carries a very significant degree of uncertainty.

In contrast, regulated industries such as the water industry have tended to be a stable and predictable business which can be forecast some way ahead. Other factors such as the level of contingency built into a forecast, levers available to management to influence the forecast result and management's historical forecasting accuracy will usually be considered when deciding whether a forecast can be reported on.

It is not uncommon for a profit forecast to be revised upwards during the offer period. This is perfectly permissible and in theory would seem logical, because as time passes, the company would become increasingly certain about its actual profitability, and there is less need to provide a contingency for unexpected developments. In practice, however, whilst such a revision sets a higher future earnings figure, it leaves the company open to the potential criticism of manipulating its financial reporting. The revision of a profit forecast during an offer period may also result in the disapplication of a waiver from requiring reports from reporting accountants and the financial adviser that may have been given by the Panel on an original forecast.

When making a profit forecast, directors should also have regard to the *Guidance on Prospective Financial Information*, published by the Institute of Chartered Accountants of England and Wales (ICAEW) in 2003. The overriding principle of PFI is that it should be useful in the context of the judgements made. The ICAEW is currently undertaking a consultation to update the guidance for preparers of PFI. The consultation sets out to update the guidance for regulatory changes and market developments as well as extending the scope to include all PFI and develop guidance for its application. The guidance is expected to be made public in the fourth quarter of 2019.

8.2.5   *The assumptions underlying the forecast*

It is a protection for shareholders that the principal assumptions upon which the forecast is based have to be published. In practice, however, it is unusual for many of the assumptions to be particularly interesting or informative in relation to the specific circumstances of the company. For example, they will almost invariably refer to there being no change in exchange rates or in the current rate of inflation.

Assumptions must identify clearly those factors that are within the directors' control and those that are not. Thus, an assumption that a new product will be launched would not be in the directors' control if the launch was subject to approval by a regulatory authority, but its introduction would be within the directors' control if there were no authorisations still awaited.

The directors have sole responsibility for the assumptions in the forecast, although in practice they often need advice and guidance from their reporting accountants and financial advisers in formulating and wording the assumptions. The directors of a substantial, multi-location group would typically need more assistance, given the range and complexity of factors potentially affecting such a group's results.

In order to arrive at the directors' best estimate of the likely results, assumptions must clearly be realistic, and the directors cannot cover themselves by making an assumption on something which may well be wrong, for example, assuming that the company will not suffer a strike when in fact one is threatened would not be allowable.

There are certain assumptions that are not generally considered acceptable. For example, an assumption which in effect says nothing more than "we assume the forecast will be achieved" is not permitted. An example of this would be the assumption that "sales will be in accordance with budget". This is meaningless for the shareholders who do not know how demanding the budget is, and therefore are none the wiser regarding the preparation of the forecast. An assumption that is allowed would be, for example, "market demand will continue in line with recent trends and seasonal patterns". In this example, market demand is an uncertainty beyond the company's control.

That latter assumption is an example of what assumptions are supposed to be, that is, useful to shareholders in helping them to form a view as to the reasonableness and reliability of the forecast.

Published assumptions tend to be quite standard, but there are often one or two that are specific to a particular industry. One example was stated by Devenish in its defence against Boddington in 1991 in assuming that there would be no abnormal weather conditions, this being relevant because the level of beer sales is so highly dependent upon the weather. Predictably, Boddington referred to it as more a weather forecast than a profit forecast! A forecast by Manweb a number of years ago assumed that weather conditions would be in line with the experience of the last 30 years.

There is a second level of assumptions which are always in existence but are not published and these could be described as the detailed working assumptions. These will be reviewed by the reporting accountants and financial advisers and discussed with the company in the same way as the published assumptions. It is important that such assumptions are identified because some could be critical to the achievement of the forecast and hence require careful consideration.

8.2.6 *Responsibility*

The Code is quite clear about who is responsible for making a profit forecast. Sole responsibility for a forecast lies with the directors. The reason for this is entirely logical. The people in the best position to determine the likely profits, and to take account of all relevant factors, and to know about current problems which could affect profits, are the directors. Having sole responsibility focuses the directors' minds and is designed to ensure that the directors do not merely rely on their staff to produce the numbers without reviewing the outcome, nor wholly rely on their professional advisers. It is, after all, the forecast made by the directors.

However, this does not mean that the financial advisers and reporting accountants have no responsibilities. They are expected to carry out their duties with appropriate care and skill so as to express an opinion on the forecast. Indeed, failure to do so could involve legal liability.

One principal way in which the directors are able to demonstrate that they have taken due care in compiling the forecast is to commission a commentary "long-form" report from the reporting accountants, which will then be discussed with the directors. Such a report is of particular use to non-executive directors or directors who are executives of particular divisions or subsidiaries but who nevertheless have to take responsibility for the forecast as a whole. It is also an important benefit to the financial advisers in meeting its own responsibilities in relation to the forecasts.

Having discussed the long-form report with the reporting accountants and the financial advisers, the directors often refine or amend their forecast in the light of the matters which have been raised. Such a revision sometimes involves either taking a different view on a particular item in the forecast or, more typically, including a contingency element which the directors decide is necessary to take account of the various uncertainties which inevitably exist in a forecast. One thing that experience suggests is that if anything is not going to go as expected in a forecast, it is far more likely to have an adverse effect on profits than a positive one. This is a further reason why early involvement of all advisers prior to making any announcement is important, therefore allowing suitable time to work through the diligence process.

Forecasts are often put together and reviewed in a very short period of time to meet the requirements of the Code timetable. A company may not have adequate resources to do all the work necessary and so it is sometimes the case that external accountants provide assistance in elements of the preparation of a profit forecast. However, such work must be appropriate and clearly distinguished from the reporting work; a reporting accountants' independence would be impaired if it both prepared a forecast and then had to report on it in public. Moreover, only the directors and staff of the company have sufficient detailed knowledge of the company's affairs to prepare a forecast of the required quality.

8.2.7 *Preparation of a long-form report*

There are a number of key matters that would typically be investigated by the reporting accountants and reported in the long-form report in order to review and comment on the compilation of a forecast. Normally a review would address the following:

1. how much of the forecast profit has already been achieved according to the company's management accounts;
2. how reliable those management accounts have been in the past, or if certain items typically needed adjusting, for

      example, the stock figure which has always been found to be incorrect when the stock was actually counted;

3.   whether the same accounting policies had been followed as in the past—it would be inappropriate for the forecast to assume plant and machinery was written off over 20 years when in last year's audited accounts it was written off over 15;

4.   commentary on the assumptions and a comment if the reporting accountant believes any assumptions to be unrealistic;

5.   an explanation of how the forecast had been prepared;

6.   the reliability of the forecast, and thus the extent to which there should be a contingency provision. This will depend upon whether such a forecast had been done in exactly the same way many times before or whether it was a rushed, one-off exercise using short-cut methods;

7.   the accuracy of previous forecasts, as a prudent contingency would be required where there is evidence of major inaccuracies in forecasting in the past;

8.   a comparison of the figures included in the forecast with those of equivalent periods in previous years with explanations for the changes; and

9.   analysis of the sensitivity of profits to changes in the assumptions. Such an analysis is key, for example, if sales are 2% less than budget, how much might this affect profits?

The forecast will have been based upon information available at the time it was prepared. After the main review work has been completed and immediately prior to issue of the forecast, further information may become available and appropriate. This should be compared with that used in the preparation of the forecast to ensure it is consistent.

The same updating exercise will be required when any subsequent documents are issued to shareholders by the company since the validity of the forecast has to be reconfirmed by the directors, and in addition, the reporting accountants and financial advisers have to confirm that they have no objection to their published reports continuing to apply.

Although the directors have sole responsibility for the forecast, the financial adviser is required to discuss the forecast with the company and report that it has satisfied itself that the forecast is being made by the directors with due care and consideration.

The way in which the financial adviser satisfies its obligation to report on whether the forecast has been prepared with due care and consideration will differ depending upon the investment bank. The extent of the bank's work will depend upon the approach of the bank involved, the firm of reporting account-ants involved, the difficulty of the industry in terms of forecasting, and the extent to which the bank knows the client.

The reporting accountants have their explicit responsibility under the Code to examine the accounting policies and calculations and to report on them in the relevant documents issued by the company. In accordance with the Standard (SIR 3000) issued by the Auditing Practices Board, the reporting accountant will report that:

- "the forecast has been properly compiled on the basis of the assumptions made by the directors"; and
- "the basis of accounting used is consistent with the accounting policies of the company".

At first sight such a report might appear to be very limited in scope. After all, if the forecast adds up and there is no distortion arising because different accounting policies have been used, then the job might appear to be done. However, whilst there is no overt statement about the assumptions, reporting accountants should not allow an assumption to be published which appears to be unrealistic and there is a general expectation that, if a firm of accountants reports on a profit forecast, it implies a reliability which goes beyond this restricted form of wording. Therefore market practice guides reporting accountants to effectively satisfy themselves that the profit forecast on which they are reporting;

- has been made by the directors with proper care and consideration;
- taking into account all relevant factors; and
- that the forecast is credible.

It is perhaps of interest to note that the UK is very different from the US environment as regards profit forecasts. In the UK, it is recognised that forecasts depend upon subjective judgements and are subject to inherent uncertainties. Consequently, although reporting accountants are not able to verify profit forecasts (a misconception, at times, of the press and others), they are nevertheless able to express an opinion thereon. In the US, no doubt influenced by the litigious environment, profit forecasts are not part of takeover defences and, despite "safe harbor" rules in certain circumstances, auditors or reporting accountants do not issue reports on them in the same way.

8.2.8   Conclusion

A forecast of profits is an extremely important piece of information for an investor during a takeover. Forecasts can often result in an increased offer being made by the bidder. They sometimes persuade shareholders not to accept an offer. Where forecasts prove to be wrong, particularly when the actual result is less than the forecast, this can cause loss to investors and is clearly a serious matter. Whilst the Code is designed to minimise the risk of a forecast not being met, this can and does on occasion happen, either because of circumstances which could not reasonably have been envisaged when the forecast was drawn up, or because a forecast was not drawn up with the requisite care and the review process was inadequate.

The Panel does investigate situations where forecasts have not been met to see whether there has been a breach of the Code. Whilst there have not been any completed legal cases in the UK, some legal actions have been mounted against financial advisers and reporting accountants which have reached a compromise settlement. However, until a case is actually completed in court, there will remain some doubt regarding the precise responsibilities of directors, financial advisers and reporting accountants in this area.

It is, of course, open to question whether the increasingly litigious environment in the UK, combined with a legal system that can still make accountants liable for 100% of a claim (irrespective of what proportion they were actually responsible for), will lead us down the US route and result in profit forecasts not being made and much less information on the future being provided to shareholders during takeovers.

A point to note in conclusion is that this Chapter only considers the Rules and reporting requirements of the Takeover Code. There is a complex web of other rules and legislation in the UK and abroad that could also require reporting on profit forecasts. For instance, disclosure on a profit forecast might be required under the Prospectus Rules. Therefore advisers are reminded to consult all applicable rules and legislation before reaching conclusions.

8.3 Quantified financial benefits statements

8.3.1 Introduction

During the Granada takeover of Forte in 1996, Granada published a circular which included a statement that the ongoing profit of Forte could be improved by over £100 million under Granada's ownership. At the time, no specific Rule in the Code governed such a statement although it was subject to the general standards of care. The Code was amended in 1997 to cover "merger benefits" and "earnings enhancement statements" (i.e. a statement that an acquisition will enhance the acquirer's earnings per share) published during the course of a takeover. The Code was further amended in July 2013, introducing a new definition "quantified financial benefits statements", covering "merger benefits" and "earning enhancement statements" as well as extending the Code requirements to cost savings statements made by target companies.

The update to the Rules in 2013 did not change the extent of the Board's responsibility for quantified financial benefit statements, they previously had and retain sole responsibility for such statements. The amendments to the rules did however significantly increase the number of circumstances requiring reporting by reporting accountants and financial advisers.

The Code is periodically reviewed and amended following public consultation. A recent example of this was seen in 2017, when the definition of quantified financial benefits statements was extended to include asset sale scenarios:

> "Where, in competition with an offer or possible offer, an offeree company announces that it has agreed terms on which it intends to sell all or substantially all of the company's assets (excluding cash and cash equivalents) and that it intends to return to shareholders all or substantially all of the company's cash balances (including the proceeds of any asset sale), a statement by the offeree company quantifying the cash sum expected to be paid to shareholders (either as a specific amount or as a range) will be treated as a quantified financial benefits statement."

Given that this amendment is still relatively new there has been little opportunity for its application. It will be interesting to see how market practice will develop in connection with the application of this new requirement.

8.3.2 *Quantified financial benefits statements: Code requirements*

The Rules concerning quantified financial benefits statements reside in Rule 28 together with the Rules concerning profit forecasts. These statements are required to be reported on if quantified merger benefits or cost saving measures are published for the first time (or previously announced cost savings are reiterated) during an offer period. Merger benefits and earnings enhancement statements are now regularly seen in supporting the rationale for merger-style transactions and in bid defence documents published by target companies.

The Rules were originally introduced in order to ensure a high standard of rigour underlying any statements that offeror companies make during the course of an offer. Rule 28.6 specifically covers disclosure requirements for quantified financial benefits, and requires sufficient disclosure to enable target companies to identify weaknesses in the proposed level of benefits being put in front of shareholders or support cost savings the target company expects to achieve if the takeover does not proceed. The Rule requires disclosure of the bases of belief underlying the directors' statement, an analysis of the constituent elements of the estimate, and a base figure for comparison.

Where a target company has published cost savings measures prior to the receipt of an offer such a statement is not subject to the reporting requirements of Rule 28. However, if the Board make any amendments to the statement during the offer period, the revised cost savings statement will be treated as a quantified financial benefits statement and Rule 28 will apply.

Quantified financial benefits statements are typically stated net of a contingency to reflect a level of prudence in light of the amount and quality of evidence available to support the initial quantification. In respect of synergies statements, this will reflect any restrictions with respect to access to and sharing of financial information and integration planning discussions that are permissible between the offeror and the offeree during the offer period.

Quantified financial benefit statements are typically included in the Rule 2 announcement at the very start of an offer period as part of the rationale for the deal. Companies and advisers should be mindful of the timetable to make this initial quantification and the risk that it may be amended. They should also remain vigilant as to the expectations of various stakeholders with respect to amending (often increasing) the targeted synergy or cost savings during the offer period.

As with profit forecasts, if any document or announcement published by a company includes a quantified financial benefits statement, any subsequent document published by that party in connection with the offer must, unless superseded by a revised benefits statement included in the document, include a statement by the directors reaffirming the quantified financial benefits statement. Where reports were obtained in respect of the original quantified financial benefits statement, the document must include a statement that the reporting accountant and financial adviser have confirmed that their reports continue to apply.

8.3.3 *Quantified financial benefits statements: reporting requirements*

The Rules include the requirement for public reporting from the reporting accountants and financial advisers, to include all quantified financial benefit statements made during an offer period by either the bidder or the target. Prior to 2013, reporting was only required in connection with a hostile offer but is now required in all offer situations. This has therefore resulted in an increase in the number of public reports required from reporting accountants and financial advisers for inclusion in offer and defence documents.

Reporting accountants and financial advisers are required to publicly report whether a quantified financial benefits statement has been "properly compiled on the basis stated" and made with "due care and consideration" respectively.

The work involved in order for the directors to be satisfied that it is appropriate to make such a statement and for the reporting accountants and financial advisers to report on it should not be underestimated. Consistent with the approach taken for profit forecasts, most Boards request a long form style report from the reporting accountants to provide the Board with detailed diligence upon the approach taken by management in the preparation of the quantified financial benefits statement and the underlying assumptions used. The key aspects of the long form report for a synergies savings statement will involve:

1. consideration of the planned target operating model of the enlarged business;
2. the appropriateness and robustness of the basis of preparation of the synergy calculations, including the baseline financials of the offeror and offeree;
3. the reliability of the evidence to support individual synergy savings and in turn the risk and hence the discount, or contingency, applied to the targeted gross savings; and
4. costs to achieve the synergies based on the supporting evidence available.

In 2019, the Financial Reporting Council has opened a consultation on SIR 6000 which will establish specific additional Investment Reporting Standards and provide guidance on the reporting accountant's responsibilities and procedures when engaged to report publicly on the proper compilation of such quantified financial benefits statements.

8.3.4 *Quantified financial benefits statements: other considerations*

There can be a risk that the initial quantification is done quickly in order to meet an announcement timetable, and with limited or restricted information given the statement is being made at the beginning of deal negotiations. Indeed Rule 21.3 restricts the extent of information that can be shared between offeror and offeree, even in an agreed deal. Typically there will also be restrictions due to Competition Law which will likely be prevalent in the majority of deals, as well as the risk of interlopers.

Precision is therefore often difficult and hence care is needed, especially given that the statement is likely to exist for a long period (i.e. the whole offer period), giving rise to a higher likelihood of new or improved information coming to light and changing the assumptions.

There is an increased focus of the Panel on these statements, and therefore further detail, for example as to phasing of savings and plans for employees, including headcount reduction, may be requested after the headline savings figures are announced, even if the targeted savings are not being revised. Companies and advisers also need to be mindful about what constitutes a new statement. For example, in the 2015/16 acquisition of Rexam by Ball Corporation an original statement was made that synergies of "approximately $300 million" could be achieved. Later in the offer period this was updated to be "less than $300m". The change in the statement from "approximately" to "less than" led the Panel to consider this a new statement and therefore the Panel required new reports to be issued by the reporting accountant and financial adviser. This situation would also occur where companies are required to update synergies or costs statements for any planned divestments that are required on completion of a merger, for example due to competition requirements.

Companies may also wish to announce revenue synergies in connection with a merger or acquisition. Such statements are typically made in narrative form only. The challenge of producing sufficient and appropriate evidence to support numerical revenue synergies disclosures in order for the reporting accountants and financial adviser to issue the required reports, is typically not capable of being met during the offer period before completion of the transaction.

Parties wishing to make quantified financial benefit statements which are not intended to be interpreted as profit forecasts should include an explicit and prominent disclaimer to the effect that such statements should not be interpreted to mean that earnings per share will necessarily be greater than in the preceding year. If, from a quantified financial benefit statement, a reader is able to calculate or infer the prospective profits of the enlarged group or at least determine a floor or ceiling for such profits, the statement will be subject to the Rules governing profit forecasts. Parties to a takeover who are in doubt as to the interpretation of such a statement are encouraged to consult the Panel in advance.

Some recent examples of quantified financial benefits statements are included within the OneSavings Bank plc offer for Charter Court Financial Services Group plc (2019), Takeda Pharmaceutical Company Limited offer for Shire plc (2018), Hammerson Plc offer for intu properties plc (2017), the merger between Standard Life Plc and Aberdeen Asset Management Plc (2017) and the London Stock Exchange Group Plc merger with Deutsche Börse AG (2016).

8.3.5 Conclusion

Quantified financial benefit statements are a key disclosure during a takeover, given they go directly to the strategic and financial rationale for the takeover or defence of an unwelcome offer. They will have a significant bearing on whether shareholders accept or reject an offer. Where announced savings are not realised, as with profit forecasts, this can cause loss to investors and is clearly a serious matter. The level of scrutiny applied to such statements by various stakeholders, including employees and the Panel itself is high and companies and advisers should be fully aware of the focus and questions that will be received from stakeholders in respect of such statements.

8.4   Asset valuations

Asset valuations are very similar to profit forecasts as far as the Code is concerned. Valuations are used, principally by a target company, to defend against an offer or to argue for a higher price, based upon furnishing information to shareholders about the asset value of the company. The Code, through Rule 29, ensures that such information is given only where it is properly supported by a report from an independent valuer unconnected with the parties to the transaction.

During the Granada bid for Forte, Forte used a number of defences including a valuation of their hotels—this resulted in a revalued net assets per share of 334 pence, which can be compared to Granada's initial lower offer of 323 pence, and their final offer of 373 pence per share.

A more recent example of an asset valuation made in accordance with Rule 29 of the Code was the inclusion of property valuations of intu property plc's property portfolio in a trading statement made in October 2018 in connection with the possible offer from The Peel Group, The Olayan Group and Brookfield Property Group.

Following consultation during October 2018, the Takeover Panel published some amendments to Rule 29 of the Code. These amendments were aimed at providing clarity over the type of assets covered by Rule 29 as well as when the Rule should be applied. These amendments took effect from 1 April 2019.

8.4.1   *Valuations and offers*

Valuations given in connection with an offer typically apply to companies whose share prices tend to be influenced by asset values as opposed to profits, and good examples of this are oil exploration companies and property companies. Rule 29.1(b) provides that Rule 29 applies to:

- land, buildings, plant or equipment;
- mineral, oil or gas reserves; and
- unquoted investments representing in aggregate 10% or more of the gross asset value of the party to the offer which published the valuation.

The recent amendments specifically introduced the requirement in relation to unquoted investment. In addition to these assets however, the Panel still retains the ability to apply Rule 29 to any other kind of asset or liability valuation and therefore the Panel should be consulted at the earliest opportunity.

Prior to the update in April 2019, the Code did not specify when Rule 29 applied other than "in connection with an offer", the changes to the Code added clarity that Rule 29 will apply to an asset valuation published:

- during the relevant offer period;
- in the 12 months prior to the commencement of the offer period; or
- more than 12 months prior to the commencement of the offer period, but only if attention is drawn to that valuation in the context of the offer.

However, where the Panel considers the valuation is not material to the offeree shareholders in making a properly informed decision as to the merits or demerits of the offer, Rule 29 may not apply.

The Code requires a valuation to be supported by an opinion from an appropriately qualified valuer, which in the UK is likely to be a member of the Royal Institution of Chartered Surveyors (RICS), or the Institute of Revenues Rating and Valuation (IRRV). In addition, the valuer must have sufficient current knowledge of the asset being valued, together with the skills and understanding necessary to make the valuation.

The Code also deals with valuations of the other parties' assets. The bidder or target can only publish a valuation of the other parties' assets if a valuation is unqualified and up to appropriate standards. In exceptional cases, it is permitted for one party to comment on the others' valuation. The interpretation of this part of the Rule by the Panel leads to an interesting consequence: until one party has issued a formal valuation during the offer, the Panel does not allow the other party to refer to an old valuation. Accordingly, a bidder is unlikely to be able to comment on the trend in net assets per share shown by a target's financial statements until an up-to-date valuation has been issued by the target. The Panel needs to be consulted on this area in advance.

Unlike a profit forecast that is "on the record" and has to be reaffirmed, withdrawn or amended and reported on, an asset valuation has to be reported on only if it is made in connection with an offer. So, for example, the directors' estimates of asset values, which are frequently included in audited accounts, can be reproduced in offer or defence documents when setting out statements of assets, and need not be supported by an independent valuer, provided the asset values are not a particularly significant factor and are not given undue prominence.

8.4.2   Basis of valuation

Clearly, a valuation is of little use to shareholders or any other party unless the basis of that valuation is set out clearly.

The appropriate basis of a valuation depends on the type of asset, for example properties in use by a company should be valued at open market value for existing use, whereas investment properties should be valued at open market value. The detailed requirements are set out in the Code.

Furthermore, the valuation of land, buildings and plant must be made in accordance with the Appraisal and Valuation Standards issued by RICS. A point of detail came up in the Bilton defence in 1998 concerning whether or not the valuation should be gross or net of purchasers' costs. Normal practice is for it to be net of purchasers' costs, although Rule 29 is not explicit on this point.

The Panel may, in certain circumstances, permit the provision of information in addition to the basic valuation. For example, in the hostile offer for Wolverhampton & Dudley Breweries, a valuation report was also prepared based upon the value of the pubs if sold as one block rather than individually. In addition, in the hostile offer for Blue Circle a "calculation of worth" valuation was presented to illustrate the potential development value of certain properties which would not be reflected in the open market values. However, the Panel should be consulted in advance in such circumstances and may require additional disclosures if an alternative valuation is to be used.

Where there is a material tax liability which would arise on sale of the asset, this should be disclosed. There are also detailed disclosures required for land with development potential including the costs of development and an estimated value once development has been completed, together with confirmation of whether planning consent has been obtained and the nature of any conditions to consent which might affect value.

8.4.3 Exemptions

There is one exemption to the Rule in which a valuation must be fully supported by a report. Where the target company has a portfolio of assets—perhaps a retailer with hundreds of high street shops, or a house builder with many half-built houses— the Panel is sometimes prepared to allow a valuation of a representative sample by the professional valuer which is then extrapolated by the directors to give a value for the portfolio as a whole. This is not because the costs of a full valuation would be prohibitive, but rather that the time required to carry out a valuation is not available.

Any valuation must state the effective date at which the assets were valued, which is particularly relevant in times of rapidly changing property prices. It is possible to use a valuation that is not current but, since the valuer must state that he is satisfied that a valuation at the current date would not be materially different, it must effectively be up to date before it can be published.

8.4.4 Conclusion

In an asset rich business an Asset Valuation can be a key factor in supporting the valuation for both a defence or an offer. Companies should ensure that they allow sufficient time for the independent valuer to complete their work on the valuation, which may involve extensive work depending upon the nature of the assets.

Chapter 9

Application of the Market Abuse Regime to Takeovers

Mark Bardell
Partner
Herbert Smith Freehills LLP

Antonia Kirkby
Senior PSL
Herbert Smith Freehills LLP

9.1 Introduction

It is a stated purpose of the Code to provide an orderly framework within which takeovers are to be conducted and to promote, in conjunction with other regulatory regimes, the integrity of the financial markets (see 1.1 above and para.2(a) of the Introduction to the Code). Indeed, the fourth of the six General Principles of the Code specifically provides that:

> "False markets must not be created in the securities of the offeree, of the offeror or of any other company concerned by the bid in such a way that the rise or fall of the prices of the securities becomes artificial and the normal functioning of the markets is distorted."

Likewise, the market abuse regime is designed to ensure the integrity of financial markets and promote investor confidence. The EU Market Abuse Regulation (EU/596/2014) (MAR) states:

> "An integrated, efficient and transparent financial market requires market integrity. The smooth functioning of

securities markets and public confidence in markets are prerequisites for economic growth and wealth. Market abuse harms the integrity of financial markets and public confidence in securities and derivatives." (Recital (2).)

Even at the policy level of the stated purposes of the Code and the market abuse regime, the potential for significant overlap is apparent. However, the rules of the Code and the provisions of the market abuse regime have not been designed to fit together as one coherent regulatory regime (not least because the Code is a domestic UK regime and the market abuse regime, through MAR, is an EU-wide directly applicable regime). Consequently, compliance with the Code will not in itself ensure compliance with the market abuse regime (for example a target acquiring an interest in shares in compliance with the Rules of the Code regarding share buying—see Ch.3 above—while in possession of inside information disclosed to it during a due diligence exercise will likely constitute market abuse—see 9.3 and 9.5.1 below); and, vice versa, compliance with the market abuse regime will not in itself ensure compliance with the Code (for example a director of a target company who has recommended that shareholders reject an offer and who wishes to sell shares in the target company at a time when he or she is not in possession of inside information may only do so under the Code with the consent of the Panel and after giving sufficient public notice of their intention together with an appropriate explanation—see Note 5 on Rules 4.1 and 4.2).

Accordingly, it is essential for practitioners in this area to be aware of the provisions of the market abuse regime as well as the rules of the Code and to consider each separately.

The market abuse regime in the UK is currently set out in MAR, and the implementing measures under it, which came into force in the UK, and other EU Member States, with effect from 3 July 2016. MAR replaced the regime previously contained in ss.118–137 (Pt VIII) of the Financial Services and Markets Act 2000 (the FSMA). The likely impact of Brexit is described at 9.2.3 below.

The Financial Conduct Authority (the FCA) is responsible for enforcing MAR in the UK and can take enforcement action against a person who commits market abuse (see 9.3.3 below for the sanctions).

Market abuse remains a civil offence (the UK, along with certain other EU Member States, e.g. Denmark, having opted out of the EU criminal sanction regime that accompanies MAR) but the market abuse regime sits alongside the criminal offences relating to insider dealing (contained in the Criminal Justice Act 1993) and market manipulation (contained in ss.89 and 90 of the Financial Services Act 2012). It also applies in addition to relevant regulatory requirements of the FCA, the rules of the relevant markets and the Code.

There are some important areas of overlap between the jurisdiction of the FCA and that of the Panel in the context of transactions governed by the Code. Accordingly, the purpose of this Chapter is to provide:

1.   an explanation of how MAR is implemented in the UK;
2.   an overview of what constitutes market abuse under MAR;
3.   a description of the obligation to disclose inside information under MAR; and
4.   an insight into how MAR may impact a takeover in practice in the UK.

9.2   The implementation of MAR in the UK

9.2.1   *The background to the market abuse regime*

The UK introduced a market abuse regime in 2001 under the FSMA, to supplement the existing criminal offence of insider dealing under the Criminal Justice Act 1993. The regime created (and not without controversy) what is often referred to as a "civil offence"; it was not, and still is not, a criminal offence. As such, a lower standard of proof is required to enforce it and an offence can be committed by any legal person (including a body corporate) rather than just by an individual. With effect from 2005, this UK regime was amended when the EU Market Abuse Directive (2003/6) (MAD) came into force. MAD sat alongside the existing UK offences rather than replacing them. The original UK offences of market abuse were retained, with their original broader scope, in addition to the new offences introduced into the FSMA as a result of MAD. In 2014 the European Commission approved a new regime in the form of MAR and a new criminal sanctions directive (CSMAD).

MAR came into force on 3 July 2016 and applies to companies with securities admitted to an EU regulated market (such as the main market of the London Stock Exchange), companies admitted to an EU multilateral trading facility (such as AIM) and companies with securities admitted to trading on an organised trading facility (OTF) in the EU. MAR also applies to any financial instruments whose price or value depends on, or has an effect on, the price or value of a financial instrument which is traded on one of those markets.

The UK has opted out of CSMAD and instead retained the criminal offence of insider dealing under the Criminal Justice Act 1993, which is broader than CSMAD.

9.2.2 The implementation of MAR in the UK

MAR is directly applicable in the UK and other EU Member States. It did not therefore need to be implemented through the enactment of domestic legislation.

The choice of a regulation (which is directly applicable in all Member States) rather than a directive (which has to be implemented by each individual Member State) is a signal of the European Commission's desire for greater harmonisation and to create a single, directly applicable, EU market abuse rule book. EU Member States were, therefore, required to amend and, where appropriate, repeal the provisions in their national legislation which applied the market abuse regime under MAD, in order to reflect the creation of the new directly applicable rules.

MAR is supplemented by a series of implementing regulations, which are also directly applicable in EU Member States and which give further detail on certain aspects of the regime. The key regulations under MAR likely to be relevant on a takeover are the Inside Information Implementing Regulation (EU/2016/1055), the Insider Lists Implementing Regulation (EU/2016/347), the Delegated Regulation (EU/2016/522), which covers a range of topics including restrictions on and notifications in relation to PDMR transactions, and the Market Soundings Delegated Regulation (EU/2016/960) and Implementing Regulation (EU/2016/596).

The European Securities and Markets Authority (ESMA) is also required to publish guidelines on certain aspects of the MAR regime. Those of relevance on a takeover are its Guidelines on delaying disclosure of inside information (ESMA/2016/1478) and its Guidelines for persons receiving market soundings (ESMA/2016/1477). Issuers are required to make every effort to comply with these guidelines. ESMA has also published a Q&A document on MAR (ESMA70-145-11) which it updates from time to time, the most recent version at the time of publication being version 14.

In the UK, the provisions in FSMA relating to market abuse were repealed when the provisions of MAR came into effect. There were also substantial changes to the FCA Handbook, in particular the Disclosure Rules and Code of Market Conduct. Where the provisions of MAR directly replaced provisions in the FCA Handbook, the FCA deleted those rules and replaced them with "signposts" to the relevant MAR provisions (rather than copying the MAR provisions out). Some additional guidance in the Handbook which is not reflected in MAR has also been retained (to the extent it is not inconsistent with the provisions of MAR). These sections are no longer rules and instead guidance, so in particular the Disclosure Rules have become the "Disclosure Guidance". The Disclosure Guidance in DTR 2 contains some useful additional guidance on the regime. There is also a section in the Market Conduct Sourcebook of the FCA Handbook on market abuse (FCA MAR) which contains guidance on the market abuse offences and the definition of inside information.

9.2.3 The impact of Brexit on the market abuse regime in the UK

The vote in June 2016 for the UK to leave the EU and the service by the UK in March 2017 of notice, under art.50 of the Treaty of the European Union, of the UK's intention to leave the EU does not have any direct legal effect on its own and the FCA confirmed that EU legislation remains applicable until any changes are made.

It is currently expected that when the UK leaves the EU, the European Union (Withdrawal) Act 2018 will preserve and convert into domestic law all EU law that applies to the UK at the time it leaves the EU. If the UK and EU agree terms for the UK's exit from the EU, the current draft of the Withdrawal Agreement provides for a transitional period (currently expected to end in December 2020). During the transitional period, EU law would continue to apply in the UK and the legislative impact of Brexit would be delayed until the end of the transitional period. The market abuse regime would therefore remain unchanged during that period. Even after the end of any such period, it will likely remain unchanged, with the provisions of EU MAR being converted into domestic law, unless and until the Government decides to make any changes.

If the UK were to leave with no deal, there will be no transitional period and the provisions of EU MAR will be converted into domestic UK law on Exit day. Again, the impact for issuers is likely to be limited. The greatest impact will be on issuers which have securities admitted to markets in the UK and the EU and which may therefore be subject to both UK MAR and EU MAR. Such issuers will, for example, have to notify any delay in disclosure of inside information both to the

FCA in the UK and to the national competent authority in the relevant EU Member State in which their securities are admitted to trading.

The FCA published the final changes to its Handbook that will apply in the event of a no deal Brexit in FCA PS 19/5. It also gave guidance to issuers on the changes in relation to MAR in the event of a no-deal Brexit in Primary Market Bulletin Issue no 21.

The FCA has said that, post-Brexit, it expects firms and market participants to continue to apply Level 3 Guidelines such as the Q&A and Guidelines published by ESMA to the extent they remain relevant but that they will not be incorporated into UK law or FCA rules/guidance.

9.2.4   The Takeover Panel and market abuse

The Panel has always sought to preserve its exclusive jurisdiction over matters relating to takeovers because it is only too well aware of the tactical opportunities which overlapping regulatory jurisdictions can provide and the risk of allegations of market abuse being used tactically to deter or delay takeovers.

However, it is important to note that it is not the Panel which determines whether behaviour in the context of a takeover constitutes market abuse. It is a question of law, as interpreted ultimately by the European Court of Justice (ECJ), but as applied and enforced by the FCA in the UK. This raises the possibility of different interpretations under the two different regimes because it is not open to the FCA simply to adopt the Panel's views.

In practice, however, the FCA will take into account the Code rules and the views of the Panel. For example, FCA MAR contains a list of provisions of the Code "conformity with which will be unlikely to, of itself, amount to market abuse". The relevant provisions are listed in FCA MAR 1.10.4G–1.10.6G. FCA MAR also says, in the context of the offence of unlawful disclosure of inside information, that in determining whether disclosure was in the normal exercise of a person's employment, profession or duties, it will take into account whether the disclosure was permitted by the Code (FCA MAR 1.4.5G). In some areas though, the Panel is more permissive than the FCA and, as discussed above, parties to an offer should bear in mind that compliance with the Code does not necessarily mean there is no risk of committing market abuse. Take, for example, shareholders or counterparties to negotiations who are made insiders in relation to an approach regarding a possible takeover offer. The Panel's practice is to allow selective disclosure to a limited number of persons (see Practice Statement No.20), whereas under MAR disclosure must be for a legitimate purpose (that is, in the normal exercise of a person's employment, profession or duties) and the recipient must owe a duty of confidentiality even where selective disclosure is permitted. If the selective disclosure constitutes a "market sounding" (for example where a bidder is raising equity financing for its offer or speaking to target shareholders to seek irrevocable undertakings), onerous procedures and record-keeping requirements may also apply under MAR (see 9.3.2.3 below).

Whilst it is for the FCA to determine whether behaviour amounts to market abuse, there is FCA guidance in the Decision Procedure and Penalties Manual which says that, in relation to behaviour in the context of a takeover bid, it will refer to the Takeover Panel and attach due weight to its views (DEPP 6.2.22G).

Where a Code breach is potentially also market abuse, even under MAR it is still expected that the FCA will not necessarily get involved. As Sir Howard Davies, the then Chairman of the FSA (the predecessor to the FCA), made clear in June 2000:

> "We fully share the objective of ensuring that the FSA is not unhelpfully dragged into takeover battles, with damaging consequences for the way in which takeovers

are handled in London… We believe that outcome can be achieved … by means of good cooperation between the FSA and the Panel."

The Decision Procedure and Penalties Manual (DEPP 6.2.22G– 6.2.27G) and the Enforcement Guide give details on how the FCA and the Takeover Panel will interact.

First, the FCA will refer to the Panel and give due weight to its views and will consult the Panel before exercising its powers if it considers that the exercise may affect the timetable or outcome of a takeover offer.

Secondly, the FCA expects parties to exhaust procedures for complaint available under the Code. The Takeover Panel's powers will often be sufficient. The FCA says in DEPP that it will not, save in exceptional circumstances, take action in respect of behaviour to which the Code is relevant before the conclusion of procedures available under the Code nor exercise its powers during the currency of a takeover offer.

The principal circumstances in which the FCA is likely to consider exercising its market abuse related powers are stated to be:

1. where the behaviour falls within the prohibition in art.14 of MAR (which prohibits insider dealing and unlawful disclosure of inside information);
2. where the FCA's approach in previous similar cases (whether or not in a bid context) suggests that a sanction should be imposed;
3. where the market abuse extends to securities or a class of securities which may be outside the Panel's jurisdiction;
4. where the market abuse threatens or threatened the stability of the financial system; and
5. where the Panel requests the FCA to consider the exercise of its powers.

Intervention by the FCA in relation to Code governed matters is likely to be a rare event and it is likely to be very unusual for intervention to be contemporaneous. Where appropriate, the Panel and the FCA are likely to organise and run simultaneous and co-operative decision-making processes to minimise disruption to the takeover timetable and the possibility of parties to a bid playing them off against one another.

Whilst this jurisdictional overlap does provide scope for litigation in takeovers, in practice it has not emerged to date. Assuming the Panel and the FCA continue a close and constructive working relationship, the scope appears limited. Indeed the back-up of the wide-ranging powers that the FCA has in respect of market abuse (in particular, the power to fine) provides useful additional support for the Panel. The fact that the FCA (in the context of a decision on whether to impose a penalty in respect of market abuse) clearly attaches importance to co-operation with regulators and to the swift taking of appropriate action should also assist the Panel as it is likely to provide an additional incentive to remedy or compensate for market abuse and to do so quickly.

9.3   Market abuse offences explained

The market abuse offences under MAR most likely to apply on a takeover are those of insider dealing and the unlawful disclosure of inside information which are described further below. As mentioned above, the criminal offence of insider dealing in the Criminal Justice Act 1993 remains unchanged.

9.3.1   Insider dealing and legitimate behaviour

The offence of insider dealing is set out in arts 8 and 14 of the MAR. Article 9 of the MAR sets out certain types of behaviour that will be viewed as legitimate and in those situations a person will not be deemed to have committed the offence of insider dealing. It is worth noting, however, that a person may still be deemed to have engaged in insider dealing, even if they fall within one of these examples of legitimate behaviours, if there was an illegitimate reason for the transaction or behaviour concerned (see art.9(6)).

9.3.1.1   The offence of insider dealing

Article 14 provides that a person shall not engage or attempt to engage in insider dealing. This is expanded upon in art.8 which defines insider dealing as occurring in circumstances where a person possesses inside information and uses that information by acquiring or disposing of, for its own account or the account of a third party, directly or indirectly, financial instruments to which that information relates. The offence is similar to the insider dealing offence that was previously in the FSMA. Two key points to note are that: (i) it is an offence to *attempt* to engage in insider dealing; and (ii) there is a presumption under MAR that, if a person deals while in possession of inside information, they will be considered to have used the inside information as part of the basis for dealing (Recital (24) of the MAR). This presumption is a codification of the ECJ's decision, under MAD, in *Spector Photo Group and Van Raemdonck v Commissie voor het Bank-, Financie-en Assurantiewezen* (C-45/08) (EU:C:2009:806; [2010] Bus. L.R. 1416). The use of inside information to cancel or amend pre-existing orders or bids is also expressly caught.

FCA MAR gives the following as examples of behaviour that may amount to insider dealing in the context of a takeover: a bidder or potential bidder entering into a transaction in a financial instrument that provides merely an economic exposure to movements in the price of the target company's shares, using inside information concerning the proposed bid (for example, a spread bet on the target company's share price); and a person who acts for the bidder or potential bidder dealing for his own benefit in a financial instrument using information concerning the proposed bid (FCA MAR 1.3.2G).

The Code also includes a Rule relating to insider dealing (Rule 4.1) which broadly prohibits any dealings in target company shares, in derivatives relating to target company shares and, even, except where the proposed offer is not price-sensitive in relation to such securities, in bidder shares (or related derivatives) before the announcement of a bid by any person,

other than the bidder, in possession of price-sensitive information concerning the bid. In practice, however, almost all cases
within Rule 4.1 also involve insider dealing and would
therefore be likely to be passed on by the Panel to the FCA. It is
expected that the FCA would, however, consult the Panel if it
thought its proposed action in respect of an insider dealing
matter might have an impact in relation to the takeover bid.

9.3.1.2   Legitimate behaviour on a takeover

A person who deals while in possession of inside information
is not presumed to have used that information, and thus
engaged in insider dealing, where: (i) the information was
obtained in the conduct of a takeover; and (ii) the person uses
the information solely for the purpose of proceeding with the
takeover (art.9(4)). Unlike under the previous MAD regime,
however, stakebuilding is expressly excluded from this safe
harbour. In practice, bidders will have to rely on the exemption
for trading pursuant to one's own intention in art.9 when
stakebuilding (see 9.3.1.3 below).

When a person relies on art.9(4), any inside information that
the person possesses must have been made public by the time
of acceptance of the offer or approval of the merger (unless it
has otherwise ceased to be inside information).

FCA MAR says that examples of using inside information
solely for the purpose of proceeding with a takeover under
art.9(4) may include the seeking of irrevocable undertakings to
accept an offer, as well as making arrangements in relation to
offering securities as consideration and making arrangements
to offer cash consideration (FCA MAR 1.3.17G).

9.3.1.3   Dealing in knowledge of own intentions

The fact that a person uses its own knowledge that it has
decided to acquire or dispose of financial instruments when
acquiring or disposing of those instruments does not of itself
constitute insider dealing. As discussed above, a bidder

462

wishing to stakebuild will have to rely on this to avoid committing the offence of insider dealing (see also 9.5.1 below).

9.3.1.4   *Dealing pursuant to a pre-existing obligation*

A person who acquires or disposes of financial instruments while in possession of inside information will not be deemed to have used that information and engaged in insider dealing where the transaction is to discharge an existing obligation, provided the obligation arises from an agreement concluded before the person possessed inside information.

9.3.2   *Unlawful disclosure*

The offence of unlawful disclosure is again broadly the same as under the previous regime under MAD. There is a safe harbour for "market soundings", provided prescribed procedures are followed, when selectively disclosing inside information, most notably when a bidder is sounding out target shareholders about their willingness to accept the offer. (Although in practice, in most recommended deals, it is usual for the target itself to conduct this process and therefore for the process to fall outside of the market soundings regime.) This safe harbour is discussed in 9.3.2.3 below.

9.3.2.1   *The offence of unlawful disclosure*

Article 14 provides that a person shall not unlawfully disclose inside information. This is expanded upon in art.10 which defines unlawful disclosure of inside information as occurring in circumstances where a person possesses inside information and discloses that information to any other person, except where the disclosure is made in the normal exercise of an employment, a profession or duties.

9.3.2.2   *Disclosure in the normal exercise of employment, profession or duties*

The exception for disclosure in the normal exercise of an employment, a profession or duties is similar to the previous safe harbour, found in s.118(3) of the FSMA, for disclosure in "the proper course of the exercise" of his employment, profession or duties. It is suggested that, in the UK, the decision of the Upper Tribunal in *Hannam v the Financial Conduct Authority* ([2014] UKUT 233 (TCC); [2014] Lloyd's Rep. F.C. 704) remains relevant when considering this safe harbour. In that case, mention by a financial adviser of an unannounced takeover approach to a third party was found to be outside of that safe harbour.

When inside information is selectively disclosed in the normal exercise of an employment, a profession or duties, the recipient must also owe a duty of confidentiality under art.17(8) of the MAR.

The requirement for disclosure to be in the normal exercise of an employment, profession or duties (often referred to as the legitimate purpose test) means that parties will have to consider whether it is appropriate to disclose the information. Simply having a non-disclosure agreement in place is not sufficient. In the UK, the FCA has kept the guidance in DTR 2.5.7G and DTR 2.5.8G on selective disclosure. The guidance emphasises that the disclosure must be justified and that selective disclosure cannot be made to any person simply because they owe a duty of confidentiality. It also sets out an indicative list of persons to whom issuers may selectively disclose inside information, including advisers and major shareholders.

9.3.2.3 *Market soundings*

There is a safe harbour (in art.11 of the MAR) for disclosure of inside information in the course of a market sounding (i.e. in circumstances of wall crossing) in certain situations. The safe harbour provides protection from the offence of unlawful disclosure but at the cost of imposing some onerous require-ments on the participants to the market sounding.

A market sounding under MAR is the communication of information prior to the announcement of a transaction either to gauge the interest of potential investors in a possible transaction or for a bidder to sound out target shareholders on a takeover (whether a cash or securities bid).

A market sounding conducted in accordance with MAR art.11 (and the relevant implementing regulations about how the sounding must be conducted and recorded) will be deemed to have been made in the normal exercise of a person's employment, profession or duties and so will mean that the disclosure is not unlawful for the purposes of art.10 of the MAR.

As art.11 is designed to provide a safe harbour from the offence of unlawful disclosure (i.e. an optional defence), non-compliance with the market sounding requirements in art.11 and the implementing regulations does not automatically mean that the communication is unlawful. The only require-ment which must be complied with in all cases is in art.11(3), which requires a disclosing market participant (i.e. the person conducting the market sounding) to consider in advance whether the sounding will involve disclosure of inside information and to make a written record of its conclusions and the reasons for it. This is the view taken by the City of London Law Society and the Law Society's Company Law Committees' Joint Working Parties in their Market Abuse Regulation Q&A, the most recent version of which was published in May 2018.

However, whilst strict compliance with the market soundings procedures is optional, the regime under MAR is drafted in prescriptive terms (a brief overview of the requirements is set out below). Therefore, whenever any selective disclosure of inside information falls within the definition of market sounding, it may be advisable to follow the market soundings procedures. In any event, even if the bidder and its advisers choose not to comply with the procedural requirements for a market sounding, they should always consider in advance whether the sounding will involve the disclosure of inside information and keep a record of their conclusions and reasoning.

On a takeover a bidder will be conducting a market sounding if it sounds out target company shareholders about its offer. If the bidder is subject to MAR and the bid is to be equity financed, the bidder may also conduct a market sounding if it sounds out its own shareholders as potential investors in the shares that the bidder intends to issue. A bidder's advisers should also follow the procedures and in practice a bidder should only conduct a market sounding in conjunction with its advisers.

In practice, in most recommended deals, it is usual for the target itself to sound out its own shareholders and therefore for the process to fall outside of the market soundings regime as, the definition of a market sounding does not include a target company sounding out its own shareholders. The target would however have to ensure that it meets the criteria for selective disclosure, as described in 9.3.2.2 above (so the disclosure must be in the normal exercise of the person's employment, profession or duties and the recipient must owe a duty of confidentiality).

The procedures required to be followed on a market sounding are more onerous and prescriptive than under the previous regime for wall-crossings.

Under MAR, both the parties conducting the sounding ("disclosing market participants" or "DMPs") and the parties being sounded out ("market sounding recipients" or "MSRs") must follow prescribed procedures. The detailed requirements are set out in the Market Sounding Delegated Regulation and Implementing Regulation. For disclosing market participants, the key points to note include the requirement to establish procedures, prior to any sounding, for how that sounding will be conducted and to provide a set of materials, with prescribed contents, to all MSRs. During the sounding, recorded phone lines should be used when available. Where not available (or if the MSR does not consent to the use of recorded phone lines), records of the market sounding communications should be kept. The requirements envisage that written notes or minutes of the conversation must be kept and furthermore, where possible, agreed and signed by both the DMP and the MSR.

MSRs should be given an estimate of when the information will cease to be inside information. When DMPs assess that the information disclosed has ceased to be inside information, they should inform the MSR as soon as possible. Cleansing must therefore be addressed more rigorously under MAR than was previously the case.

There are also detailed record-keeping requirements, which apply for five years, post-sounding.

ESMA takes the view that there is a risk that inside information will be passed during a market sounding even if the DMP has categorised it as not containing inside information. DMPs must therefore keep records of market soundings even where the DMP has concluded that no inside information will be disclosed.

In addition to the measures for DMPs in the implementing regulations, ESMA has published guidelines containing requirements for MSRs.

Practitioners must also keep in mind the Code requirements relating to the communication and distribution of information during an offer. In particular, the Code requires that any documents or presentation referred to during the course of seeking irrevocables from target shareholders must be published on a website when the offer is announced (Rule 20.1(c) and Note 6 on Rule 20.1).

9.3.3   *The penalties for market abuse*

If the FCA finds that market abuse has taken place, it can impose a fine, or issue a public censure, or it can seek an injunction or impose a restitution order on any person, including companies, other legal entities and individuals.

Market abuse can be committed anywhere in the world in relation to financial instruments admitted to trading on a relevant EU market (see 9.2.1 for the markets to which MAR applies).

9.4 The obligation to announce inside information and delaying disclosure

As well as the market abuse regime, MAR also contains the regime for disclosing inside information. The overall regime for announcing inside information, and when disclosure can be delayed, is broadly the same as the previous regime. The main change to the regime relates to the procedural requirements that have to be followed when delaying disclosure which require, amongst other things, companies to identify the precise time and date at which inside information arose.

9.4.1 The definition of inside information and the obligation to announce it

MAR requires inside information to be announced as soon as possible (unless disclosure can be legitimately delayed).

The core definition of inside information is set out in art.7(1)(a) of the MAR, which provides that inside information is information that:

1. is of a precise nature;
2. has not been made public;
3. relates directly or indirectly to one or more issuers or to one or more financial instruments; and
4. if made public, would be likely to have a significant effect on the prices of those financial instruments or on the price of related derivative financial instruments.

The definition of inside information is for practical purposes the same under MAR as under the previous regime. The changes simply reflect case law and guidance developed under MAD.

MAR makes it clear that where information relates to future circumstances or events, there must be a realistic prospect of the event (or circumstance) occurring in order for it to be sufficiently precise for the purposes of the definition of inside information and that intermediate stages leading up to a particular event can themselves be inside information, if they meet the criteria for inside information.

In December 2017, an AIM company, Tejoori Ltd, was fined £70,000 by the FCA for failing to disclose inside information as soon as possible. It had been notified that it was likely to have to sell shares it held in another company pursuant to a drag along notice that other shareholders in the company intended to issue. It would receive no initial consideration for the shares and might receive deferred consideration over five years, which would be materially lower than the value of its investment in the company. The FCA concluded that the information given to Tejoori was sufficiently precise to amount to inside information when it was given a draft of the drag along notice as the information gave rise to a reasonable expectation that Tejoori would be required to sell its shares and the information about the consideration was sufficiently specific to enable a conclusion to be drawn that the transaction would have a negative effect on Tejoori's share price. Although the drag along notice had not been signed, it was an intermediate step in a protracted process which met the test for inside information.

In the context of a takeover, the decision as to whether inside information has arisen will remain fact-dependent. In practice, it is likely that for a target company it will arise on receipt of an approach (bearing in mind that, although the bid may still be speculative at that stage, an intermediate stage can itself be inside information and that bidders are required to disclose to the Panel the date of an approach). For bidders that are within the scope of MAR, it will depend on: (i) whether the transaction is price-sensitive in relation to it; and (ii) at what point the information becomes sufficiently precise to be inside information.

It has been noted by many commentators that the procedural requirements that apply when the disclosure of inside information is delayed (discussed at 9.4.3 below) mean that the point at which inside information arises must be analysed more frequently and rigorously than was sometimes the case under the previous regime.

It is also important to continue monitoring for inside information as the transaction progresses. Further developments in the course of a transaction (e.g. in relation to anti-trust clearance) might also amount to inside information and the decision-making process and procedures if disclosure is to be delayed must be followed each time inside information arises.

9.4.2   *When can disclosure of inside information be delayed?*

The ability to delay disclosure of inside information is for practical purposes the same as under the previous regime under the DTRs, so delay is permitted:

1. so as not to prejudice the issuer's legitimate interests;
2. if the omission would not be likely to mislead the public; and
3. if the issuer can keep the information confidential.

ESMA has published Guidelines on the circumstances in which a delay is permitted. The guidelines provide a non-exhaustive list of situations in which the legitimate interests of the issuer are likely to be prejudiced by the immediate disclosure of inside information. These broadly mirror those previously contained in guidance published by the FCA and ESMA, including negotiations in course where the outcome would be jeopardised by disclosure. The Guidelines also give examples of when a delay might mislead the public. These include where the inside information that the issuer intends to delay disclosing is materially different from the last public announcement of the issuer on the matter to which the inside information relates. In the *Tejoori* case discussed above, the FCA said that Tejoori could not delay disclosure after the information became inside information because it had commented on the shareholding in its February interim results, saying that "the Board remains confident of the future prospects of this investment". Any delay in disclosing the information would therefore have misled the market because of this statement. Whilst not legally binding, issuers are required to make every effort to comply with ESMA Guidelines.

The FCA has also retained some limited guidance in DTR 2.5 on delaying disclosure of inside information.

9.4.3 Procedural requirements when delaying disclosure

It is essential that, when delaying disclosure of inside information, issuers and their advisers bear in mind and comply with the record-keeping and notification requirements under MAR.

If an issuer delays disclosing inside information, it must (when the information is announced) notify the FCA that disclosure was delayed. It will have to include in that notification details of when the inside information first existed (including the precise time, as well as the date, that it first existed); and the names of the persons responsible for the decision to delay.

The FCA can also require a written explanation from the issuer of how the conditions for delay (including confidentiality) were satisfied during the period of delay.

This means that companies subject to MAR must identify when inside information arises and, if disclosure of the information is delayed, keep a record of when the information arose, who was responsible for the decision to delay and the grounds on which delay was permitted. They should also monitor and record their continued compliance with the conditions for delay whenever they delay the disclosure of inside information.

If an issuer does decide to delay disclosure of inside information, it must also create an insider list recording those persons working for it who have access to the inside information (MAR art.18). It must also ensure their advisers keep an insider list recording who has access to the inside information. The insider list must be in a prescribed form and record prescribed information (including each person's name, date of birth and addresses, as well as the reason why they are on the insider list). The detailed requirements, and the prescribed template, for an insider list are set out in the Insider Lists Implementing Regulation. MAR requires an insider list, and the information recorded on it, to be kept up to date at all times and the FCA can ask for a copy at any time. Issuers on SME Growth Markets, which includes AIM, only have to prepare an insider list when asked to do so by the FCA. However, they must still be able to provide the FCA with an insider list upon request. They must also take all reasonable steps to ensure that any person with access to inside information acknowledges the legal and regulatory duties entailed and is aware of the sanctions applicable to insider dealing and unlawful disclosure of inside information (MAR art.18(6)).

9.5 Impact of MAR on takeovers in practice

Market abuse will need to be considered and reviewed throughout each stage of a takeover and practitioners must remember that compliance with the Code does not mean that there is no risk of market abuse. The impact of the market abuse regime under MAR on each of the key stages of an offer is considered in this section.

9.5.1 Stakebuilding

A bidder may want to go into the market to buy shares in the target company ahead of a formal offer.

The reasons for a bidder wishing to acquire a stake in the target company may include increasing the likelihood of its bid being successful or helping to defeat a competing bid. Stakebuilding may also reduce the bidder's acquisition costs (if it can acquire shares at a price lower than the offer price) or enable the bidder to recover some of its costs in the event that another (higher) bid is successful.

Various legal and regulatory restrictions and disclosure requirements apply where a bidder stakebuilds (see Ch.3 above for discussion of these). Under MAR, if the bidder is in possession of inside information relating to the target company when it acquires shares in the target company, it may commit the offence of insider dealing.

Stakebuilding is defined in art.3(31) of the MAR as "an acquisition of securities in a company which does not trigger a legal or regulatory obligation to make an announcement of a takeover bid in relation to that company".

There are two different categories of inside information that need to be considered in the context of stakebuilding: the bidder's intention to make the offer; and any inside information provided by the target company to the bidder as part of the bidder's due diligence.

In order to be certain to avoid committing the offence of insider dealing, the bidder should ensure that its behaviour is legitimate for the purposes of art.9.

Stakebuilding is specifically excluded from the takeover safe harbour in art.9(4) (as discussed in 9.3.1.2 above). This means that the only available safe harbour for stakebuilding is the "own intention" safe harbour in art.9(5) (see 9.3.1.3 above). If the only inside information that the bidder has is the fact that it intends to make a takeover offer, stakebuilding will be permitted under the "own intention" safe harbour in art.9(5). However, if the bidder has obtained inside information about the target company through due diligence, there is no safe harbour available and the bidder will not usually be able to stakebuild, because of the presumption that a person who deals while in possession of inside information has used that information. This does not preclude a bidder from taking a view having taken appropriate legal and financial advice that, in the circumstances of a particular case, there is in fact no inside information in its possession following due diligence access, but there would be a need for particular caution to be taken in such circumstances.

9.5.2 *Irrevocable undertakings*

The obtaining of irrevocable undertakings is an acquisition and disposal (or an attempt to acquire or dispose) of shares at the point the irrevocable is entered into.

The bidder will have inside information when it obtains the irrevocables (i.e. knowledge of the intention to bid and possibly inside information relating to the target company) and so prima facie it would be committing the offence of insider dealing in obtaining an irrevocable.

However, regardless of the type of inside information that the bidder has (i.e. knowledge of its intention to bid or due diligence information which is inside information), obtaining an irrevocable will fall within the takeover safe harbour in art.9(4) of the MAR as the purpose is to proceed with the offer. FCA MAR includes the obtaining of irrevocables as an example of what is permitted under the takeover safe harbour exemption in art.9(4) (FCA MAR 1.3.17G).

Bidders will have to bear in mind, when relying on the takeover safe harbour, that one of its requirements is that any inside information that the bidder has must be disclosed by the time of the acceptance of the offer. In a recommended bid, this is likely to be satisfied after any irrevocable undertakings have been entered into and the offer announced, on the basis that the target directors' recommendation should have priced in all information disclosed in the due diligence process and it therefore ceases to be "inside information" upon publication of the recommendation. This issue is more difficult for a bidder which has received potentially inside information during a due diligence process and which wishes to proceed with the bid in the absence of a recommendation. Such a scenario will require specific and fact-dependent legal and financial advice.

The giver of an irrevocable will also have to consider whether it is permitted to give an irrevocable. The analysis described above in relation to the bidder will generally also apply to the giver of an irrevocable. The exception is where the giver is a "person discharging managerial responsibilities" (or PDMR) of the company. PDMRs include the directors and other senior executives of the company who are not directors but who have regular access to inside information relating directly or indirectly to the company and power to take managerial decisions affecting the future developments and business prospects of the company.

Under MAR art.19(11), a PDMR cannot conduct any transactions, on their own account or for the account of a third party, during "closed periods", that is in the 30 days before the announcement of an interim financial report or a year-end report. ESMA has confirmed that where an issuer releases a preliminary results announcement ahead of its annual report, the MAR closed period will be the 30-day period prior to the preliminary results announcement, provided that the preliminary results announcement contains all the key financial information relating to the financial figures expected to be included in the year-end report (see the ESMA Q&A on MAR).

Whilst there was an exemption under the previous regime (in the Model Code in the Annex to LR 9 in the Listing Rules) for the giving of an irrevocable during a prohibited period, the only exceptions from the prohibition on PDMRs dealing during the closed periods under MAR are for transactions in exceptional circumstances, such as severe financial difficulty, and transactions under or related to employee share schemes, qualification or entitlement of shares or transactions where the beneficial ownership does not change (art.19(12)). The giving of an irrevocable by a PDMR would not come within any of these exceptions.

This means that PDMRs are not permitted to give irrevocable undertakings during a closed period. In practice though, for commercial reasons, most bidders are reluctant to announce a bid until after the results are ready and have been published.

Outside of the MAR closed periods, there is no specific restriction on PDMR dealings, even if there is inside information in relation to the company. PDMRs may however commit market abuse if they give an irrevocable undertaking when they are in possession of inside information unless they can find a safe harbour to rely on.

9.5.3 Announcements on an offer

As a rule of thumb, in the context of holding announcements, if the parties are preparing a holding announcement as required by the Code, it is likely that at that point there will be inside information. The parties should (if they have not already) record the fact that inside information has arisen, the grounds for delaying disclosure and the other requirements discussed in 9.4.3. If it is a target holding announcement post-approach it will be inside information; if it is a bidder holding announcement pre-approach it might not be inside information (see 9.4.1 above).

Any announcements containing inside information must comply with the MAR requirements for such announcements, that is state that they contain inside information and give the identity of the person making the announcement.

9.5.4 Making the offer

As discussed in 9.3.1.2 above, MAR provides a safe harbour for making a takeover in art.9(4). The bidder can rely on this safe harbour when making the offer. This is the case regardless of whether the inside information that the bidder possesses is information about the proposed offer or information obtained as part of due diligence (because it refers to information obtained "in the conduct" of the offer or merger). However, under MAR the bidder needs to be sure that, at the time that the offer is accepted (rather than made), all information that it has received has been cleansed i.e. is no longer inside information.

9.5.5 *The target company board's recommendation*

MAR includes provisions on investment recommendations. However, whilst the provisions are aimed at producers of investment research, the definition in MAR of "information recommending or suggesting an investment strategy" is drafted so broadly that it could arguably apply to target company directors' recommendations to shareholders to accept an offer.

The relevant provisions are art.3(1)(34) and (35) (Definitions) and art.20 (Investment recommendations and statistics) of MAR:

> "(34) 'information recommending or suggesting an investment strategy' means information:
> (i) produced by an independent analyst, an investment firm, a credit institution, any other person whose main business is to produce investment recommendations or a natural person working for them under a contract of employment or otherwise, which, directly or indirectly, expresses a particular investment proposal in respect of a financial instrument or an issuer; or
> (ii) produced by persons other than those referred to in point (i), which directly proposes a particular investment decision in respect of a financial instrument;
> (35) 'investment recommendations' means information recommending or suggesting an investment strategy, explicitly or implicitly, concerning one or several financial instruments or the issuers, including any opinion as to the present or future value or price of such instruments, intended for distribution channels or for the public."

Anyone producing an investment recommendation must:

1. take reasonable care to ensure that information is objectively presented;

2. disclose conflicts of interest; and
3. ensure that all substantially material sources of information are clearly and prominently indicated.

The detailed requirements are set out in implementing regulations.

Taking a purposive construction, this element of MAR is not intended to capture directors' recommendations and so should not apply. This is the view taken by the City of London Law Society and the Law Society's Company Law Committees' Joint Working Parties in their Market Abuse Regulation Q&A, the most recent version of which was published in May 2018. In any event, taking a practical approach even if it does apply the requirements would largely be met already due to existing company law and regulatory requirements (e.g. Rule 19 of the Takeover Code on standards of care and Rule 25 on disclosure of interests). Nonetheless, it is a point for practitioners to be aware of and additional attention to disclosure may be required in offer documentation.

Index

This index has been prepared using Sweet & Maxwell's Legal Taxonomy. Main index entries conform to keywords provided by the Legal Taxonomy except where references to specific documents or non-standard terms (denoted by quotation marks) have been included. These keywords provide a means of identifying similar concepts in other Sweet & Maxwell publications and online services to which keywords from the Legal Taxonomy have been applied. Readers may find some minor differences between terms used in the text and those which appear in the index. Suggestions to *sweetandmaxwell.taxonomy@tr.com*.